Professional Software Testing with Visual Studio® 2005 Team System

McWHERTER

Professional
Software Testing with
Visual Studio® 2005 Team System

Professional
Software Testing with
Visual Studio® 2005 Team System

Tools for Software Developers
and Test Engineers

Tom Arnold

Dominic Hopton

Andy Leonard

Mike Frost

Wiley Publishing, Inc.

Professional Software Testing with Visual Studio® 2005 Team System: Tools for Software Developers and Test Engineers

Published by
Wiley Publishing, Inc.
10475 Crosspoint Boulevard
Indianapolis, IN 46256
www.wiley.com

Copyright © 2007 by Wiley Publishing, Inc., Indianapolis, Indiana

Published simultaneously in Canada

ISBN: 978-0-470-14978-2

Manufactured in the United States of America

10 9 8 7 6 5 4 3 2 1

Library of Congress Cataloging-in-Publication Data

Professional software testing with Visual Studio 2005 team system :
tools for software developers and test engineers / Tom Arnold ... [et
al.].
        p. cm.
  Includes index.
  ISBN 978-0-470-14978-2 (paper/website)
  1.   Computer software–Testing. 2.   Microsoft Visual studio.   I.
Arnold, Tom, 1967-
    QA76.76.T48P76 2007
    005.1′4–dc22
                                                    2007026308

For Siobhan. I love you.
— *Tom Arnold*

To all the underappreciated testers in the world.
— *Dominic Hopton*

To Christy, Stevie Ray, and Emma Grace.
— *Andy Leonard*

To my family for their love and support all these years,
especially Dad for encouraging my interest in computers.
And to Sarah, who makes my life complete.
— *Mike Frost*

About the Authors

Tom Arnold was a program manager for Microsoft Visual Studio 2005 Team System, specifically for the testing tools. He has also managed other commercial testing tools projects by Microsoft and Rational Software and has spoken at such industry conferences as STAR, Microsoft Tech Ed, Internet World, and many others. In addition to two other books on software testing, he has produced three video series on the topic and co-founded a 250-employee software testing company (later sold to Lionbridge/Veritest). Tom is currently a program manager at Microsoft on the OfficeLive.com team. Tom can be reached at http://www.msvstest.com.

Dominic Hopton is a software development engineer on the Visual Studio Enterprise Test team at Microsoft. One of the original team members, Dominic helped fashion the new development and testing tools in Visual Studio 2005. He is currently working on the next version of testing tools for Visual Studio.

Andy Leonard is a SQL Server database developer, MVP, and engineer. He is a co-author of *Professional SQL Server 2005 Integration Services*. He founded and manages VSTeamSystemCentral.com. Andy's experience includes web application architecture and development, VB.NET, ASP, and ASP.NET; SQL Server Integration Services (SSIS); data warehouse development using SQL Server 2000 and 2005; and test-driven database development.

Mike Frost is a senior "software design engineer in test" (i.e., a software tester who mostly writes code) at Microsoft. Over the last 10 years he has worked on several releases of Visual Studio with a focus on the infrastructure and architecture used for testing software. Currently he is working on the new OfficeLive.com service product.

Credits

Executive Editor
Robert Elliott

Development Editor
Kelly Talbot

Technical Editors
Paul Schafer
Chris Massie
Bill Barnett
Michael Fanning

Production Editor
Debra Banninger

Copy Editor
Cate Caffrey

Editorial Manager
Mary Beth Wakefield

Production Manager
Tim Tate

Vice President and Executive Group Publisher
Richard Swadley

Vice President and Executive Publisher
Joseph B. Wikert

Proofreader
Nancy Carrasco

Indexer
Melanie Belkin

Project Coordinator, Cover
Adrienne Martinez

Anniversary Logo Design
Richard Pacifico

Acknowledgments

Tom Arnold: Thank you to Wiley Press and Wrox for inviting me to participate: Bob Elliott, Kelly Talbot, Debra Banninger, and everyone else. Siobhan Quinn, thank you for joining me at countless coffee shops while I typed and you laughed at my cheesy jokes. To the Visual Studio team — specifically Sam Guckenheimer, Jim Sather, Chris Lucas, Gabriel Marius, and my fellow Program Managers — thank you for the chance to be a part of something that reaches literally millions of developers worldwide. Rob Arnold, my brother and mentor, thank you for your constant encouragement. My co-authors — Dominic, Andy, and Mike — thank you guys for signing up! Thank you to our technical editors — Paul, Chris, Bill, and Michael — for keeping us honest. Mikky Anderson, Bruce Johnson, and Sridhar Chandrashekar, thank you for supporting my efforts. Thank you, Mom and Dad, for everything.

Dominic Hopton: Thanks have to go to the people who enabled me to understand and learn my product and be part of it. Without their guidance and encouragement, I wouldn't have understood enough to be able to write this book. I won't remember all your names, but I must thank Tom Marsh, Joe Rohde, James Su, and David Williamson for nurturing me. I also have to thank Tom Arnold for encouraging me to do the book with him — and his constant nagging! Finally, I have to thank Joanne Cunningham for the special and unique encouragement she provided that allowed me to put pen to paper. Thank you.

Andy Leonard: Thanks to Rob Caron, Gert Drapers, Matt Nunn, Sachin Rekhi, and Cameron Skinner for their blog posts about Visual Studio Team Edition for Database Professionals. I learned a lot about creating custom test conditions from blog posts and samples by Sachin Rekhi and Gert Drapers. For help with C# coding, thanks to my friends: John Brown, Craig Dahlinger, Jason Gerard, Frank La Vigne, and Chris Massie. Many thanks to the author team: Tom, Mike, and Dominic — you guys are awesome! Thanks to Kelly Talbot, editor and ''coach,'' and our entire Wrox Team at Wiley: Bob Elliott, Colleen Hauser, and Helen Russo; to name a few. Whenever I sign on to write, so does Christy. Thanks for your encouragement and inspiration, Beautiful.

Mike Frost: Thanks to Bill Barnett for his technical knowledge and reviewing; to Cullen Waters, Mei-Fang Huang, and the rest of the Office Live stress testing team for their help and examples; and to Sean Lumley and Ed Glass for their informative blogs and helpful e-mails.

Professional

Software Testing with
Visual Studio® 2005 Team System

Contents

Contents

Contents

Contents

Introduction

I've had the good fortune of being a part of many startups, both where there were three of us working to build a company that eventually went to 250 employees and $14 million in sales annually, and also in a corporate setting where a new division was being formed. In every case, we struggled with the question of what tools we needed to use on our team, how they would integrate, and how the team would put those tools to use effectively so that we could bring a quality product to market in as short a period of time as possible.

Typically this has meant building our own "stack" of tools: an open source version control system like CVS (Concurrent Versions System), a defect and issues tracking system such as Team Track by Serena Software, automation tools for web and load testing by Mercury Interactive, open source unit testing tools such as JUnit and NUnit, code coverage analysis tools such as C Cover by Bullseye Testing Technology, test library manager by Rational Software, collaboration software for sharing documentation by Plumtree (BEA Systems) or SharePoint (Microsoft Corporation), and more.

Once we figured out our tool stack, we also had to agree on the process we were following for our project's life cycle. Were we taking a waterfall approach, Agile, spiral, Rational Unified Process (RUP), Microsoft Solution Framework (MSF), or something completely new? These were the questions that had to be answered if we expected to move effectively as a team.

With our tools and process selected, the team then had to weave a thread between those tools to allow version control, code coverage, dynamic analysis, test results, and a host of other applications by using our ad hoc queries and applications like Microsoft Excel to paint a picture of how our project was doing. This would answer the important question of whether we were going to be shipping our software on time.

While having the big picture of the health of our project was important to us as a team, it was critically important when we had investors — whether they were venture capitalists, the corporate VP sponsoring the new effort, or our friends and family who loaned us the start-up capital — who wanted to know what progress was being made with the money they had so graciously provided and placed at risk.

Enter Visual Studio 2005 Team System: a suite of tools addressing the needs of software architects, developers, test engineers, program managers, and those footing the bill for the project. Not only does VSTS provide the "stack" of tools right out of the box, but it also has critical integration points allowing those tools to work together, whether it's helping the team get a large build completed each night or getting a current snapshot of the bug trends. This was a huge undertaking by Microsoft to create such a suite, and they created and delivered it to rave reviews.

It all sounds so daunting when I look back on it, but it was a matter of taking things one step at a time and breaking each of our needs and requirements into manageable components. This book breaks out two of those components from VSTS and explores the tools provided by developers and test engineers *for* developers and test engineers. Specifically, we are looking at Visual Studio Team Edition for Software

Developers (VSTESD) and Visual Studio Team Edition for Software Testers (VSTEST), which are part of the overall Visual Studio Team System.

The goals of this book are to:

❑ Introduce you to the Visual Studio Team System big picture.

❑ Walk you through the overall user interface of the VSTEST and VSTESD development and testing tools.

❑ Dive deep into each of the test types available to test engineers and software developers.

❑ Help you understand how to effectively put the code analysis and dynamic analysis tools to use.

❑ Pull together the pieces to see how they integrate into a team setting.

My co-authors, editors, and I wrote this book because many of us were either on the Microsoft team that helped create these testing tools or are in the industry putting those tools to use effectively day in and day out. We want to share with you what has worked for us and how these tools are intended to be used so that you can be effective as a software developer or test engineer on your team as quickly as possible.

Who This Book Is For

VSTS blurs the line between software test engineers and developers, and as a result we have two main audiences who will find this book essential in their use of the test and analysis tools. Software developers will be interested in the unit testing, code analysis, and profiling tools to help them better understand how to write quality code. Test engineers will want to use the unit tests written by the developers and possibly write some of their own unit tests, as well as create web, load, and manual tests to help create a complete approach to testing their product. Both testers and developers will want to make use of the code coverage results from running their tests and the user interface for creating, organizing, and maintaining those tests; as well as leveraging the libraries they create for such things as having those tests run against each new build before it is determined worth installing for testing purposes. Both audiences will also want to understand the integration points of where the tools plug in to other aspects of VSTS.

The assumption is that you already have a working knowledge of Visual Studio. This is an easier assumption to make for the audience comprised of software developers since many of them are already using Visual Studio. This is not so easy for those who are focused on the tool from a software tester's role if they haven't already been writing source code, because this is the first time testing tools have been integrated into Visual Studio from the ground up. Regardless, there is not sufficient space for us to go into great depth regarding Visual Studio itself. We instead focus mainly on the testing and analysis tools found specifically in the VSTEST and VSTESD editions of VSTS.

We do not discuss in detail any specific testing methodologies or recommend any particular software development life cycle. VSTEST and VSTESD stand on their own and are able to integrate into whatever approach your team chooses to take in applying them to your project. We have recommended links to further educate you on such practices in Appendix F.

What This Book Covers

This book looks at the tools found in the Visual Studio Team Edition for Software Developers (VSTESD) and Visual Studio Team Edition for Software Testers (VSTEST) editions of the Visual Studio 2005 Team System.

This includes:

- ❏ The user interface for creating, authoring, executing, and managing tests, including:
    - ❏ Unit tests (including database unit tests)
    - ❏ Web tests
    - ❏ Load tests
    - ❏ Manual tests
    - ❏ Ordered tests
    - ❏ Generic tests
    - ❏ Third-party tests
- ❏ Analysis tools:
    - ❏ Code analysis (also known as static analysis)
    - ❏ Dynamic analysis (profiling and code coverage)
- ❏ Integration points into Visual Studio Team Foundation Server

The scope is very simple in the case of this book because we don't have to worry about previous versions of these tools. This is the first time these test types and analysis tools have been integrated into Visual Studio. We will be looking in detail at how these tools are put to use in your project.

How This Book Is Structured

It is not an easy task to write a book for two disparate audiences — software testers and developers. It is true that testers and developers are both engineers and will be using testing tools to ensure the quality of the software project. However, depending on the team's approach and methodologies, the tools can come into play at different stages of development. As noted above, there are many different testing methodologies and software development life cycles. Rather than limiting the book to one particular methodology or life cycle, we have focused, instead, on how you actually use VSTEST and VSTESD and how you can integrate them into your processes, regardless of what type they might be.

Here is how we organized this book:

- ❏ **Chapter 1, Introduction to VSTEST and VSTESD** — An introduction to where VSTEST and VSTESD fit into the big picture.
- ❏ **Chapter 2, A Quick Tour of VSTEST and VSTESD** — Exploring the user interface necessary to create, author, execute, and manage tests.
- ❏ **Chapter 3, Unit Testing with VSTEST and VSTESD** — Using unit tests in general.
- ❏ **Chapter 4, Testing the Database** — Leveraging unit tests to test against a database.
- ❏ **Chapter 5, Web Testing** — Recording your interactions with a web site and optionally rendering it into source code.
- ❏ **Chapter 6, Using Manual, Ordered, and Generic Test Types** — How to place one or more tests into a ''container'' for added flexibility and value.
- ❏ **Chapter 7, Load Testing** — Conducting load tests to simulate multiple users accessing your application at the same time.

- ❏ **Chapter 8, Using Code Analysis and Dynamic Analysis** — Analyzing your code as part of the compilation step as well as at run time.

- ❏ **Chapter 9, VSTEST and VSTESD within the Software Development Life Cycle** — Using the tools as part of a team setting, specifically with Visual Studio Team Foundation Server (VSTFS).

- ❏ **Appendixes** — How-to's and walk-throughs to help you see the workflow at a quick glance:

  - ❏ **Appendix A, Installing Team Explorer** — Connecting your installation of Visual Studio to your team's VSTFS server.

  - ❏ **Appendix B, Creating and Running a Web Test: A High-Level Walk-Through** — Web test walk-through.

  - ❏ **Appendix C, Creating and Running a Unit Test: A High-Level Walk-Through** — Unit test walk-through.

  - ❏ **Appendix D, Creating and Running a Load Test: A High-Level Walk-Through** — Load test walk-through.

  - ❏ **Appendix E, Creating and Running a Manual Test: A High-Level Walk-Through** — Manual test walk-through.

  - ❏ **Appendix F, Other Sources of Information** — Information about Web sites, forums, conferences, and more.

If you are completely new to VSTS, you will want to start with Chapters 1 and 2 to understand what exactly defines the VSTEST and VSTESD tools and then move into the chapters for the tools most applicable to your situation. If you are familiar with these tools already and are looking more for in-depth coverage of a particular type of test or tool, you can jump directly to those particular chapters, found in Chapters 3 through 8. If you want to understand how the tests and tools integrate with Visual Studio Team Foundation Server (VSTFS) used in a team setting, Chapter 9 will be immediately helpful to you. If your goal is to get a quick understanding of the flow of how a particular test type is added to your project, authored, and finally executed, then Appendixes B through E are where you will want to start.

Conventions

To help you get the most from the text and keep track of what's happening, we've used several conventions throughout the book.

> **Boxes like this one hold important, not-to-be forgotten information that is directly relevant to the surrounding text.**

Tips, hints, tricks, and asides to the current discussion are offset and placed in italics like this.

As for styles in the text:

- ❏ We *highlight* new terms and important words when we introduce them.
- ❏ We show keyboard strokes like this: *Ctrl+A*.
- ❏ We present code in two different ways:

```
In code examples we highlight new and important code with a gray background.
```

The gray highlighting is not used for code that's less important in the present context, or has been shown before.

Source Code

As you work through the examples in this book, you may choose either to type in all the code manually or to use the source code files that accompany the book. All of the source code used in this book is available for download at `http://www.wrox.com`. Once at the site, simply locate the book's title, *Professional Software Testing with Visual Studio 2005 Team System* (either by using the Search box or by using one of the title lists), and click the Download Code link on the book's detail page to obtain all the source code for the book.

> *Because many books have similar titles, you may find it easiest to search by ISBN; this book's ISBN is 978-0-470-14978-2.*

Once you download the code, just decompress it with your favorite compression tool. Alternately, you can go to the main Wrox code download page at `http://www.wrox.com/dynamic/books/download.aspx` to see the code available for this book and all other Wrox books.

Errata

We make every effort to ensure that there are no errors in the text or in the code. However, no one is perfect, and mistakes do occur. If you find an error in one of our books, like a spelling mistake or faulty piece of code, we would be very grateful for your feedback. By sending in errata you may save another reader hours of frustration, and at the same time you will be helping us provide even higher-quality information.

To find the errata page for this book, go to `http://www.wrox.com` and locate the title using the Search box or one of the title lists. Then, on the book details page, click the Book Errata link. On this page you can view all errata that have been submitted for this book and posted by Wrox editors. A complete book list including links to each book's errata is also available at `www.wrox.com/misc-pages/booklist.shtml`.

If you don't spot "your" error on the Book Errata page, go to `www.wrox.com/contact/techsupport .shtml` and complete the form there to send us the error you have found. We'll check the information and, if appropriate, post a message to the book's errata page, and fix the problem in subsequent editions of the book.

p2p.wrox.com

For author and peer discussion, join the P2P forums at `p2p.wrox.com`. The forums are a Web-based system for you to post messages relating to Wrox books and related technologies and interact with other readers and technology users. The forums offer a subscription feature to e-mail you topics of interest of your choosing when new posts are made to the forums. Wrox authors, editors, other industry experts, and your fellow readers are present on these forums.

At `http://p2p.wrox.com` you will find several different forums that will help you not only as you read this book, but also as you develop your own applications. To join the forums, just follow these steps:

1. Go to `p2p.wrox.com` and click the Register link.
2. Read the terms of use, and click Agree.

3. Complete the required information to join as well as any optional information you wish to provide and click Submit.

4. You will receive an e-mail with information describing how to verify your account and complete the joining process.

You can read messages in the forums without joining P2P, but in order to post your own messages, you must join.

Once you join, you can post new messages and respond to messages other users post. You can read messages at any time on the Web. If you would like to have new messages from a particular forum e-mailed to you, click the Subscribe to this Forum icon by the forum name in the forum listing.

For more information about how to use the Wrox P2P, be sure to read the P2P FAQs for answers to questions about how the forum software works as well as many common questions specific to P2P and Wrox books. To read the FAQs, click the FAQ link on any P2P page.

1

Introduction to VSTEST and VSTESD

As part of introducing you to Visual Studio Team Edition for Software Testers (VSTEST) and Visual Studio Team Edition for Software Developers (VSTESD), we need to see where these tools fit within the life cycle of software development. To give you, the reader, a better understanding of this, we're going to discuss briefly the general software development process.

The Software Development Process and Software Development Life Cycle (SDLC)

The software development processes provide a general framework for developing software. The "software development process" in and of itself is not a set of guidelines by which to develop software. Rather, it's a set of terms in which you can describe and discuss many different development methodologies — Waterfall, CMMI, Scrum, and eXtreme are all different software development processes that vary greatly in their actual implementation but share common phases in one form or another. These are all under the larger umbrella of "Software Development Life Cycle (SDLC)."

Often, these different processes are formalized by different organizations, and sometimes government organizations. CMMI, for example, is managed by the Software Engineering Institute, or Rational Unified Process by IBM.

Planning, Analysis, Design, and Development

Within any software design process, there are many common sections. Here, we'll discuss in brief the sections in which VSTEST and VSTESD do not play a huge role. These are catered for by many tools, and in a large part by the rest of the members of the Visual Studio Team System set of tools from Microsoft (Team Foundation Server, Team Architect, Database Professional) and other companies (Borland, IBM).

Planning

Planning is the phase in which you decide what needs to be built (e.g., the problem that the ultimate end product will solve) and who is to be involved in the project, set target dates, and make other decisions that need to be determined before you can start developing an application.

You must understand at a very high level the problem you are trying to solve. You will also begin to set some preliminary dates and time periods for the task at hand.

The planning phase is something that varies significantly from business to business, and project to project. With the ever increasing desire of teams to produce more and produce it faster, agile processes are changing how people think about planning. Instead of it being a lengthy process in which many details are set out (dates, what language to use, etc.), they are being moved out in the development process to be considered closer to the point at which they are needed, rather than in a disconnected process that may have little or no context related to the questions that need to be answered at the time.

Analysis

During the analysis phase, you gain knowledge of what the software needs to do to be considered successful. Through gathering of requirements and analysis of these requirements, you can scope the project into that which is truly needed to solve the problems that your customers (be they internal or external) need to be solved.

There are tools and processes in the marketplace that can help you manage your requirements and your requirements gathering. These provide a great way to track requirements against actual implementation — something that can be lost in the heat of software development. Some of these tools include CaliberRM from Borland and MindManager from Mindjet software. CaliberRM has integration into TFS to provide a rich linking interface with other work items such as test results, bugs, and any other work item type.

Design

After one has collected and digested the requirements, it is possible to start designing the application. This ranges from the high-level component architecture to the layout of the UI. This could easily stray into the development of the project, but ideally one usually avoids the nitty-gritty at this stage.

Development and Testing

These two phases are where, in case you hadn't deduced it, the Visual Studio toolset can really help. However, we'll save that discussion for later. Right now, it's important to note that both of these phases are catered to extensively by Visual Studio. Development is the process of taking your design and turning it into a real living and breathing piece of software. This is what we all know and love as "programming" — writing lines of code, creating UI, and building new functionality and experiences.

However, once you've built your application, you need to test it. How you do this varies widely from complex, forward-thinking processes to simple exploratory testing. Each different type of testing brings something unique to the table, along with many different advantages and disadvantages. Some processes don't have a formal testing phase; however, somewhere there is testing.

Implementation and Maintenance

Once you've built an actual system, your job is not done. You need to deploy the system to your customers so that they can reap the benefits of the wonderful application you have created. Often this is called deployment or implementation, in which you roll out the application in your customer's environment and your users use it every day, which will undoubtedly result in issues and defects being reported. This neatly brings us to maintenance.

Even after your application has shipped, its development is not complete. There will be issues with your application once it's been deployed to customers, and these often will need to be resolved. This is where you will need to maintain your application.

Existing Tools in the Marketplace

Testing has been around since the first computer programmers. This has often been a painful and laborious process: calling multiple functions with different inputs; moving through long, drawn out steps in an end-to-end scenario; making specific HTTP requests — the list goes on. Because of the need to perform these actions often and repeatedly, several different tools have been created over the years. We're going to take a look at some of the most common tools that match VSTEST for functionality, specifically unit testing and web/load testing. There are other features around testing and development, but for the purposes of this discussion, these are the ones that are standout features.

Unit Testing (NUnit, MbUnit)

Unit testing has been recently popularized by Kent Beck as part of eXtreme programming. By no means does this mean that the only use of unit testing is within eXtreme programming — it has many uses in many different development processes ranging from the standard waterfall model to the most agile processes today. It even has a place in the hobbyist developer's toolbox, providing a great way to validate the units of your code in an automated and repeatable fashion that, no matter how small or large your development project is, provides an enormous amount of value.

The name *unit testing* is the key to understanding what unit testing brings to the table: the ability to test individual units of code. A class, function, SQL stored procedure, web page, or even a specific part of a protocol (or maybe the whole protocol) can be considered a "unit." Similar to the way the manufacturing world may have different units that combine to produce a complete product, units combine to form the complete application.

Using this approach, you can see that, as you build the units of your application, creating a set of validation tests to validate your components can give you significantly higher confidence when combining those units later on. By extension, this allows you to develop and fix bugs with greater confidence.

It is important to note that unit testing does not always have to be about testing specific units. It can also be used to perform any other type of programmatic testing. Examples include the way in which the VSTEST team made use of the unit testing features in VSTEST as the foundation for testing all the areas of the products, not only for the developer unit tests, but also for writing scenario tests, integration tests, UI tests, web tests, and even database tests, all using the VSTEST tools and technology.

NUnit

NUnit is the .NET port of the xUnit framework created by Kent Beck. However, it is more than a straight port — the NUnit team embraced some of the advantages provided by the .NET platform to create a much more holistic feel to the tests that are written. As a platform, NUnit provides a command line and GUI runner with different user experiences depending on the intended use. Additionally, it provides attributes, assertion classes (above the standard `Debug.Assert` classes), and configuration files for manipulating the environment for running the tests.

At the simplest level, a unit test within NUnit is simply a method appropriately attributed to indicate that they should be considered tests. However, those methods must reside within a class that has a different set of attributes on it. Here is a canonical example:

```
[TestFixture]
public class SampleTestFixture
{
    [Test]
    public void Test1()
    {
        Assert.Fail("This test does nothing meaningful");
    }
}
```

As one can see, the attributes make it easy to create and identify the test classes and test functions within a set of source code.

When you run this test in the GUI runner, you get an output like that in Figure 1-1.

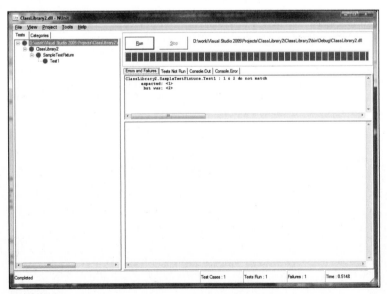

Figure 1-1

As can be seen, you are provided with a list of test classes, and the tests contained within those test classes. You can run at the different levels (assembly, namespace, class) and see your results in the right-hand pane. As you can see from the sample test, our single test case failed — with the error message that was provided to the `Assert.Fail` call. This allows for easier diagnosis when your tests fail; having an error like

```
ClassLibrary2.SampleTestFixture.Test1 :
    expected: <1>
     but was: <2>
```

is unhelpful. However, an error like

```
ClassLibrary2.SampleTestFixture.Test1 : 1 & 2 do not match
    expected: <1>
     but was: <2>
```

is much more helpful, providing you with some context as to what the assertion was actually intended to validate, which can be invaluable when trying to diagnose test-case failures with code that you do not understand well. In the case of one specific test — or even tens of tests — this is not an issue, as the set of code that you have to understand is small. But when you have many hundreds of test cases, the code that you need to understand to diagnose and fix the failures may be prohibitively large.

In addition to the standard "unit testing" duties of providing an execution environment and assertion framework, NUnit actually goes to the next level by providing unit testing for both Windows forms and ASP.NET. These provide simple, but powerful, object model type unit testing functionally for the Windows forms and ASP.NET frameworks. It should be noted that these are not functional tests that simulate user clicks and mouse movements, but rather, they merely invoke and wrap the necessary methods that are required to simulate the events being fired on the controls. This is often just as powerful as functional testing, but it has its own set of caveats.

The last remaining piece of the NUnit puzzle is that it provides mock objects' functionality. Mock objects allow you to simulate the implementation of an interface or class without having to do the full implementation of that interface or class. This is performed by providing skeletal code that allows your real code to function as though it were using a real implementation. This is extremely powerful for validating when your code is consuming interfaces without having the potential headaches of a real implementation (e.g., IHeartMonitor is difficult to test without a real heart monitor).

MbUnit

On the surface, MbUnit looks like any other unit testing framework: It provides assertions, declarative markup, and execution tools. However, MbUnit is potentially very much more powerful than the other unit testing frameworks. This is because of the focus that MbUnit has on extensibility and allowing people easily and simply to extend and customize how tests are executed. The most obvious scenario is data-driven tests, which with MbUnit can be declared inline:

```
[TestFixture]
public class DivisionFixture
{
    [RowTest]
    [Row(1000,10,100.0000)]
    [Row(-1000,10,-100.0000)]
    public void DivTest(double num, double denom, double result)
```

```
    {
        Assert.AreEqual(result, num / denom, 0.00001 );
    }
}
```

As can be seen, you can simply, easily, and clearly declare that a test is minimally data driven while providing a small set of values to be passed into the test. Additionally, because of the strong typing on the test methods' parameters, the actual test can be more clearly written. It's important to remember that these types of extensions can be written such that your custom attributes appear as first class citizens within your tests. This means that rather than having some alternative and unclear way of setting test behavior, it is right there with the test in a way that is integrated and clear. This gives a very different experience from creating your own solutions to the same problem, which results in you ending up with code that just isn't as clear.

It is interesting to note that it is the NUnit model that VSTEST is following rather than MbUnit. MbUnit is a recent entrant into the market and has certainly shaken it up somewhat, with the NUnit team looking closely to see what can be learned in the area of extensibility.

Web and Load Testing

With today's typical application being more than just a single form-based application written in Visual Basic sitting on a single user's computer, load testing has become a much more significant part of the software life cycle. This combined with the primary platform these days being a web-based one, web testing and load testing are the most common types of non-developer-orientated testing being done by organizations. Within this market there is only one clear leader today — Mercury Load Runner. This is a very expensive product, but it provides the whole gamut of load and web testing, from simple http testing through to SOAP testing, and profiling of those services.

Additionally, the Mercury toolset provides a tight integration across a wide range of testing tools, from test-case management to business process testing.

Where VSTEST and VSTESD Fit in the SDLC

The Visual Studio Team System attempts to provide tools and technology to cover the whole life cycle — bug/work item tracking, source code control, automated build system, testing, architecture, and so on. From the names *Visual Studio Team Edition for Software Developers* and *Visual Studio Team Edition for Software Testers*, it should be clear in which part of the SDLC these products fit — testing and developing.

VSTEST provides an ability to author tests, run tests, and, most importantly in the context of SDLC, publish and share the results with your team and the management of your team. This is thanks to the reporting functionality of the Team Foundation Server (TFS), which allows you to create reports covering all aspects of the data within TFS — Source Control checkins (number of files, number of changed lines, changes, code reviewer), work item changes, code coverage, and test results — over time within a SQL Reporting Services environment.

Where you see *testing* as part of your software life cycle (no matter what specific methodology it may be), VSTEST is a product that can help you fulfill those tasks. It's also important to note that SDLC is a huge topic that could be a separate book on its own. However, in the context of the Team System, we have covered the SDLC in more detail in Chapter 9.

What VSTEST and VSTESD Do

Visual Studio Team Edition for Software Testers and Visual Studio Team Edition for Software Developers are editions of Microsoft Visual Studio that go above and beyond the Visual Studio Professional Edition experience by providing role-specific extensions to the IDE experience. VSTEST is specifically targeted at the tester role by providing a set of features for testing applications and services. VSTESD provides tools enabling people in developer roles to have a greater understanding of their code — through performance, code analysis tools, and unit testing. This section only provides a very high-level overview of the features in VSTEST and VSTESD. For more information, see Chapter 2 (a general overview of VSTEST and VSTESD) and the specific chapters and appendixes for the specific areas of functionality.

VSTEST Features

With the focus in VSTEST being on testing, one can see that all of the extra functionality is testing based, focusing on several different test types that the user can take advantage of to test his or her application. Some of these are useful to the developer-focused tester (such as unit testing and web testing), while others are very much for the non-developer-focused tester (such as load testing and manual tests).

The experience for the user is intended to be the same across all test types — whether you are running a unit test or a load test, the basic experience is intended to be the same. This enables you to take advantage of a core set of experience when working with tests in VSTEST. Later in this book, all the test types and areas of the product will be covered in much more detail, where some of this shared user experience will become evident.

Unit Testing

The unit testing functionality provided by VSTEST is very similar to that of NUnit. You author the actual test code in the same fundamental way as NUnit, by adding appropriate attributes to the methods and classes that you wish to be considered tests. Additionally, unit testing in VSTEST supports being data driven, and also another type of test called ASP.NET tests. These are not to be confused with web tests. All of the main Microsoft programming languages are supported out of the box — Visual Basic, C#, and C++/CLI (formerly called Managed C++). Other languages are also supported; however, there is no integrated IDE support for running tests in those languages. An example here might be Visual J#: You can author tests in this language, but you will have to use the command line tools to execute these tests.

The data-driven support revolves around each test being executed N times (where N is the number of rows in a database table) and the test being provided with the data row for each invocation. Any ADO.NET consumable database may be used for data driving a unit test; however, XML (as an arbitrary markup) is not supported.

The ASP.NET support is twofold. Firstly, it allows your tests to be executed under the ASP.NET runtime environment, allowing access to all the standard System.Web namespace objects you have access to in a normal ASP.NET application. Secondly, your test has access to the System.Web.Forms.Page object that represents the page being requested for that unit test. This allows access to the controls, methods, and other items that are relevant to unit testing ASP.NET code.

More detailed information on unit testing can be found in Chapter 3, which covers all aspects of unit testing in VSTEST and VSTESD. Also, database unit testing is covered in detail in Chapter 4.

Web Testing

The underlying technology used to implement the web testing functionality in VSTEST is HTTP requests. The testing that VSTEST provides here is not a browser-based web testing solution — it won't drive your mouse clicks through your HTML and script. However, it is a very powerful HTTP-based web testing solution, providing everything from an easy-to-use browser-based recorder to a set of complex extensions for data validation of the returned data (extraction and validation rules), and being drivable from a database.

The Web Test Recorder allows you to simply record a web test by navigating between pages, filling any forms along the way. All the data are captured and turned into a full web test, which can be customized to your heart's content.

At a basic level, as long as your requests return "OK" responses as determined by the HTTP response code, then your tests will pass. But as is always the case, this is unlikely to meet your needs, which is where extraction and validation rules become useful. They allow you to extract certain pieces of information from the HTTP response and also to validate that response against a set of criteria. Additionally, it is possible to create your own rules — these require programming, but can be very powerful. All parts of the request (URL, form data, etc.) can be driven out of a database to ensure that not every test is identical. An example is if you have a URL that takes a query string parameter (such as `http://localhost/viewOrder.aspx?orderid = 1234`), you can use a database to fill in the "1234" part with different order ID, using the URL as a template.

Finally, any web test can be turned into a "coded Web test," a code-based web test that will allow the authors of a test to have extremely fine-grained control over the test. This includes request parameters, choices/branches based on certain responses, and anything else one chooses to put in code.

Chapter 5 contains a deep overview of all the web testing functionality to be found in VSTEST. A walk-through of creating your first unit test can be found in Appendix C, which is a step-by-step guide showing you details of each step.

Load Testing

Within VSTEST, there are many test types, and those test types can be extended by third parties. It may be that many of these test types are exactly the kind of test that you would like to run against a server as a set of load tests. Both unit tests and web tests fit this criterion out of the box, and one can imagine many other types of tests that might fulfill the same role.

The load test functionality in VSTEST and VSTESD is a container test type. It contains many other tests (of any test type) and allows the user to set parameters for execution (number of users, variance over time). This powerful feature allows for great flexibility in how you author your tests. It allows you to author the test in the most appropriate way, rather than having to shoehorn one type of testing paradigm into another, that is, web tests as unit tests.

As a load test is executed, it will collect a large range of Windows performance counters from the local machine, any agents being used to distribute the test load, and any servers that the user specifies. All of these counters are stored for later review, allowing you to see bottlenecks and drill deeper into any that are found. The remote agent and controller functionality in VSTEST and VSTESD exists primarily to support running load tests under high load.

Chapter 7 contains a thorough discussion of the load testing functionality found in VSTEST, including discussion of analyzing the graphs of performance. Appendix D contains a walk-through for creating your first load test. Additionally, there is a discussion of performance analysis in Chapter 8 in the context of profiling your application.

Manual Testing

The manual testing functionality in VSTEST is somewhat limited, as it only provides a simple text document of steps that need to be performed along with pass/fail results and user comments. This is useful for small-scale projects but does not really scale out to managing thousands of test cases that need to be performed by many users who need to report bugs, screenshots, issues, and other pieces of information that may be relevant to the test.

It is important to note that there are two types of manual test in VSTEST, text-based and Microsoft Word-based. The text-based tests are just that, simple text documents. The Word-based tests allow you to author the test documents in Microsoft Word in any way that can be exported to HTML. Note that one area of the HTML that is restricted is the support for inline ActiveX objects — this is to ensure a secure environment when running manual tests.

Chapter 6 covers manual testing in more detail, with a walk-through for creating manual tests being provided in Appendix B.

Generic Testing

One problem that the Visual Studio Team Test development team encountered during the development was requests from users to be able to integrate their existing custom test harnesses into the Visual Studio Team System. People were looking for a low cost of entry, and a custom test type did not have this. Additionally, the existence of custom test types implies a desire to keep authoring tests in that manner. Many customers wanted to switch over to the Visual Studio Team System without having to lose many thousands of test cases. The solution was generic tests.

Generic tests are a test type that merely invokes a given executable with a specific environment and waits for the process to terminate, and depending on the return code determine a pass/fail of that test. This allows many automated tests to be integrated into VSTEST quickly and easily.

In the case of the pass/fail, or one high-level result not being fine-grained enough, the test harness can also output XML conforming to a specific schema. This output will be interpreted to provide detailed results and better integration of legacy test harnesses.

Chapter 6 provides detailed coverage of generic tests, and a walk-through is provided in Appendix E.

Ordered Testing

The general approach that VSTEST takes to the execution order of your tests is "undefined": Your tests can execute in a different order between runs, and VSTEST makes no guarantee of that order. However, there are times when you want your tests to execute in a very specific order. Take the example of unit testing databases, either stored procedures or a data access layer, for which you may have expensive test cases that make significant changes to the contents of the database. While you can back up/restore the state of the database, this could significantly increase the time to run your tests.

Ordered tests are the VSTEST solution to this problem. They allow you to combine any set of tests (including different types, such as unit with web tests) and specify an explicit order for them to run in. You can also choose to have the ordered test "fail" if any of its contained (or "inner") tests fail, or it can continue. When you run the tests, the order is as you explicitly specified it. When you are viewing results, you have to drill down into the ordered test results to see any specific results of the contained tests.

Chapter 6 covers ordered testing detail, and Appendix F provides a walk-through of creating ordered tests.

Code Coverage

The final high-level feature of VSTEST is code coverage. Code coverage allows you to see which parts of your application are being executed by your automated and manual test cases. It provides line-by-line information as to which have been executed and which have not. This allows for some great insights — both from the "we're not testing enough" and the "this code is never executed, it is dead code" perspectives — providing valuable insight into your testing and your application.

Code coverage works through instrumenting the application binaries on disk. One of the things VSTEST can do is to instrument the binaries each time you run tests to ensure that your coverage is collected.

VSTESD Features

It's important to note that the only shared feature area between VSTEST and VSTESD is unit testing (and ordered testing). This is the exact same feature that you see in VSTEST, but transplanted into VSTESD. It is the only part of the testing functionality that is available in VSTESD. The rest of the features are targeted toward developers.

Code Analysis

Static analysis or code analysis is a technique for inspecting the correctness of applications without actually executing the applications. This can include inspecting source code directly or using tools to examine the binary code directly. Within VSTESD, there are two sets of tools to analyze your code: PREfast (for C++) and FxCop, referred to as *Code Analysis* inside the Visual Studio IDE.

Both of these tools check for common programming errors and validate against a set of rules, which in the case of FxCop are extensible to enable an organization to enforce its own common programming rules. These may be as simple as spelling errors or naming conventions but also extend to ensuring that certain code-based security practices are taken into account.

Profiling

When your application is having a performance problem, it can often be very difficult to identify where the bottleneck is at the code level. Through the use of profiling, one can find these bottlenecks. This involves either running your application through the scenarios that show the performance bottleneck while sampling CPU-based "counters," or using instrumentation. After the data have been collected, the Visual Studio toolset will allow you to see where that bottleneck is.

Main Differences Between VSTEST and VSTESD

It should now be clear that there is a large difference between the feature sets of VSTEST and VSTESD. When one steps back, the sharp demarcation between the intended roles for the two editions can be seen — testing versus development.

VSTEST provides a set of testing tools that encompass all aspects of testing — test types (from web, to unit, to manual testing), remote execution, and simple test-case management. On the other hand, VSTESD provides tools enabling you to write better applications as a developer — unit testing, profiling, and code analysis.

Feature	VSTEST	VSTESD
Unit testing	X	X
Web testing	X	
Load testing	X	
Generic testing	X	
Manual testing	X	
Ordered testing	X	X
Code coverage	X	X
Test manager	X	
Remote execution	X	
Code analysis		X
Profiling		X

Remote execution is a feature of VSTEST that enables you to run your tests on a remote set of machines — an *agent* in the terms of the product. However, all the components to run your tests remotely are not provided with VSTEST, and additional software is required. The Visual Studio 2005 Team Test Load Agent product provides both Controller and Agent components of remote execution that are licensed per CPU. Installing these two pieces of software is a simple process, and enabling remote execution from a VSTEST is as simple as editing the Test Run Configuration to set the remote machine to execute on. For more details about editing the test run configuration, see Chapter 2. It is important to note that the Load Test Agent is not a free product and must be purchased.

How Do They Help the SDLC?

One of the biggest challenges in any software team is being able to manage and track the work that is being undertaken. In the context of testing, this means being able to see your results over time as well as being able to actually perform the work that is required (i.e., test your product).

VSTEST helps you achieve this through its many testing features: unit testing, web testing, load testing, manual testing, generic testing, result publishing, and code coverage. Each of these individual components allows you to fulfill a different part of the SDLC, but when they are combined, they allow you to succeed with your testing across your entire product.

It's clear that the "Testing" sections allow you to fulfill the need to test your product. However, the other parts are less clear. Results publishing is a good example of where it goes beyond simply getting the results into some other system to be reviewed by others. It allows, in combination with the Team Foundation Server, tracking and analysis of results over time. This should not be underestimated.

While seeing that you have 90 percent of your tests passing today is great, you need context to see what has happened over time. What were the results last week? What were the results a month ago? Tomorrow, when the results show only a 10 percent passing rate, you can see that this is a significant change from the previous day. This moves you from merely testing your product into being able to know about the state of your product *over time*. You can then plan throughout the product cycle, knowing your history and trends across both testing and development.

The key factor here is that there is an integrated experience across the whole of the Visual Studio Team System products that provides an integrated experience for the whole of the SDLC, and VSTEST dovetails into this by providing a great solution for testing.

Why Choose VSTEST Over Other Tool Sets?

The primary advantage VSTEST provides over other tool sets is the integration into Visual Studio. No other set of tools integrates into Visual Studio as VSTEST does. It is a first class citizen within the IDE, providing high-level windows for authoring, executing, and managing tests that have a consistent look and feel with the rest of the Visual Studio IDE. Although there might be programs in the industry that can compete in a limited capacity, when you look at VSTEST and VSTESD as part of an integrated solution, their power and reliability are much more compelling than a set of cobbled together tools from around the industry.

Integration into the IDE

Within the IDE, VSTEST provides several integration points: test projects and the Test View, Test Manager, and Test Results windows. These all serve a specific purpose. Note that Test Manager is not available in VSTESD — it is a VSTEST-only feature. These windows are what you need to know about to get around the product. For a deeper look at the individual parts of the IDE, take a look at Chapter 2, which will walk you through all the basic functionality of VSTEST and VSTESD.

Test Project

Test projects are the biggest unit of granularity when it comes to managing your tests. A test project is just like a class library project, except that it holds tests as well as source code. It provides all the normal project features (source control, folders, debugging, etc.) and comes in the three language flavors — Visual Basic, C#, and C++/CLI. You can find test projects under File ⇨New ⇨ Project ⇨ <Language> ⇨ Test in the Visual Studio IDE. When looking in the other test windows, it's important to note that only tests in test projects in the currently open solution will show up.

Test View

Test View is the primary window for viewing and running tests. It provides a linear, flat list of all the tests currently loaded. Double clicking a test in this window will open the test in its editor. You can use the Test View toolbar for running, debugging, grouping (one level tree like view), and filtering the list of tests. You can access this window from either the Test toolbar, or from the Test ⇨ Windows menu item at the top of the IDE.

Test Manager

Categorization is an important factor when you have many hundreds of tests, and it is Test Manager that provides a simple way to categorize your tests. It does this through a concept of test lists, and the use of a "metadata" file that is shared across the solution. It provides a very similar interface to Test View, but with the added functionality of categorization, both for viewing and running the tests.

Test Results

This is the primary window where you will monitor and view your results. It provides both a flat list as well as a category view (a la Test Manager), with the same filtering/grouping functionality from Test View/Test Manager. You can re-run, pause, and stop a run that is currently in progress, as well as see results that have already completed during a run in progress. One important feature when you are using remote agents is the ability to disconnect from the run. This means you don't need to be connected for a 12-hour load test run. You can also save specific results and full runs from here for sharing with your team.

Integration with TFS

The final part of the VSTEST puzzle when being compared against other toolsets, is the integration with the Team Foundation Server. VSTEST provides several valuable integration points with TFS, allowing you to get test data into TFS easily. A step-by-step guide for installing and using the Team Explorer functionality of TFS can be found in Appendix A.

The simplest of these is being able to file a bug directly from a test result: When you see that failing test case, you can right-click on the test result and select "Create Work Item." This will open the Create Bug form in TFS, pre-filling in the title and description with error details and attaching the results file to the bug. This means that when someone else comes to look at the bug, they have all the relevant information required to take a first pass at investigating the bug without having to try re-running the test.

Secondly, and arguably much more complicated, is the ability to publish your results into TFS. These results are associated with a build within TFS and are tracked as part of those builds over time. You can also associate failing test cases with bugs and see which bugs are tracking which failures at any given time. As you publish your results, you slowly build up a historical view over time, being able to see the total number of test cases, pass/fail rates, trending, and code coverage numbers for your test cases over time. While initially the data appear to be mostly academic in nature, they allow you to start building reports in which you can compare the actual performance of your team against the predicted/required performance to hit milestones.

Summary

The SDLC is a complex and huge area of discussion whose surface cannot even begin to be scratched with what we've covered here. However, we have shown that there are several areas where testing can help improve the quality of your applications by allowing those tools to fulfill parts of the SDLC.

We've also looked at the tools that are out there other than VSTEST and VSTESD, and what unique advantages those tools have. Also, we took a very brief overview of what features VSTEST and VSTESD have and what they bring specifically to the SDLC.

With this basic understanding of VSTEST and VSTESD, the context for discussion of the specific features and how they can be used and help you with developing and testing your application has been set.

2

A Quick Tour of VSTEST and VSTESD

Now that you have an overview from Chapter 1 of Visual Studio Team Edition for Software Testers (VSTEST) and Visual Studio Team Edition for Software Developers (VSTESD), let's look at what has changed in the Visual Studio integrated development environment (IDE), then dive into each of those areas in Chapters 3 through 9.

This chapter first looks at the test types in VSTEST and VSTESD and moves on to the user interface (UI) directly related to working with those test types. The chapter finishes by looking at additional tools useful for testing that do not fit into a specific test type (that is, static and dynamic analysis tools incorporated into Visual Studio).

After you complete this chapter, you will have a good understanding of what has been included in the editions of Visual Studio for Testers and for Developers and be ready to dive into the specific details of each of the features.

Test Types

The Microsoft team that designed the testing tools, framework, and overall architecture in Visual Studio 2005 put a stake in the ground and started with the most popular test types on the market today. This includes addressing how to create and manage manual tests, unit tests, web tests, and load tests. This also included creating a type of container test that encapsulates the most basic test types.

Microsoft also kept an eye on the future not only to allow itself the opportunity to continue to add new test types to its repertoire, but also to offer the opportunity for third-party companies to integrate their testing tools into the VSTEST and VSTESD testing framework. The most obvious omission to anyone who has used software testing tools is a test type that supports UI automation. Providing this ability to integrate into Visual Studio opens that door to all of the third-party vendors who already have such UI automation solutions in place.

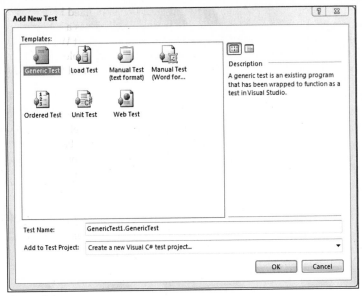

Figure 2-1

The six test types (see Figure 2-1) included in VSTEST (with a subset included in VSTESD) are:

- ❑ Manual (two formats: rich-text and plain text) (available only in VSTEST)
- ❑ Unit (available in both VSTEST and VSTESD)
- ❑ Web (available only in VSTEST)
- ❑ Load (available only in VSTEST)
- ❑ Ordered (available in both VSTEST and VSTESD)
- ❑ Generic (available only in VSTEST)

You should note that manual, web, load, and generic test types are available only in the Visual Studio Team Edition for Software Testers version of Visual Studio Team System 2005, and as a result, the screenshots you see may differ depending on whether you are using VSTEST or VSTESD.

The Manual Test Type

The simplest of the test types, the manual test provides you with a way to integrate those tests to be completed by human interaction with the rest of your tests. For example, if you have a test that is too difficult or time-consuming to write code to complete, enter it as a manual test. Many developers and testers will later turn these tests into coded solutions, but complete them manually in the interim (we go into more detail on manual tests in Chapter 6).

Consider the following scenario. As a test engineer you have been assigned the task of verifying how your application handles errors when transferring data over a network. One of your scenarios checks for losing the connection mid-transfer. This could be simulated by writing some code to interact with the network drivers to "lose" the connection. But this is a bit time-consuming, especially if you're new to working with the network drivers in Microsoft Windows. Instead, you can create a manual test whereby you physically unplug the network cable while transferring data. Should you wish to automate it later, you can then remove the manual test and replace it with the automated version.

This test type is available in two formats. One is called a Word Format, which allows for richer formatting capabilities, such as bold, italic, and underlined text, as well as a choice of fonts and the option of embedding graphics. The other format is a text file that can be edited in Visual Studio's editor. The thinking behind this is that if you have Microsoft Word installed, why not give you the option of creating a richer manual test document? However, it was not the goal to require that Microsoft Word be installed.

> *The manual test type is available only in Visual Studio Team Edition for Software Testers. For a walkthrough of using this test type, see Appendix E. Chapter 6 also goes into more detail about using this test type.*

The Unit Test Type

A unit test, in short, is code that tests code. One of the most popular tools on the market is JUnit (for Java programmers) with an NUnit version available for .NET programmers. The unit test type is Microsoft's approach to unit testing: Developers write test methods (unit tests) that call methods in their production code to verify they receive the expected results. Testing each unit of code in this way, to verify that key functionality in their code has not broken because of other teammates' efforts in a shared codebase, is extremely valuable in catching bugs quickly and early. On some teams, for example, it is a requirement that a developer run unit tests for a given code module prior to submitting any changes. (Chapter 3 has a more in-depth analysis of unit tests, Chapter 4 goes into detail on using the unit test type for testing databases, and Chapter 9 discusses tests as a whole, including unit tests, being required as part of the check-in process.)

Another approach to using unit tests is to write the tests before writing the code. Commonly referred to as test-driven development (TDD), this helps developers think through the parameters and return values for the methods they will be writing in the future. Tests continue to report as "failed" until the developer implements the actual code. The Visual Studio IDE is not completely set up to support TDD, that is, stubs (method declarations with minimal or no definition) must be written for the code to compile. The refactoring support in Visual Studio can help somewhat with this approach, but because it was not designed to be used in this way, taking a TDD approach is limited.

> *For a step-by-step example of using the unit test type, see Appendix C.*

The Web Test Type

The web test type is created by recording your interactions with a web site from a Microsoft Internet Explorer browser. With each click of the mouse, the HTTP request that is generated by the browser is captured for later playback. This includes the GET and SUBMIT approaches to sending requests and data from forms. You can even parameterize your tests should you wish to send different sets of data for a recorded test. Such a test is called a *coded web test* (see Chapter 5 for more details).

The web test type is available only in the Visual Studio Team Edition for Software Testers. For a step-by-step example of using the web test type, see Appendix B.

The Load Test Type

The load test type is the first of what we will call a *container test type*. This test comprises other tests, specifically web and unit tests. The load test type can be run from your local computer or by submitting it to the Visual Studio Team Test Load Agent (VSTTLA), which runs on a separate computer and manages the distribution and execution of the load tests by simulating many users running your tests at the same time, potentially on multiple computers called *agents*. You are limited only by the number of VSTTLA computers you have and the configuration of those computers (i.e., processor speed and memory). Results are then returned to your local computer when those tests complete. (Chapter 7 goes into great detail about how to create, execute, and evaluate the results of a load test.)

The load test type is available only in the Visual Studio Team Edition for Software Testers. For a step-by-step example of using the load test type, see Appendix D.

The Ordered Test Type

Another container test type, the ordered test type, allows you to arrange any of your tests into a specific order of execution. For example, if you select a group of unit tests that are not part of an ordered test and then execute those tests, there is no way to control the order in which those tests execute; nor is there a guarantee that they will execute in the same order the next time. Place those same tests into an ordered test type, however, and that order of execution is ensured. This comes in most handy when you have a test that helps initialize an environment prior to testing and is also helpful for any tests that have the goal of cleaning up after all tests have completed. You can also control whether the execution of tests within that type short-circuits when an error is encountered or continues on regardless of the results of the previous test.

The Generic Test Type

The last of the container test types, the generic test type allows you to utilize any tests that your organization may already have created. This is commonly used to support legacy tests by providing a command line to execute your tests.

For example, many teams write batch files or create simple command-line programs for running tests against their applications. If the command line for their homegrown tool is `MyTest.exe/run_all`, then a generic test can be created and configured to execute that same command line. The benefit is that the generic test appears in Visual Studio alongside your other tests and can be part of a larger execution of tests. For a more complete discussion of the generic test type, see Chapter 6.

Future/Third-Party Test Types

The Microsoft team thought ahead by providing an open architecture through their Visual Studio Integration Program (VSIP) efforts allowing third-party companies like Compuware Corporation, Mercury Interactive (now HP), Rational Software (now IBM), and many others to integrate with Visual Studio. Several companies that wanted future versions of their test tools to be available as a "test type" in Visual Studio worked with the VSTEST and VSTESD teams at Microsoft to have a tight integration, including the ability for those third-party companies to either use the Visual Studio IDE or launch their own editors, while still allowing Visual Studio to manage the execution of all of the tests (third-party tests and tests intrinsic to VSTEST and VSTESD).

The Test User Interface

In 1994 Microsoft included a software testing tool called "Microsoft Visual Test 4.0" as part of the Visual Studio IDE. Microsoft Visual Test was sold to Rational Software in 1996, and the tool was retired in 2001. With Visual Studio Team System, Microsoft came full circle and started offering testing tools not just to software test engineers, but also to software developers, resulting in the VSTEST and VSTESD editions of Visual Studio. The result is that, for the first time, a top-level Test menu (see Figure 2-2) appears in the Visual Studio IDE, and believe me, it was no small feat to get this menu placed in such a prominent location.

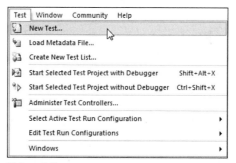

Figure 2-2

Not only did the feature team get a top-level menu in place in the IDE, they added several key windows to help manage, maintain, execute, and evaluate tests and the results of running those tests. The challenge was to not crowd out the main window, where all of the coding takes place. The idea was to think of the developer and tester using the tool being in different modes.

Instead of parading out the different UI windows and menus in an incoherent way, I'm going to take the approach of what modes in which these elements are typically used: creation and coding of tests, management of those tests, and execution of tests.

The UI for Creation and Authoring of Tests

The user interface is not simply the Test menu or some additional windows. Test functionality has wider-reaching effects as it was incorporated into the New Project dialog box, right-click menus in the

Solution Explorer and Code Editor window, the Options dialog box used to configure your Visual Studio IDE experience, and the Properties window.

For step-by-step walk-through examples of some of the test types, see Appendixes B through E.

The New Project Dialog Box

Selecting the File ➪ New Project menu item displays the New Project dialog box shown in Figure 2-3. There are different types of projects that can be created, such as Windows, Office, Database, and now, Test (for each of the supported languages: C#, C++, and Visual Basic).

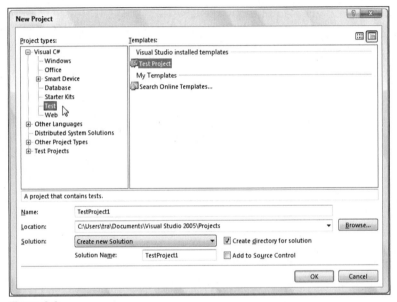

Figure 2-3

Tests live in their own projects, which makes it easier to extract them prior to shipping. This comes in very handy when you're working on a team and you want to have your own tests to run against production code but you don't want to impose them upon others by having them in production-code projects.

Creating a new test project is like creating any other kind of project for the language you've chosen. That is, the coded tests (unit tests, e.g.) will be written in the language you've selected, whether it is C#, C++, or Visual Basic.

You will notice as you scroll to the bottom of the list of project types that there is a Test Projects node with Test Documents as its subnode. This was created for non-programmers who want to create manual tests but don't see a need to pick a language.

As you create a new test project, place it in the same solution as the code you plan to test. This simplifies things when it comes to auto-generating tests against new code, instrumenting binaries for code coverage, and so on.

The Components of a New Test Project

When you create a new Test project in your chosen language, the project is added to your Solution. Also, several files are created and even opened on your behalf. Some files are in the Solution Items folder, and others are the Test project itself, all of which can easily be viewed in the Solution Explorer.

In the Solution Items folder in the Solution Explorer, you have two files (see Figure 2-4):

❑ **localtestrun.testrunconfig** — A test run configuration file holds information about how your tests are executed. This includes such settings as where the test will be executed (locally or remotely), whether or not code coverage data will be gathered during the test's execution, what scripts need to be run prior to execution or to clean up when tests complete, and so on. (This file is used and modified in several scenarios. See Chapters 3, 5, 7, and 9 for more details.)

❑ **TestProject1.vsmdi** — Assuming your solution is called *TestProject1*, you will see this Visual Studio metadata file. This file is used to store the organization of your tests as well as their dependencies, such as the test run configuration that is set as the current default. This metadata file is modified by the Test Manager window and is used by the IDE for executing tests. It can also be used optionally by the command line utility (`mstest.exe`) for running your tests. In addition, when you use a team build that executes tests when the compilation completes, this file is needed to specify how to run those tests.

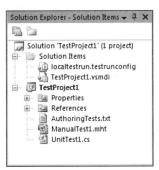

Figure 2-4

In addition to the Solution Items folder, the actual test project (in the case of Figure 2-4, a test project called *TestProject1*) comes equipped with several files. These files were created simply as examples to help you get started. You can delete them without worry and even stop their creation in the first place via a setting in the Options dialog box (see "The Options Dialog Box" section later in this chapter).

In the TestProject1 project (this is based on the name you gave it when creating the project), you will find:

❑ **AuthoringTests.txt** — This file is not only added to your project, it is displayed in the main editing window to help you get started in understanding the basics of working with a Test project.

❏ **ManualTest1.mht** — This .mht file (in the Multipurpose Internet Mail Extension HTML format) is an example of a manual test. You can create more of these if you wish, but the goal was to get at least one into a project so that people who are completely new to Visual Studio would have a starting point. Double-clicking the file will launch Microsoft Word, which gives you a very rich manual test template that supports Microsoft Word formatting. This hypertext formatted file is displayed nicely within the Visual Studio IDE when the test is executed. It is also worth noting that there is a text version of the manual test template for those who do not have Microsoft Word installed.

❏ **UnitTest1.cs** — The extension (in this case, ''.cs'') depends on the language you've selected. It might be .cpp or .vb for C++ or Visual Basic, respectively. This file is a template to help you get started coding your unit tests. Happily, while writing unit tests has been made easy, there are even easier ways to create such tests when you have already written the code you plan to test (that is, generating test code based on your production code). More on this in Chapter 3, ''Unit Testing with VSTEST and VSTESD.''

If you already have a Solution open with one or more projects, those using the C# or C++ developer settings may add a Test Project to the current solution by right-clicking the top node in the list in the Solution Explorer and selecting Add ➪ New Project from the context menu, as seen in Figure 2-5.

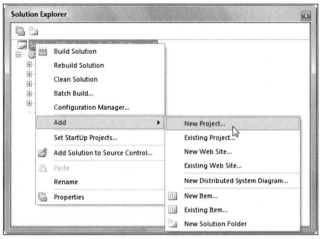

Figure 2-5

Remember to right-click. Context menus abound in Visual Studio, and there are great shortcuts to be found, including a quick way to add a Test Project to an existing solution.

The Test Menu's 'New Test' Menu Item

The first menu item in the Test menu (shown in Figure 2-2) is New Test. Selecting this item displays the Add New Test dialog box, as seen in Figure 2-6.

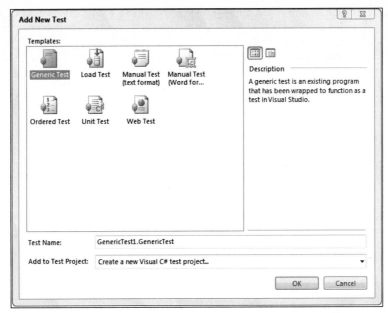

Figure 2-6

Select the test type you want, change its file name to something understandable to you and your team, and then, if you have more than one test project in your current solution, select which test project to add the new test to.

Each test type has a different editing experience. Three examples: selecting the Manual Test (text format) opens a template in the IDE ready for editing, the Manual Test (Word format) launches Microsoft Word (if installed) with the template ready for editing, and Load Test opens a wizard to guide you through filling and configuring that container of tests. As we explore each of these test types in the following chapters, we will look more closely at each editing experience.

> *Again, remember to right-click in Visual Studio; there are many shortcuts to be found. Another example is right-clicking an existing Test Project and selecting Add ⇨ New Test from the context menu. Also, if you look further down that context menu, you will see some of the common test types listed, which lets you cut one more step out of creating a test by avoiding the New Test dialog box.*

The unit test type is a very special animal. This feature-rich test type extends its context menu/right-click support into the editor. For example, if you have open one of the code modules that you'd like to run tests against, you can right-click a namespace, class, or individual method and select the Create Unit Tests menu item. This launches the Create Unit Tests dialog box (see Figure 2-7), which you can use to auto-generate tests against your existing source code. (A lot of effort went into the design of this feature, and it is very convenient and a great time saver. Chapter 3 will give you all the details.)

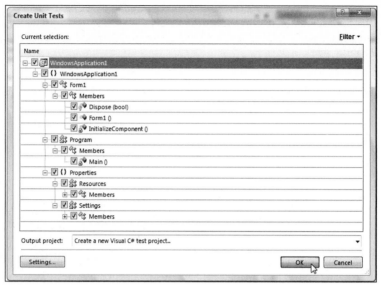

Figure 2-7

The Test View Window

Shown in Figure 2-8, the Test View window is used in the authoring and execution of your tests. Available to both the VSTEST and VSTESD, it is a simplified version of the Test Manager window, discussed later in this chapter. The main idea for this window is to provide an easy way to view all of the tests you have authored. In this view you can set properties, delete tests, and run those tests to help you fine-tune their execution.

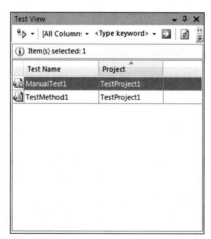

Figure 2-8

To avoid overloading the Visual Studio editor and taking up more screen space (and thereby crowding out the editing window where the majority of the work gets done), the Test View window defaults to docking with the Solution Explorer window.

In this window, two run commands are available (run normally or in debug mode), simple filtering is provided to help you manage when the number of tests increase, and a Group By option lets you group tests by different properties, including the name of its parent project, the test type, the name of the person who created the test, and so on.

The Options Dialog Box

While the Options dialog box isn't tied solely to the topic of Test Authoring, I thought it better to visit it sooner rather than later. In general, the Options dialog box allows you to customize your Visual Studio experience. This is also true for working with the new Test features (see Figure 2-9).

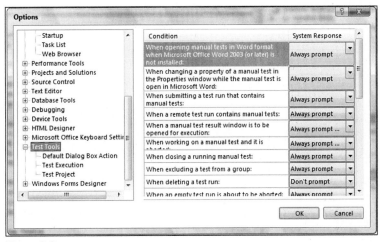

Figure 2-9

The Options dialog box is opened using the Options menu item found under the Tools menu. There you will find a Test Tools node that, when expanded, shows three available groupings of options:

❑   Default Dialog Box Action

❑   Test Execution

❑   Test Project

If you have "Visual Basic Development Settings" as your default Visual Studio environment settings, the Test Tools node will not be immediately visible in the Options dialog box. You will need to click the "Show all settings" checkbox first.

Default Dialog Box Action

Shown in Figure 2-10, the Default Dialog Box Action set of options allows you to specify how Visual Studio should behave in specific situations — that is, to prompt or not to prompt. You know the "Don't show me this dialog box again" checkbox? This is where you can turn that on or off. When prompting doesn't occur, this helps you understand what action will then be taken on your behalf.

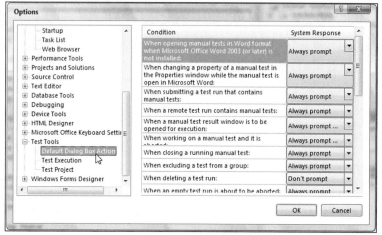

Figure 2-10

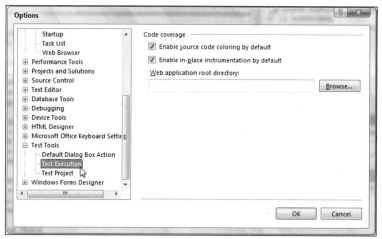

Figure 2-11

Test Execution

A smaller but no less powerful set of options is the default settings for how your tests should be executed. Figure 2-11 shows three options controllable by the user:

❑ **Enable source code coloring by default (checked by default)** — Centered around the code coverage feature (discussed in Chapter 8), this allows you to control whether your source code's text color is changed based on whether it was exercised by a test, partially exercised, or completely skipped.

❑ **Enable in-place instrumentation by default (checked by default)** — We will provide more detail on this when we look at Code Coverage in Chapter 8. It is necessary to modify a binary (or instrument it) to keep track of what sections of code were visited during execution. Copies of the binary file are made prior to this instrumentation and placed in a separate directory. There are times when it is necessary for a binary file to remain in the same location, and thus the option is available to instrument it in place (and not move it).

❑ **Web application root directory** — When you test an ASP.NET application, you must specify where that application resides.

Test Project

The last and simplest set of default options can be found in the Test Project grouping, shown in Figure 2-12. Here you have two options:

❑ **Default test project type** — This honors the settings you selected when you first ran Visual Studio (or changed through the Tools menu using the Import and Export Settings menu item). That is, if you selected C# as your preferred setting, the language associated with your test project will by default be C#. This is where you can override that default.

❑ **Files added by default** — Do you remember all those default files added to your test project? If you don't find them helpful and end up deleting them each time you add a new project, this is where you can select which files are (or are not) added to your test project.

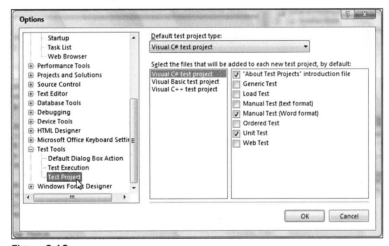

Figure 2-12

Having looked at the UI for the creation and authoring of tests, we next move to managing those tests.

The UI for Management of Tests

Much of the key functionality for managing a huge library of tests is limited to VSTEST. The thinking that goes into this decision is that VSTESD focuses more on the authoring of unit tests and the execution of those tests to verify their accuracy and correctness. This, for example, is why Test View is available in both the Developer and Tester versions, but the Test Manager window is available only in the Tester version.

If you have Visual Studio Team Suite, you have everything, and calling out these exclusions does not apply to you.

In a team setting, everyone's tests are moved into a larger collection, typically with more than just the unit test type. This conglomeration of tests helps validate the success of a given team build. Visual Studio Team Edition for Software Testers adds much of its value not only in the additional test types, but in the organization and complex execution of those tests that cannot be accomplished with Visual Studio Team Edition for Software Developers alone. As you read through this section, the italic paragraphs will call out some of the differences.

The Test Manager

The Test Manager window, shown in Figure 2-13, is like the Test View window, but larger, and with the important ability to organize tests. Because it is meant to be used after tests are authored, it occupies the space typically inhabited by the all important text editor/code window. It's also a straightforward window to master, which is one of its key strengths.

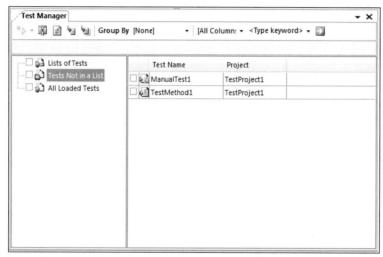

Figure 2-13

The Test Manager is available only in VSTEST.

Defaulting to a tabbed document layout, this window style affords you the flexibility of quickly being able to *Ctrl+Tab* between your other views. If you find that you are also authoring tests at the same time, you can still jump between editing and organizing your tests. Like any of the other tabbed documents, it also support other views, such as floating and docked, simply by right-clicking the tab at the top of the window labeled Test Manager.

Across the top is a toolbar with some of the same buttons found on the Test View window. Running longitudinally is a slide-able divider that separates the Test Lists (left side) from the view of a particular list's contents (right side).

A word on nomenclature: Many discussions were had by the Microsoft team designing the testing tools about what to call groupings of tests. Should they be suites, categories, lists, or a dozen other recommended words? After speaking directly with the testing community at conferences, on message boards, and in late-night sessions where we invited one particular users group into our office at 11 p.m. for a private pre-release demonstration, we landed on lists. *The consensus was that* suites *has many different connotations from one company to another. Does it include test configuration data, does it contain other suites within a suite, and so on? And thus, a* test list *(or list of tests) is simply that: a container holding a list of tests. It can even hold other lists, which lets you organize your tests in whatever way makes the most sense to you.*

Test Lists

In addition to the left side of the Test Manager showing the organization of the tests, it also controls the group selection of those tests. When initially opened it has three top-level nodes:

❑ **Lists of Tests** — Initially empty, this is where your newly created test lists will live.

❑ **Tests Not in a List** — Just as it sounds, this is a way to quickly find unorganized tests that need to be placed into an appropriate list.

❑ **All Loaded Tests** — A flat view of all available tests, both loaded in your current solution as well as those that had been previously organized using Test Manager, saved to disk, and then imported into your current Test Manager session.

Creating a new test list is as simple as selecting the Create New Test List menu item from the Test menu, or right-clicking the List of Tests node in the Test Manager window. This displays the Create New Test List dialog box shown in Figure 2-14.

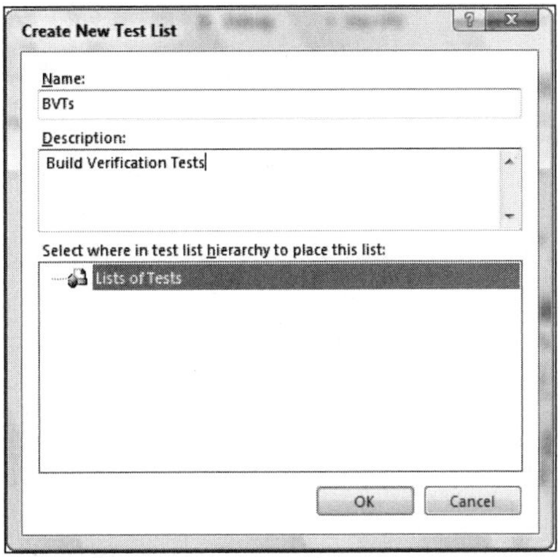

Figure 2-14

Since the Create New Test List menu item applies only to the Test Manager window, the menu item is only available in VSTEST (or the full Visual Studio Team Suite).

After you type the name of your test list, it is placed under the List of Tests node in the left pane. Adding a test list to a test list is just as simple: right-click the test list to which you want to add a new list, and select Create New Test List. The dialog box also lets you select where to place your new test list if you didn't select the correct parent test list. Also supported is dragging and dropping of test lists so that you can reorganize their positions.

Once you are satisfied with your organization of tests — or even if you're not, knowing full well that you can easily reorganize later — you can start adding content (i.e., tests) into those test lists.

Tests are added into a test list by simply clicking on the nodes on the left to get the view best suited to your needs. Next, select the tests you want to add to your test list, but do this by clicking the test name, *not the checkbox next to the test*. The checkbox is used to identify which tests are part of the test execution. As you'd expect, in addition to being able to drag and drop tests individually into a folder, you can select a range of tests by using *Shift-click* or *Ctrl-click*.

> *To place a test in multiple test lists, hold the* Ctrl *key while dragging the test into another test-list folder. (This action shows the "+" symbol to confirm that it is adding the test to another folder.) What's important to note is that it is not copying the test; it is creating another reference to that test. Changes to the test's execution will affect that test for all test lists that reference it.*

While organizing your tests, your changes are saved with each change you make. These changes live in the .vsmdi (Visual Studio test metadata) file that was added to the Solution Items folder in your current solution when you created your first test project. By using this metadata file, you can check tests into the Visual Studio Team System source code control to be shared with others.

The Test Manager Toolbar

Figure 2-15 shows the Test Manager's toolbar. It resembles the Test View toolbar (see Figure 2-8), but it sports three additional buttons:

❑ **Add/Remove Columns** — Although not on Test View's toolbar, this is available on its right-click menu. In either window the functionality allows you to display many of the test's properties as columns that can be used in grouping and filtering tests.

❑ **Load Metadata File** — The same behavior as the "Load Metadata File" menu item on the Test menu, this allows you to open a .vsmdi file that is not part of your current solution. This is especially useful to those who are focused only on organizing and executing other's tests.

❑ **Import Metadata File** — This allows you to combine a metadata file with the one that is currently open, giving you more power to create an overall library of tests created by your team.

Figure 2-15

The UI for Test Execution and Results

With the tests authored and organized, next comes the execution of those tests. As part of authoring your tests, you've likely been verifying your efforts by running those tests as you go and already have encountered some of the UI surrounding test execution and test results, specifically the Run Configuration dialog box and Test Results window. This section looks at the UI around executing your tests.

If you are someone focused solely on the management and execution of tests and therefore selected the Team Test Settings when you started Visual Studio, only the Test Manager window, Test menu, and a limited few other menus and windows are displayed by default (that is, the Build menu is not visible by default, the Solution Explorer window is set to auto-hide, and so on). Whatever your settings, this section continues our quick overview of the UI, specifically looking at running tests and viewing results of their execution.

We will look at the UI for configuring how tests run, verify that the correct run configuration is selected, select some tests to execute, and then view the results.

The Test Results window can also be seen in use in the walk-throughs provided in Appendixes B through D.

Test Run Configurations

A test run configuration file (.testrunconfig) was added to your Solution Items folder when you initially created your test project. Alternatively, if you loaded a Visual Studio test metadata file (.vsmdi), it also references a run configuration file.

The test run configuration file allows you to specify *how* your tests are run. Consider the potentially huge library of tests you have at your fingertips. Now imagine those tests being used in a myriad of ways:

❑ **Check-in requirements** — Tests that a developer must run on code before checking in that code.

❑ **Nightly build process** — Execution of tests automatically by the build process as a large team build completes that night (providing a go/no-go decision on whether or not to take the build in the morning).

❑ **Locally as part of a test pass** — Testers augment their efforts by not only having planned tests execute locally on their computers but also performing their own ad hoc tests.

❑ **Execution in a lab setting** — Tests dispatched to remote computers, likely with different hardware and software configurations, allowing for compatibility testing.

❑ **Execution as part of a load test** — Tests bundled up and sent to a controlling server to simulate hundreds or thousands of users accessing a web site or service to help find bottlenecks, and other related problems.

Each of these scenarios has a different run configuration file but uses the same test. In many cases, testers will have multiple run configurations on their computer, allowing them to quickly specify whether they want code coverage results gathered in the test run (slower execution because of a necessary instrumentation step) or to run their tests quickly for a sanity check. Whatever the need, this is the strength of a run configuration file.

The test run configuration file is saved in XML format. Most of its settings can be edited using the dialog box shown in Figure 2-16; the remaining settings can be edited directly in the XML document. Display the dialog box by selecting the "Edit Test Run Configurations" option on the Test menu and then choosing the appropriate .testrunconfig file.

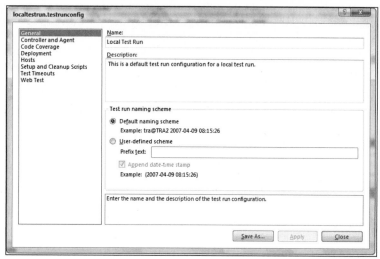

Figure 2-16

There are eight sections of the run configuration that can be modified. We will go into more depth in each of these sections in the next chapters, but for now, here they are at a high level:

❑   **General** — In this section, you can control the naming of your test runs and subsequent results that may be eventually shared with others.

❑   **Controller and Agent** — If your team has installed the controller software on another computer on your network (in a lab setting, for example), this section allows you to specify which computers to use when running your tests.

❑   **Code coverage** — Do you ever wonder exactly how effective your tests are in exercising your code-under-test (production) code? With this feature, you can determine which sections of code were exercised as part of your test run.

❑   **Deployment** — If you have additional files that are required as part of the test run (data files relied on by your tests or by your code-under-test), this is where you add those files, which will then be deployed along with your tests.

❑   **Hosts** — This allows you to specify the type of host your tests are running on. For example, are you running tests against a Windows application, or are you running them on an ASP.NET assembly?

❑   **Setup and Cleanup Scripts** — This section allows you to specify a script (such as a .bat file) that should be executed before or immediately following the test run. This way you can both set the scene and clean up after yourself in the event that temporary files were created as part of the execution of those tests.

❑   **Test Timeouts** — These settings help your test run recover from tests that do not complete because of a crash. Here you can specify how long VSTEST and VSTESD will wait before considering an individual test as failed, and how long to wait before an entire test run is considered failed. If a particular test is known to take a long time, the value set in this dialog box can be overridden by setting the test's individual timeout property.

❏ **Web Test** — These settings are specific to the web test type. You can use them to control the default execution behavior of the web test, including how many times each web test should be run as part of the test run, the browser type to simulate, network type to simulate, and whether or not to recognize the "think times" or delays made when the web test was originally recorded.

You can have more than one test run configuration file available. For this reason, click the Select Active Test Run Configuration option on the Test menu before you run your tests to verify that the correct test run configuration file is active.

The Test Results Window

You've run your tests, whether it was from the Test View or Test Manager windows, or by using the Test menu, where you can click on a Test Project in your Solution Explorer and run all of the tests it contains. Now you want to know what happened. The Test Results window is designed to tell you both what has happened and to let you re-run those tests (or a subset of those tests — such as the ones that failed) to help you diagnose what went wrong.

The Test Results window, shown in Figure 2-17, appears along the bottom of the IDE, in the same footprint used by the Output window, again with the goal of avoiding the crowding of the editor area. Comprising a toolbar, light-yellow status field spanning the width of the window, and columns showing the results and details of the tests, the Test Results window has a wealth of functionality.

Figure 2-17

The Test Results Toolbar

In addition to the right-click/context menu, much of the Test Results window's functionality lies in its toolbar. You'll notice at once that the Test Results window's toolbar is crowded with buttons grouped and divided out by a vertical separator bar to help in their organization. From left to right, the buttons are the following:

❏ **Views buttons** — There are two buttons to control how you view results.

  ❏ **View All Results button** — A flat list view of the results for each of the tests.

  ❏ **View Results by Result List button** — A list of the test results as they map back to their original Test List groupings that were created using the Test Manager window.

❏ **Runs grouping** — There are two buttons for selecting and getting more information about a test run.

  ❏ **Run Details button** — Displays a Result Summary as a tabbed document allowing you to see which Test Run Configuration file was used, the person who ran the test, start and stop times, and high-level results.

- ❑ **Select Run dropdown box** — A list of the test runs that have completed during this session of Visual Studio. Select a specific test run to review or show all the results combined.

- ❑ **Run/Pause/Stop buttons** — These buttons give you control over running your tests.

  - ❑ **Run dropdown button** — Gives you the option of how to re-run the results you've checked in your test results list: Run (using all original settings in the original run), Run with (allowing you to select another run configuration file when re-running the check-marked tests), and Debug (allowing you to re-run the checkmarked tests under debug mode so that you can use breakpoints and watch windows).

  - ❑ **Pause** — You may pause a test run if necessary, but only after the test currently executing completes (i.e., you cannot pause a test once it has started its execution).

  - ❑ **Stop** — Abort your test run.

- ❑ **Publish/Export/Import/Close buttons** — These four buttons allow you to save test runs or open previous test run results.

  - ❑ **Publish button** — If you are connected to a Team Foundation Server and have reporting enabled, you can push your test results to the team database using this button.

  - ❑ **Export Test Run Results dropdown button** — Provides two options: Export all results from the current view of test results, or export only those results that are selected (not to be confused with checked, which is used only for specifying which test to re-run). This feature is especially helpful when sharing your results with others on the team.

  - ❑ **Import Test Results button** — If you have some old test results you've previously saved, or results someone has shared with you, this allows you to load, view, and even re-run those tests if you still have the files necessary for the test to run on your computer.

  - ❑ **Close Results button** — Free up some memory and clear out your Test Results window by clicking on the Close Results button.

- ❑ **Group By dropdown box** — Similar to Test View and Test Manager, you can create a view that shows your test results grouped by a particular property, such as the owner/author, priority, result (e.g., pass or fail), and so on.

- ❑ **Filter dropdown box and text box** — Also like the Test View and Test Manager windows, here you specify a keyword and the column to apply that keyword to. Clicking the green right-arrow button next to the keyword text box applies the filter so that you see only those items that match.

- ❑ **Show Code Coverage Results button** — This button displays the Code Coverage Results window, shown in Figure 2-18, and the next piece of UI we will look at.

The takeaway for you in the Test Results window is that it has close ties to the Test Manager and Test View windows. Once you're familiar with working with any of these three windows, you'll work well with the others. They all can be used for executing tests, but the Test Results window is where you go to see the final results.

As you would expect, test results are typically passed or failed. Another result, one that is still considered a failed state, is the inconclusive result. This exists to flag auto-generated tests that have not yet been modified by the author of the test and is seen specifically when auto-generating unit tests. The goal is to avoid auto-generated tests showing passed when no one took the time to actually inspect the generated test. Further results exist that indicate less frequently encountered conditions such as Not Runnable, Aborted, and Timeout.

The Code Coverage Results Window

There is a setting in the Test Run Configuration dialog box that allows you to specify whether to gather code coverage data during the execution of your tests. If configured to gather coverage data, part of the test execution includes a step where the binaries are modified (instrumented) to allow the tools to watch which segments of code are executed as a result of your tests' execution.

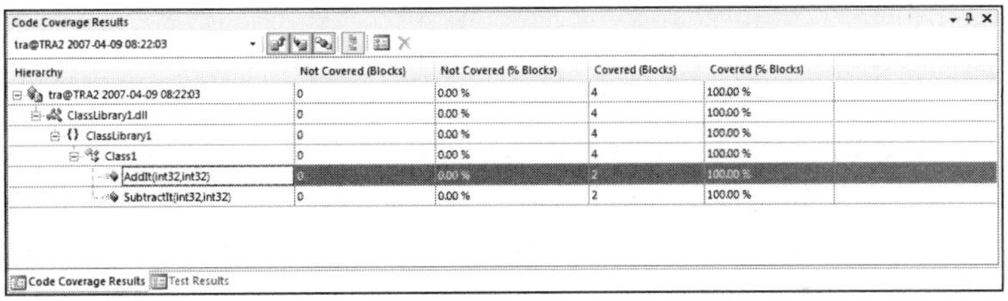

Hierarchy	Not Covered (Blocks)	Not Covered (% Blocks)	Covered (Blocks)	Covered (% Blocks)
☐ tra@TRA2 2007-04-09 08:22:03	0	0.00 %	4	100.00 %
☐ ClassLibrary1.dll	0	0.00 %	4	100.00 %
☐ {} ClassLibrary1	0	0.00 %	4	100.00 %
☐ Class1	0	0.00 %	4	100.00 %
AddIt(int32,int32)	0	0.00 %	2	100.00 %
SubtractIt(int32,int32)	0	0.00 %	2	100.00 %

Figure 2-18

The Code Coverage Results window, shown in Figure 2-18, is a straightforward window. With the customary toolbar across the top, the main area of the window shows a hierarchy of the binaries, namespaces, classes, methods, and so on that were instrumented as part of the test run.

While many code coverage tools list coverage numbers by a line of code, Visual Studio uses blocks, which are finer detailed than a line of code. Take an IF-statement, for example. If the statement includes an && (AND for VB users) or an || (OR), portions of that single line are evaluated separately. The line could be considered in two, three, or more evaluated blocks where only a portion of that line would receive coverage. (In the example of AND, if the first condition evaluates to False, the rest of the line is skipped, which results in partial coverage of that line and a completely uncovered block.)

Should you prefer lines of code to be covered instead of blocks (e.g., because the rest of your team's metrics are based on lines of code), you can right-click a column in the Code Coverage Results window and add/remove the appropriate columns to meet your needs.

While the Code Coverage Results window provides a great wealth of information about the percentages covered, there is yet another way to visualize the results. Assuming you have the source code available on your computer, you can double-click a method, for example, to jump to that section of code. There you will see coloring that signifies which sections were covered, not covered, and partially covered by your tests.

The default colors are light red for untouched, light orange for partially touched, and light blue for areas touched by the test execution. For example, although it is difficult to see in black and white in Figure 2-19, the colors show up quite clearly on a monitor. In this instance, the block of code in the AddIt() method is light blue, and the block of code in the SubtractIt() method appears as light red.

```
namespace ClassLibrary1
{
    public class Class1
    {
        int AddIt(int a, int b)
        {
            return (a + b);
        }
        int SubtractIt(int a, int b)
        {
            return (a - b);
        }
    }
}
```

Figure 2-19

For more examples of working with the dynamic analysis capabilities of code coverage, see Chapter 8.

You can change these colors from the Tools menu by selecting the Options menu item. Under the Environment node, click the Fonts and Colors section. The Display items list box has three entries relating to code coverage:

- Coverage Not Touched Area
- Coverage Partially Touched Area
- Coverage Touched Area

The wording used by the code coverage team is deliberate, that is, "touched" instead of "covered." This is to help people understand that the test may have visited or touched a section of code, but just because it was able to cause execution to run through that segment does not mean it was fully tested. Different conditions and variable values will cause each segment to behave differently. A high level of code coverage does not necessarily mean a low number of bugs. Take a `switch` *statement as an example: Just because it handles the situations in which values* X, Y, *and* Z *are handled, that doesn't mean it's impossible for value* N *to somehow get passed to the statement, which was never expected by the programmer. Code coverage cannot predict unexpected values passed to a method, only confirm that the values that were passed caused specific branches of code to be executed.*

The Test Runs Window

The Test Runs window, shown in Figure 2-20, gives a top-level view of your test runs. It sounds simple enough, and it is, but it's not just for viewing the test runs you've completed on your computer. It's also used for connecting to test runs completed, queued, or currently executing on remote computers.

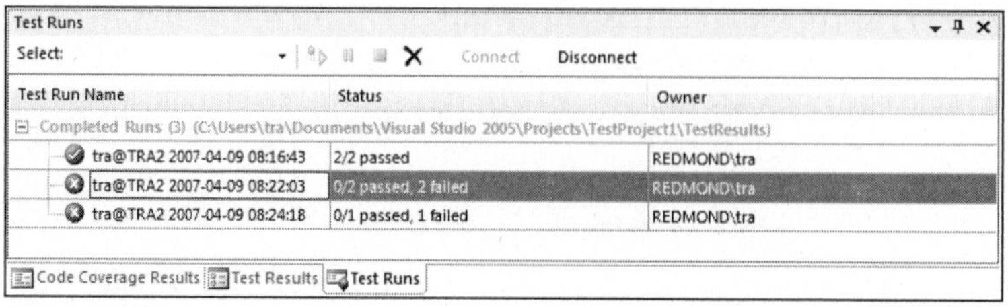
Test Runs
Select:
Connect
Disconnect
Test Run Name
Status
Owner
Completed Runs (3) (C:\Users\tra\Documents\Visual Studio 2005\Projects\TestProject1\TestResults)
tra@TRA2 2007-04-09 08:16:43
2/2 passed
REDMOND\tra
tra@TRA2 2007-04-09 08:22:03
0/2 passed, 2 failed
REDMOND\tra
tra@TRA2 2007-04-09 08:24:18
0/1 passed, 1 failed
REDMOND\tra
Code Coverage Results
Test Results
Test Runs

Figure 2-20

The Select dropdown list box in the window's toolbar is where you specify whether you are looking at local or remote test results. This displays the Connect to Controller or Local Results dialog box, shown in Figure 2-21.

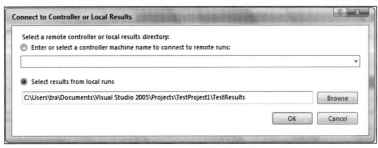

Figure 2-21

Opening a test run allows you to pause the entire run, stop it, or re-start it using the buttons on the toolbar, similar once again to the Test Manager, Test View, and Test Results windows. A button not available in the other windows, however, is the Delete (X) button, which you click to remove the results from a computer. This is important to note because if you do not delete test results through this UI, you will need to search the computer's hard drive for a TestResults folder to delete results manually. These files can grow quite large as the binaries of the code-under-test are copied here as part of the test execution. Be sure to take the necessary time to clean up, or you will slowly run out of drive space.

Analysis Tools

Included in the Visual Studio Team Edition for Software Developers (VSTESD) are tools for analyzing your program. These take the form of code analysis (more commonly referred to as *static analysis*) as well as performance and code coverage (also known as *dynamic analysis*).

These tools are explored in greater detail in Chapter 8.

Code Analysis

The code analysis feature analyzes your project without actually running the source code. Tools like this have been around for years, including one tool called Lint for analyzing C source code. In the case of the code analysis functionality in Visual Studio, however, it's not the source code that is reviewed, it is the compiled intermediate language (MSIL) that is analyzed.

The simplicity of using this tool belies its sophistication and overall value. To have such a powerful tool enabled by simply clicking a checkbox or selecting a menu item seems contrary to most other tools. Fortunately, it really is that simple.

To enable the code analysis feature, you simply edit the properties of your project and select the Enable Code Analysis checkbox, as shown in Figure 2-22. As the program is checked for syntax and compiled, one additional step is added to the process, which is running the code analysis tool against the compiled objects.

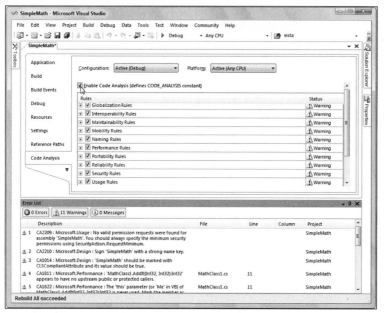

Figure 2-22

Another way to invoke the tool is to right-click the project in the Solution Explorer window. Then, select the Run Code Analysis menu item from the context menu. This is a helpful approach if you do not wish to have the analysis performed each time the code is compiled, as will happen when turning on this feature through the project's properties.

Performance Measurements

The Performance tool that is included with VSTESD works by measuring the execution of your program, unlike the static analysis/code analysis tool, which merely looks at the results of your non-executing compiled code. The *dynamic analysis* capabilities come in two flavors: code coverage (mentioned earlier in this chapter) and performance analysis — sometimes known as a *profiler*. Both are explored in greater depth in Chapter 8.

Found under the top-level Tools menu, the Performance tool is invoked through its Performance Wizard, as shown in Figure 2-23. Here you can profile an executable, a dynamic-link library (DLL), or even an ASP.NET application. To have real-world measurements, it is recommended that you profile a non-debug version (that is, a Release build) of your project. This is because a debug build has additional instrumentation in place to help in the debugging of your source code and potentially results in slowing down your program's execution. When measuring your program's performance, you want it as close to the shipping version as possible, hence running the tool against a Retail build.

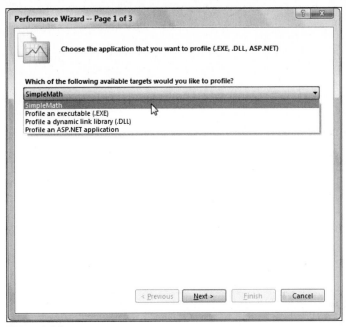

Figure 2-23

There are two methods that can be used for profiling your application:

- ❑ **Sampling** — Focuses on the overall execution of your entire program in an unobtrusive manner.
- ❑ **Instrumentation** — Inserts markers into your compiled source code to allow for greater detail in measuring the performance of your program, even to the detail of looking at specific modules.

Summary

It's an understatement to simply say that a lot of work has gone into Visual Studio to incorporate testing tools that are useful to both software developers and test engineers. This undertaking included laying a foundation that both Microsoft and their partners can build on and leverage for years to come.

Even with all of the forward-thinking work to provide a strong foundation, Microsoft was able to also include six key test types with the tool. External companies like Compuware also integrated their tools into Visual Studio through the Microsoft VSIP program. All of this new functionality is supported by a straightforward UI for making effective use of these testing features.

The authoring, management, and execution of tests cater to several roles. Not just software developer and tester, but manager levels can get into the act by managing and executing tests with little or no exposure to the code through the Test Manager window. Results can be seen easily and even shared with the team through exporting the results to a file or publishing them to a team database.

In addition, tools for analyzing the compiled source code both in a static, non-executing state as well as taking readings and measurements at run time are available to help further finetune your project.

Now that we've had a high-level tour of the UI and how it all fits together, in Chapter 3 we begin our deep dive into the first test type: unit tests.

3

Unit Testing with VSTEST and VSTESD

Often developers ask when they are writing their applications, "Am I doing this right? Did I break anything else?" Unit testing provides a simple, efficient, and flexible way to achieve a greater peace of mind through fast, reproducible, automated tests. However, unit tests can go beyond simple unit tests toward scenario testing — it all depends on the problem you're trying to solve.

Overview of Unit Testing

When I first heard about unit testing I didn't understand it, and I didn't see the point. Why should you write some tests that don't really test anything specific? You're just testing some small, minimally functional method. How does that help? Over time I saw that so many fixes broke simple functionality, which would bubble up the layers of an application to the point that it would cause major issues. I realized that if I had written a small test that I could run every time I made a change, I would have saved myself an enormous amount of work.

Why Unit Test?

When you are building an application, over time you create a number of layers — each layer relying on the assumptions, assertions, and implied behaviors of the layer below it. It is when these beliefs start to be broken and torn down that you start to see issues in your applications. Unit tests allow you to revalidate these assumptions after every change. You are asserting your beliefs about the application layers.

As a lone developer of an application (or "on a project"), it is often easy to understand your code base from end to end, and understand all the interactions of different components of the application. However, as soon as you become a team (that is to say, more than one person), your personal knowledge starts to wane. The other people with whom you are working are not able to read your mind, and conveying your assumptions and interactions becomes more and more difficult. While to a certain extent it is possible to rely on clan knowledge, this does not survive the ravages of time and begins to wane as people leave the team and move onto different projects. Unit tests become a great way to translate this knowledge into code — a universal language that reflects what is really going on rather than what is believed to be going on. If your project has a collection of unit tests, whenever anyone in your team makes a change, they can revalidate the application behavior quickly, allowing them to be confident that the changes they have made are the correct ones.

Approaches to Unit Testing

While unit testing is itself a specific approach to testing your application, there are actually several different approaches within the world of unit testing. The basis of these is often much more ideological than practical, but there are lessons to be learned from each different approach.

The major differences revolving around the question of what to test with your unit tests is related to public versus private implementation. There are many drawbacks and benefits to each — often determined by what you are actually building. But using public versus private as the only deciding factor is unwise. This is why the following sections are broken into "Test What You Want" and "Test Only Publics." The first imposes no pre-defined suggestions on what you should test, whereas the second implies that you should and encourages you to test all your publicly exposed code. The other major approach is actually more of a development methodology rather than a flavor of unit testing. Instead of starting with coding, you start by building tests to validate that which you have not yet written. This is often counterintuitive but can turn out to be an especially powerful approach.

Test What You Want

When the author of the tests sits down to start creating unit tests, one of the biggest questions he or she faces is what to test. With new code this can be easy: Just start testing everything that you are writing, section by section. However, as your code base starts to grow, this can become unwieldy and also complex. What about that legacy code base that you need to shore up to ensure that it stays stable? That's even harder. There are thousands of lines of code and hundreds of classes, all of which have complex interactions that are ever so difficult to untangle to a state such that you can test.

This brings us to the important realization that you test what you want to test, not what some prescribed mandate has dictated you should test. You don't test everything, and you don't test nothing. You use your understanding of the code base, the bug history, and your intuition to know what to write tests for. This can be very useful, and is also a pay-as-you-go model. There is no huge cost upfront, and you can incrementally build out the test set for your application.

The only major drawback with this approach is the level of trust you place in yourself and the rest of your team to author your tests.

Test Only Public Implementations

When one performs proper encapsulation, there is a set of public and private methods, each performing different and more locally scoped operations. These provide a clear boundary for types that are shared between components. Only the public members are the entry points between your application layers.

Because of the assertion that your most likely area for defects is changes in behavior between layers, why bother testing that the behavior of the private implementations of the types is correct? The private implementation details are just that — private details that are irrelevant to anyone and should not be tested. If they are private they will be fluid, and the overhead of having to test privates (and maintain those tests) will be too significant to provide any value.

The very basic premise here is that you have tests to test the publics, and if you break one of the privates, your tests for those publics will ensure the validation of the privates. Depending on your understanding of the code, this can also have the drawback of having to track back through the failure to understand exactly which private method has failed.

Test-Driven Development (TDD)

Test-Driven Development (TDD) is a very different approach to unit testing — insomuch as it is not in reality a way of testing, but a way of development. It provides a significant change to your development process and appears on the surface to be very similar to "test-first development"; however, this is an oft held misconception. A great example of this was the Visual Studio Team Test team, who published an article on how to do test-driven development in VSTEST, only to have the TDD community cry out against the article. Fundamentally, the team had misunderstood what was meant by *Test-Driven Development* — believing it was test-first development. The TDD community is very passionate about ensuring that the underlying design process of TDD does not get confused or lost, and because of this they were very passionate about ensuring that the article portrayed TDD correctly. Test-first development is an approach in which all your tests are authored up front, and then you author the code, running the tests as you go. This seems very similar to TDD, but the fundamental difference here is in what the tests look like. Test-first development results in tests that take a typical form of attempting to test functionality as described below. TDD takes a much more fine-grained perspective.

Within the team there was great discussion about the article and how to resolve the concerns with the community — both by publishing an updated article and also by investigating unit test IDE (integrated development environment) integration feature improvements for future versions of Visual Studio by actively engaging the TDD community.

It's important to understand that TDD changes the whole workflow of your code authoring. You write your tests before you have written even one line of application code: Your tests start to dictate the design of your application, as you write only the minimal amount of code to ensure that the tests pass. As you build out of your tests, you may go so far as to create empty methods in your application code that return immediately — a dummy implementation of that method. This reiterates the tenet that your tests are validating assumptions. Knowing that your code is "good" and your tests pass means you can move forward on the implementation and allows you to validate immediately that your new, expanded implementation is good. If your test fails, you need to resolve that issue before progressing forward.

TDD is a very powerful approach and is something that can only really be understood through experience. It also is very difficult to talk about from an abstract perspective, or even to provide a step-by-step guide for. It's about how you approach the problem, and your thought processes. Learning through application is the key here.

What Unique Unit Testing Features Do VSTEST and VSTESD Have?

VSTEST and VSTESD are Microsoft's first entry into the market of unit testing, a market that is dominated by NUnit. The aim was to meet NUnit's core unit testing abilities such as marking up of test cases and command-line execution. However, because of the greater set of testing tools that the unit testing feature is part of, there was significant opportunity to enable unit testing to take advantage of those features. These enabled some unique scenarios and behaviors in VSTEST's and VSTESD's unit testing support.

Host Adapters

When you author a unit test that relies on a large infrastructure, your unit test will have a significant problem in providing that same infrastructure to your application code. An example of complex infrastructure may include a set of services or technology that requires significant infrastructure to support but is fundamentally required by the application. If you need to unit test these classes that build on this infrastructure, then you are going to have a tough time enabling those classes to function without effectively reimplementing that infrastructure. Sometimes this can be resolved by refactoring your services or technology to be a much more reusable component. However, this is not always an option because of the complexities of the environment. Within Visual Studio, there was a problem with the large amount of infrastructure in the IDE itself. How could this problem be overcome? The solution was something that within VSTEST is called a *host adapter*.

Host adapters are a powerful way to run the unit test infrastructure in-process, enabling the environment for your unit tests to match that of the application. They are not simple to implement and may require your application to expose some sort of connection (more commonly called *a hook*) to the host adapter. While the level of investment is very high and implementation of the host adapter is complex, the return can be huge if your application is significantly complex.

For more details on developing a host adapter, see the VSIP SDK (`http://www.vsipdeveloper.com`). This includes full documentation and also a small, sample implementation.

ASP.NET Unit Testing

One of the host adapters shipped with VSTEST and VSTESD is an ASP.NET host adapter. This is different from the Web Testing features in VSTEST and VSTESD, which provide HTTP-level testing, rather than specifically ASP.NET.

This host adapter allows your unit tests to run within the ASP.NET hosting process — either IIS or Web Development Server (previously codenamed Cassini). It enables access to all the standard ASP.NET APIs such as the Page object, HttpContext, application state, and the Session object. This enables you to test your ASP.NET application fully in a realistic environment.

Deployment

With all testing, you will often require data files, additional DLLs, and other files. Because of the way that VSTEST runs tests, having the files in a single location is not possible. This means that you need to ensure that the files that are needed are, in fact, available to the application. However, despite the ability to add them as items in the run configuration, it makes more sense to declaratively mark the items with each test method. This means that it is easy to see the requirements for each test.

One complaint with this model is that there is a time period for each deployment item to be copied to the run location, which is done at the beginning of the entire run rather than per test. However, one clear advantage is that you can re-run your tests with impunity because your source data are untouched by any edits and changes your tests may make to them.

Private Accessors

Despite the contention around the validity and justification for testing private members, VSTEST provides a quick and easy solution, removing the need for you to write reflection code (classes and types in the `System.Reflection` namespace). The private accessor functionality in VSTEST generates a set of wrapper classes around your application classes that are private. It does this by providing wrapper classes that mirror your actual classes. This means you can write code that appears very similar to actually writing tests directly against the application code. This is very powerful and enables you to access things that would otherwise require lots of reflection-based code to be written. When used in conjunction with the test generation functionality, it generates tests against the private accessor rather than the (inaccessible) application code.

Creating Your First Unit Test

There are two main ways to author unit tests — either through manually writing the code or using code generation. However, the end result is often similar, and in either case you have to write the true meat of the tests yourself: The code generation functionality is not smart enough to solve the complex problems of user data types and analysis of the actual function. Being able to understand what the specific implementation does is very complex. We're going to walk through creating a sample class library, generating a unit test, and customizing that unit test to properly test the class library, and then run the test to see its outcome.

Creating a Sample Library

First, let's create a new C# class library. To do this, click File ⇨ New Project, and in the New Project dialog box select "Visual C#\Windows\Class Library" (see Figure 3-1).

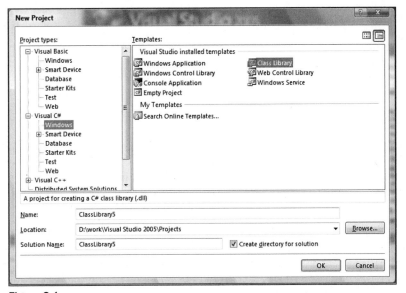

Figure 3-1

This will create a simple class library, just waiting for you to add some code. We're going to create a simple mathematical library that will provide something easy to test:

```
using System;
using System.Collections.Generic;
using System.Text;

namespace SampleLibrary
{
    public class SimpleMath
    {
        public int Add(int a, int b)
        {
            return a + b;
        }

        public float Add(float a, float b)
        {
            return a + b;
        }

        public int Subtract(int a, int b)
        {
            return a - b;
        }

        public float Subtract(float a, float b)
        {
            return a - b;
        }

        public int Multiply(int a, int b)
        {
            return a * b;
        }

        public float Multiply(float a, float b)
        {
            return a * b;
        }
    }
}
```

You should be able to type this code directly in place of the code created by the default class library. Once you've done this, you should be able to succesfully build the class library. If you cannot, check that you've copied the code clearly into your file, and rebuild. We use this sample library below for some examples.

Generating Unit Tests

With the code generation feature in VSTEST, you can generate per project, per namespace, per class, or per method tests at any given time. It generates into a test project that is currently in your solution or creates a new one. One powerful feature to note here is that you can generate from any language to any other language (e.g., C# into Visual Basic).

For the moment, we're just going to generate for one method. To do this:

1. Right click on the `Add(int a, int b)` method.
2. Select Create Unit Tests, which opens the Create Unit Tests dialog box.
3. Ensure that the Add checkbox is ticked (see Figure 3-2).
4. Select "Create a new Visual C# test project" in the output project selection at the bottom of the window.
5. Click OK.

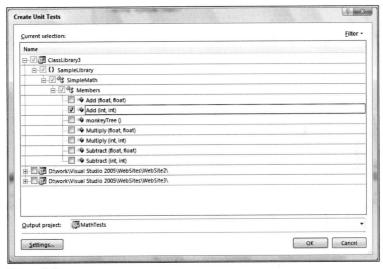

Figure 3-2

You will be presented with an opportunity to name your test project. Select an appropriate name, and click Create in the New Test Project dialog box. After a few moments, you will see the project created, and your test will be created.

We've generated your first test. The test should look something like this:

```
[TestMethod()]
public void AddTest()
{
    SimpleMath target = new SimpleMath();

    int a = 0; // TODO: Initialize to an appropriate value

    int b = 0; // TODO: Initialize to an appropriate value

    int expected = 0;
    int actual;

    actual = target.Add(a, b);
```

```
      Assert.AreEqual(expected, actual, "SampleLibrary.SimpleMath.Add
  did not return the expected value.");
      Assert.Inconclusive("Verify the correctness of this test method.");
  }
```

As you can see, this test does not test very much here. If you were to run it, it would, however, appear to pass — other than the `Assert.Inconclusive` call — this will ensure that when you run the test, you are warned that this test might not actually be validating the application code. This is where your understanding of the application under test comes in. You will need to understand what you are testing to be able to successfully test it. In this case, you can see that 0 + 0 will, in fact, result in 0. But this is very dangerous, since there is nothing meaningful being tested. In this specific example, we need to change the test to do something meaningful.

1. Change `int a = 0;` to `int a = 17;`.

2. Change `int b = 0;` to `int b = 25;`.

3. Change `int expected=0;` to `int expected=42;`.

4. Remove the `Assert.Inconclusive` line.

5. Rebuild the project.

We've now ensured that the test is providing meaningful values (17, 25) to the application and that we understand the expected results (42). We can now run the unit test.

Running Unit Tests

Obviously the goal of writing tests is to actually run them. So having now created a unit test that performs some meaningful action, we need to execute the test. You should be able to show the Test View window, and select the single test — AddTest — and select run. After a few moments, the test results window should look like Figure 3-3.

Figure 3-3

A Tour of Unit Testing in VSTEST

Within unit testing, there are many different areas, both in the UI and in the code itself, where there is opportunity to change the behavior and expose other areas of functionality. These cover all aspects of unit testing.

Anatomy of a Test Class

All test classes follow the same general form — a class, attributed with a `[TestClass]` attribute. This is used by the VSTEST infrastructure to identify that this class may contain tests that need to be executed. Also, the test class must be public. It cannot be internal. See the following code:

```
using System;
using System.Text;
using System.Collections.Generic;
using Microsoft.VisualStudio.TestTools.UnitTesting;

namespace TestProject1
{
    [TestClass]
    public class UnitTest1
    {
        [TestMethod]
        public void TestMethod1()
        { }
    }
}
```

Additionally, it must have a parameterless, public constructor.

Each test method in the test class is a public method, with no return type (a Sub in Visual Basic), and which also takes no parameters. To be considered a test method, it needs to have the `[TestMethod]` attribute on it, and it must be located within a class marked with the `TestClass` attribute.

If any of the attributes are missing, then there will be no errors reported, and there just won't be any tests executed. However, in the case of applying the attributes, but failing one of the other requirements (not public, or having parameters), then an error will be reported.

Passing and Failing a Test

One of the most fundamental aspects of unit testing is passing or failing a test case. The binary choice is based on whether an unhandled exception bubbles out through the test method into the VSTEST execution infrastructure. All the built-in assertions work this way, and it can be explicitly asserted that something has failed. More of the assertions are discussed below. Additionally, a test can "time out"; that is, if it takes longer than a specified amount of time, the test will fail, and its Result will be Timeout. Timeouts are discussed below in this chapter.

If you wish to pass a test, then you just need to ensure that no exceptions leave the test method. There is no way to explicitly say a test is in the Passed state.

Code Generation

When you are trying to build up a set of tests for an existing code base, it can often be a laborious and time-consuming process. VSTEST provides a feature that will help lessen the burden of this work, reducing it to only the required work of making the test itself — the code that really requires you to understand what you are testing and cannot be generated automatically.

When you generate for a set of methods, it creates the boilerplate tests in source files named similarly to the actual application source files, and names the test classes and test methods in a similar way. These names can be customized to your needs along with other options.

When you bring up the Create Unit Tests dialog box, which we saw above in the section "Creating Your First Unit Test," you see that it has several components (see Figure 3-4).

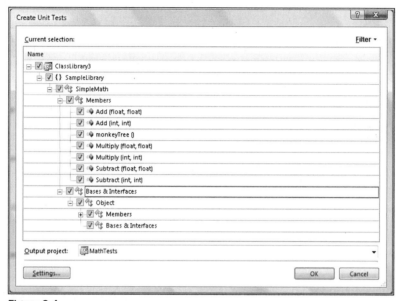

Figure 3-4

There is the main area that you will be working with. This is the type tree and lists all the types, methods, properties, namespaces, and projects that are loaded in the current solution. Also the projects that are listed are the only ones that can be generated for. Not all project types can be generated for. It's important to remember that if generation cannot be done for a project, then that project will not be shown in this tree. Each of the project's types and members will be shown in the language of the projects, for example, a Visual Basic project will show `Bar(ByVal foo as Integer())` rather than `Bar(int[] foo)`, which is what will be shown for C#.

Below the Current Selection group box, there is a dropdown list (Output Project), which will enumerate the test projects in the current solution (if there are any) and will also list the supported test project types that can be created. If you have all the supported languages (Visual Basic, C#, and C++) installed, there will be three. If you install another combination, then there will be the appropriate options listed. If you select a new test project, then you will be prompted for the name of the project, which will be added to the solution as needed.

Code Generation Options

There are two types of options in code generation — filtering and generation settings. Filtering determines what you can see in the "Current selection" tree at the center of the dialog box — non-public items, your code only, base classes, and so on. It just enables you to see a more focused selection of the members that you need to generate for. As you can probably guess, hiding all the privates will significantly reduce the items in the tree, and also the same can be said for "base classes."

Display Non-Publics

This shows all non-public methods — Private, Internal, and Protected. It also takes into account the nested nature of classes, so that public classes nested in private classes will not show if this option is not enabled.

It should be noted that any methods that you may select to generate for with this option shown will have private accessors generated for them.

Display Base Types

With Display Base Types enabled, within the type tree you will see any classes or interfaces that the parent type is explicitly deriving from, along with the ability to expand and see the members of those types.

When you select methods to generate for underneath the Bases & Interfaces node, you will see that the generated test method will have its target generated type be of that base class, with the actual class being assigned to it (see Figure 3-4):

```
[TestMethod()]
public void DisposeTest()
{
    IDisposable target = new Class2();
    target.Dispose();
}
```

With the preceding code, you can see that Class2, which implements IDisposable, is being tested. However, instead of just calling the dispose method from the perspective of Class2, it's called via the interface. This ensures that you are testing the interface implementation rather than potentially some other similarly named method. This helps you test the contract between components.

Display My Code Only

When you derive from base classes and interfaces, you may not want to retest the base implementations (in the case of base classes) that are not defined as part of the project that the class being tested is in. You only want to test that which is in that project. By using this option, you can filter out those that are not defined and implemented in this project.

Settings

These settings change the standard form of the code that is generated (see Figure 3-5). This includes naming, and also some of the code that is emitted. However, these settings do not significantly change the code that is generated; they merely allow you to change and remove some of the standard code that is emitted, without changing the basic form of the code.

❑ **Naming settings** — These options allow you to change the naming of the files, classes, and methods that will be generated. In each one there is a replacement string — [Files], [Class], and [Method]. The purpose here is primarily to allow you to force a file, class, or test name for your class, rather than allowing for customization to your heart's content — hence the limited selections for replacements.

❑ **General options** — The output of each test method can be changed with these options. Overall, they merely allow you to tidy up your generated code to your needs rather than doing anything dramatic.

   ❑ **Mark all test results Inconclusive by default** — With this option on (which is the default), the `Assert .Inconclusive` call is emitted with each test method, to ensure that people don't believe that the test can produce a valid and meaningful Passed result immediately after being generated. This will make sure that when the tests are run, you can see they need more work to become valid tests.

   ❑ **Enable generation warnings** — If for any reason the test method can't be generated, the error information will be generated as a comment in the method body.

   ❑ **Globally qualify all types** — Sometimes, when generating for a number of classes into the same file, there can be ambiguous types because the same type name is in two different namespaces that are imported at the top of the file. The solution here is to globally qualify all the types. This is because all the types have their full namespace in front of them, for example, String versus System.String.

   ❑ **Enable documentation comments** — Before each test method, there is an XML Documentation comment that describes the test. However, the default is merely saying the method that is being tested. It can easily be updated by you to reflect the true meaning of the test. If this option is off, then the comments are not generated.

Figure 3-5

Private Accessors

Private members and types are not accessible to the test project by default; in fact, they are not accessible at all. The same applies to protected members; since the test classes do not derive from the class under test, they do not have access to their protected members. Despite the suggestions from within the industry that you should not test the private members, as discussed at the beginning of the chapter, there is also a call for some sort of solution to the problem by actually calling the private methods and types in an application.

It has always been possible to access private members through reflection code, but this can be laborious and difficult, depending on the types being tested. It involves understanding the location of types, constructor parameters, method parameters, access type, and many other aspects. An additional issue is that it removes a significant amount of clarity and readability from your code. Let's look at an example of what this may look like if you created the reflection code to call a sample private method:

```
using System;
using System.Collections.Generic;
using System.Text;

class PrivateClass
{
    private void PrivateMethod() { }
}
```

The code here is an "internal" class, with one private method. Under normal circumstances, it is not possible to call PrivateMethod from another class or another assembly. However, through reflection code you can.

```
[TestMethod()]
public void PrivateTest()
{
    Assembly asm = Assembly.Load("ClassLibrary3");
    Type type = asm.GetType("PrivateClass");
    ConstructorInfo constructor = type.GetConstructor(new Type[] { });
    Object newObject = constructor.Invoke(null);

    MethodInfo privateMethod = type.GetMethod("PrivateMethod",
BindingFlags.Instance | BindingFlags.NonPublic);
    privateMethod.Invoke(newObject, null);
}
```

As can be seen, the reflection-based code is significantly less clear (see the preceding code) and significantly more complex. It increases in complexity as the constructors/methods require parameters, and those parameters are private types themselves. It balloons out enormously in both terms of lines of code and complexity. Instead of you being able to merely type the code that you mean to call that method, you need to ensure that you wrap it up in an array of objects and pass it to the invoke method, ensuring you use the right instance of the type. This is a moderate amount of code for methods that accept public types, but if the types that you need to pass are also private, there is an almost viral-like infection of all your code with these reflection calls.

Private accessors wrap all of this code and functionality into an API that looks exactly like the original code, but with new names that reflect that they are accessors. This code is completely computer generated, and there is little value in examining it because it is not very readable and contains just reflection calls to pass the parameters to the private method via reflection. However, if you wish to look at the code that is generated, open the VSCodeGenAccessors.cs that is added to your test project in the code editor. In the case of the above test, the test would look very much clearer using the private accessors. The methods are invoked as they would be in a normal test case, there is no lack of readability, and it's also clear that you are working with a private type.

53

```
[DeploymentItem("ClassLibrary3.dll")]
[TestMethod()]
public void PrivateMethodTest()
{
    object target = TestProject1.PrivateClassAccessor.CreatePrivate();
    TestProject1.PrivateClassAccessor accessor = new
TestProject1.PrivateClassAccessor(target);

    accessor.PrivateMethod();
}
```

Customizing Your Test Methods

While generation will create your boilerplate test methods, they are not enough to test your application. As you build out your test methods and create real tests that actually do something of significance with the classes and methods in your application, you will discover that there are more customizations required to make your testing even more successful. All of the customization of unit testing in VSTEST is done using attributes — a feature of the .NET platform that is exposed in all of the major languages shipped by Microsoft in Visual Studio. For more information on attributes, look at the specific documentation for the language you are using.

Initialization and Cleanup

One of the biggest areas where customization is needed is around initialization and cleanup. Often for each test case to run, some set of common initialization is needed — maybe opening a data connection and authenticating against a remote server. If this code is placed in the test case itself, it loses clarity and becomes difficult to maintain, and although the initialization is easy to abstract into a method, cleanup requires much more careful management around exception handling in error cases, and the like. After you have implemented this for several methods, it starts to become very complex.

Assembly and Class Attributes

The [AssemblyInitialize]/[AssemblyCleanup] attributed methods are run once before any tests are run in the entire assembly, and cleanup is run after all tests in the assembly run. There can only be one of these methods per assembly. An example method would be:

```
[AssemblyInitialize]
public static void AsmInit(TestContext context)
{}
```

[ClassInitlialize]/[ClassCleanup] is run immediately before any tests from that class are run:

```
[ClassInitialize]
public static void ClassInit(TestContext context)
{}
```

These enable you to set static members that may hold references to long-living and reusable types such that all test methods in the class can make use of them without having to reopen them all the time. The cleanup methods function similarly, but have no parameters.

Test Initialization and Cleanup

These initialization and cleanup methods are called before and after every test method. These are also instance, rather than static methods, because they belong to the instance of the test class that is created for each test method:

```
[TestInitialize]
public void TestInit()
{ }

[TestCleanup]
public void TestCleanup()
{ }
```

Expected Exceptions

When you are testing an application's code, it is not always the Passing case (e.g., no exception was thrown, or some set of values was compared against an expected set of values) that you are trying to validate; it is often that you want to ensure that the error cases are handled correctly. This can be done with the [ExpectedException(Type)] attributes, which will ensure that the test case will only pass if there is an exception thrown that matches the type specified and is not handled in the application code.

It is important to note that any exception type can be used except System.Exception. Additionally, there is an overload for the attribute that accepts a parameter named *message*. This does not validate the message in the exception and only provides the error message that should be reported when the exception is not caught:

```
[TestMethod]
[ExpectedException(typeof(FileNotFoundException))]
public void ExceptionTest()
{
    throw new FileNotFoundException("File.txt");
}
```

Temporarily Disabling Tests

As time progresses when authoring tests, certain tests may become unstable and begin to fail for reasons other than bugs in your application code. Because these are known failures and no investigation is needed to understand the root cause of the failures for every run of tests, it may be required to disable the test. At first look, this seems simple: remove the [TestMethod] attribute, or comment the method out. However, this makes it easy to lose the test because it now no longer shows up in any UI, or when you run all your tests. However, there is another way to exclude tests using an additional attribute, the [Ignore] attribute, which means that the test is grayed out in Test view, or errors are reported from the command line.

Deployment Items

As discussed previously, there is the need for data files and other files that are needed both by the test cases and the application under test to function. This means that there has to be a way to include files to be copied to where the tests are executed from. This is handled through deployment items. As discussed in Chapter 2, you can use the run configuration to add run level and solution-wide deployment items and directories. However, the deployment items are not always solution wide, and therefore there is a desire to have a more localized selection of deployment items. These again are just attributes with solution-relative paths — and this is an important factor to remember, these are not relative to the project:

```
[DeploymentItem("File.txt")]
[TestMethod]
public void DeploymentItems()
{
    File.Exists("File.txt");
}
```

Timeouts

When a test is executing, there may be expectations of how long it should take. These are not performance expectations. That is something for the dynamic analysis functionality to cover, along with performance targets being set in advance. But there may also be an expectation that if something takes longer than a specified period of time, there is an error, and the test case should be aborted. In these cases, it is possible to have an attribute that sets an explicit maximum time period for the test to execute. By default, all tests are set with a 5-minute timeout — this can be changed in the run configuration. This attribute allows you to override that value for a specific test case.

It is important to note that the timeout is for the total time that a test takes to execute, and this is not just the method itself, but the initialization and cleanup methods. Additionally, if this is the first method to be executed in a class, it will include the time used by the class initialize method, and if it's the first test in the entire assembly, the assembly initialize time will be included. These rules also apply for cleanups as well:

```
[Timeout(10000)]
[TestMethod]
public void TimeoutTest()
{
    System.Threading.Thread.Sleep(30000);
}
```

Unit Testing Assertions

One of the key aspects of unit testing is the assertions that are used to validate the data, assumptions, and other statements about the code under test. There are many assertions that can be used, both for single items (Assert.*), string assertions to assert various properties of a test (StringAssert.*), and collection asserts that validate the contents of ICollection (CollectionAssert.*).

Standard Asserts

There are a large number of asserts that validate equality, non-equality, reference identity, and type comparison. Each of these many methods has overloads providing strong typing for the primitive types, with parameters to provide relevant error messages for easier diagnosis. A message that says "0 does not equal 1" is not helpful (and the default), whereas a message that says "0 does not equal 1. This is because more than 0 errors were found" provides significantly more context to the person investigating the failure:

```
[TestCleanup]
public void Assertions()
{
    Assert.AreEqual(0, 1, "1, and 0 are different numbers");
    Assert.AreNotEqual(0, 1, "1, and 0, should never be the same");
}
```

Generic Overloads

For almost all the assertions there are generic overloads. This allows for strongly typed validation of the objects being compared, without having to worry about the types being coerced as System.Object, and losing potentially type-specific implementations of Equals, GetHashCode, or other similar methods.

With the generic overloads, you can get strongly typed (not System.Object) comparisons and assertions that allow for a significantly more reliable and accurate verification of your types. Generics are an advanced feature of the .NET Runtime and languages that was introduced with .NET 2.0. For more information, see Microsoft's documentation.

String Asserts

Often the data being validated is a string, and within that string you are asserting either with a regular expression or with String.Contains. However if you do this with standard asserts, your code will become a myriad of calls that again cloud the real intent of the code. The StringAssert class provides overloads and methods that take regular expressions to provide short ways to validate the strings without having to write regular expression code. These are very similar to the standard assert classes, but are focused on string verification.

Collection Asserts

Contrary to what you might assume from its name, CollectionAssert allows you to validate the quality and contents of the collection at the item level rather than the collection level, that is to say, these methods will go inside the collections and validate the items for equality and existence of items.

It should be noted that we're not going to discuss all the methods of the Assert class here. They are all very self-descriptive method names with well-named parameters, and discussing them here would be excessive.

Debugging Unit Tests

When authoring and investigating tests, there is a requirement to debug not only the tests, but also the application code. This could be difficult to work through the tests if they were in a custom harness, or with NUnit, where you would need to attach to another process (although it can be simplified) at the right time. With VSTEST, debugging of any unit test is built into the product. The debugging functionality available to you for unit tests is the same as for any other application that you are debugging. You can step through all the the code from the highest to the lowest level of your application straight from the unit test as if you were actively debugging your application as you step through method to method. You can also use *F5* to debug an entire test project: In this case, all tests, be they unit tests or any other test type, are run under the debugger.

It is important to note a couple of things when running under the debugger:

❏ All timeouts are disabled during the test run (for obvious reasons).

❏ If you turn on the "Break on all Exceptions" option in the Debug ⇨ Exceptions dialog, then you will be barraged by several exceptions from the VSTEST infrastructure itself. Because these can sometimes be noisy, it is recommended that if you need this, then you should only enable it after you have had the debugger break into the beginning of the test method. If you then enable it, you will see any exceptions thrown by your application code.

Advanced Unit Testing

We've been through the basics of unit testing — and you have at your disposal the skills required to create and run unit tests to successfully test your application. However, no application is simple enough that just calling some methods on it is going to test it. Nor will just running the tests in the IDE be enough. People will want to run tests without Visual Studio running, or in a build type environment. These tasks fall under advanced unit testing, and cover several different areas. Some of these are also not documented well in the product documentation and can only be discovered through experience or searching the support forums online.

All unit tests can have several different properties that can be added to them. These can affect the execution of a test and also provide simple metadata about that test. Here is a summary of the most common attributes:

Attribute	Editable	Description
Associated work items	Editable if part of TFS	When working on a team and connected to the Visual Studio Team Foundation Server, a *work item* can be associated with a test. Work items come in many flavors, including not only an assigned task to be completed, but also reported product defects ("bugs"). Associating a work item with a test provides a way to show that a test maps directly to this particular area of the product.
Class Name	Read-Only	The class name that this test is a member of.
Data Access Method	Editable	Decides where the rows in the database are accessed in sequential order, or randomly when doing data-driven testing.
Data Connection String	Editable	The connection string, in ADO.NET format, that is used to connect to the database being used in a data-driven test.
Data Provider	Read-Only	The ADO.NET Provider that is used for the data-driven test. This could be various values but typically is System.Data.OleDb.

Attribute	Editable	Description
Data Table Name	Editable	The table, as found in the database connected with the connection string, that is being used for the data-driven test.
Deployment Items	Editable	Allows you to specify files or folders to deploy with your test run. Specify the full path to the file or folder on one line. Specify each additional file or folder on a separate line. These files are in addition to any files specified in the test run configuration (see Chapter 2 for a description of the *Test Run Configuration* dialog box).
Description	Editable	Use this property to describe what the test is for.
Full Class Name	Read-Only	The full name of the class this test is part of, including the namespace and any nested classes.
ID	Read-Only	The unique identifier for the test. For a manual test type, this is the actual path where the test resides.
Iteration	Editable if part of TFS	When working on a team and connected to the Visual Studio Team Foundation Server, an "Iteration" can be defined. Consider this like milestones or stages within the software development life cycle (SDLC). This property allows you to specify to which part of the SDLC this test belongs.
Namespace	Read-Only	The namespace that the class is a member of.
Non-runnable Error	Read-Only	When a test is part of a test project but for some reason it cannot be included as part of a test run, this property contains a description of the problem. For example, if the file on the local drive does not exist but is listed in the project, this will contain an error value.
Owner	Editable	Used to list the name or user ID of the person who authored or maintains the test.
Priority	Editable	If your team uses this property, this helps determine which tests need to be run first.
Project	Read-Only	This property contains the name of the parent project containing this test.
Project Area	Editable if part of TFS	If part of a team project (connected to the Visual Studio Team Foundation Server), the test can be mapped directly to a "Project Area" specified for the team project.
Project Relative Path	Read-Only	The filename of the project containing the test. The path is relative to the location of the solution on the local disk.
Solution	Read-Only	This is the name of the solution that contains the test project that holds this test.

Continued

Attribute	Editable	Description
Test Enabled	Editable	This allows a test to be excluded from test runs without having to modify a test list that contains this particular test. An example is turning off a test that results in crashing the current build of the program being tested. Once a new build becomes available that fixes the crashing bug, the test can be re-enabled.
Test Name	Read-Only	The name of the test, based on its filename.
Test Storage	Read-Only	In the case of a manual test, this is the same as the test ID — the path to the file that contains the test.
Test Type	Read-Only	The type of the test — in this case, Manual Test.
Timeout	Read-Only	A manual test does not have a timeout value, that is, its value is infinite. For other test types, this value allows you to specify how long the test can take to run before it is aborted and marked as a failed test if it does not complete on its own in the allotted time.

MSTest Command-Line Tools

Within VSTEST and VSTESD there is a command-line tool for executing all types of tests, and much of what we discuss here will apply to other test types, not just unit testing. However, in all examples, we will be using the sample tests generated at the beginning of this chapter in the section "Creating Your First Unit Tests." Additionally, we will assume that the tests are in an assembly named *MathTests.dll*.

To be able to access the MSTest tool, you need to either have started a Visual Studio Command Prompt (in the tools section of the Visual Studio program group on the Start menu), or have added your Visual Studio install directory to your path.

If you are not comfortable using a command prompt in Windows, then it is suggested that you move on to the section, "Unit Test Lifetime."

Once you've opened this prompt, see what the output looks like from running just `mstest` (see Figure 3-6).

Figure 3-6

If you use `mstest`/help, you will be able to see all the switches that can be used with `mstest` on the command line. We are not going to cover all of those here, but we will cover the majority.

Switches

A large number of the switches are related to publishing the results into the Visual Studio Team Foundation Server (VSTFS), which is not something that is being covered here, and those switches will not be discussed.

Before you start to run any of these commands, make sure you have changed to the directory where your MathTests.dll project is located:

```
C:\Users\d.hopton>d:

D:\>cd "work\Visual Studio 2005\Projects\MathLibrary\MathTests"

D:\work\Visual Studio 2005\Projects\MathLibrary\MathTests>
```

Test Container

The most important switch that you will be using is the `/testcontainer` switch. This is the switch that is used to identify the files and DLLs that contain the tests that need to be executed. You need to specify the relative or absolute path to the files to be executed. If you use just the file name, only the current working directory will be used to search for the test files:

```
Example execution:
D:\work\Visual Studio 2005\Projects\MathLibrary\MathTests>mstest
/testcontainer:bin\debug\MathTests.dll
Microsoft (R) Test Execution Command Line Tool Version 8.0.50727.42
Copyright (C) Microsoft Corporation 2005. All rights reserved.

Loading bin\debug\MathTests.dll...
Starting execution...

Results             Top Level Tests
-------             ---------------
Inconclusive        MathTests.SimpleMathTest.AddTest
Inconclusive        MathTests.SimpleMathTest.AddTest1
Inconclusive        MathTests.SimpleMathTest.MultiplyTest
Inconclusive        MathTests.SimpleMathTest.MultiplyTest1
Inconclusive        MathTests.SimpleMathTest.SubtractTest
Inconclusive        MathTests.SimpleMathTest.SubtractTest1
0/6 test(s) Passed, 6 Inconclusive

Summary
-------

Test Run Inconclusive.
  Inconclusive  6
  ---------------
  Total         6
Results file:     D:\work\Visual Studio 2005\Projects\MathLibrary\
MathTests\TestResults\d.hopton_POPPLER 2007-03-06 01_06_27.trx
Run Configuration: Default Run Configuration
```

As you can see, all the tests in the DLL were run and a Results file was created, which if you open in the IDE will have the result of the test run, just as if you had run it using the tools in the IDE. You can either use the File menu inside Visual Studio or just double-click the Results file to cause it to open in the IDE.

It is possible to specify more than one assembly or test file at a time, and that is done by specifying any number of /testcontainer switches:

```
Mstest /testcontainer:MathTests.dll /testcontainer:CalcTests.dll
```

No Isolation

During the final stages of development of Visual Studio 2005, there were several complaints from the community around performance — both from the time to start running tests, to the time to run thousands of empty tests (somewhat of a benchmark within the community). Some of these couldn't be resolved so late in the game — the time to deploy tests, for example. However, there were some mitigations that could be done to help ease some of the pain, and /noisolation was one of them.

Normally, when you execute a set of unit tests, each test assembly is isolated in its own application domain. These take time to start up, but also provide significant isolation for the tests, and more importantly VSTEST, by ensuring that no rogue unit test can accidentally take down the whole test run, but only that small subset of tests. There are also various technical reasons (e.g., unloading of assemblies) that this was chosen.

It turned out that application domain startup time was actually rather significant, and on the command line for a large number of tests wasn't actually needed. If you are running just one test assembly, from the command line, there is not a lot to isolate that assembly from. It's only going to break its own tests if it crashes the whole of mstest. Thus, the /noisolation switch was added.

This switch ensures that there is no additional app domain created, and all the tests run in the same app domain as mstest and the rest of the VSTEST infrastructure. Another facet is that there is no process isolation either. Normally, tests are run in a separate process (VsTestHost.exe). With this switch, there is no other process except mstest involved in executing the tests

Test Selection

When you are running tests on the command line, you might want to only execute some tests, rather than all the tests in the assembly — because of time constraints, no requirements for running all the tests, or maybe you're just iterating on one specific test case.

In the IDE, you would use the Test View or Test Manager window to select a subset of tests to be executed. Since there is no UI on the command line, then you need another way to select the test cases. This is achieved through the use of the /test switch. With this switch, you specify the test name, and any tests that match this name will be executed. Note that this is a substring match, rather than an "if this matches, run it." Additionally, this does not provide any wildcard, regular expression, or other complex syntax for selecting test cases. It is a very simple implementation to facilitate something approaching test selection on the command line.

It is possible to get an exact match on the test case that you want to execute, by using the /unique switch. This looks for only test cases that exactly match the name supplied. However, one would expect it to run the test that matched exactly. It does not — in reality, if it finds any more than one match based on the normal /test results (e.g., substring matching), then it will fail and report that it found more than one test by that name:

```
D:\work\Visual Studio 2005\Projects\MathLibrary\MathTests>mstest
/testcontainer:bin\debug\MathTests.dll /test:AddTest /unique
Microsoft (R) Test Execution Command Line Tool Version 8.0.50727.42
Copyright (C) Microsoft Corporation 2005. All rights reserved.

Loading bin\debug\MathTests.dll...
Test AddTest is not unique. It maps to more than one test.
Starting execution...
No tests to execute.

D:\work\Visual Studio 2005\Projects\MathLibrary\MathTests>
```

This causes somewhat of a problem when one needs to execute just a single test from the command line. However, it is possible, but you must use the fully qualified name of the test method:

```
Mstest /testcontainer:bin\debug\MathTests.dll
/test:MathTests.SimpleMathTests.AddTest /unique
```

Run Configuration

If you have created a run configuration in the IDE and wish to use it on the command line, you can specify it on the command line to be used for the invocation of mstest:

```
Mstest /testcontainer:bin\debug\MathTests.dll
/runconfig:MyRunconfig.testrunconfig
```

This uses the run configuration in the same way you would using the IDE.

Results Files

By default, whenever you run on the command line, a TRX file (a test results file) is generated in line with the run name. This means that as you run over and over again, you will start to build up a large number of Results files. Additionally, the .trx generated filename is not particularly user friendly, or easy to type. By specifying the /resultsfile switch, you can choose the name for your trx file:

```
Mstest /testcontainer:bin\debug\MathTests.dll
/resultsfile:MyResultsFile.trx
```

If the file is already present, then mstest will not overwrite the trx file, and will, in fact, not run any tests. It is important that you clean up your Results files between runs if you are using a constant filename.

Metadata File

Test lists are created to help you easily select and run named subsets of tests. As mentioned in Chapter 2, these test lists are stored in test metadata (.vsmdi) files that are part of the solution. While in the IDE you see the test lists automatically, and they are immediately available. You need to use the /testmetadata switch to specify a VSMDI file:

```
Mstest /testcontainer:bin\debug\MathTests.dll
/testmetadata:MathTests.vsmdi
```

When you specify just the VSMDI file, then all the tests that are persisted in test lists in that file are executed. If you did not place a test into a test list, then it will not be executed because it is not saved into the VSMDI file:

```
Mstest /testcontainer:bin\debug\MathTests.dll
/testmetadata:MathTests.vsmdi /testlist:AdditionTests
```

However, the point of VSMDI is categorization rather than enabling you to run all the tests in your solution. Thus the ability to specify a specific test list is also provided. With nested test lists, you just specify the test list as if it were a set of folders on your computer:

```
D:\work\Visual Studio 2005\Projects\MathLibrary>mstest
/testmetadata:MathTests.vsmdi /testlist:Addition
Microsoft (R) Test Execution Command Line Tool Version 8.0.50727.42
Copyright (C) Microsoft Corporation 2005. All rights reserved.

Loading MathTests.vsmdi...
Starting execution...

Results                 Top Level Tests
-------                 ---------------
Inconclusive            (Addition/)MathTests.SimpleMathTest.AddTest
Inconclusive            (Addition/)MathTests.SimpleMathTest.AddTest1
0/2 test(s) Passed, 2 Inconclusive

Summary
-------
Test Run Inconclusive.
  Inconclusive  2
  ---------------
  Total         2
Results file:      D:\work\Visual Studio 2005\Projects\MathLibrary
\TestResults\d.hopton_POPPLER 2007-03-06 01_51_31.trx
Run Configuration: Local Test Run
```

Peccadilloes of Command Line Execution

While the runtime environment from the command line is the same as that in the IDE, some of the startup environment is different. Additionally, there are some issues with VSMDI files that you should be aware of — while not strictly on the command line (the behavior is the same in the IDE), one will encounter this more often as the test assembly changes without being able to easily see the test lists. We discuss these issues below.

Search Paths

When running on the command line, any paths that are used are relative, with the search starting in the current working directory. This applies not only to files passed on the command line, but also for deployment items (in the run configuration and in the test methods), test dlls when using only the VSMDI file, and assembly dependencies. This means that if your files are in other paths within the system, you need to ensure that all relative paths are correctly relative to where you execute the mstest command.

Test Lists and Renaming Tests

Unit tests are identified by a one-way MD5 hash of the fully qualified method name, for example:

```
Namespace1.Namespace2.Class1.Method1
```

This means, that when you change the name of the test, its MD5 hash changes, and no longer identifies it as the old test case. On the surface, this is not a problem, but as soon as you are using test lists (as described in Chapter 2), this causes a problem because you may receive orphaned test cases in test lists, and the tests will no longer be in the test list in which you placed them (because, technically, they no longer exist).

While there is nothing that can be done to solve the problem (and it is a fundamental issue with the way in which renames are performed in VSTEST for unit tests), if you are not aware of it and do not take the time to re-add the test cases to the original test lists when you rename them, you soon end up with a large number of orphaned tests and test lists full of nothing but broken tests.

Unit Test Life Time

On the surface, the lifetime of the test class, the order in which methods are executed, and the lifetime of threads seems clear. However, it is not. It is, in reality, completely the opposite of that which one would expect.

Firstly, the order in which your tests are going to be executed is officially "undefined." That is to say that Microsoft makes no guarantees or suggestions as to the order in which the tests are going to be executed. This is because of the very nature of the VSTEST toolset. It is not solely about unit tests, the infrastructure can execute many tests of many types in a single run, and the order in which these "should" be executed would be undefined. As such, this has been carried through into unit testing. A neat, unintended, byproduct of this is that it reinforces the unit testing purists' belief that any single test can be executed entirely on its own without having to execute other tests. However, there are times when order is important — and the VSTEST and VSTESD products include the ordered test type to cope with this (see Chapter 2 for more details).

Some interesting pieces of information that may help you understand the behavior you are seeing when you run in the IDE versus the command line are:

❑   On the command line, tests are executed in the order in which reflection returns the classes and methods.

❑   In the IDE, a general rule is "the order in which they are selected, is the order in which they run." If you change your sorting and change your selection, the order may change dramatically.

❑   When using test lists, the order is the order in which the tests are discovered within the test lists.

❑   The only way to ensure order is to use ordered tests.

Test Class Lifetime

Most users expect there to be one test class instance for the duration that all the test methods that belong to that test class are being executed. That is to say, one test class is instantiated for N number of tests.

This would allow you to acquire resources and maintain state within the test class instance for the life of tests. This is not what happens — in a completely orthogonal way, for each test method a new test class is instantiated. This means that any assumptions around state that may be set up by previous test methods are invalid.

So, to be clear, if you run 20 test methods on a test class, then the test class will be instantiated 20 times.

Initialization/Cleanup Ordering

When you have multiple test classes, with multiple test methods, and each class has its own ClassInitialization/Cleanup defined, the timing and order of these methods being called is not 100% clear — and it is not that which you think it is. Given the following sample code:

```csharp
using System;
using System.Text;
using System.Collections.Generic;
using Microsoft.VisualStudio.TestTools.UnitTesting;

namespace SampleTests
{
    [TestClass]
    public class UnitTest1
    {
        [AssemblyInitialize]
        public static void AsmInit(TestContext context)
        { Console.WriteLine("UnitTest1.AsmInit"); }

        [AssemblyCleanup]
        public static void AsmCleanup()
        { Console.WriteLine("UnitTest1.AsmCleanup"); }

        [ClassInitialize]
        public static void ClassInit(TestContext context)
        { Console.WriteLine("UnitTest1.ClassInit"); }

        [ClassCleanup]
        public static void ClassCleanup()
        { Console.WriteLine("UnitTest1.ClassCleanup"); }

        [TestInitialize]
        public void TestInit()
        { Console.WriteLine("UnitTest1.TestInit"); }

        [TestCleanup]
        public void TestCleanup()
        { Console.WriteLine("UnitTest1.TestCleanup"); }

        [TestMethod]
        public void TestMethod1()
        { Console.WriteLine("UnitTest1.TestMethod1"); }

        [TestMethod]
        public void TestMethod2()
        { Console.WriteLine("UnitTest1.TestMethod2"); }
    }
```

```
[TestClass]
public class UnitTest2
{
    [ClassInitialize]
    public static void ClassInit(TestContext context)
    { Console.WriteLine("UnitTest2.ClassInit"); }

    [ClassCleanup]
    public static void ClassCleanup()
    { Console.WriteLine("UnitTest2.ClassCleanup"); }

    [TestInitialize]
    public void TestInit()
    { Console.WriteLine("UnitTest2.TestInit"); }

    [TestCleanup]
    public void TestCleanup()
    { Console.WriteLine("UnitTest2.TestCleanup"); }

    [TestMethod]
    public void TestMethod1()
    { Console.WriteLine("UnitTest2.TestMethod1"); }

    [TestMethod]
    public void TestMethod2()
    { Console.WriteLine("UnitTest2.TestMethod2"); }
}
}
```

As has been stated before, the order that the actual tests may be executed in is undefined. However, this causes an interesting issue with respect to cleanup: When should the last ClassCleanup be called? Well, since tests can be interleaved, it's not a simple answer. The path that the VSTEST team took was that cleanup for all classes will be called at the very end of the test run, before the assembly initialization.

The explicit order of calls for the preceding code is:

```
UnitTest1.AsmInit
UnitTest1.ClassInit
UnitTest1.TestInit
UnitTest1.TestMethod1
UnitTest1.TestCleanup
UnitTest1.TestInit
UnitTest1.TestMethod2
UnitTest1.TestCleanup
UnitTest2.ClassInit
UnitTest2.TestInit
UnitTest2.TestMethod1
UnitTest2.TestCleanup
UnitTest2.TestInit
UnitTest2.TestMethod2
UnitTest2.TestCleanup
UnitTest1.ClassCleanup
UnitTest2.ClassCleanup
UnitTest1.AsmCleanup
```

It is very important to understand this order, because if you are expecting cleanup to be called in the middle of your run to release resources, this is not going to happen, and you will need to ensure that your resources are managed effectively.

One solution to this problem is to not use class level init and cleanup, and instead make use of static constructors and manage your resources outside of this infrastructure.

Thread Today, Gone Tomorrow

Each test method is called on a different thread. This is to ensure that timeouts can happen. While on the surface this may seem to be OK, it causes problems when you are doing interop with unmanaged code. Because the thread disappears, anything that has been associated with that thread — Win32 windows, thread local storage — will disappear as soon as the thread goes away. If your application relies on a Win32 window existing for the lifetime of the thread, then you will need to start the window on a non-test executed thread. As a byproduct of this, the initialization and cleanup methods may in actual fact be called on different threads.

The Application Domain (AppDomain)

As was discussed as part of the /noisolation description, all unit test assemblies are run in their own unique app domain. If you run two test assemblies with the same invocation of mstest, then there are two application domains, which exist for the life of all tests in that assembly. This means if you have shared statics across multiple assemblies (in some sort of singleton pattern), then you will see that this will be recreated as one assembly of tests completes executing, and another starts to execute. This is something to be aware of, as it may confuse you as you try to share several common objects across assemblies.

App.config

Most applications these days store a large amount of their configuration in an app.config file that resides in the same location as the EXE for the application — this will be named Application.exe.config, and the settings are applied to the default app domain that is created when a managed binary is executed. However, in the case of unit tests, there is no exe to run, since it is Visual Studio that is the program "running" the tests. This causes a problem for applications that rely on their settings being in the app.config file, since when they request their setting they will just see a default app domain, created specifically for the unit tests.

Based on customer feedback, Microsoft added support for this to Visual Studio. If you have settings that need to be applied, then just ensure that there is an app.config or TestDllName.dll.config (e.g., MathTests.dll.config) that is present in the same directory as the test assembly itself. This application configuration file, and any settings (binding redirects, tracing, data sources, and anything else in them), will be applied to the app domain in which the tests are running.

Differences When Using /noisolation

When using /noisolation, there is no way to have the app.config files configuration applied — you get the "default app domain" settings, and are unable to change them. If it is required that you have app.config settings loaded for each test dll, then it is a requirement that you do not use /noisolation.

ASP.NET

As was mentioned previously, one of the unique features of VSTEST is the ability to run unit tests within ASP.NET. These can be any old unit tests, but doing this does require some additional attributes on your test methods. These attributes are used to specify what web site to run against, what URL to test, that it is an ASP.NET unit test, if it's to run under IIS, and also potentially credentials.

These attributes are the same for both the Web Development Server and IIS. However, there is one difference — for IIS, you do not specify the AspNetDevelopmentServerHost attribute on the test methods. This attribute is used to identify information for the unit test to run:

```
[TestMethod()]
[HostType("ASP.NET")]
[AspNetDevelopmentServerHost("%PathToWebRoot%\\WebSite2",
"/WebSite2")]
[UrlToTest("http://localhost/WebSite2")]
```

When you specify these attributes, the unit test is run inside the ASP.NET runtime under either IIS or Web Development Server (Cassini), and you have full access to the normal services that would be available to you on an ASPX page. You can get hold of the Page object from the test context:

```
System.Web.UI.Page = testContext.RequestedPage;
```

Once you have the page, you can call .FindControl to acquire any other control on the page to validate its value, or presence. This is in addition to just testing your App_Code helper classes that your page may be making use of. VSTEST does not support generation for code that is outside of the App_Code directory within your web site.

If you wish to specify credentials, you can use the [Credentials] attribute, which will allow you to specify a username and password combination that will authenticate with basic, NTLM, digest, and Kerberos authentication mechanisms.

Data-Driven Testing

When you have methods in your application code that may need to be called several times with different inputs to check corner cases, range of support, and specific error cases, you have various choices for implementation. You can create several test cases that call the required method with each and every input, or creating one method that just repeatedly calls the method with the supplied inputs. Both of these approaches have significant drawbacks — large amounts of code have to be written to support each method, and can be painful to maintain. In the case of the second, you lose the granularity in the reporting of the test results, which can be frustrating when diagnosing the cause of the failure.

The solution to these is data-driven testing. With data-driven testing, your test method is executed for all the rows in a database table, with an ADO.NET DataRow being provided as part of the test context, along with the DataConnection. Any database that is supported by the ADO.NET infrastructure can be used.

Before we can examine a data-driven test, we need to create a data source. To do this we are going to use Microsoft Excel:

1.   Start Microsoft Excel.

2.   Create a new worksheet.

3.   In the first column enter the numbers 1–10.

4.   In the second column enter the numbers 10–1.

5.   Save the spreadsheet in a well-known location.

Once you have done this, create an empty test method, and then in Test View select it, so that you can see its properties in the Properties window. Select the Data Connection String property, and click the ellipsis on the right (see Figure 3-7).

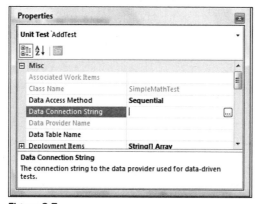

Figure 3-7

You will now see the standard .NET Data Provider dialog pop up (see Figure 3-8).

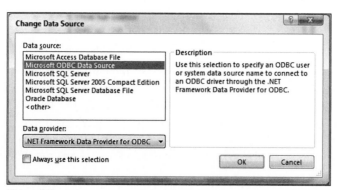

Figure 3-8

Select Microsoft ODBC Data Source, and click Continue. In the Connection Properties dialog box, select "Use connection string," and click the *Build* button. In the Select Data Source dialog box, click

"Machine Data Source," "Excel Files," and click OK. In the Select Workbook dialog box, select the file you created earlier. Click OK, and then OK again to close the Connection Properties dialog box. You should be returned to the Properties window in Visual Studio. Below the Data Connection String is the Data Table Name dropdown list. If you open this list, you see all the worksheets in the Microsoft Excel file. If you had used SQL or another database, you would see a list of all the tables. There is no way to filter the results with a query — you must select a whole table, or view.

If you now look at the test, it should look something like this:

```
[DataSource("System.Data.Odbc", "Dsn=Excel Files;dbq=d:
\\datasource.xls;defaultdir=d:;driverid=1046;maxbuffersize=2048;
pagetimeout=5", "Sheet1\$", DataAccessMethod.Sequential), TestMethod()]
public void AddTest() {}
```

If you now run this test, you will see that the test result window shows only one high-level result, but the roll up information in the yellow area of the test results window will report 11/11 tests. If you then double-click on the result, you will be presented with the detailed results of the data-driven test (see Figure 3-9).

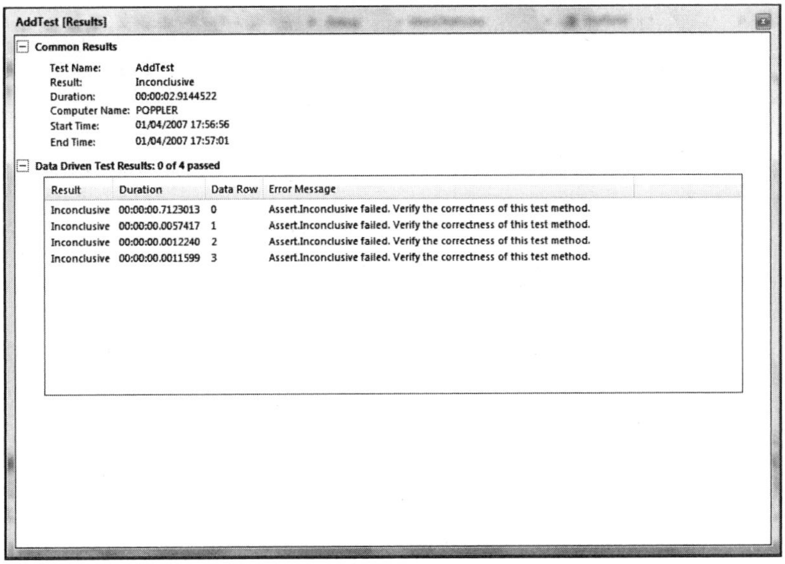

Figure 3-9

Now we can add actual access to the data rows that are returned from our data source. We do this by accessing the DataRow property on the test context, either with named columns or numbered columns. Since we did not use named columns in the Microsoft Excel worksheet, we need to use numbered access:

```
Assert.AreEqual(testContextInstance.DataRow[0],
testContextInstance.DataRow[1], 10);
```

If you now run the test again, you will see different results, some passing, and some failing. As you drill into each test case, you can see the data row that was passed to your test method.

Test Context

The test context is a helpful class that provides the test name and deployment path while your test is executing. However, it is only available if you have a specifically named and typed property on your test class — it must be called TestContext:

```
private TestContext testContextInstance;

public TestContext TestContext
{
    get { return testContextInstance; }
    set { testContextInstance = value; }
}
```

When you have this on your test class, the test infrastructure will assign a new instance of a TestContext class to it before a test method is called. It will always have the current test name, deployment directory, and logging directory set to allow you to write files into these directories. It does also have timer functionality used by load testing; however, that is covered in Chapter 7.

Summary

We have covered an enormous amount of information in this chapter, from the principles of unit testing, the different approaches to unit testing, all the way through to advanced topics such as data-driven unit testing and running your tests under ASP.NET. You now have a powerful set of tools to enable you to unit test your application successfully.

Testing the Database

The goal of this chapter is to develop and test a database project using Microsoft Visual Studio 2005 Team Edition for Database Professionals (VSTEDP).

Most applications interact with a database that also requires testing. This chapter explains how to test a SQL Server database using VSTEDP.

Database Testing Is Different

Application testing is covered very well in the rest of this book. Testing the database is comparable to testing applications on certain levels — such as testing scalar functions. Simply put, database testing is different from application testing.

Key differences surface when you consider the following scenarios:

- ❑ A new row has been added to a table. How do you test it for validity?
- ❑ Several hundred rows are returned in a query of a view. How do you determine that these rows belong in the results?
- ❑ A user belongs to a specified database role. Should this user be able to execute a stored procedure?
- ❑ A stored procedure returns a NULL value. How do you determine if this is acceptable?

Testing the results of set-based operations requires a different way of thinking about testing — and a new tool. In response, the good people at Microsoft have provided VSTEDP.

VSTEDP, originally named *Data Dude*, allows database developers to develop, test, refactor, compare, and populate SQL Server databases with test data — all inside the Visual Studio 2005 Integrated Development Environment (IDE). Integrating with the Visual Studio 2005 IDE provides a feature-rich environment from which to work, including a design-time debugger and a comprehensive test framework.

Developing a Database Project

We'll start by developing a database project with VSTEDP. We will demonstrate the database development capabilities of the product while building the schemas, tables, views, stored procedures, and a login. It'll be fun!

There's no place like code to demonstrate VSTEDP's capabilities. Let's jump in!

A SQL Server 2005 database is created in the following example. In the section "Database Project Deployment" of the chapter, it will be deployed to an instance of SQL Server Express, which is available free from Microsoft at `http://msdn.microsoft.com/vstudio/express/sql/`. *VSTEDP is also compatible with SQL Server 2000.*

We'll begin by creating a new project in the Visual Studio 2005 Integrated Development Environment (IDE). Start by opening Visual Studio 2005 and creating a new project by clicking File ⇨ New ⇨ Project. When the New Project dialog displays, expand the Database Projects node in the Project Types list on the left, then select Microsoft SQL Server. In the Templates list, select SQL Server 2005 from the "Visual Studio installed templates." Enter **TestDatabase** in the Name textbox, and make sure the "Create directory for solution" checkbox is checked as shown in Figure 4-1.

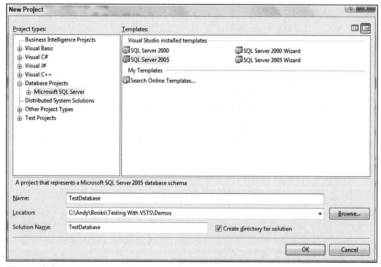

Figure 4-1

Click OK to create the new project.

If you have configured an instance of SQL Server in the Tools ⇨ Options ⇨ Database Tools ⇨ Design Time Validation Database, you will be prompted here to verify that selection.

After a moment, the TestDatabase project loads into the Visual Studio 2005 IDE and is ready. There are familiar items in the project that are common to most Visual Studio projects, and there are some not-so-familiar items. See Figure 4-2.

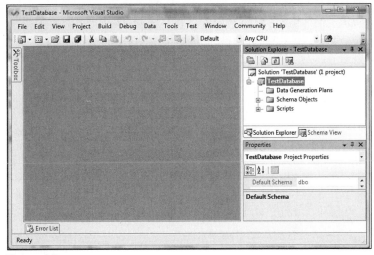

Figure 4-2

Exploring the Project

Solution Explorer contains the TestDatabase project file at its top level. A solution file, also named TestDatabase, was generated, although it is not displayed in the Solution Explorer at this time. Located beneath the TestDatabase project are three logical folders for categories of objects: Data Generation Plans, Schema Objects, and Scripts.

The logical folder named *Data Generation Plans* is only used for data generation plans and is empty at project creation.

The logical folder named *Schema Objects* contains myriad logical subfolders — each representing a major category of SQL Server database objects as shown in Figure 4-3.

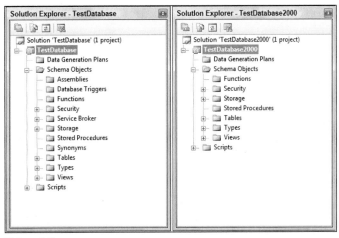

Figure 4-3

This list of database schema objects is SQL Server version–specific. The Schema Objects on the left in Figure 4-3 represent a SQL Server 2005 database. The smaller set of Schema Objects shown on the right of Figure 4-3 represents a SQL Server 2000 database.

This chapter will demonstrate SQL Server 2005 database projects.

Database objects defined beneath the Schema Objects hierarchy are referred to *en masse* as "Database Object Definitions." Database Object Definitions are stored as SQL scripts but are interpreted by the VSTEDP engine as database schema objects.

The logical folder named *Scripts* contains two subfolders, Post-Deployment and Pre-Deployment, as shown in Figure 4-4.

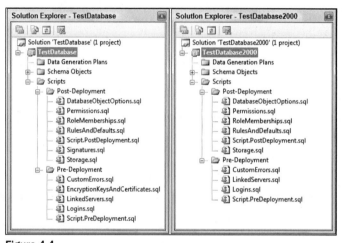

Figure 4-4

As before, there are differences between versions of SQL Server. SQL Server 2005 projects contain a Signatures.sql file in the Post-Deployment folder and an EncryptionKeysAndCertificates.sql file in the Pre-Deployment folder.

The files in the Scripts subfolders are named by function. Pre-Deployment scripts include:

❑   **Logins.sql** — This script is generated first and contains logins specified in the source database. It uses the sp_addlogin stored procedure in SQL Server 2000 and the CREATE LOGIN SQL statement in SQL Server 2005.

❑   **LinkedServers.sql** — This script is generated second and contains SQL statements that create linked servers. It uses the sp_addlinkedserver stored procedure to script linked servers.

❑   **CustomErrors.sql** — This script is generated third and contains user-defined error messages. It uses the sp_addmessage stored procedure to script custom errors.

❑   **EncryptionKeysAndCertificates.sql** — This script is only used for SQL Server 2005 databases. When importing a SQL Server 2005 database schema, this script is generated last and contains placeholders for each CREATE__ KEY and CREATE CERTIFICATE statement in the source database.

❑ **Script.PreDeployment.sql** — This script contains SQLCmd statements that control the order of execution of the Pre-Deployment scripts listed above.

Post-Deployment scripts include

❑ **Storage.sql** — This script is generated first and contains files and filegroup information.

❑ **Permissions.sql** — This script is generated second and contains object permissions (GRANT, DENY, and REVOKE) for the target database.

❑ **RoleMemberships.sql** — This script is generated third and contains role associations for the target database. It uses the sp_addrolemember stored procedure.

❑ **RulesAndDefaults.sql** — This script is generated fourth and contains SQL statements that define defaults and rules for the target database. In SQL Server 2000, the script uses:

   ❑ sp_bindrule to bind a rule to a column or alias a data type.

   ❑ sp_binddefault to bind a default to a column or alias a data type.

   ❑ sp_addrolemember to add a security account to an existing database role.

❑ In SQL Server 2005, the script uses:

   ❑ ALTER TABLE *TableName* ADD CONSTRAINT *ConstraintName* CHECK to bind a rule to a column or alias a data type.

   ❑ ALTER TABLE *TableName* ADD CONSTRAINT *ConstraintName* DEFAULT to bind a default to a column or alias a data type.

   ❑ sp_addrolemember to add a security account to an existing database role.

❑ **DatabaseObjectOptions.sql** — This script is generated fifth and contains SQL statements that are applied to the target database after deployment. An example is adding extended properties using sp_addextendedproperty.

❑ **Signatures.sql** — This script is only used for SQL Server 2005 databases. When importing a SQL Server 2005 database schema, this script is generated last and contains SQL statements that define signatures for the target database.

❑ **Script.PostDeployment.sql** — This script contains SQLCmd statements that control the order of execution of the Post-Deployment scripts listed above.

At this stage of project development, some Pre-Deployment and Post-Deployment script files may be empty (or, in the cases of the Script.PreDeployment.sql and Script.PostDeployment.sql files, hollow templates containing only comments).

When a project is built, the Pre-Deployment, Database Objects Definitions, and Post-Deployment scripts are merged into a single script.

The Project in the File System

The collected scripts are interpreted by VSTEDP in a manner consistent with a database. In other words, although we will create a collection of scripts, the project will respond to them as if they are an actualized database. There's a reason for this: VSTEDP will, behind the scenes, render these files into a temporary database on a server you designate. This database has already been created when the project was first created.

When I close the VSTEDP Integrated Development Environment (IDE), this database will be dropped. When I reopen the project, the same working database is created. On my development server I now have a database named *TestDatabase_DB_03033680-46ed-4f1d-9442-7b43c9d493fc*. The database name is generated during project setup and is stored in the [*ProjectName*].dbproj.user file. If you named your database project TestDatabase, your file is named TestDatabase.dbproj.user. The version of this file for my project contains the following:

```
<Project xmlns="http://schemas.microsoft.com/developer/msbuild/2003">
  <PropertyGroup Condition=" '$(Configuration)' == 'Default' " />
  <PropertyGroup>
    <DesignDBName>TestDatabase_DB_
03033680-46ed-4f1d-9442-7b43c9d493fc</DesignDBName>
  </PropertyGroup>
</Project>
```

If you look, you probably have a similarly named database on your local or development server.

You can edit the name of the development database in TestDatabase.dbproj.user. If the TestDatabase project is open in the Visual Studio IDE, close it before making edits to the TestDatabase.dbproj.user file. Edit the filename inside the DesignDBName tag. Save and close the file, then reopen the project in the Visual Studio IDE. If you open SQL Server Management Studio and look at the development instance, you will notice the new database name.

Adding Schemas, Tables, and Constraints

Tables are arguably the base object of databases. In SQL Server 2005, tables can be assigned to schemas. Schemas in SQL Server 2005 are more than glorified aliases for logins as in previous versions of SQL Server. Constraints define and enforce relationships and perform basic data validation.

Let's continue building our project by adding schema objects. First, take a look at the Schema View. To open Schema View click View ⇨ Schema View as shown in Figure 4-5.

Figure 4-5

There are virtual folders for the various types of database objects. There's also a folder for Orphaned Objects.

Right-click the project name in Schema View, hover over Add, and click Table. The Add New Item dialog displays. Click Tables and Views in the Categories list, Table in the Templates list, and enter the table name Contact.

When you click the Add button, a generic table script is created and added to the Tables virtual folder. The table is assigned to the dbo schema by default. In this exercise we want to make the table part of a new schema named Person, but we must first add the schema.

The good news is we're almost where we need to be to add a new schema to the TestDatabase project. There's a better way to add a table to a schema, so close this script before proceeding. Delete the dbo.Contact table by right-clicking the table object in the Tables logical folder in Schema View and clicking Delete. Click Yes on the Confirmation dialog to complete the delete process.

In the Add New Item — TestDatabase dialog displayed, click Security from the Categories list on the left, and select the Schema template as shown in Figure 4-6.

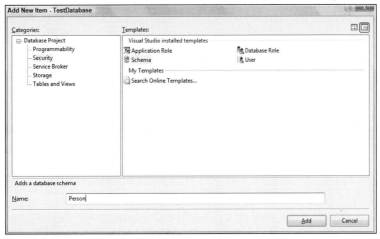

Figure 4-6

Set the schema name to Person and click Add. The new Person schema appears in Schema View beneath Security\Schemas as shown in Figure 4-7.

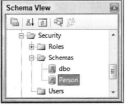

Figure 4-7

Now we can add a table to the new Person schema. The most straightforward means of adding a table to the Person schema is to right-click the schema object named Person in Schema View, hover over Add, and click Table as shown in Figure 4-8.

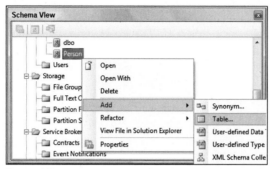

Figure 4-8

When the Add New Item dialog displays, Tables and Views is selected from the categories list and the Table template is selected in the Templates list. Enter *Contact* as the table name (as shown in Figure 4-9), and click the Add button.

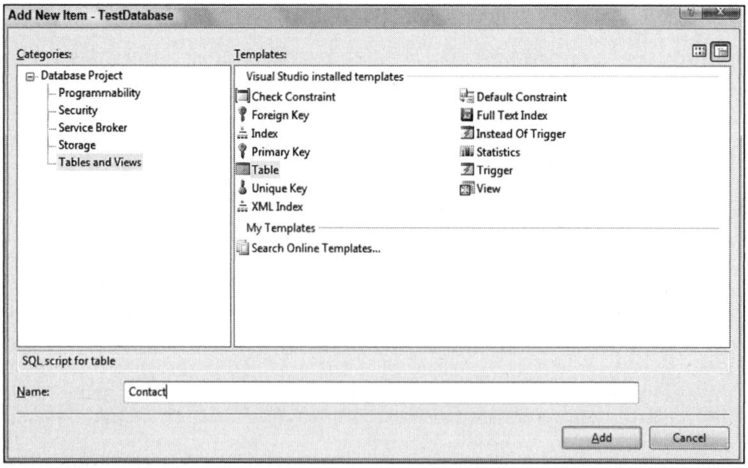

Figure 4-9

Note the schema of the table just created: It's in the Person schema! How did it get there? When you created the table by right-clicking the Person schema object, the table was created in the context of the Person schema.

There are now two new files open in the Visual Studio Integrated Development Environment: Person.schema.sql and Person.Contact .table.sql. Person.schema.sql contains the Data Definition Language (DDL) script for creating the Person schema object:

```
CREATE SCHEMA [Person]
;
```

Since this script serves our purposes and requires no changing, close this script. Person.Contact.table.sql contains the generic table DDL contained in the table template:

```
CREATE TABLE [Person].[Contact]
(
    column_1 int NOT NULL,
    column_2 int NULL
);
```

Edit the Person.Contact DDL, changing it to the following:

```
CREATE TABLE [Person].[Contact](
    [ContactID] [int] IDENTITY(1,1),
    [NameStyle] [bit] NOT NULL CONSTRAINT [DF_Contact_NameStyle]
DEFAULT (0),
    [Title] [nvarchar](8) NULL,
    [GivenName] [nvarchar](50) NOT NULL,
    [MiddleName] [nvarchar](50) NULL,
    [FamilyName] [nvarchar](50) NOT NULL,
    [Suffix] [nvarchar](10) NULL,
    [EmailAddress] [nvarchar](50) NULL,
    [EmailPromotion] [int] NOT NULL CONSTRAINT
[DF_Contact_EmailPromotion] DEFAULT (0),
    [Phone] [nvarchar](25) NULL,
    [PasswordHash] [varchar](40) NOT NULL,
    [PasswordSalt] [varchar](10) NOT NULL,
    [AdditionalContactInfo] [xml] NULL,
    [rowguid] [uniqueidentifier] NOT NULL CONSTRAINT
 [DF_Contact_rowguid] DEFAULT (newid()),
    [ModifiedDate] [datetime] NOT NULL CONSTRAINT
 [DF_Contact_ModifiedDate] DEFAULT (getdate()),
 CONSTRAINT [PK_Contact_ContactID] PRIMARY KEY CLUSTERED
(ContactID ASC)
);
```

Save the file after making these changes by clicking the diskette icon or File ⇨ Save Person.Contact.table. sql, or by holding the Control (*Ctrl*) key and pressing the *S* key.

If the Transact-SQL is incorrect, the validation check will detect the error, and the Error List dialog will display as shown in Figure 4-10.

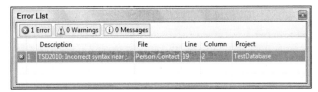

Figure 4-10

To demonstrate an error, I omitted a closing parenthesis in the Primary Key constraint, changing the line from

```
(ContactID ASC)
```

to

```
(ContactID ASC
```

Saving the file triggered validation, and the error shown in Figure 4-10 was detected. Clear the error by replacing the end parenthesis and saving the file.

Continue building the database project by adding another schema to the project. Navigate to Security, Schemas in the Schema View. Right-click Schema, hover over Add, and click Schema. Name this schema *HumanResources* and click the Add button.

To create a new table in the HumanResources schema, right-click the HumanResources schema object in Schema View, hover over Add, and click Table. Name the table *Employee*, and change the template code to the following:

```
CREATE TABLE [HumanResources].[Employee](
    [EmployeeID] [int] IDENTITY(1,1),
    [NationalIDNumber] [nvarchar](15) NOT NULL,
    [ContactID] [int] NOT NULL,
    [LoginID] [nvarchar](256) NOT NULL,
    [ManagerID] [int] NULL,
    [Title] [nvarchar](50) NOT NULL,
    [BirthDate] [datetime] NOT NULL,
    [MaritalStatus] [nchar](1) NOT NULL,
    [Gender] [nchar](1) NOT NULL,
    [HireDate] [datetime] NOT NULL,
    [SalariedFlag] [bit] NOT NULL CONSTRAINT
[DF_Employee_SalariedFlag] DEFAULT (1),
    [VacationHours] [smallint] NOT NULL CONSTRAINT
[DF_Employee_VacationHours] DEFAULT (0),
    [SickLeaveHours] [smallint] NOT NULL CONSTRAINT
[DF_Employee_SickLeaveHours] DEFAULT (0),
    [CurrentFlag] [bit] NOT NULL CONSTRAINT
[DF_Employee_CurrentFlag] DEFAULT (1),
    [rowguid] [uniqueidentifier] NOT NULL CONSTRAINT
[DF_Employee_rowguid] DEFAULT (newid()),
    [ModifiedDate] [datetime] NOT NULL CONSTRAINT
[DF_Employee_ModifiedDate] DEFAULT (getdate()),
    CONSTRAINT [PK_Employee_EmployeeID] PRIMARY KEY CLUSTERED
([EmployeeID])
);
```

Let's add some constraints to HumanResources.Employee. First, save the file. In Schema View, navigate to Tables and expand HumanResources.Employee. Right-click the Keys node, hover over Add, then click Foreign Key.

To demonstrate the functionality, accept the default name for the foreign key (ForeignKey1) and click the Add button. Replace the template code in the foreign key statement with the Transact-SQL below.

```
ALTER TABLE [HumanResources].[Employee]
WITH CHECK ADD CONSTRAINT [FK_Employee_Contact_ContactID]
FOREIGN KEY([ContactID]) REFERENCES [Person].[Contact] ([ContactID]);
```

Before saving the file, look at the Key object name in Schema View: ForeignKey1. Note that when the Transact-SQL is updated and saved, the object name in Schema View changes to match the name defined in the code: FK_Employee_Contact_ContactID.

Add a second foreign key named *FK_Employee_Employee_ ManagerID* to HumanResources.Employee:

```
ALTER TABLE [HumanResources].[Employee]
WITH CHECK ADD CONSTRAINT [FK_Employee_Employee_ManagerID]
FOREIGN KEY([ManagerID]) REFERENCES [HumanResources].[Employee] ([EmployeeID]);
```

Adding Views and Stored Procedures

SQL Server views allow database developers to recombine data stored in other database objects without duplicating the data or even adding to required storage. Stored Procedures are compiled Transact-SQL statements that execute very quickly in the SQL Server relational engine.

Create a view containing a summary of the Contact information stored in the Person.Contact table. Return to Schema
View and navigate to Security, Schemas, and Person. Right-click the Person schema, hover over Add, and click View.

Name the view *vContactSummary*, and change the template code to the following:

```
CREATE VIEW [Person].[vContactSummary]
AS
    SELECT [ContactID]
    ,[Title]
    ,[GivenName]
    ,[MiddleName]
    ,[FamilyName]
    ,[Suffix]
    ,[EmailAddress]
    ,[Phone]
  FROM [Person].[Contact]
;
```

Add a second table named *Department* to the HumanResources schema. Change the DDL to match the following:

```
CREATE TABLE [HumanResources].[Department](
    [DepartmentID] [smallint] IDENTITY(1,1),
    [Name] nvarchar(50) NOT NULL,
    [GroupName] nvarchar(50) NOT NULL,
    [ModifiedDate] [datetime] NOT NULL CONSTRAINT
 [DF_Department_ModifiedDate]  DEFAULT (getdate()),
 CONSTRAINT [PK_Department_DepartmentID] PRIMARY KEY CLUSTERED
 ([DepartmentID])
);
```

Create a stored procedure to return individual rows from the Person.Contact table. Return to Schema View, and navigate to Security, Schemas, and Person. Right-click the Person schema, hover over Add, and click Stored Procedure.

Name the stored procedure *uspGetContactDetails*, and change the template code to the following:

```
CREATE PROCEDURE [Person].[uspGetContactDetails]
      @ContactID int
AS
      SELECT
      [NameStyle]
      ,[Title]
      ,[GivenName]
      ,[MiddleName]
      ,[FamilyName]
      ,[Suffix]
      ,[EmailAddress]
      ,[EmailPromotion]
      ,[Phone]
      ,[PasswordHash]
      ,[PasswordSalt]
      ,[AdditionalContactInfo]
      ,[rowguid]
      ,[ModifiedDate]
   FROM [Person].[Contact]
   WHERE [ContactID] = @ContactID
RETURN 0;
```

Add another stored procedure to the Person schema — this one named *uspGetContactSummary*. Change the template code to the following:

```
CREATE PROCEDURE [Person].[uspGetContactSummary]
      @ContactID int
AS
      SELECT [ContactID]
      ,[Title]
      ,[GivenName]
      ,[MiddleName]
      ,[FamilyName]
      ,[Suffix]
      ,[EmailAddress]
      ,[Phone]
      FROM [Person].[vContactSummary]
RETURN 0;
```

Create a new stored procedure in the dbo schema named *uspGetEmployeeManagers*, and edit the DDL as shown here:

```
CREATE PROCEDURE [dbo].[uspGetEmployeeManagers]
    @EmployeeID [int]
AS
BEGIN
    SET NOCOUNT ON;
    -- Use recursive query to list out all Employees required
  for a particular Manager
    WITH [EMP_cte]([EmployeeID], [ManagerID], [GivenName],
  [FamilyName], [Title], [RecursionLevel]) -- CTE name and columns
```

```
    AS (
        SELECT e.[EmployeeID], e.[ManagerID], c.[GivenName],
c.[FamilyName], e.[Title], 0 -- Get the initial Employee
        FROM [HumanResources].[Employee] e
            INNER JOIN [Person].[Contact] c
            ON e.[ContactID] = c.[ContactID]
        WHERE e.[EmployeeID] = @EmployeeID
        UNION ALL
        SELECT e.[EmployeeID], e.[ManagerID], c.[GivenName],
c.[FamilyName], e.[Title], [RecursionLevel] + 1
-- Join recursive member to anchor
        FROM [HumanResources].[Employee] e
            INNER JOIN [EMP_cte]
            ON e.[EmployeeID] = [EMP_cte].[ManagerID]
            INNER JOIN [Person].[Contact] c
            ON e.[ContactID] = c.[ContactID]
    )
    -- Join back to Employee to return the manager name
    SELECT [EMP_cte].[RecursionLevel], [EMP_cte].[EmployeeID],
[EMP_cte].[GivenName], [EMP_cte].[FamilyName],
        [EMP_cte].[ManagerID], c.[GivenName] AS 'ManagerFirstName',
c.[FamilyName] AS 'ManagerLastName'  -- Outer select from the CTE
    FROM [EMP_cte]
        INNER JOIN [HumanResources].[Employee] e
        ON [EMP_cte].[ManagerID] = e.[EmployeeID]
        INNER JOIN [Person].[Contact] c
        ON e.[ContactID] = c.[ContactID]
    ORDER BY [RecursionLevel], [ManagerID], [EmployeeID]
    OPTION (MAXRECURSION 25)
END;
```

Add another stored procedure to the dbo schema named *uspGetManagerEmployees,* and edit the DDL:

```
CREATE PROCEDURE [dbo].[uspGetManagerEmployees]
    @ManagerID [int]
AS
BEGIN
    SET NOCOUNT ON;

    -- Use recursive query to list out all Employees required for a
particular Manager
    WITH [EMP_cte]([EmployeeID], [ManagerID], [GivenName],
[FamilyName], [RecursionLevel]) -- CTE name and columns
    AS (
        SELECT e.[EmployeeID], e.[ManagerID], c.[GivenName],
c.[FamilyName], 0 -- Get the initial list of Employees for Manager n
        FROM [HumanResources].[Employee] e
            INNER JOIN [Person].[Contact] c
            ON e.[ContactID] = c.[ContactID]
        WHERE [ManagerID] = @ManagerID
        UNION ALL
        SELECT e.[EmployeeID], e.[ManagerID], c.[GivenName],
c.[FamilyName], [RecursionLevel] + 1 -- Join recursive member to anchor
```

```
            FROM [HumanResources].[Employee] e
                INNER JOIN [EMP_cte]
                ON e.[ManagerID] = [EMP_cte].[EmployeeID]
                INNER JOIN [Person].[Contact] c
                ON e.[ContactID] = c.[ContactID]
            )
        -- Join back to Employee to return the manager name
        SELECT [EMP_cte].[RecursionLevel], [EMP_cte].[ManagerID],
    c.[GivenName] AS 'ManagerFirstName', c.[FamilyName] AS
    'ManagerLastName',
            [EMP_cte].[EmployeeID], [EMP_cte].[GivenName],
    [EMP_cte].[FamilyName] -- Outer select from the CTE
        FROM [EMP_cte]
            INNER JOIN [HumanResources].[Employee] e
            ON [EMP_cte].[ManagerID] = e.[EmployeeID]
            INNER JOIN [Person].[Contact] c
            ON e.[ContactID] = c.[ContactID]
        ORDER BY [RecursionLevel], [ManagerID], [EmployeeID]
        OPTION (MAXRECURSION 25)
END;
```

Click File ⇨ Save All to save this script and the project changes.

At this point, we have a simple database project:

❑   Three schemas:

  ❑   Dbo

  ❑   HumanResources

  ❑   Person

❑   Three tables:

  ❑   HumanResources.Department

  ❑   HumanResources.Employee

  ❑   Person.Contact

❑   One view:

  ❑   Person.vContactSummary

❑   Four stored procedures:

  ❑   Dbo.uspGetEmployeeManagers

  ❑   Dbo.uspGetManagerEmployees

  ❑   Person.uspGetContactDetails

  ❑   Person.uspGetContactSummary

The database project we just created is based on the AdventureWorks sample database that ships with SQL Server 2005. I made a few changes:

❑   I've replaced some user-defined types (UDTs) with their native data types for brevity. But the UDTs could just as easily have been created inside this project.

❑ I renamed a couple of columns in the Person.Contact table (for demonstration purposes — we will change the name to match AdventureWorks shortly).

❑ I added Person.vContactSummary, Person.uspGetContactDetails, and Person. uspGetContactSummary.

The other objects are from AdventureWorks.

Inside the Development Database

If you open the SQL Server Management Studio, connect to your development instance of SQL Server, and look at the objects in the Development Database, you will see they represent the schema designed in the database project. If you make a change in the project by altering one of the .sql files, the change is propagated to the database when you save the .sql file.

Try it. Make sure the project is open in the Visual Studio IDE (remember the working database project is dropped unless the project is open in the VS IDE). Open SQL Server Management Studio, and connect to your development instance of the Database Engine. Navigate to the working database, expand Views, expand Person.vContactSummary, and expand Columns. You should see a list of the columns defined in the Person.vContactSummary CREATE VIEW statement earlier.

Now in the VS IDE, open the Person.vContactSummary .sql file. You can open it by double-clicking the object in either Solution Explorer or Schema View. Add an alias of "NameTitle" to the Title column, but don't save the file (yet). The script should now appear as follows:

```
CREATE VIEW [Person].[vContactSummary]
AS
    SELECT [ContactID]
    ,[Title] AS 'NameTitle'
    ,[GivenName]
    ,[MiddleName]
    ,[FamilyName]
    ,[Suffix]
    ,[EmailAddress]
    ,[Phone]
  FROM [Person].[Contact]
;
```

Return to SQL Server Management Studio. In Object Explorer, right-click the Columns folder for the Person.vContactSummary view, and click Refresh. You should observe no change in the name of the Title column.

Return to VSTEDP and save the .sql file. Refresh Person.vContactSummary's columns in SQL Server Management Studio. You should now see that the Title column has been changed to *NameTitle*. This is one way to manually rename columns in VSTEDP, but there is a much better way.

If you attempt to save the project at this point, an error is generated. uspGetContactSummary still references the Title column in Person.vContactSummary. Renaming the Person.vContactSummary.Title column breaks uspGetContactSummary.

Before proceeding, delete the alias to the Title column in Person.vContactSummary, and save the script.

VSTEDP provides support for database development. Before we dive into the test-related features, let's take a brief look at a couple of these features: Rename Refactoring and Database Project Deployment.

Rename Refactoring

How often has the following happened to you: Somewhere near the end of the application development cycle, you are tasked with developing the database? You are handed a set of specifications or (more likely) sent e-mail with attached .bak files and, if fortunate, given just enough time to evaluate the stored procedures, functions, tables, and relationships for performance. You are tasked with completing the development and deploying the database to an integration server for testing.

When about 80 percent finished with these tasks, you realize a column name is less intuitive than it could be. Being a conscientious database developer, you think to yourself, "Someday, someone is going to look at this column and misunderstand the data stored here. I should fix this." But how? Perhaps the database schema already contains a couple dozen tables, 50 or more stored procedures, and several views and functions. Finding all of them and testing the changes is going to be a nightmare — and will almost certainly delay deployment of the database to the test server. To further complicate matters, the name of the column is not unique to the table. The column name is used elsewhere, adding to the reasons for changing it *and* complicating the change process (so much for Find and Replace).

Rename Refactoring in VSTEDP provides a solution.

Refactoring means many things to many people. For application and web developers, it can mean coding cycles in which code is first built in a single object or class, then refined into a more object-oriented architecture. Common functionality is identified, and methods are created to manage subtle variations.

Rename Refactoring provides a means for standardizing the interface to the database.

Open the TestDatabase project in VSTEDP. In Schema View, navigate to the columns of the table for Person.Contact. Right-click the GivenName column, hover over Refactor, and click Rename as shown in Figure 4-11.

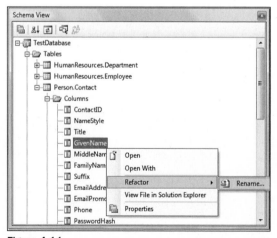

Figure 4-11

The Rename dialog diaplays with "[GivenName]"in the New Name textbox. Change this to "[FirstName]" and make sure that the "Preview changes" and "Generate refactoring log" checkboxes are checked as shown in Figure 4-12.

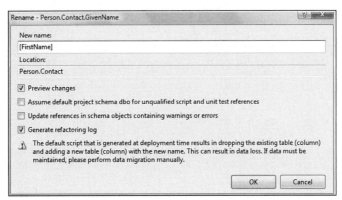

Figure 4-12

Click the OK button to proceed. The Preview Changes — Rename dialog displays the identified locations of the Person.Contact.GivenName column. This lists the objects containing the Person.Contact.GivenName column that will be renamed to Person.Contact.FirstName.

A few important things to note here:

❑   Dynamic SQL containing Person.Contact.GivenName will not reflect the change.

❑   Any Pre-Deployment and Post-Deployment scripts containing Person.Contact.GivenName will be unaffected.

❑   The only column affected by this change is the column named *GivenName* in the Person.Contact table.

Dynamic SQL and Pre-Deployment and Post-Deployment scripts will need to be updated manually. If your intention is to change all references named *GivenName* in all objects — and there are legitimate reasons for this — Find and Replace is a better mechanism.

One legitimate reason for making a Find and Replace change is to maintain consistency across database tables. Consider the following scenario: A database contains two tables with columns named GivenName. *In this instance, you could conceivably wish to rename all references of* GivenName *to* FirstName. *Find and Replace would accomplish this in a single step, whereas Rename Refactoring would require two steps (one for each table column).*

To apply the rename refactor, click the Apply button shown in Figure 4-13.

Use the step described earlier to rename the Person.Contact .FamilyName to Person.Contact.LastName. Save all changes to the project.

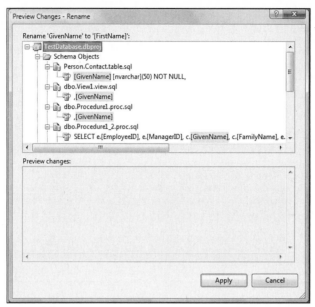

Figure 4-13

Database Project Deployment

Our project has reached a stage where we want to deploy it to our development server before proceeding. The target server has to be configured before proceeding.

Here I deploy to a named instance of SQL Server Express: [MachineName]\SQLExpress.

To configure the target server, open a database project (I am using the TestDatabase project created earlier) in the Visual Studio 2005 IDE. Right-click the project name in Solution Explorer, and click Properties. On the project properties page, click the Build tab as shown in Figure 4-14.

Click the Edit button beside the Target Connection textbox. When the Connection Properties dialog displays, configure the connection properties as shown in Figure 4-15.

Note that the database name defaults to the name of the project. If this is the first time you have configured this connection and you click the Test Connection button on the Connection Properties dialog without changing the default database name, an exception is thrown. The database does not yet exist. Click OK to proceed.

Accept the default options on this and the other tabs of the Project Properties page. A detailed examination of the options is beyond the scope of this chapter, but more information is available at http://msdn2.microsoft.com (search for "Team Edition for Database Professionals").

To deploy, return to Solution Explorer, right-click on the project name, and click Deploy. That's all there is to it.

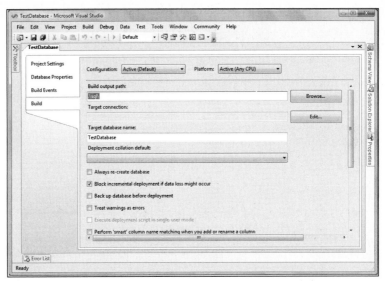

Figure 4-14

Figure 4-15

Generating Test Data

Let's review: We have created and developed a VSTEDP database project for SQL Server 2005 and deployed it to a local SQL Server Express instance on our development server.

Recall our goal from the start of the chapter — to develop and test a database project using VSTEDP. We are halfway there: Our database has been developed. Now it needs to be tested.

Before the database can be tested, we need some data. This is accomplished easily enough. Just fire up the Import/Export Wizard, and copy some data from Production. To quote one of my high school gym teachers, "Wrong!"

"Why 'Wrong!'" you ask? There remain scenarios in which linking to Production data is fine and legal; thus this isn't always wrong. But it is increasingly incorrect in the age of regulations such as the US laws Sarbanes-Oxley Act of 2002 (Sox) and Health Insurance Portability and Accountability Act of 1996 (HIPAA). Rest assured, if your company is public and your database contains personal identification information, pulling Production data for development purposes can be hazardous to your CEO's (and CIO's, and CFO's) constitutional liberties in the United States.

Fortunately, VSTEDP provides a means to generate data, against which there is no law.

To begin, open the TestDatabase project. In Solution Explorer, right-click Data Generation Plans, hover over Add, and click Data Generation Plans. Change the name of the plan to TestDataGenerationPlan1. dgen, and click the Add button.

The "Table" column allows you to select the tables included in the Data Generation Plan. Check the checkbox beside the table name to include the table. The next column, "Rows to Insert," contains the number of rows to generate for the selected table.

"Related Table" contains a dropdown list. It is based on foreign key constraints read from the schema. The "Related Table" dropdown list for the HumanResources.Employee table contains Person.Contact and None. Person.Contact is related to HumanResources.Employee through two foreign keys: FK_Employee_Contact_ContactID and FK_Employee_ Employee_ManagerID. Note that although two foreign key constraints relate the tables, Person.Contact is listed only once.

Select Person.Contact from the "Related Table" dropdown list for the HumanResources.Employee table. When a table is selected, "1:1" appears in the "Ratio to Related Table" column. Change this to **1:5**. Note that the Rows to Insert for HumanResources.Employee changes from 50 to 10 — reflecting the ratio of one HumanResources.Employee for every five Person.Contact rows as shown in Figure 4-16.

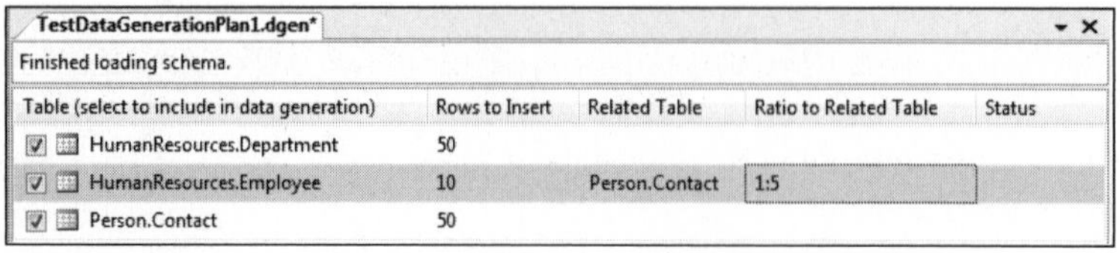

Table (select to include in data generation)	Rows to Insert	Related Table	Ratio to Related Table	Status
☑ HumanResources.Department	50			
☑ HumanResources.Employee	10	Person.Contact	1:5	
☑ Person.Contact	50			

TestDataGenerationPlan1.dgen*
Finished loading schema.

Figure 4-16

In the TestDataGenerationPlan1.dgen window, click Person.Contact. Click Data, then Data Generator, then Column Details to configure data generation for the Person.Contact columns. In the Column Details window, click on the "FirstName" column. To see an example of the data that will be generated for this column, click Data ⇨ Data Generation ⇨ Preview Data Generation. The Data Generation Preview window displays. I find it much easier to work with Data Generation Plans with the Column Details and Data Generation Preview side-by-side as shown in Figure 4-17.

Figure 4-17

In the Data Generation Preview, note that the data in the FirstName column are pure gibberish. This is by design, but you can customize it in many ways.

In the Column Details window, click on the "Generator" column for the FirstName field. It currently defines the String generator for FirstName. A glance at the Properties window demonstrates that these generators are configurable. A complete walk-through of available properties is beyond the scope of this chapter, but a selection of properties and descriptions follows:

Property	Generator	Description
Percentage Null	All	The percentage of NULL values generated for the selected column. 0% is no NULL values; 100% is all NULL values.
Seed	All	The seed value is used to generate repeatable values for the given field.
Maximum/Minimum Length	String	Specifies the maximum and minimum length of the random string values generated.
Uniform	Numeric (BigInt, Integer, SmallInt, TinyInt)	The approximate shape of the distribution curve represented by the random data.
Min/Max	Numeric (BigInt, Integer, SmallInt, TinyInt)	The minimum and maximum values for randomly generated integers.
Expression	Regular Expression	A regular expression used to generate the random data.
Connection Information	Data Bound Generator	Specifies the connection to the data source.
Select Query	Data Bound Generator	Contains one or more Transact-SQL SELECT statements (separated by semicolons) to retrieve data.

In the Column Details window, change the Generator from String to Regular Expression. In the Properties window, change Expression from

```
[a-zA-Z0-9]*
```

to

```
[A-Z][a-z]*
```

This regular expression generates something that looks more like a first name. Make the same change for the MiddleName and LastName fields, and note the changes in the Data Generation Preview.

Press the F5 key, click Data ➪ Data Generator ➪ Generate Data, or click the Generate Data button to populate the test database with this data. The Generate Data for Target Database dialog displays. If you configured a test location on the Build tab of the Project Properties, the connection you configured will be displayed here by default. If you did not configure a Build location, you can create a target connection by clicking the New Connection button as shown in Figure 4-18.

Figure 4-18

When ready to generate data, click the OK button. A dialog will appear asking if you wish to delete existing data before proceeding. Clicking Yes will truncate existing data from the database — clicking No will leave existing data in the database and append data generated here.

You want to be careful in answering this dialog. If you test using row counts and you add the generated data twice, it will skew the test results. If you accidentally duplicate data via the data generation plan, simply re-generate it and answer "Yes" in the Delete Existing Data dialog.

Repeatable data are generated. If you clear the database and re-generate the data without changing the data generation plan, the same data will populate the database.

If no errors were thrown, you should now be able to verify the existence of test data in your database.

Unit Testing

Create a Database Unit Test Project by clicking Test ➪ New Test. When the Add New Test dialog displays, select Database Unit Test. You can create database unit test projects in VB.Net, C#, or C++. For this demonstration, I chose C# as shown in Figure 4-19.

When you click the OK button, the New Test Project dialog displays, prompting for a project name. Enter UnitTests_TestDatabase, and click the Create button. The Project "UnitTests_TestDatabase" Configuration dialog displays next. Select or create a connection to the test instance of the database (deployed earlier, not to be confused with the development database created when you created the project) for the first Database connection. Under Deployment, check the "Automatically deploy the database project before unit tests are run" checkbox, and select the TestDatabase.dbproj project and "Default" for the deployment configuration. You can choose to populate the test database with generated data from the Data Generation Plan (created earlier). You can also elect to truncate the data in the test database before generating data. If you configure the Test Project as described above and use objects built thus far in this chapter, your dialog will appear as shown in Figure 4-20.

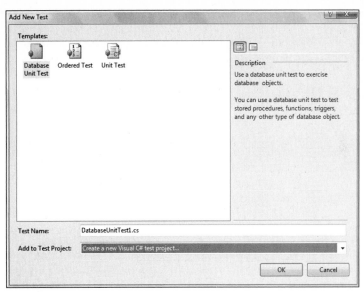

Figure 4-19

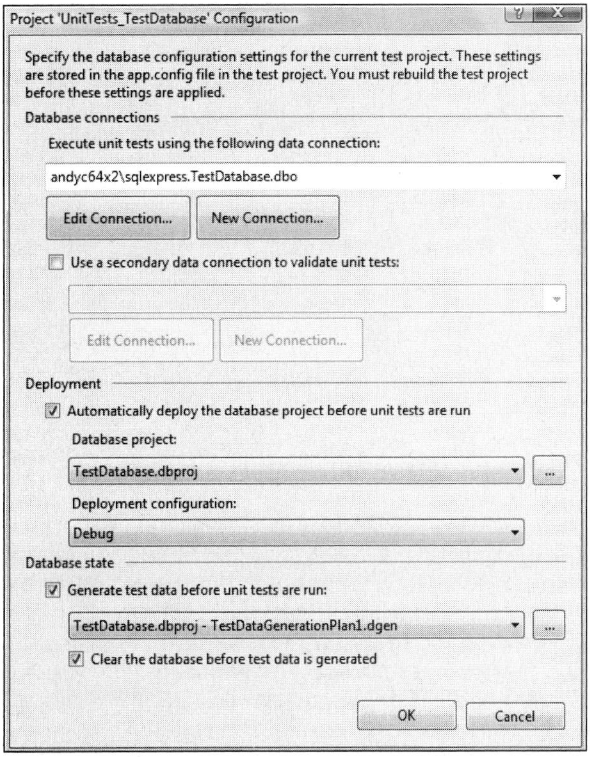

Figure 4-20

Two files open on the Visual Studio IDE:

❑ **DatabaseUnitTest1.cs** — an empty container for developing automated database unit tests.

❑ **AuthoringTests.txt** — a text file containing useful information about testing in general.

See Chapter 2 for details about the testing GUI and test types and Chapter 3 for more information about Unit Testing in general.

On DatabaseUnitTest1.cs, click the "Click here to create" link to create a new database unit test script. A new empty test is created. If you do not see the Test Conditions window, click Test ➪ Windows ➪ Test View to see a default Inconclusive Test as shown in Figure 4-21.

Figure 4-21

What happens when we execute an inconclusive test? Let's test it and find out! Start the selected test by clicking the Start Selected Test button on the Test tools toolbar, clicking Test ➪ Start Selected Test Project with Debugger, or pressing *Shift+Alt+X*.

The test project takes a moment to compile for this first execution, and then the test results are displayed as shown in Figure 4-22.

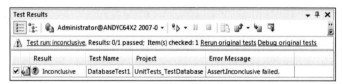

Figure 4-22

Not surprisingly, the Inconclusive test results are . . . inconclusive. While this may seem an obvious result (and something to be filed with the Department of Redundancy Department), there's more to this than initially meets the eye.

First, the test does not pass. Why? Inconclusive tests should return any result except a passing result. "So why create a test that won't pass by default?" you ask. That is an excellent question!

If a unit test created a default test condition that passed, an empty test could be considered a successful test. This is not ideal: Empty tests should provide, at a bare minimum, an indication that more work needs to be done to this test. The inconclusive result accomplishes this nicely.

What should we test with our first unit test? Let's check for the existence of our database. Beneath the comments, enter the following T-SQL statement into the UnitTests_TestDatabase.cs window:

```
SELECT Count(*)
FROM master.sys.databases
WHERE name = 'TestDatabase'
```

Remove the default Inconclusive Test by clicking the Delete button to the right of the Test Conditions dropdown. In the Test Conditions dropdown, select Row Count, and click the Add (+) button to the right of the Test Conditions dropdown.

A new Row Count test condition is created and named rowCountCondition1 (or something similar). In the Test Conditions list, double-click the row containing rowCountCondition1 to bring up the Properties window. Change the name property from rowCountCondition1 to DatabaseExists. Change the Row Count property to 1 to indicate that we expect a single row to be returned by this query.

This test queries the master.sys.databases view in SQL Server 2005, returning the number of rows where the name column contains "TestDatabase." If our database exists in this instance of SQL Server 2005, there will be a row here defining it.

Execute the test, and observe the results in the Test Results window, as shown in Figure 4-23.

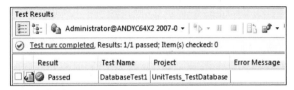

Figure 4-23

The results prove it: The database has been successfully deployed.

Some development methodologies suggest (imply, or even require) a failed test before any development is accomplished. These methodologies are categorized as Test-First Development (TFD). The general idea can be summarized thus: If the creation of a test is a prerequisite before any application coding, you will end with a comprehensive set of regression tests. The pros: Regression tests improve code and application quality and are a fantastic mechanism for validation — even during unit testing. The cons: TFD nearly doubles development effort (and therefore development time) for the first application release.

Unit Test Stored Procedures

Open Schema Explorer, and expand the TestDatabase database object, expand the Stored Procedures object node, right-click Person.uspGetContactDetails, and click "Create Unit Tests. . . ." The Create Unit Tests dialog displays with the checkbox beside `Person.uspGetContactDetails` checked. You can opt to create unit tests for other stored procedures from this dialog. Click the OK button to proceed.

The following default stored procedure unit test code is generated:

```
-- database unit test for Person.uspGetContactDetails
DECLARE @RC INT,
    @ContactID INT

SELECT @RC = 0,
@ContactID = 0

EXEC @RC = [Person].[uspGetContactDetails] @ContactID

SELECT RC=@RC
```

Notice that the unit test generator parsed the stored procedure for parameter names and data types. They are included in the default unit test T-SQL. Note also that an Inconclusive Test Condition is included.

If it is not visible, open the Test View window by clicking Test ➪ Windows ➪ Test View. Right-click Person_uspGetContactDetailsTest, and click Run Selection. Again, since the only test defined is an Inconclusive test, the test fails.

The test T-SQL is executing the stored procedure, passing a ContactID parameter value of 0. If you open the Person.Contact table in your deployed TestDatabase, you will note that the Data Generator populated this table with gibberish, but the ContactID column is an integer with the IDENTITY flag set to start seeding at 1 and increment by 1 each time. Therefore, there is no ContactID equal to 0.

Remove the Inconclusive Test condition, and add an Empty ResultSet Condition. Name this condition *NoContactID0* and re-execute the Person_uspGetContactDetailsTest. When executed, this test passes because an empty resultset is returned.

Multiple Test Conditions

Select and copy to the clipboard the test Transact-SQL listed earlier (for Person_uspGetContact DetailsTest). In the DatabaseUnitTest1.cs designer window, click the Add Test button as shown in Figure 4-24.

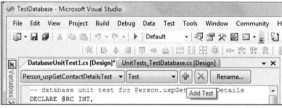

Figure 4-24

When prompted, name the new test *uspGetContactDetails_ ContactID8*. Paste the code you copied from the other test into the designer window and modify as shown:

```
-- database unit test for Person.uspGetContactDetails
DECLARE @RC INT,

    @ContactID INT
SELECT @RC = 0,
    @ContactID = 8

EXEC @RC = [Person].[uspGetContactDetails] @ContactID
```

It's almost the same code as before with the ContactID parameter set to 8 instead of 0.

Delete the default Inconclusive Test Condition, and add a Scalar Value Test Condition. In Properties, name the condition *FirstNameTest*. Open SQL Server Management Studio, and connect to your Test instance of the TestDatabase database. Execute the following Transact-SQL statement to determine the value of the "FirstName" column in Person.Contact for ContactID 8:

```
USE TestDatabase;

SELECT FirstName
FROM Person.Contact
WHERE ContactID = 8;
```

In my instance, the result is Ctqwbhe. In SQL Server Management Studio, select and copy the result. Return to Visual Studio 2005, and paste this value into the Expected Value property of FirstNameTest. As the "FirstName" column is the third column returned by Person.uspGetContactDetails, change the Column Number property to 3.

In Test Conditions, create a new test condition by clicking the Add Test Condition button. Select Execution Time from the Test Condition dropdown. View the properties of this new condition, and rename it *FirstNameExecTime*. Change the default execution time (30 seconds) to 00:00:00 (0 seconds).

In the Test View window, right-click uspGetContactDetails_ ContactID8, and click Run Selection. This test fails, but that was by design. No script can execute in less than 0 seconds (in the current version of our universe, anyway). Double-click the Failed notification in the Test Results window to view Results. In the Error Message section you will see something like "ExecutionTimeCondition Condition (FirstNameExecTime) Failed: 00:00:00.0800000 was longer than 00:00:00."

Close the Results window, and change the Execution Time property for the test to 00:00:01 (1 second). This should pass because the script executed in less than one second previously. When you re-execute the uspGetContactDetails_ContactID8 test, it passes.

A couple of things to note here: Execution Time only includes the actual run time of the Transact-SQL script — and not the entire test. On my laptop, the test takes about 45 seconds to build and execute the first time. Subsequent executions consume about 18 seconds.

Why?

Why did we test Person.uspGetContactDetails in this way?

We executed three unit tests:

❑   We tested exclusion. We verified a row that we did not expect to exist (ContactID = 0).

❑   We tested inclusion. We verified a row that we expected to exist (ContactID = 8).

❑   And we tested performance. We chose a time limit (1 second) and verified the script executed in that amount of time.

These are some of the conditions you will want to test in real life. Was it necessary to break them into two tests? Not necessarily. This is more a question of testing style than anything. Some shops like to have all functionality tested in a single unit test with multiple conditions, as we did with our second test. Others prefer one test condition per unit test. I encourage you to do what works best for you — just be aware that there are other ways to accomplish the same goal.

In our inclusive and exclusive tests of Person.uspGetContactDetails, we hard-coded the values of ContactID and the expected results. Data-driven tests provide a means to compare test values against centrally stored data sets.

Developing Data-Driven Database Tests

As described in Chapter 3, data-driven tests simplify repeatable testing. In database testing, data-driven tests can be used to validate schema and data integrity.

Test Data

There are debates in the database developer community surrounding test data. We arrive at one such debate topic here: Should we leave test data in the deployed production database?

I am a test-it-and-see guy — I always have been. While that answer may be little help, here are some questions, considerations, and rules of thumb:

❏ Are the data metadata? Metadata is "data about data." In database application development, metadata can be divided into two categories:

   ❏ **Database metadata:** — This includes extended properties, schema-comparison tables, and performance information.

   ❏ **Application metadata:** — This includes application configuration and localization information.

❏ What is the performance impact of storing test data in the production database?

Allowing metadata to remain in the production database requires a design with enough flexibility that the test data will be ignored unless desired. The overhead of some designs is considerable. For instance, I've seen data warehouses implement a TestData column with a bit data type. A bit may not consume much space in a typical database application, but they add up fast in a 250-million-row data warehouse table!

Data-Driven Database Testing

Before we begin, let's purge and reload our test instance of TestDatabase. Connect to TestDatabase on your test instance, and execute the following Transact-SQL in a new query window in SQL Server Management Studio:

```
USE [TestDatabase]
GO
IF  EXISTS (SELECT * FROM sys.foreign_keys WHERE object_id =
  OBJECT_ID(N'[HumanResources].[FK_Employee_Contact_ContactID]') AND
  parent_object_id = OBJECT_ID(N'[HumanResources].[Employee]'))
ALTER TABLE [HumanResources].[Employee] DROP CONSTRAINT
[FK_Employee_Contact_ContactID]
GO

truncate table HumanResources.Department
truncate table HumanResources.Employee
truncate table Person.Contact
GO
```

This Transact-SQL drops the foreign key named *FK_Employee_Contact_ContactID* and then truncates each of our three tables. Why? The foreign key interferes with truncating (and reloading) Person.Contact. We'll replace FK_Employee_Contact_ContactID when reloading is complete.

There are several approaches to populating test data:

❏ You can write INSERT Transact-SQL statements.

❏ We've already seen and used Data Generators.

❏ You can copy or import data using a utility or programming language.

Writing INSERT Transact-SQL statements can be tedious, but SQL Server Management Studio facilitates this by allowing you to automatically generate INSERT Transact-SQL statements. To demonstrate, open SQL Server Management Studio (if it's not already open). Connect to an instance of SQL Server with the AdventureWorks database installed, and navigate to the Person.Contact table.

Right-click on the Person.Contact table, hover over "Script Table as," hover over "INSERT To," and click "New Query Editor Window." Voila — an autogenerated INSERT Transact-SQL statement!

SQL Server Integration Services provides several means to transfer data between data sources. You can write applications in any of the .NET languages that generate or move data into databases. There are also many off-the-shelf utilities for performing data migration.

One such utility for moving data ships with SQL Server — the Import and Export Wizard. Let's use the Import and Export Wizard to import some data from the AdventureWorks database.

> We are going to import a subset of the data stored in three AdventureWorks tables. There are a couple of approaches we can take to complete this task. One approach is to only import the data we want. If we choose this route, we will have to build and execute three Import and Export Wizard packages. Another approach is to import all the data in the three tables and then execute queries to prune the full data set into the desired subset. This approach involves one Import and Export Wizard package and some custom Transact-SQL. Less operations equals less work! We'll go with option 2.

> The AdventureWorks database and other useful samples are available from the Microsoft Download Center http://www.microsoft.com/downloads. Search the "All Downloads" category for "SQL Server 2005 Samples and Sample Databases."

To begin, right-click TestDatabase in SQL Server Management Studio, hover over Tasks, and click Import Data. Click the Next button on the Welcome screen if displayed.

When the Data Source screen displays, navigate to an instance of SQL Server containing the AdventureWorks database, select the AdventureWorks database, and click the Next button. The Data Destination screen should be configured properly (since you clicked Import Data from the Destination database). Click the Next button to proceed.

On the Specify Table Copy or Query screen, accept the default "Copy data from one or more tables or views" option, and click the Next button. When the Select Source Tables and Views screen displays, check the checkboxes to select the [AdventureWorks].[HumanResources].[Department], [Adventure-Works].[HumanResources].[Employee], and [AdventureWorks].[Person].[Contact] tables as shown in Figure 4-25.

Hold down the *Ctrl* (Control) key to multi-select the three checked tables, and click the Edit Mappings button. On the Transfer Settings dialog, select "Enable identity insert" as shown in Figure 4-26.

Click the OK button on the Transfer Settings dialog, and the Next button on the Select Source Tables and Views screen to proceed.

The Save and Execute Package screen is interesting. The Import and Export Wizard builds a SQL Server Integration Services (SSIS) package based on your selections. You can store the package for later execution if desired. Accept the defaults on the Save and Execute Package screen and click the Next button.

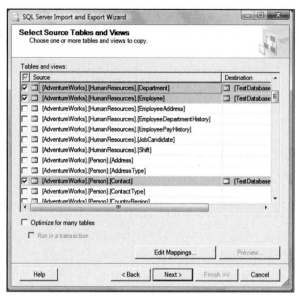

Figure 4-25

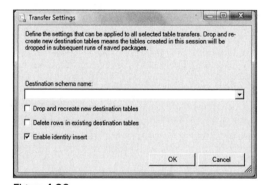

Figure 4-26

The Complete the Wizard screen summarizes the actions it is about to take. Click the Finish button to build and execute the SSIS package. If all goes well, you should see error-free progress until the process completes and displays an image similar to that shown in Figure 4-27.

Prune the Person.Contact data (we don't need 19,972 rows), removing the rows that do not have corresponding rows in the HumanResources.Employee table, using the following Transact-SQL statement:

```
USE TestDatabase;

DELETE Person.Contact
WHERE ContactID NOT IN
(SELECT ContactID
FROM HumanResources.Employee);
```

In my database, this trims the Person.Contact table down to 290 rows.

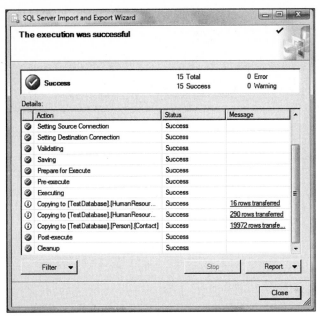

Figure 4-27

Earlier, we truncated the tables in our test database. Prior to truncating the tables, we dropped a foreign key on the HumanResources.Employee table. Let's replace it now before proceeding with tests. Execute the following Transact-SQL to add and check the contraint:

```
-- after the import...
ALTER TABLE [HumanResources].[Employee] WITH CHECK ADD
CONSTRAINT [FK_Employee_Contact_ContactID] FOREIGN
KEY([ContactID]) REFERENCES [Person].[Contact] ([ContactID])
GO
ALTER TABLE [HumanResources].[Employee] CHECK CONSTRAINT
 [FK_Employee_Contact_ContactID]
```

Now that our test data are in place, let's execute some data-driven unit tests!

Return to the TestDatabase solution in the Visual Studio 2005 IDE, and Click Test ➪ New Test. Click the "Click here to create" link to create a new test. Accepting the naming defaults creates a new test named *DatabaseTest1*. This is a good place to note the Rename button above the Transact-SQL canvas. This button allows you to rename tests.

The name of the test appears in the Test View window. If you create new test C# files using the defaults, the first test in each C# class will be named *DatabaseTest1*. Since the Test Name is the only identifying property visible in Test View, having more than one test named *DatabaseTest1* will be confusing.

Click the Rename button to rename this test. Change the name to *Employees_NotIn_Contacts*, and click the OK button to complete the rename procedure. Delete the Inconclusive test condition, and add an Empty Resultset test condition. On the Transact-SQL canvas, add the following code:

```
-- A relationship test.
SELECT ContactID
FROM HumanResources.Employee
WHERE ContactID NOT IN
(SELECT ContactID
 FROM Person.Contact)
```

You can now execute the test by right-clicking Employees_NotIn_Contacts in Test View and clicking Run Selection. Because of the test preparation earlier, this test Passes.

> *Note that the data we just imported will be overwritten the next time we start the test project. The reason? Our Database Test Configuration (Test ⇨ Database Test Configuration) is set to "Generate test data before unit tests are run" using TestDataGenerationPlan1.dgen (see Figure 4-20).*

The purpose of this test is to determine if HumanResources.Employee contains only records found in Person.Contact. This relationship is enforced by the FK_Employee_Contact_ContactID foreign key constraint.

Before testing the constraint, we're at a good place to discuss different methods of implementing customized assert functionality in database testing. The two basic methods are:

❑　Write the Transact-SQL in a way that will accomplish custom assertion.

❑　Alter the test project C# or Visual Basic.Net code, or add a custom test condition.

One benefit of both approaches is that this allows developers and test engineers to leverage the power of declarative *or* imperative languages to accomplish testing. Another advantage provided by this flexibility is that it allows test engineers and developers to work in whichever language they're more comfortable: Developers and Test Engineers with a database development or administration background may prefer to utilize Transact-SQL, while those with application development experience may prefer altering the C# or Visual Basic test application code.

In the next test, we will write Transact-SQL to test for and validate a custom condition. Let's use this approach to test how the constraint is enforced. We'll accomplish this by utilizing a test-first approach and attempt to add a record to HumanResources.Employee that doesn't currently exist in our subset of Person.Contact.

Click the Add button in the current Unit Test class. Name the test AddANonExistentContact, and place the following code on the Transact-SQL canvas:

```
INSERT INTO [TestDatabase].[HumanResources].[Employee]
           ([NationalIDNumber]
           ,[ContactID]
           ,[LoginID]
           ,[ManagerID]
           ,[Title]
           ,[BirthDate]
```

```
             , [MaritalStatus]
             , [Gender]
             , [HireDate]
             , [SalariedFlag]
             , [VacationHours]
             , [SickLeaveHours]
             , [CurrentFlag])
      VALUES
             ('123-45-6789'
             , 0
             , 'None'
             , 1
             , ''
             , '1/1/1980'
             , 'S'
             , 'M'
             , '11/30/2006'
             , 0
             , 80
             , 40
             , 1)
```

Remove the default inconclusiveCondition1 test condition, and add a Not Empty ResultSet test condition. In Test View, select AddANonExistentContact, and run the selection.

This script should generate an exception. The goal of this test is to prove that the constraint will prevent a new HumanResources.Employee record from insertion into this table, unless the ContactID already exists in the Person.Contact table.

The test Fails because of an exception returned from the SQL Server database engine. In Test Results, double-click the Failed result to view details. The SQL Server exception returned is similar to:

```
Test method UnitTests_TestDatabase.DatabaseUnitTest3.AddANonExistentContact
    threw exception:  System.Data.SqlClient.SqlException: The INSERT statement
    conflicted with the FOREIGN KEY constraint "FK_Employee_Contact_ContactID".
    The conflict occurred in database "TestDatabase", table "Person.Contact",
    column 'ContactID'.
The statement has been terminated..
```

You might assume that the exception generated by the test run qualifies as a "Not Empty ResultSet," but it does not. Errors don't count as ResultSets. Searching the list of Test Conditions, we do not find Error or Exception listed.

What's really needed here is a means to *assert* this error should be returned. Asserting this error would indicate that we expect this particular exception to be returned by the SQL Server database engine. Successful assertion results in a Passed test. If another exception is returned, the test should Fail.

Let's alter the Transact-SQL to assert we expect this error condition. Replace the existing AddANonExistentContact Transact-SQL test script with:

```
begin try
INSERT INTO [TestDatabase].[HumanResources].[Employee]
            ([NationalIDNumber]
            ,[ContactID]
            ,[LoginID]
            ,[ManagerID]
            ,[Title]
            ,[BirthDate]
            ,[MaritalStatus]
            ,[Gender]
            ,[HireDate]
            ,[SalariedFlag]
            ,[VacationHours]
            ,[SickLeaveHours]
            ,[CurrentFlag])
     VALUES
            ('123-45-6789'
            ,0
            ,'None'
            ,1
            ,''
            ,'1/1/1980'
            ,'S'
            ,'M'
            ,'11/30/2006'
            ,0
            ,80
            ,40
            ,1)
end try
begin catch
  select Error_Number()  -- "throw" the exception number...
end catch
```

Remove the Not Empty ResultSet test condition, and add a Scalar Value test condition. Go to the test condition properties, and set the expected value to 547. In Test View, right-click AddANonExistentContact, and click Run Selection. This test succeeds.

The script utilizes a feature in Transact-SQL 2005 — Try-Catch. The original statement is wrapped into the Try clause — enclosed between Begin Try and End Try statements. The Try clause is followed by the Catch clause. Inside the Catch clause is logic to return the Error_Number value of ("throw") any exception raised by the SQL Server database engine.

If more than one constraint exists on the table, it's possible for any of them to generate Error_Number 547, and you need to isolate the error to the offending Foreign Key constraint. One solution is to return the Error_Message system function instead of the Error_Number. Simply replace Error_Number() with Error_Message() in the earlier script to throw the error message text instead of the error number. An Error_Message for an FK_Employee_Contact_ContactID violation looks like this:

```
The INSERT statement conflicted with the FOREIGN KEY constraint
    "FK_Employee_Contact_ContactID". The conflict occurred in database
    "TestDatabase", table "Person.Contact", column 'ContactID'.
```

In preparation for the next example, change the text condition Expected Value property to the previous text.

One thing to note regarding this test is that it doesn't test what happens if we add a valid Person.Contact to the HumanResources.Employee table. There's a good reason for this: Individual test conditions should test for one and only one function. Can we edit the script to catch other errors (or no error)? Certainly. But if we do, is the source of the problem immediately apparent when a test fails? No. If we change the script to add a valid ContactID instead of ContactID 0, the test also passes.

Obtain a valid ContactID by executing the following query:

```
SELECT Top 20 ContactID
FROM TestDatabase.Person.Contact;
```

When I execute this statement I get a list of valid ContactIDs. I choose to work with ContactID 11. Because the purpose of this test is to check the status of FK_Employee_Contact_ContactID, we should modify the test to Fail if the INSERT statement succeeds.

> *Before you browse over to* Wrox.com's *P2P Forums* http://p2p.wrox.com *and submit a nasty post about this, please consider the following: If this test passes in its current state you will* not *know why. It will either pass because FK_Employee_Contact_ContactID is functioning correctly* or *because someone accidentally added a valid ContactID.*

Let's edit the test script to fail if we unintentionally use a valid ContactID value:

```
declare @Msg nvarchar(4000);

begin try
begin transaction
insert into [TestDatabase].[HumanResources].[Employee]
           ([NationalIDNumber]
           ,[ContactID]
           ,[LoginID]
           ,[ManagerID]
           ,[Title]
           ,[BirthDate]
           ,[MaritalStatus]
           ,[Gender]
           ,[HireDate]
           ,[SalariedFlag]
           ,[VacationHours]
           ,[SickLeaveHours]
           ,[CurrentFlag])
     values
```

```
              ('123-45-6789'
              ,11
              ,'None'
              ,1
              ,''
              ,'1/1/1980'
              ,'S'
              ,'M'
              ,'11/30/2006'
              ,0
              ,80
              ,40
              ,1)
  -- "No Error" check...
  if (@@error = 0)
    begin
      set @Msg = 'No error returned'
      rollback transaction
      raiserror(@Msg,16,1)
    end

  end try

  begin catch
    select Error_Message()
  end catch
```

Execute the test and verify a failed test result. Note the following changes to the Transact-SQL script:

❑   A valid ContactID (I used 11; yours may vary) is used as the value to insert.

❑   A no-error check is performed immediately after the INSERT statement.

❑   To keep the undesired data out of HumanResources.Employee, we introduce a transaction.

This script attempts to load ContactID 11 into the HumanResources.Employee table. ContactID 11 is a valid ContactID in Person.Contact. Since this test is designed to validate FK_Employee_Contact_ContactID *exceptions*, we desire the test to fail if a valid ContactID is submitted in the INSERT statement.

The no-error check performed immediately after the INSERT Transact-SQL statement provides this additional functionality. We check the internal parameter @@error for no-error (0). If this is true, the INSERT statement has succeeded. If the INSERT statement succeeds, the code inside the Catch block will never execute. Catch is only called when an exception — something to "catch" — exists.

Here we use Transact-SQL to assert that "No Error" is, in fact, an exception by using the RAISERROR statement to introduce an error.

Just prior to asserting an error condition, the Rollback Transaction statement performs an "undo" operation, reversing the results of the INSERT statement and maintaining HumanResources.Employee in its pre-test state. Using transactions in this manner is one way to keep unwanted test data out of your test database. One downside to using transactions: Transactions maintain a verbose history in the SQL Server transaction logs. Managing large amounts of test data in this fashion will cause the transaction logs to grow, regardless of the SQL Server database recovery model selected.

For more information about SQL Server transaction logs and database recovery models, see Books Online.

The RAISERROR statement inside the Try block introduces a SQL Server exception. This causes the Catch block to execute. The RAISERROR statement is fed the exception text "No error returned," and this message becomes the Error_Message value returned from the Catch block Transact-SQL — and the value compared to the Expected Value of the Scalar Value Test Condition. The test result details appear conspicuous to those new to testing: "Unexpected error returned: No error returned."

This test now passes only when ContactIDs that are not found in Person.Contact are supplied and the exception returned is a violation of FK_Employee_Contact_ContactID. Validate this by changing the ContactID value from 11 to 0, and re-execute the test. It should now Pass. Perfect.

To be complete, let's add a test for valid data inserted into HumanResources.Employee. Click the Add Test button, and name the new test *AddAnExistingContact*. Remove the default Inconclusive test condition, and add a Scalar Value test condition. Replace the default comments with the following Transact-SQL script:

```
declare @Msg nvarchar(4000);
begin try
begin transaction
insert into [TestDatabase].[HumanResources].[Employee]
        ([NationalIDNumber]
        ,[ContactID]
        ,[LoginID]
        ,[ManagerID]
        ,[Title]
        ,[BirthDate]
        ,[MaritalStatus]
        ,[Gender]
        ,[HireDate]
        ,[SalariedFlag]
        ,[VacationHours]
        ,[SickLeaveHours]
        ,[CurrentFlag])
    output inserted.EmployeeID
    values
        ('123-45-6789'
        ,11
        ,'None'
        ,1
        ,''
        ,'1/1/1980'
        ,'S'
        ,'M'
        ,'11/30/2006'
        ,0
        ,80
        ,40
        ,1)

-- "No Error" check...
  if (@@error = 0)
    begin
```

```
      rollback transaction
    end

end try

begin catch
 select Error_Message()
end catch
-- safety net...
if @@trancount > 0
 rollback transaction


-- rollback identity...
declare @RecCount int;
set @RecCount = (select count(*) from HumanResources.Employee)
dbcc checkident('HumanResources.Employee', reseed, @RecCount)
```

Note that we again use ContactID 11 — a known valid ContactID in our deployed test instance of TestDatabase. Also note the use of another new Transact-SQL 2005 feature, the Output clause.

The Output clause give us access to the Inserted and Deleted virtual tables used internally by SQL Server for Insert, Update, and Delete operations. These virtual tables were previously available in SQL Server 2000 triggers. The Output clause in this statement returns the value of the inserted HumanResources.Employee.EmployeeID identity column — without requiring a second Transact-SQL statement (or worrying about concurrency, locking, etc.).

For more information about the Output clause, see the Books Online, topic: "OUTPUT Clause (Transact-SQL)."

If there is no error on INSERT, the no-error check executes and rolls the transaction (the INSERT statement in this case) back. If there is an error, the Catch block fires and returns the Error_Message. The transaction "safety net" is in place to ensure we don't leave an open transaction.

As a rule of thumb, always manage all possible transaction states.

When the transaction rolls back, nearly all of the changes applied to HumanResources.Employee by the script are reversed. One change that is not reversed is the identity field increment. Human Resources.Employee.EmployeeID is an identity column. It increments to the next value when the INSERT statement executes but does not decrement to the previous value when the transaction rolls back. The "rollback identity" code uses the dbcc `checkident` function to reset the next value for the identity to the next available value based on the current number of rows in HumanResources.Employee.

Execute the test by right-clicking AddAnExistingContact in Test View and clicking Run Selection. The test Passes. If you change the ContactID to 0, the test Fails and reports violation of FK_Employee_Contact_ContactID as the reason. Again, perfect!

This pattern provides a non-empty resultset, which satisfies the test condition. But it also provides intelligence regarding the current value and state of the identity column in the table under test. Such information should be recorded for later analysis.

In this section, we've examined developing unit tests that are based on data values. One way that database testing differs from application testing is in how security testing is conducted. In many application tests, security testing relies heavily on database security. In the next section, we examine security unit-testing in SQL Server 2005.

Unit Testing Security

Permissions and security are the foundation of any enterprise database application. And yet security is considered — and often tested — as if database permissions were a nuisance. Granted, testing security is no fun — mainly because there is precisely no room for error. As Test Engineers and Developers charged with delivering a secure database application, we must be right 100 percent of the time, whereas the ''bad guys'' only have to be right once.

Before conducting this test, we need to add a SQL Login to our test database. Why did we wait until now to add the SQL Login? Until the database project is deployed, the script that creates the login will fail.

Adding a SQL Login

SQL Server allows users to connect via two methods: Windows Authentication and SQL Logins. Both provide access to SQL Server databases and database objects. Windows Authentication uses Active Directory security credentials to authenticate users; SQL Logins provide authentication via the SQL Server Login username and password.

Let's create a SQL Login next. Execute the following Transact-SQL statement to create the test login SQLLogin1 and assign permissions for the login:

```
USE master
GO
IF Not Exists(SELECT * FROM sys.server_principals WHERE name =
N'SQLLogin1')
CREATE LOGIN SQLLogin1 WITH PASSWORD=N'SQLLogin1',
 DEFAULT_DATABASE=TestDatabase, CHECK_EXPIRATION=OFF, CHECK_POLICY=OFF
GO
USE TestDatabase
GO
IF Not Exists(SELECT * FROM sys.database_principals WHERE name =
N'SQLLogin1')
CREATE USER SQLLogin1 FOR LOGIN SQLLogin1
GO
GRANT SELECT ON Person.Contact TO SQLLogin1
GO
GRANT EXECUTE ON Person.uspGetContactSummary TO SQLLogin1
GO
DENY EXECUTE ON dbo.uspGetManagerEmployees TO SQLLogin1
GO
GRANT EXECUTE ON Person.uspGetContactDetails TO SQLLogin1
GO
DENY SELECT ON HumanResources.Department TO SQLLogin1
GO
DENY SELECT ON HumanResources.Employee TO SQLLogin1
GO
DENY EXECUTE ON dbo.uspGetEmployeeManagers TO SQLLogin1
GO
```

Let's develop a unit test to check permissions for our SQL Server Login: SQLLogin1.

Click Test ⇨ New Test to create a new database unit test, and name the test SecurityTests.cs. Change the Add to Test Project dropdown from the existing Test Project to "Create a new Visual C# test project." Click the OK button, and, when prompted, add it to a new test suite we will name *SecurityTests_TestDatabase*. When the test loads, click the "Click here to create" link to build a new test.

When the Project Configuration dialog displays, click the New Connection button. Enter the name of your test server, and click the "Use SQL Server Authentication" option. Enter the SQLLogin1 credentials, and select or enter TestDatabase in the database name dropdown as shown in Figure 4-28.

Figure 4-28

Click the OK button to proceed. Then click the OK button on the Project Configuration to complete this step. Click the "Click here to create" link to start developing a new test. Click the Rename button, and change the name of this test from *DatabaseTest1* to *SecurityTest_uspGetEmployeeManagers*.

You can generate the test Transact-SQL manually if you wish, but I like using SQL Server Management Studio to build test Transact-SQL. In SQL Server Management Studio, browse to your test instance of

TestDatabase, and locate uspGetEmployeeManagers. Right-click the stored procedure, hover over "Script Stored Procedure as," hover over "EXECUTE To," then click "New Query Editor Window" as shown in Figure 4-29.

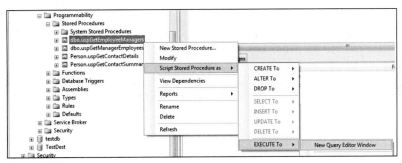

Figure 4-29

This auto-generates almost all of the Transact-SQL code I need to execute a test of this stored procedure. Copy the code, and paste it into your test window in VSTEDP. Add a SET statement for the EmployeeID parameter so your code appears as follows:

```
DECLARE @RC int
DECLARE @EmployeeID int
SET @EmployeeID = 9
EXECUTE @RC = [TestDatabase].[dbo].[uspGetEmployeeManagers]
   @EmployeeID
```

In Test View, right-click and Run SecurityTest_uspGetEmployeeManagers. If your code matches mine at this point, the test will Fail with the following error:

```
Test method SecurityTests_TestDatabase.SecurityTest.SecurityTest_uspGetEmployee
    Managers threw exception:  System.Data.SqlClient.SqlException: The EXECUTE
    permission was denied on the object 'uspGetEmployeeManagers', database
    'TestDatabase', schema 'dbo'..
```

SQLLogin1 has permissions on a couple of stored procedures, so let's test to make sure the account can reach and execute one of them. Click the Add Test button, and name the new test *SecurityTest_ uspGetContactDetails*. Remove the default Inconclusive Test Condition, and add a Non-Empty Resultset Test Condition. Paste the following code over the default text and run the test:

```
DECLARE @RC int
DECLARE @ContactID int
SET @ContactID = 8;
EXECUTE @RC = [TestDatabase].[Person].[uspGetContactDetails]
   @ContactID
```

The test should Pass.

In this section, we've lightly touched on security testing. In practice, proper security testing is the most important and should be the most robust testing we endeavor to pursue.

For more information about Permissions, see the Books Online, topic: "Permissions."

Developing Custom Unit Tests

VSTEDP is extendable, allowing you to create your own custom Unit Test conditions.

In this section, we walk through everything you need to do to create a custom test condition. The test condition we will build is more complex than the handful of examples that existed online at the time of this writing. This walk-through is designed for people with little experience with C# because the majority of database administrators have little experience developing application software or using platforms similar to C#.

Our custom test condition, ColumnListCondition, will compare the results of a Transact-SQL query to a delimited list. This has many uses, but we will be using it to check for the proper number, name, and position (ordinal) of columns in a given table.

The agenda for this section is as follows. We will:

❑   Add a C# Custom Test Condition project to the existing TestDatabase project.

❑   Build a Custom Test Condition for VSTEDP.

❑   Configure the Custom Test Condition to integrate ("hook") with VSTEDP.

❑   Develop a new Unit Test using our test condition.

Adding the Custom Test Condition Project

Let's get started! In Solution Explorer, right-click the TestDatabase solution, hover over Add, and click on New Project. Select a new C# Class Library project and name it CustomTestConditions. Click the OK button to proceed.

A new project is created and added to the TestDatabase Solution. A default Class1.cs file is created. Rename this class file to *ColumnListTestCondition.cs*. Under the CustomTestConditions project, right-click References, then click Add Reference as shown in Figure 4-30.

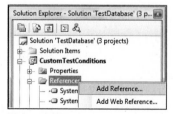

Figure 4-30

As shown in Figure 4-31, you can hold down the Control key and multi-select to add the following references to the C# project:

❑ Microsoft.VisualStudio.QualityTools.UnitTestFramework.dll

❑ Microsoft.VisualStudio.TeamSystem.Data.UnitTesting.dll

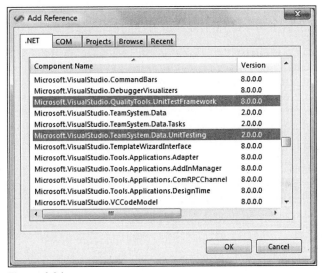

Figure 4-31

Building the Custom Test Condition

Click the OK button after selecting these references. In Solution Explorer your CustomTestConditions project will now look like Figure 4-32.

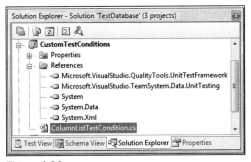

Figure 4-32

Double-click ColumnListTestCondition.cs to open this class for editing. Replace the default code in ColumnListTestCondition with the following:

```
using System;
using System.Collections.Generic;
using System.Text;
using System.Data;
using System.Data.Common;
using System.ComponentModel;
using System.ComponentModel.Design;
using System.Text.RegularExpressions;
using TestTools = Microsoft.VisualStudio.TestTools.UnitTesting;
using Microsoft.VisualStudio.TeamSystem.Data.UnitTesting;
using Microsoft.VisualStudio.TeamSystem.Data.UnitTesting.Conditions;

namespace CustomTestConditions
{
    [DisplayName("Column List")]
    public class ColumnListCondition : TestCondition
    {
        private int _resultSet;
        private string _columnList;
        private char _delimiter;
        private int _batch;
        private int _colCount;

        public ColumnListCondition()
        {
            _resultSet = 1;
            _columnList = "";
            _delimiter = ' ';
            _batch = 1;
            _colCount = 1;
        }


        #region Properties

        //property specifying the resultset for which
        //you want to check the column list
        [Category("Test Condition")]
        [DisplayName("ResultSet")]
        [Description("ResultSet Number")]
        public int ResultSet
        {
            get { return _resultSet; }

            set
            {
                //basic validation
                if (value < 1)
                    throw new ArgumentException("ResultSet cannot
be empty");

                _resultSet = value;
            }
        }
```

```csharp
        //property specifying the delimiter between
        //fields in the column list
        [Category("Test Condition")]
        [DisplayName("Delimiter")]
        [Description("Column List Delimiter")]
        public char Delimiter
        {
            get { return _delimiter; }

            set
            {
                //basic validation
                if (Convert.ToChar(value).Equals(""))
                    value = Convert.ToChar(",");

                _delimiter = value;
            }
        }

        //property specifying
        //expected column list
        [Category("Test Condition")]
        [DisplayName("Column List")]
        [Description("Column List")]
        public string ColumnList
        {
            get { return _columnList; }

            set
            {
                //basic validation
                if (value.Equals(""))
                    throw new ArgumentException("Column List cannot
be empty");

                _columnList = value;
            }
        }

        #endregion

        //method you need to override
        //to perform the condition verification
        public override void Assert(DbConnection
validationConnection, ExecutionResult[] results)
        {
            //call base for parameter validation
            base.Assert(validationConnection, results);

            //verify batch exists
            if (results.Length < _batch)
                throw new TestTools.AssertFailedException
(String.Format("Batch {0} does not exist", _batch));
```

```
                ExecutionResult result = results[_batch - 1];

                //verify resultset exists
                if (result.DataSet.Tables.Count < ResultSet)
                    throw new TestTools.AssertFailedException
        (String.Format("ResultSet {0} does not exist", ResultSet));

                DataTable table = result.DataSet.Tables[0];

                // get column count...
                if (_columnList.Contains(Convert.ToString(_delimiter)))
                    _colCount = _columnList.Split(new
        char[]{_delimiter}).Length + 1; else
                    _colCount = 1;

                //actual condition verification
                //verify resultset column list matches expected
                if (table.Rows.Count != _colCount)
                    throw new TestTools.AssertFailedException(String.Format(
                        "ResultSet {0}: {1} column count did not
         match the {2} columns expected",
                        ResultSet, table.Rows.Count, _colCount));
                string[] fields = new string[_colCount];
                fields = _columnList.Split(_delimiter);
                int x = 0;
                while (x < table.Rows.Count)
                {
                    if (table.Rows[x].ItemArray[0].ToString() !=
        fields[x].ToString())
                    {
                        throw new TestTools.AssertFailedException
        (String.Format(
                            "Column {0} is expected at ordinal {1} but
         {2} is at ordinal {1}",
                            fields[x], x,
         table.Rows[x].ItemArray[0].ToString()));
                    }
                    x++;
                }

            }

            //this method is called to provide the string shown in the
            //test conditions panel grid describing what the condition tests
            public override string ToString()
            {
                return String.Format(
                    "Condition fails if ResultSet {0} does not
        contain {1} columns",
                    ResultSet, ColumnList);
            }
        }
    }
}
```

The first part of this code contains a list of using statements. These statements define the libraries that will be accessed by the remaining C# code. The namespace definition is next and is important: It identifies our library to other applications, VSTEDP, in this case. Our namespace is CustomTestConditions.

The next thing our example does is define the class. [DisplayName("Column List")] defines the name of the Test Condition as it will appear in the Test Condition dropdown inside VSTEDP. The class definition follows: public class ColumnListCondition : TestCondition.

Immediately below the class definition we initialize the class-level variables:

Variable	Data Type	Description
_resultSet	Int	An identifier for the current resultset under test. The current maximum is 1 resultset per test condition, but this will likely change in future releases.
_columnList	String	Contains the delimited list of columns to compare with the results of the query.
_delimiter	Char	Contains the delimiter used by _columnList.
_batch	Int	An internal iterator for looping through multiple resultsets. This value could be hard-coded to 0 at this time, but it's good programming practice to plan for the future as much as possible.
_colCount	Int	Contains the number of columns detected in _columnList, and therefore expected in the results.

The class-scoped variable declaration is followed by the default constructor for the class: public Column-ListCondition. Inside the curly braces that follow, we initialize all class-scoped variables.

In the Support region, a private helper method named countNumberOfCharsInString provides a mechanism for counting the occurrences of the _delimiter character in _columnList. It uses Regular Expressions to accomplish this.

For more information on Regular Expressions, see .NET Framework Regular Expressions http://msdn2.microsoft.com/en-us/library/hs600312.aspx.

The next region groups the class properties together. There are three class properties: Resultset, Delimiter, and ColumnList. Resultset can contain any integer value and can be used as an identifier for a given test or test batch execution.

These properties are read/write so they contain code to set and get values. Text descriptors for the property name and description are defined by setting Category, DisplayName, and Description.

The next section of C# code contains the Assert method. The Assert method does most of the work we see in our custom test condition. This method is inherited from a base class named TestCondition. In fact, this method overrides the code contained in TestCondition's Assert method to perform the checks and comparisons we desire.

This method is passed the connection — a connection to a SQL Server in this case — and an object of type `ExecutionResult`. The `ExecutionResult` (results) contains an ADO.NET data set object, which, in turn, contains an ADO.NET table object. The table object contains the results of our query and can be visualized as the Grid Results Pane in SQL Server Management Studio.

The checks include calls to make sure:

❑ The current batch exists.

❑ A resultset exists inside the `ExecutionResult`.

❑ The number of rows in the resultset matches the number of rows predicted by the `ColumnList` property.

When these preliminary checks are complete, the `ColumnList` values are split into an array of string data type (`fields`) by the `Delimiter`. A loop is initiated, and the values of the `fields` string array are compared to the values in the resultset `table`. When the first mismatch is detected, an exception (`AssertFailedException`) is generated and thrown.

The final method provides feedback in the Test Conditions panel grid describing what this test condition actually tests. It's dynamic in that as the Resultset and ColumnList properties change, the value of the string changes.

That's all there is to it! (Well, that's all there is to the code, anyway. . . .) If this is your first foray into C#, you're not in the shallow, "Hello World" end of the pool. You're building something that will hook into Visual Studio and help you and those with whom you work be more productive while producing higher-quality database code. This is what Unit Testing is all about!

Building the 'Hook'

In order for VSTEDP to use the custom test condition code we just built, we have to take actions to "hook" it into the Visual Studio application. The two things we must do at this stage are:

❑ Add security.

❑ Define an interface that lets VSTEDP know our test condition is out here and ready for use.

Security for Custom Test Conditions

Code Access Security (CAS) is a field in its own right, and we will merely scratch the surface with our example. Our foray into CAS will consist of using the Strong Name signing utility provided with Microsoft Visual Studio to sign the assembly.

There are several ways to accomplish code signing. For details, see the "How to: Sign an Assembly with a Strong Name" in Microsoft help or at MSDN.

To sign the assembly, we need a key file containing a public and private key pair. One way to generate a key file is by using the Strong Name tool (`sn.exe`). To generate a key file for our custom test condition assembly, execute the following in a command prompt window:

```
"C:\Program Files\Microsoft Visual Studio 8\SDK\v2.0\Bin\sn.exe" -k
"C:\Andy\Books\Testing With
VSTS\Demos\TestDatabase\CustomTestConditions\ctcsn.snk"
```

Your file paths may vary depending on where you installed Visual Studio and the location of your TestDatabase project files.

When I successfully execute the command on my computer, it looks like Figure 4-33.

Next, attach the key file to the C# custom test condition code so that it will be used whenever you build your project. To accomplish this, right-click the CustomTestConditions project, and click Properties. Click the Signing tab, and then check the "Sign the assembly" checkbox. In the "Choose a strong name key file" dropdown click Browse, and navigate to the file we just created (ctcsn.snk), as shown in Figure 4-34.

Whenever we build this project, the assembly will be signed automatically using ctcsn.snk.

Before we leave project properties, let's add some post-build-event commands. In CustomTestConditions project properties, click the Build Events tab. Paste or carefully type the following statements into the post-build-event command-line textbox:

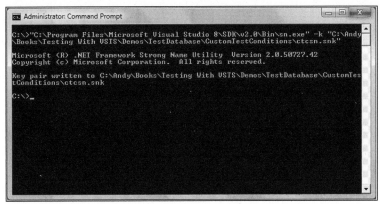

Figure 4-33

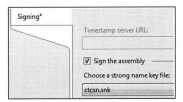

Figure 4-34

```
copy "$(TargetDir)$(TargetName)$(TargetExt)" "$(ProgramFiles)\Microsoft
Visual Studio 8\DBPro\Extensions\$(TargetName)$(TargetExt)" /y
copy "$(ProjectDir)$(TargetName).Extensions.xml" "$(ProgramFiles)\Microsoft
Visual Studio 8\DBPro\$(TargetName).Extensions.xml" /y
"$(ProgramFiles)\Microsoft Visual Studio 8\SDK\v2.0\Bin\gacutil.exe" /if
```

```
"$(ProgramFiles)\Microsoft Visual Studio
8\DBPro\Extensions\$(TargetName)$(TargetExt)"
```

If Visual Studio 2005 is not installed in your default Program Files directory (which is most likely C:\Program Files), you will need to replace "$(ProgramFiles)" above with the fully qualified path to your Visual Studio 2005 installation.

The first copy command copies the assembly file into the Extensions directory for VSTEDP. The second copy command copies the Extensions XML file (yet to be created) into the proper directory. Finally, the third command registers the assembly with the Global Assembly Cache (GAC).

The Global Assembly Cache is a machine-wide code cache containing assemblies intended to be shared among several .NET applications. The GAC is created on every machine when the Common Language Runtime libraries of the .NET Framework are installed. Any application can reference assemblies in the GAC.

For more information about assemblies and GAC, see the help topic "Assemblies and the Global Assembly Cache (C# Programming Guide)" in Visual Studio 2005 Help.

Defining the Interface

Next we need to construct the Extensions XML file used by VSTEDP to identify and load our signed assembly. To accomplish this, right-click the CustomTestConditions project in Solution Explorer, hover over Add, and click New Item. When the Add New Item dialog appears, select XML file, and name the file *CustomTestConditions.Extensions.xml*. Click the Add button to proceed.

Paste or carefully type the following over the default code in the CustomTestConditions.Extensions.xml file:

```
<?xml version="1.0" encoding="us-ascii"?>
<extensions  assembly="CustomTestConditions, Version=1.0.0.0,
Culture=neutral, PublicKeyToken=[Public Key Token]" version="1"
xmlns="urn:Microsoft.VisualStudio.TeamSystem.Data.Extensions"
xmlns:xsi="http://www.w3.org/2001/XMLSchema-instance"
xsi:schemaLocation="urn:Microsoft.VisualStudio.TeamSystem.Data.Extensions
Microsoft.VisualStudio.TeamSystem.Data.Extensions.xsd">
    <extension type="CustomTestConditions.ColumnListCondition" enabled="true" />
</extensions>
```

One key portion of this code is missing and cannot be located until after we build the project (which signs and deploys the assembly to the GAC): the *[Public Key Token]*.

To obtain the Public Key Token, build the assembly by right-clicking the CustomTestConditions project in Solution Explorer and clicking Build. If all goes well, you should see the following in the Output window:

```
Assembly successfully added to the cache
========== Build: 1 succeeded or up-to-date, 0 failed, 0 skipped ==========
```

If you see this message, you should now be able to browse to the GAC using Windows Explorer (the GAC is located in *%Windows%*\assembly). Locate the CustomTestConditions assembly in the GAC, right-click the file, and click Properties as shown in Figure 4-35.

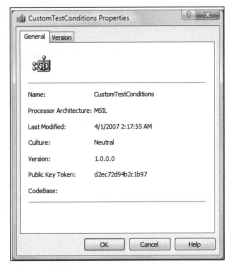

Figure 4-35

Double-click the Public Key Token value to select it, and then copy the selected value to the clipboard. Return to Visual Studio, and paste this value over *[Public Key Token]*. Then build the assembly again to refresh this file.

To verify, browse to the location where you installed Visual Studio, drill down to the DBPro subdirectory (on my computer, this location is C:\Program Files\Microsoft Visual Studio 8\DBPro), and open the default code in the CustomTestConditions.Extensions.xml file.

If all has gone according to plan, we now have a custom test condition registered and ready to use.

To load our custom test condition, we must first close all instances of Visual Studio and reopen them. Custom test conditions are loaded when Visual Studio starts.

Developing a Unit Test with the Custom Test Condition

To test our new test condition (sounds redundant, I know), create a new database unit test named *ColumnListConditionTest*. Once the new test is loaded, click the "Click here to create" link to build a new test.

Replace the default Transact-SQL in the test window with the following code:

```
select name
from sys.columns
where object_name(object_id) = 'Contact'
order by column_id;
```

Remove the default Inconclusive Test Condition, and select our new Column List Test Condition. Press F4 to view properties, and add a comma (",") as the single character in the Delimiter property. Add the following to the ColumnList property:

```
ContactID,NameStyle,Title,FirstName,MiddleName,LastName,Suffix,EmailAddress,
EmailPromotion,Phone,PasswordHash,PasswordSalt,AdditionalContactInfo,rowguid,
ModifiedDate
```

Click the Rename button to change the name of the test from DatabaseTest1 to ColumnListTest. In Test View, right-click ColumnListTest, and select Debug Selection. If all goes as planned, this test execution should Pass.

Try removing columns from the ColumnList property and swapping the column order. Both conditions should cause the test to fail and provide informative feedback about why and where. For instance, if I place the Title column first in the ColumnList property, the test fails with the error:

```
Column Title is expected at ordinal 0 but ContactID is at ordinal 0
```

This test condition checks for an ordered list of columns (or anything, really). It's very handy for schema validation.

Summary

In this chapter, we examined developing and testing a VSTEDP project for SQL Server 2005.

We touched on database test theory and the differences between database and application testing.

We used VSTEDP to conduct various tests against the database, SQL Server login security, and ultimately the schema itself.

We walked through development and deployment of a custom test condition, and then proceeded to conduct tests of its functionality.

Web Testing

One of the types of tests that you can create in VSTEST is a web test. This is a test specifically designed for testing a Web-based application. This could be a simple web page, a full web site, a set of web services, or (usually) a combination of all of them. Web tests use HTTP requests (POST/GET) to test your Web application.

They are also the easiest tests to create in VSTEST because of the built-in test recorder that allows you to record the HTTP requests that occur as you access and use your site. You then replay those recorded HTTP requests (as is, or with some editing) as a web test.

There are two types of web tests that you can use. The first is the "Basic Web Test," which will work for most scenarios that you need to test. It is very simple to create and edit using a very easy UI and has a recorder for quick test creation. While these web tests are flexible enough for most testing needs, because the test is made up of a list of HTTP requests with no exposed code, there are some cases in which you need more control. For those cases, VSTEST provides a "Coded Web Test" that is essentially a web test converted into C# or Visual Basic code. This allows you to edit the test scenario in a more complicated fashion and allows more flow control (e.g., conditionals and looping). But, of course, this flexibility comes at the cost of increased complexity and maintenance from using code. Coded web tests are discussed at the end of this chapter.

> *Web tests are also very closely linked to load testing because one of the major concerns for a web site is whether it can handle thousands of users at a time. For this reason, many of the settings and properties of web tests are only useful in the context of a load test. This chapter focuses on covering web tests and will call out such load test–related issues. But we cover the load testing aspects in much more detail in Chapter 7.*

Basic Web Tests

While basic web tests are easy to create, they are still very powerful and can handle many of the needs of testing a web site. Creating a simple web test is very quick and easy, and the steps to enhance it are also easy. If you find you need the additional control of a coded web test, it is easy to convert the existing basic web test to a coded web test.

Recording a Test

The easiest way to create a web test is to record it using the Web Test Recorder. This gets you a simple working test in a matter of minutes. Even when you need a more complicated test, this is the best way to start. It gives you a solid base to start from and a good understanding of what is happening in the system you are testing. There may be requests happening that you don't expect, ones that you do expect but are not there, and so forth. In fact, I have found bugs in a product I was preparing to test just by recording a scenario and examining the requests that VSTEST recorded. Even when I want to create a coded web test and I already have a similar coded web test (where one would be tempted to copy and modify the coded test), it can be useful to record it from scratch to verify that what you think is happening is what is actually occurring in the product. In addition to recording a web test, you can also create a new web test manually, adding the requests by hand, or copying the requests from another test. Coded web tests, because they are normal Visual Basic or C# code, can, of course, be written by hand as well. But in most cases, it is much easier to start by recording the web test and using that as a starting point.

> **When using recorded web tests, be sure to examine the requests to make sure they are correct. Because your product might have bugs in it (that's why you're testing), there is a danger of recording incorrect behavior in your product. Then when you run the test, you are replaying the incorrect behavior.**

Recording a Simple Test

The Web Test Recorder allows you to record a browser session in Internet Explorer to create a web test.

1. Select your Test Project. (To create a new test project, see "The New Project Dialog Box" in Chapter 2.)

2. From the Test menu, select New Test (or right-click on the project, and select Add ⇨ Web Test).

3. A new instance of Internet Explorer will open up with the Web Test Recorder window on the left of the page (see Figure 5-1).

Figure 5-1

4. Navigate to the page(s) that you want to be included in the web test, and follow the steps that you want to record as your test. As you do this, you will see the requests appear in the Web Test Recorder window.

You can pause the recording if you need to navigate through pages you do not want included in the test and then start recording again when you need to. It is very easy to edit the recording afterward. Often it is easier to just walk through the site following the steps of the test and edit out any extraneous HTTP requests later.

Stopping the recorder ends the web test recording session and closes IE. You will now see the new test listed under your test project, and it is open in the Web Test editor so that you can work with the web test.

Inserting Comments

The Web Test Recorder allows you to insert comments into the recording as you go. Just like comments in code, comments in the recording can be a very useful method for keeping track of what is happening during the test. For example, if your test covers a user browsing through several sections of your site, then you should probably add comments marking when the test enters each of the different sections. Or if there is (or might be) a difference in how you are moving from one page to another (clicking a button as opposed to the link at the top of the page), you might want to add a comment explaining how the request is being generated (e.g., "Navigating to SignUp page via the 'sign me up' button"). It is also useful for making notes about places where you might need to use dynamic data or how the page should be validated, since these things can be obvious while looking at the page and harder to remember later.

> **To add a comment, simply click the Add Comment button (the folder with the spark on it) on the Web Test Recorder toolbar, and a comment will be inserted at the end of the recording.**

Think Time

While you are recording, VSTEST keeps track of the time you spend on each page (between each request) and stores that in the Think Time property of the request. During playback of the test this can be useful in simulating an actual user. Don't worry too much about it during recording as this property is easy to edit and because it's often hard to duplicate closely the time a user would spend on a page (for one thing, you are probably more familiar with it than they are); you will almost always want to modify this value a bit from your recording. If you can keep the time that you spend on a page to roughly the same time that a user would spend on the page on average, you have a very good start. I've found that by actually walking through the same steps a user would perform, even the ones that will not affect the recording, you can get a good set of think times.

> *During test playback in a load test, you can choose to use the exact think times, vary them (but use the think time as the average), or ignore the think time (and just run the test as fast as possible). Outside of a load test, when you are just running the web test by itself, you can only turn the think times on or off.*

Think times are not very important when running an individual test but can be crucial in determining what the load your tests generate during a load test is like. For this reason, you will probably want to turn off the Think Time when running a single test and turn it on and override the settings during load testing. (We go into this in much more detail in Chapter 7.)

Using the Web Test Editor

Once you have your web test recorded, it will open up in the Web Test Editor. In the Editor you can fine-tune the various properties that govern the web test. You can also create a new web test without recording one by either copying an existing test and editing it or by adding a new test but stopping the Recorder without recording anything (there is no way to create a blank test without going through the Recorder).

Features of the Web Test Editor

The Web Test Editor has several practical and easy-to-use features:

❏ **Toolbar** — Each web test "document" that is open has a toolbar in its document window that exposes some of the basic commands.

❏ **Request Tree** — When you open up a web test to edit it, instead of seeing a code file what you see is a tree view listing the requests in the order they are executed during the test. Each request can be expanded to see the internal details of the request such as the form post parameters or the query string parameters.

❏ **Properties Window** — Many important properties and settings related to the various aspects of a web test are only editable from the Properties window. When working on web tests, it is usually a good idea to have the Properties window open all the time.

You will see various aspects of using these features throughout the chapter.

Adding a New Request

You can manually add a new request to your web test simply by right-clicking on the request just after the place where your new request should execute and choosing Add New Request. Then you need to enter in all of the URL data for the request.

You can also copy a request and paste it into the web test in another spot. You can then either leave it as is (to have the test hit the same page more than once) or edit the request properties to create a new request.

Cleaning Up Your Recorded Test

VSTEST records each "initial" HTTP request but does not record any subrequests that occur based on the content of the response to the original request. In other words, VSTEST records just the user-initiated requests and does not record redirects or in-page requests. It does a very good job of this but can have problems with pages where there is a large amount of client-side scripting as in AJAX style pages (see the section "Web Tests and AJAX" below in this chapter).

Removing Unneeded Requests and Modifying the Order

Sometimes the steps that have been recorded for your web test are exactly what you wanted, but as with any type of recording, sometimes you need to do some editing afterward. Occasionally when you record a web test, you will get extraneous steps that are not part of what you want to test. This could be due to stopping/starting the recording at the wrong time, accidentally clicking the wrong button, or just that there are some pages that you do not want included in this particular test. You should browse through the list of recorded steps and delete any steps that are not needed for the test.

You can also modify the steps in other ways, changing the order, copying them to create multiple similar requests, and so forth. This is all done using standard keyboard commands (*Ctrl* + *C*, etc.) or drag-and-drop. This can be useful if you recorded a simple walk-through of some pages but then want to better simulate a user browsing your site. For example, copying a step (request) so that you have more than one identical step in a row can simulate a user hitting Refresh.

> **You need to be careful about changing the order of requests. For example, if Request A has an extraction rule to extract a value used by Request B, an error will occur if Request B is moved before Request A.**

Subpage Requests and Redirects

In the recorded test you won't see dependent (or "subpage") requests, such as images and other files that are loaded when that page is loaded. In other words, only the GET/POST request for the page is recorded, not all of the individual Get requests for the elements on the page. They will be requested when the test is run, based on the contents of the page at run time (just as when the browser opens the page during normal use). This means that changes to the contents of the page (e.g., adding or removing an image) will be reflected in your tests without needing to update the web test.

> You will not see any redirects that may be occurring on your site. Because that is an action that is not user initiated, VSTEST does not record it. This is good because, for example, if your site changes so that a certain request now returns a redirect, your test will not need to change.

Components of a Web Test

All web tests are made up of a set of components and properties that determine how the web test works and what it does. There are some overall properties that control the general behavior of the Web Test. These properties set behaviors such as what (if any) proxy server to use for all requests and what credentials to authenticate with.

In addition to the properties of the web test, there is the list of requests that the test performs (essentially the steps of the test), including any comments. Each of these requests itself has a set of properties that determine the specifics of that individual request. These requests can be grouped into transactions that let you consider a set of requests as a single operation for timing and other purposes.

And finally, each web test has a list of context parameters that are, essentially, global variables for the web test. These allow you easily to change certain parameters of your test, for instance, the base URL the test is running against. This is a powerful way to re-use the tests in different situations.

All these key components of Web Tests are discussed in the next few sections.

Properties of a Web Test

The web test itself has some properties that control the overall execution of the requests that make up the test:

Property	Description
Description	A brief description of the test. This can be useful for documenting the test case, but this property does not actually show up anywhere except in the Web Test Properties page.
Pre-authenticate	A setting that determines if the test should automatically include an authentication header with every request or if it should only send the authentication headers as part of a challenge/response with the server. If this property is true, then every request will include the authentication header, and if it is false, then the authentication header will only be sent when asked. It defaults to True.

Continued

Property	Description
User Name and Password	The User Name and Password properties are the properties set when you use the Set Credentials button on the Web Test Editor toolbar. (See the "Credentials" section below in this chapter.)
Proxy	If your web test is making requests that need to go outside a firewall through a proxy server, then you will need to set this value to the proxy server that the test should use.
Web Test Plug-in	Sets the Assembly reference information for your custom web test if you are using custom code for these. (We go into this feature in more detail below in this chapter; see the "Plug-ins" section.)
Request Plug-in	Sets the Assembly reference information for your custom request plug-ins if you are using custom code for these. (We go into this feature in more detail below in this chapter; see the "Plug-ins" section.)

Credentials

You can set the credentials that your test will use to interact with the web site if needed. This lets you run your tests against pages on your site that use either basic authentication or integrated Windows authentication. You just enter in the user name and password to be used by the test. You can also bind these to a data source to allow you to run the test multiple times using different credentials (see the section on "Making Web Tests Dynamic" below in this chapter).

Clicking the Set Credentials button (the file with the lock on it) on the Web Test Editor toolbar opens the Set Credentials dialog (see Figure 5-2) so that you can enter the username and password values to use. The Bind buttons are used to link these values to a data source to allow using multiple values for this.

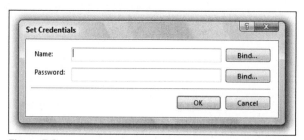

Figure 5-2

You can also edit these properties directly through the web test's properties, but if you are binding them to a data source, it is easier to use the Set Credentials dialog.

Requests

Requests are the steps that the web test will perform. Each step is a single HTTP request that VSTEST will execute and then process its response. The list of requests (also called the *request tree*) shown in the Web Test Editor are the requests that make up this test in the order in which they will be executed.

Properties of a Request

When you select a request (with the Properties window open), you will see the following properties:

❑ **Cache Control** — True/False to set whether or not you want VSTEST to simulate the standard browser caching behavior. If this is set to True, then the test will run as if it is a browser with optimal caching turned on, so that it will only request a URL the first time. In other words, if the same image file is included on all of your site's pages, turning on Caching will mean that the image is only requested from your server once. Turning off caching will mean the image is requested for every page.

This setting affects only the primary request and does not affect dependent requests (such as images embedded in the response). Caching of dependent requests is determined by whether or not you are running the web test by itself or as part of a load test. When you are just running a web test (outside of a load test), caching is turned off for all dependent requests. During a load test, dependent requests are always cached for an iteration. This means that each instance of a web test executing during a load test is considered a separate "user," but each request inside the web test is the same user. And any repeated dependent requests will be cached just like a normal user browsing a site. The load test scenario property Percentage of New Users lets you control if the web test should use caching for the initial requests or if it should act like a user that has never browsed the site before.

> *Turning caching on can more accurately simulate a user's experience and the load they generate on your server. But it does reduce the actual stress/load that your web test is generating.*

The default for this property is False, and it is usually a good idea to leave it off except for when you specifically want to measure user page load times with caching.

❑ **Encoding** — Sets the text encoding format to use for the requests. This is almost always set to UTF-8 because most HTTP traffic is in UTF-8 encoding.

❑ **Follow Redirects** — Determines if VSTEST should honor an HTTP status code of 300-307 (Redirect) and continue to the new page or if it should stop and treat the redirect as the final response of the request. Usually you will want your requests to follow any redirects automatically and end on the final page just as if it were a normal browser. But if your site is performing complicated redirects (passing values through, etc.) and you need to perform test validations on the redirect response instead of the final response, then you would turn this off (set it to False).

❑ **Method** — This is the transport method to use in this request, either GET or POST.

❑ **Parse Dependent Requests** — Determines if the internal requests in the response page should be parsed and executed or if they should be ignored. For example, any JPEGs on the page are dependent requests that, when you loaded the page in a browser, the browser would automatically execute the additional HTTP requests to get the image files. Setting this property to True means that the test will run like a standard browser, parsing and executing any dependent requests on the page.

Usually you want this set to True so that your test properly simulates a normal user. But there may be cases in which you wish to turn this off.

> **Because VSTEST does not execute any scripts on the page (including things like `<![if !IE]>`, any dependent requests that are script-dependent will always be executed. Thus if you have script on a page that conditionally loads a file, you may want to turn this off and manually add just the requests that you want to execute for the page.**

❑ **Record Results** — This property is only used during load testing and determines if the timing and performance data should be included in the load test results. In most cases, you do want to include the timing data in your load test results, but some pages may not be important in terms of timing measurements and performance. To reduce the amount of Result data (which can be very large in a load test), therefore, you can turn off the results collection for certain requests.

❑ **Response Time Goal** — This is the goal for how long (in seconds) it should take for the server to respond to this request. This property is only used during load test reporting. The load test results will then display the percentage of these requests that had a response time less than or equal to the goal. This is very useful for spotting periods during a load test when server response time was slower than you consider acceptable.

The default value is 0, which means there is no goal to which to compare the response time. And if the Record Results property is set to False, then the Response Time Goal is ignored.

❑ **Think Time** — As mentioned above in the "Recording a Test" section, the think time is an amount of time (in seconds) to pause on a page before processing the next request. The Think Time property of a request is the amount of delay before moving on to the next request. Modifying this value changes the base think time for this request. The actual think time is affected by the overall Think Time settings in the active Test Run Configuration and/or the load test.

❑ **Timeout** — This is simply the maximum time (in seconds) to wait for a response to the request before timing out and marking the request as Failing.

❑ **URL** — This is the URL of the request. Editing this property changes the URL that the request will be calling.

❑ **Version** — Sets the HTTP version to use for the request, which can be either 1.0 or 1.1. In almost all cases, you will want to use the default value of 1.1, but if you wish to simulate a user hitting your site using an older version of HTTP, to ensure compatibility you would set this to 1.0.

As you can see, there are quite a few properties that let you control and fine-tune the behavior of each request. This lets you simulate almost any type of HTTP request that you might need to test your web application.

Several of these properties operate differently during a load test and/or are overridden by the load test settings. This allows a great deal of flexibility and reuse of a single web test in many different load tests, but it does make some of these settings quite a bit more confusing.

In addition to the properties that control the behavior of the request, a request can have sub-items. These items allow you to control the data that are included in the request and how to handle and verify the data returned in the response from the request.

Sub-Items of a Request

Depending on what was recorded for the request and what has been manually added to it, various sections will appear under the request as sub-items. These sub-items allow you to control various aspects of the request and processing of the response. A very simple HTTP request may not have any sub-items, but in most cases each request will have a few of these items. Since it is always a good idea to at least have one validation rule to verify that the response is correct, most requests will have at least that. Each of these sub-items can be added by right-clicking on the request and choosing "Add <item>."

Following are the sub-items that can appear under a request:

❏   **Dependent Requests** — These are the HTTP requests due to the content of the original response. The common example is an image on a page. In most cases, where dependent requests are handled automatically, this is controlled by the request's Parse Dependent Requests property (see above). If you have turned off automatic handling of the dependent requests, then you will need to manually add any that you want to occur.

A dependent request is a normal request (except that it has a parent request) and can have all of the sub-items, including its own dependent requests. This is the other reason to explicitly add a dependent request: if you need to validate or extract a value from the response of the dependent request itself. In this case, you can add an extraction or validation rule to the dependent request to handle it.

❏   **Query String Parameters** — If there are query string parameters in the request, they are listed in the Query String Parameters section. For example, if you recorded a request `http:/temp.com/ myClient.dll?Get=AD&PG=VSTT&AP=123`, it would appear in the UI as shown in Figure 5-3.

Figure 5-3

You can edit each of these Name = Value pairs as individual items using the Properties window. Each parameter has a Name and a Value property that can be set in the Property window. There are also two other properties that can be set for each query string parameter:

❏   **Show Separate Request Results** — This property is only used for load testing and allows you to add an additional layer of grouping of the results in a load test. Normally all of the result data for a request are grouped together, but if this is set to True, then you will see the result data (response time, etc.) grouped by the different values that were used in this parameter. This is only useful if this parameter is dynamic; either with a context parameter or bound to a data store (see the "Making Web Tests Dynamic" section below in this chapter).

❏   **URL Encode** — Determines if the Name and Value will be URL encoded using the request's settings. The default is True.

❏   **Form Post Parameters** — If the request method type is POST, then it will have some form post parameters. There are two types of form post parameters: the "normal" form post parameter that handles common post request style data and a special type specifically for use with requests that upload files.

❏ **Common Form Post Parameter** — These are handled in the UI just like the query string parameters; that is, each form post parameter has a Name and a Value property. There is also a URL Encode property (again, just like a query string parameter) that determines if the Name and Value will be URL encoded using the Request's settings. The default is True.

❏ **File Upload Parameter** — A special type of form post parameter that allows simulating a file upload as part of a post request. A file upload parameter has a Name property and a URL Encode property that work just like those for the normal form post parameter. There are also two other properties specific to the file upload operation — Content Type, the MIME type of the file being uploaded; and File Name, the name of the file to upload. Note that the file needs to be included in the test project. If you bind this field to a dynamic data source (to allow uploading different files for different iterations), it still needs to refer to a file in the project.

❏ **Headers** — This parameter collection allows you to specify Name=Value pairs that will be included in the HTTP header — for example, `Referer=www.microsoft.com` or `Accept-Encoding=gzip`.

❏ **Validation Rules** — Validation rules are a very important method of verifying that the response that was returned from the request is the expected one. By default, VSTEST checks that the response does not have an HTTP status indicating an error. To get a more detailed verification requires a validation rule. We go into more detail on validation rules below in the "Verifying the Response with Validation Rules" section in this chapter.

❏ **Extraction Rules** — Extraction rules allow capturing data from the response so that it can be used in later requests. A common example is a variable that is passed from page to page to track various bits of state information (e.g., the ASP.NET `__VIEWSTATE` field). If your site does this, you will need to have extraction rules for any data that need to be passed from a response to a later request.

The good news is that VSTEST handles a lot of this work for you. For each request, VSTEST will extract data from the response that can be used in the parameters of later requests. Upon recording, any hidden fields or `VIEWSTATE` items are automatically detected and extraction rules for them are added. You can also add your own extraction rules if you need to (see the section below in this chapter, "Capturing Data During a Web Test").

Transactions

Transactions are a way of grouping requests together into a set. This does not affect the order or the way in which they are executed. It does help document the requests (e.g., "these are all part of the sign-up process") and groups them so that you move or copy them as a unit.

The main benefit of transactions is that you get timing data for the transaction as well as the individual requests. This lets you measure the total time to perform an action even if the action covers more than one request.

To add a transaction, follow these steps:

1. At the spot where you want to add the transaction, right-click and choose Add Transaction. This opens the Add Transaction dialog (see Figure 5-4).

2. Enter a name for the transaction, and pick the starting request and the ending request for the transaction.

You can move requests into and out of the transaction simply by dragging and dropping them in the Web Test Editor.

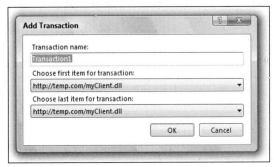

Figure 5-4

Comments

As mentioned earlier, comments in the web test can be useful to document what is happening at any particular step. It is not always clear what is happening from just the URL of the request. Any comments added during recording will show up in the web test. You can add more comments if you need to, by simply right-clicking where you want the comment added and choosing Add Comment.

Context Parameters

The Context Parameters node will appear at the bottom of the list of requests in the web test if you have any parameters set. Under this node are all of the context parameters. Context parameters are used to provide variables in your request properties, making your test more flexible and dynamic. Context parameters are covered in more detail in the next section, "Making Web Tests Dynamic."

Making Web Tests Dynamic

The output of a Web Test Recording session is a fully working web test that can be (usually) used as is to test your site. The problem with this is that every step is hard-coded to perform the exact same action each time, and if your test is doing anything more than simply browsing the site, you will probably want to make it a bit more dynamic. In some cases this may be required in order for your test to run successfully more than once. For example, if you recorded a web test that creates a new account, it may work the first time, but running the exact same steps again will probably fail with an "account already exists" error. There is a great deal of flexibility provided through the data-driven support, context parameters, and other extensibility points that allow you to customize behaviors.

You will probably need to target different web servers at various stages of the web site development (initial testing, final test server, beta server, production, etc.). Having to edit each individual request to change the URL would be time-consuming and error-prone.

Furthermore, it's often very useful to be able to run the same web test multiple times with slightly different data so that you can get a high amount of test coverage from a single web test. For this, web tests support the same data-driven features that unit tests use.

2. Select the web server that you need to set to use your local ASP.NET Development Server.

3. Click the Change button to open up the Change Web Server dialog box (see Figure 5-6). The Change Web Server dialog allows you to set up the web servers parameters to work with your ASP.NET Development Server.

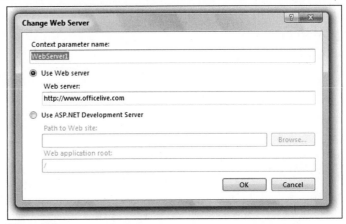

Figure 5-6

4. Select the Use ASP.NET Development Server and set the path to the web site and the web application root.

Examining the Web Server Parameters

After closing the Parameterize Web Servers dialog, you will see that the Context Parameters node has been added to your web test. Expanding it, you will see an entry for each of the servers as a `parametername=value`. You can edit these as needed using the Properties page.

You will also see that the URLs in all of the requests in the web test have been modified to use the context parameters that were just created. Each URL will now look something like: `{{WebServer1}}/Signup/Accept.html` and you have a context parameter named *WebServer1* (with a value of the web server URL that was in all of the request strings before).

> To change the web server that the test is running against, all you need to do is change the value of the appropriate context parameter, and it will be applied to each request that uses it.

Adding a New Context Parameter

To create a new context parameter, simply right-click on the Web Test node (the root node in the Web Test Editor) or on the Context Parameters node (if it is showing), and choose "Add Context parameter."

The new context parameter appears in the Context Parameters node with a default name (e.g., *Parameter1*) and no value. Select it, and set the name and value you want using the Properties page.

Using a Context Parameter

As you can see from parameterizing the web servers above, the {{...}} notation indicates a context parameter. You can make any value dynamic simply by replacing the static value with {{contextname}}. It does not have to be the entire value either; the context parameter will be expanded and concatenated with the rest of the value. You can have more than one context parameter in a value, and you can use context parameters just about anywhere you can enter in a string value.

For example, if you have a Form Post Parameter that passes in the user's e-mail address, you can make it dynamic by changing it from

```
emailaddress=test@testdomain.com
```

to

```
emailaddress={{UserName}}@{{DomainName}}.com
```

Now whenever the test is run, it will generate an e-mail address using the `UserName` and `DomainName` context parameters.

Context parameters are best used to set values that define the scenario for the current test run, settings like which web server is being used or the base domain name that will be used for every e-mail address. These are values that change in between test runs but not during the test run.

> **If you want to run the web test multiple times using a different value for a parameter or parameters each time, then you should use the data-driven support instead of a context parameter.**

Just to be a little confusing, extraction rules use context parameters to store and reference the data that are extracted from the responses.

Determining the Value of a Context Parameter

While you can just use context parameters as simple global settings that you set by manually editing the context parameter's properties before you start the test, there are several other ways that the value of a context parameter can be set. This really expands the value of using context parameters and allows you to create and manage a very dynamic set of tests.

❑ **Extraction Rules** — When an extraction rule runs on the contents of a response, it puts the extracted data into a context parameter. This context parameter can then be referenced by later requests. We go into extraction rules in much more detail in the "Capturing Data During a Web Test" section below in this chapter.

❑ **Load Test Run Settings** — A load test can also define context parameters, and when a web test is run as part of a load test, the load test's context parameters override the web test's context parameter's. This is where the use of context parameters becomes very powerful and allows you to use a single test to simulate several different user scenarios simultaneously.

❑ **Environment Variables** — You can also use environment variables with context parameters. Any environment variable that begins with "Test." can be referenced in the web test. (You leave off the "Test." when referring to environment variables from inside the test.)

For example, suppose you have a context parameter in your web test called *MyContext* (i.e., you are referencing it using {{MyContext}} in your web test. If you set an environment variable called

Test.MyContext, then this value will be used at run time in place of {{MyContext}}. While this may not be very useful when running a web test from the VSTEST UI, it can be useful when running the test from the command line (e.g., as part of a build verification test).

Data-Driven Web Tests

Just as with the other test types that VSTEST supports, web tests can be attached to a data source to allow you to run the test multiple times using a different set of data each time. Because you can have multiple data sources with table-level control of how each is accessed, VSTEST allows very complicated scenarios. You can have a test scenario that randomly selects a Login from a list of 20 accounts and then enters a unique set of data that is pulled from a separate list of 1000 records and never re-used.

Properties That Can Be Data-Bound

You can bind the following properties to a data source:

Property type	Description
Web Test Credentials	The User Name and Password that the web test uses to authenticate with the web site can be bound to a data source.
Form Post Parameters.Value	The Value property of a form post parameter (but not the Name).
QueryString Parameters.Value	The Value property of a query string parameter (but not the Name).
Request.URL	The URL used in the request can be bound to a data source.

By binding a data source to one or more of the preceding properties, you can execute the test multiple times with a new value pulled from the data source each time.

Binding different properties to the same data source (usually a different field in that source) allows you to use a set of data that is linked, for example, "user name" and "password," or the request.url and a query string parameter value.

Each property can also be bound to different data sources with different settings for how the data are accessed (randomly, sequentially, etc.). This means that you can generate a large matrix of tests from even a small set of data — 10 user credentials and 11 Form Post parameter values can give you 110 tests if you run it sequentially to get all of the variations.

Types of Data Sources

You can use any SQL database as well as any OLE DB data source like an Excel or Access file or even a plain .CSV file. Unfortunately, VSTEST does not yet support referencing an XML-based data source. It is possible to access other types of data (such as XML files) by creating a web test plug-in (see the section on "Plug-ins" below in this chapter) that loads the data and adds them into context parameters.

Adding a Data Source

To add a data source to your web test:

1. Click the Add Data Source button (the yellow canister with the spark on it) in the Web Test document toolbar.

Note that the Data menu on the Visual Studio main menu bar has an "Add Data Source," but it does not *do the same thing and is unrelated to web testing.*

2. The Connection Properties dialog appears.

3. Fill in the appropriate values to connect to your data source.

4. Use the Test Connection button to verify that your connection is set up correctly.

5. The Choose Tables dialog will appear, letting you specify which tables in the data source should be used. Check each table that will be used.

6. The data source will appear under the Data Sources node in the web test with a default name like *DataSource1*. Rename it to something more descriptive, like *TokenDB*.

> **Editing of a data source after you have added it is not supported. If you need to change the properties of a data source, like the connection string, you need to delete the existing data source and recreate it. If you create it with the same name and it has the same table values, then you will not need to change any of the data-bound properties in the test.**

Referencing a Data Source

When you look at a parameter that has been bound to a data source in the Web Test Editor, it looks very similar to a context parameter, but there are a few differences. If you look at the same parameter's properties in the Property window (see Figure 5-7), you can tell that it is a data-bound value because the reference string has three parts separated by periods: {{ a.b.c}}, whereas a context parameter just has the context name: {{contextname}}.

The text inside the {{...}} is the reference to the data source. The data source reference is a string made up of three parts: {{DataSourceName.TableName.ColumnName}}. Therefore in Figure 5-7, you can see that the QueryString parameter with the Name Get will pull its value dynamically from the data source named *DataSource1* using the data in the Key column of the table named *Tokens*.

Figure 5-7

To bind a value to a data source:

1. Select the value to bind (e.g., a Form Post Parameter).

2. In the Properties window, select the value you wish to bind to the data source.

3. Open the dropdown for the field; you will see a list of data sources and context parameters (see Figure 5-8).

4. Expand the data source that you want until you find the field in the table that you need, and select it.

You should now see the value showing as a data-bound property.

One major difference between data binding and context parameters is that while you can mix static text and one or more context parameters in a field, when you bind a field to a data source, it only gets its value from the data source. You cannot mix a data source and any other data in a field.

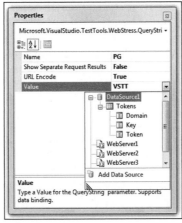

Figure 5-8

Accessing the Data During Test Run Time

Each iteration of a web test gets a single record from each data source to which it is bound. If you bind two properties to two fields in the same DataSource.Table, then they will be from the same record so that DataSource.UserTable.User and DataSource.UserTable.Password will match correctly.

Each Table in your Data Source(s) has an Access Method property that controls the order in which the records are read from the data source. To set the Access Method, simply select the table and set the Access Method property appropriately. The different Access Methods are as follows:

Access Method	Description
Sequential	Starting with the first record in the table, each successive iteration of the web test will use the next record in the table. if your web test is set to run only one iteration (the default for non-load testing), then it will always just use the first record. If you have the run settings (or your load test) configured to run the web test more times than there are records, it will loop and continue with the first record.
Unique	Unique is the same as Sequential except that it will never use the same record twice regardless of other settings. In a load test, the web test will stop running when it has used all of the records. If there are no other tests in the load test, then the load test will stop regardless of the remaining duration. If there are other tests in the load test, then those tests will continue running, but the web test will not continue once it has used all of the records.
Random	Random randomly picks a record from the table and uses it. Records may be re-used depending on the random selection.

Capturing Data During a Web Test

Often you will come across a situation in which your web test needs to capture some data contained in the response that was returned from a request. Many web sites have data that are passed from one page to the next in the POST/GET request and then included in the response. Usually this is because those data need to be included in subsequent requests. For example, if your web site responds to the "Create new Account" request with a response page containing the UserID that needs to be included in the next few requests (to finish the account creation process), then you would need to capture that data and use it in later requests. Basically any data that are generated dynamically on the server and sent to the client that need to be included in later requests will need to be extracted from the response. This is done using extraction rules. Extraction rules define how to pull data out of the response. These data are then stored in context parameters that can be used in later requests. VSTEST will automatically create some for you during recording to extract the values of Hidden Fields if it detects them.

The other reason to use extraction rules is to better expose useful debugging information. If there are values in the responses that are needed for debugging what is happening during the test run, extracting that out so that it appears in the Results UI without having to read through the response body yourself can be very helpful. Note that if you want to examine data in the response to determine if the request succeeded, then you should use *validation rules*, which are very similar to extraction rules but control the test passing or failing (see the "Verifying the Response with Validation Rules" section below in this chapter).

Extraction Rules

Extraction rules define what data to gather (or extract) from the contents of the HTTP Response. When you define an extraction rule on a request that instructs the test system to examine the response to that request, pull out the piece of data needed and store it in a context parameter. This allows the test to use dynamic data that are generated on the server in later steps of the test. A single request can have multiple extraction rules defined on it, and all of the defined rules of a request will be executed after the response is received.

Types of Rules

There are several built-in types of extraction rules that allow you to extract most types of data from a response. These rules operate as specialized text searches of the response body and header HTML. The built-in rules handle the common scenarios, but if your test needs a more specialized extraction rule, you can write a custom rule (see the section "Custom Rules" below in this chapter). Here are the rules:

❑ **Extract Attribute Value** — Extracts the value of the specified attribute from an HTML Tag. You must specify the HTML Tag that contains the attribute and the name of the attribute to get the value of. To better specify the tag, you can also specify another attribute and value. For example, if you specify `Tag Name=a; Attribute Name=href`, `Match Attribute Name=ID`, and `Match Attribute Value='register'`, it would return the value of the HREF attribute of the tag: `<a ID="register" HREF ... >`

❑ **Extract Form Field** — Extracts the value of the specified field.

❑ **Extract HTTP Header** — Extracts a value from one of the HTTP headers in the response. You can also specify whether or not a failure to find the value causes the request to fail.

❑ **Extract Regular Expression** — You can specify the text to extract using a regular expression. It will extract the entire matching string. You can specify which match to extract in case there are multiple matches.

❑ **Extract Text** — This is a simple text using a "between start and end." You specify the "starts with" text and the "ends with" text, and it extracts the text that is between the two, not including the "starts with" and "ends with" text. If there are multiple text matches in the response, then you can use the Index property to specify a match other than the first one (Index defaults to 0, which is the first match in the response).

❑ **Extract Hidden Fields** — This special rule extracts the values for all of the hidden fields in the response. Usually this will be added for you by the Recorder. Because of the fact that it extracts an unknown number of multiple values, it is very tricky to add yourself and be able to reference it. It's better to let the Recorder add this and take care of it and if you need to manually extract the value of a hidden field, use one of the other extraction rules.

How to Add an Extraction Rule to a Request

To add an extraction rule to a request, simply do the following:

1. Right-click the request and choose Add Extraction Rule. The Add Extraction Rule dialog will appear (see Figure 5-9).

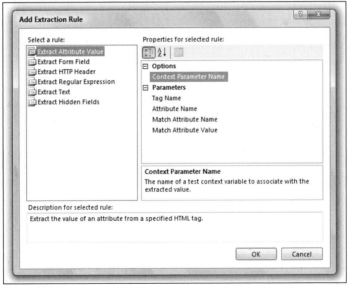

Figure 5-9

2. Fill out the parameters as needed for the data extraction you need to perform.

3. Set the Context Parameter Name to an appropriate value. It should be a name that is unique from other context parameters used in the web test to avoid overriding another context parameter when the test is run.

> The context parameter for an extraction rule is created dynamically at run time and will not show in the Context Parameters node of the web test. You can reference it in other properties only in requests that occur after the request containing this extraction rule.

Default (Auto-Captured) Fields

By default, VSTEST adds extraction rules to automatically capture all of the hidden fields in the response. The Recorder also automatically attaches the matching references in the QueryString and Form Post parameters. This is a good thing because it is not easy to add a reference to them yourself.

The format for referencing a Hidden field is {{$HIDDENn.fieldname}}, where n is the Context Parameter Name property listed in the Extract Hidden Fields rule's property page, and *fieldname* is the name of the hidden field. To get the field names yourself, you have to examine the source code of the response.

> *I recommend not using the Extract Hidden Fields rules yourself. Let the Recorder handle the hidden fields where possible, and use the other extraction rules for any extractions you need to do, including handling extracting the values of hidden fields when the Recorder does not do what you need.*

Verifying the Response with Validation Rules

By default, VSTEST determines if a step in a web test succeeded based on the HTTP return code (any HTTP error code between 400 and 599 is a failure). In many cases, you will need to be more specific as to what you consider to be a valid or passing response to the request. Many web sites prefer to handle their own errors and return a valid (200/OK) response page that contains the error message or handling. Or if the response web page is going to contain certain text or data if the operation succeeded and some other text if it failed, then you will need to create your own verification rule for the response.

Validation rules generally check for the existence for some HTML component or text in the response page received from the request. This verification is performed after all dependent requests and any redirects are completed (i.e., when the page load has completed). If the validation rule fails, then that request is marked as Failing, and therefore the whole web test fails as well. If you have more than one rule defined on the request, then they all have to pass in order for the request to pass.

Built-in Validation Rules

VSTEST includes a set of predefined validation rules that can handle the common page verifications needed. In general, these rules are checking the contents of the raw text data of the response, meaning that you cannot check if a specific string is displayed or not, especially if that display is based on script on the page. It can take a little bit of work to get the right set of things to look for. Often you can get the verification that you need by using more than one rule, both of which need to pass in order for the request to pass. For example, to verify that the response was the correct page and that there are no errors, you could create two FindText rules, one that verifies that the text `<title>CorrectPage</title>` is in the response HTML and another that verifies that "Error Message" is not in the response HTML.

All of these rules have properties that control their behaviors, allowing you to edit their settings through the Property page. Many of the validation rules are very similar to the extraction rules except that instead of extracting the data, the validation rule is checking for the existence of the data.

The following validation rules are pre-defined in VSTEST and provide enough functionality for validating most types of responses:

Validation Rule	Description
Form Field	This rule checks for the existence of a form field that has a Name and Value that you specify in the properties.
Find Text	This rule checks for the existence of a given string (the Find Text property) using either a simple text match or a regular expression. The Pass If Text Found property lets you look for the existence or non-existence of this text. For example, if you created a FindText rule with {FindText=="Error" and PassIfTextFound=="False"} properties, then it would verify that the string "Error" was *not* in the response.
Maximum Request Time	Verifies that the request finishes within a specified amount of time (in milliseconds). If it took longer than this time for the request to finish, it will be considered failing.
Required Attribute Value	Verifies that in the response there is a tag with the specified name (*Tag Name*) that has an attribute with an expected value ("Attribute Name" and "Expected Value"). In addition, you can specify another attribute name=value pair as part of determining if the tag should be checked for the expected value.
Required Tag	Verifies the existence of a specified HTML tag in the response. You can set the minimum number of occurrences that are required for the rule to pass. If the specified tag does not occur at least that many times, in the response the rule will fail.

If these rules do not provide the verification that you need for your test, VSTEST allows you to write your own custom validation rules (see "Custom Rules" below in this chapter). If you have set up a custom validation rule, it will also appear in this list.

Adding a Validation Rule to a Request

Adding a validation rule to a request works in very much the same way as adding an extraction rule. To add a validation rule to a request, simply do the following:

1. Right-click the request and choose Add Validation Rule. The Add Validation Rule dialog will appear.

2. Fill out the parameters as needed for the validation that should be performed to verify that the response is correct. See the preceding "Built-in Validation Rules" section for descriptions of the different validation rules and their settings.

A request can have multiple validation rules and a mix of validation rules and extraction rules. It is important to have at least one validation rule whenever possible to ensure that you are getting the correct response from the request, because you cannot always depend on the HTTP error codes to tell you when the response is incorrect.

But it is also important to consider the amount of time and resources that the validation will cost to perform. Adding several validation rules that require a lot of processing to perform can slow down your test. Validation rules that require a lot of memory will limit the number of users who can be running the test during a load test. Both of these can limit your ability to generate enough load to properly stress-test your system. Finding the right balance can be tricky and can take a bit of trial and error. Because sometimes you need to focus more on the functional testing than on stress testing and in that case want to have those additional validation rules even though they do slow things down, VSTEST provides a way for you to scale the validation being performed in the load test.

Validation Level

Each validation rule has a setting as to its validation level. Setting this value lets you scale how much validation is performed at run time on this request. This setting is only used during a load test to enable you to alter the validation performed depending on the type of load testing that is being performed. The more validation that is performed, the slower the test runs. This setting does not have any effect when running a single web test but can be a factor in large load test runs, especially when stress-testing a system. For more on this, see Chapter 7.

It can be a little confusing to remember how this setting works; setting the validation level on a rule to "low" means that it will always be run. In this case, *low* means that it is a low-level, or fundamental, verification; *low* does *not* refer to the priority of the verification. Setting the level to "high" means that it will *only* be run if the load test has been set to a validation level of "high."

Setting the load test level to:	Will run only the rules with a setting of:
Low	Low
Medium	Low, Medium
High	Low, Medium, High

This can be a very useful way of tuning how much validation is performed during the load test. For example, suppose that there are three ways in which you can verify that the request's response was correct: (1) checking that the value of the `<title>` tag is correct, (2) verifying that a specific form filed is in the response, and (3) verifying that the text "error" is not in the body of the response. To be completely sure that the response is correct, you want to do all three, but some of them (particularly the last one) take longer and might slow down the test, reducing the amount of load you can create. By setting the expensive check to "High," you can control if and when that validation is performed. This allows you to do one load test run that is more focused on verifying the product's functionality than it is on stress testing. Then, once the product's functionality has been verified, you can turn off the additional verification to allow putting more pressure on your server.

This can also be useful with the Maximum Request Time rule to turn on and off your performance requirements — for example, when you are testing the system's ability to function in a fault condition (e.g., all but one server in the cluster is down) where you may not have any timing requirements; you just want to make sure that the response is correct.

Custom Rules

VSTEST also allows you to write your own rules (both extraction and validation) as a managed code plug-in. The process is essentially the same for each type of rule with just a couple of differences.

You can create the custom `ValidationRule` or `ExtractionRule` class in the same file as your test, in a separate file in your test project, or in a separate (class library) project. Whichever way you choose, the important thing is that your test project has a reference to your custom classes (which happens automatically if the class is in the project or in the same file with the test). It is recommended that you put your custom validation rules and extraction rules into a separate class library project. Putting them in the test project makes it harder to re-use them in tests in other projects. Usually you can just put them all in one project that is then referenced by all of your test projects.

To write a custom rule, you need to write a class that inherits from `Microsoft.VisualStudio` `.TestTools.WebTesting.ExtractionRule` or `Microsoft.VisualStudio.TestTools.WebTesting` `.ValidationRule`. You must implement the following properties and methods:

❏ **RuleName** — This method has a string property that is the name of the rule. This is the value shown in the Extraction Rule section of the web test. Here is how you implement RuleName:

```
public override string RuleName
{
  get { return "My Custom Rule"; }
}
```

❏ **RuleDescription** — This is a string property that is the description that will display in the Add Extraction Rule dialog box, providing a detailed description of the rule. Here is how you implement RuleDescription:

```
public override string RuleDescription
{
  get
  {
    return "This class provides for the custom extraction of a value";
  }
}
```

❏ **Extract(object sender, ExtractionEventArgs e)** — This is used for extraction rules only. This is the method that performs the data extraction. It must add an item to `e.WebTest.Context` with a key equal to the context parameter name and the value that has been extracted. In other words, in your `Extract()` method code there must be a line of code something like:

```
e.WebTest.Context.Add(this.ContextParameterName, value);
```

It should set `e.Success=true;` or `e.Success=false;` depending on whether or not it successfully extracted the value.

You can access the response object using `e.Response`, which will then give you various parts of the response. For example, `e.Response.HtmlDocument` is the HTMLDocument object representing the response.

The following is an `Extract` method that examines the body of the response, looking for a property with the same name as the `ContextParameterName` setting, and extracts the value of that property, assuming the body is formatted like this: `{"Property1":"Value1", "Property2":"Value2"...}`. Thus if the extraction rule was set to extract the value of "Owner" it would look for `{..., "Owner":` `"Mike",...}` and set the context parameter Owner in the test to the value of `Mike`.

147

The extraction rule also has a property to set if the returned value should be URL and HTML decoded.

```
/// <summary>
/// Specifies whether or not any encoded url string should be decoded
/// </summary>
private bool m_decodeUrl = false;
public bool DecodeUrl
{
    get { return m_decodeUrl; }
    set { m_decodeUrl = value; }
}


/// <summary>
/// This method extract value for specified property. Body Content should format as
/// {"Property1":"Value1","Property2":"Value2"....}
/// </summary>
/// <remarks>Used primarily with Ajax requests (application/json)</remarks>
/// <param name="sender">The object raising the event</param>
/// <param name="e">The arguments that accompany the event</param>
public override void Extract(object sender, ExtractionEventArgs e)
{
    string body = Encoding.UTF8.GetString(e.Response.BodyBytes);
    string value = "";
    int loc = body.IndexOf(this.ContextParameterName,
            StringComparison.CurrentCultureIgnoreCase);
    if (loc > -1)
    {
      value = body.Substring(loc + this.ContextParameterName.Length + 3);
      int loc_end = value.IndexOf("\"");
      value = value.Substring(0, loc_end);
    }

    if (this.DecodeUrl)
    {
      value = System.Web.HttpUtility.UrlDecode(value);
      value = System.Web.HttpUtility.HtmlDecode(value);
       }

  e.WebTest.Context.Add(this.ContextParameterName, value);
    e.Success = true;

    return;
  }
```

❑ **Validate(object sender, ValidationEventArgs e)** — This is used for validation rules only. This is the method that performs the validation. It must set e.IsValid True if the response has passed the validation and False if it failed.

In the case of a failure, you should also set the e.Message string to an error message explaining the failure. This will display in the web test results, explaining what the failure was.

Just like extraction rules, you can access the response object using e.Response, which will then give you various parts of the response. For example, e.Response.HtmlDocument is the HTML-Document object representing the response.

The following is a `Validate` method that compares the entire body of the response with an expected string:

```
/// <summary>
/// The string to match to the response body
/// </summary>
private string m_expectedString = string.Empty;
public string ExpectedString
{
    get { return m_expectedString; }
    set { m_expectedString = value; }
}


/// <summary>
/// This method performs a string comparison of the entire body of a response,
  against a specified search
/// string.
/// </summary>
/// <param name="sender">The object raising the event</param>  ·
/// <param name="e">Values that accompany the event.</param>
public override void Validate(object sender, ValidationEventArgs e)
{
    string body = string.Empty;

    //Either the body is encoded as a string, or
    if (!String.IsNullOrEmpty(e.Response.BodyString))
    {
      body = e.Response.BodyString;
    }
    //... we need to convert the bytes of the body into a UTF-8 encoded string
    else if (e.Response.BodyBytes != null && e.Response.BodyBytes.Length > 0)
    {
      body = Encoding.UTF8.GetString(e.Response.BodyBytes);
    }

    //Check the body, to see if it equals the search string
    e.IsValid = body.Equals(m_expectedString,
        StringComparison.InvariantCultureIgnoreCase);


    if (!e.IsValid)
    {
      e.Message = String.Format(
          "String '{0}' does not match the response body '{1}'",
                  m_expectedString, body);
    }
}
```

> Any public read/write properties of your custom rule class will show up as properties on the Property page for a rule of your type in the VSTEST UI. This lets users set the behaviors of your custom rule in the same fashion as the built-in rules.

The Response Page

It is important to remember that the extraction and validation rules are performed on the *response* that comes from the request that the rule is attached to. The verification and extraction rules defined under RequestA will be examining the data contained in the response that comes back after making that request. Therefore, if you have a request that needs to include some data contained in the current page in its request, you need to put the extraction rule in the previous request.

> *Any redirects or other automatic actions happen before any validation or extraction rules are run. In other words, if the response to RequestA is a redirect, the Web Test engine will create a new request to follow the redirect, execute that request, and then run the extraction and validation rules on the response to the second request.*

Testing a Web Service

Web test requests that are made against a web service have a slightly different UI to make it easier to set up a web service request. If you add a web service request to your web test project, you will see a request that is very similar to the standard request. The only difference is that a web service request has a String Body parameter that allows you to specify the XML (usually a SOAP request).

To add a web service request, follow these steps:

1. Right-click in the web test where you want to insert the web service test and choose Insert Web Service Test.

2. The new web service request is added to your web test with a default URL and an empty String Body parameter.

3. Set the URL property of the request to that of the web service, such as http://localhost/myservice/Accounts.asmx.

4. Open a browser and navigate to that URL. You should see the documentation page for the web service. (If this is turned off or inaccessible, then you will need to get the Header and SOAP information from the owner of the service.)

5. Select the method that you want to test and look at the SOAP message. There will be a SOAPAction listed. The value shown for SOAPAction will be something like http://tempuri.org/Accounts and needs to be added to the request's Header.

6. Back in the Web Test Editor, right-click on the web service request, and choose Add Header to add a new header parameter.

   ❑ Set the Name property to SOAPAction.

   ❑ Set the Value property to the value that you got in Step 5, listed under SOAPAction on the web service page.

7. Select the String Body parameter under the request, and set the Content Type property to text/xml.

8. Copy the XML listed on the web service page for the SOAP request, and paste it into the String Body property (open up the property by clicking the "..." button, and paste the XML into the dialog).

9. Edit the XML to replace any placeholder text with actual values.

You can make the data in the SOAP request dynamic by using data-bound values instead of static data. The XML is parsed for data-bound values with the following syntax:

```
{{DataSourceName.TableName.ColumnName}}
```

In the end the XML should look something like this:

```
<?xml version="1.0" encoding="utf-8"?>
<soap:Envelope xmlns:xsi=http://www.w3.org/2001/XMLSchema-instance
xmlns:xsd="http://www.w3.org/2001/XMLSchema"
xmlns:soap="http://schemas.xmlsoap.org/soap/envelope/">
    <soap:Body>
        <Accounts xmlns="http://tempuri.org/">
            <UserName>{{AccountsData.UserInfo.UserName}}</UserName>
            <Password>{{AccountsData.UserInfo.Password}}</Password>
            <AccountID>{{AccountsData.UserInfo.AccountID}}</orderID>
        </Accounts>
    </soap:Body>
</soap:Envelope>
```

HTTP Request-Based Testing Does Not Test the UI

It is very important to keep in mind that a web test simulates the HTTP request traffic that is generated when a user exercises your web site. It does *not* exercise any of the UI elements or JavaScript on your pages. As such, it does not test the UI that your users see, but it does test the core functionality of your system. Often with a web site the amount of functionality that is in the client UI is pretty minimal, but it can be an issue if much of your site has script-heavy pages or uses AJAX.

This is good for a couple of reasons. It means that your tests are not affected by UI changes. UI-based testing is often fragile because the UI changes more frequently than the underlying HTTP requests being used. The other benefit is that UI tests cannot effectively be used for load testing. Having the web tests not be UI-based means that when they are included in a load test, you can execute multiple instances of the test at the same time, allowing simulating 100 users, for example, all executing the same web test on a single computer.

But the drawback of using HTTP requests is that your UI and the scripts on the page do not get exercised. This has two main effects that you need to watch out for: inability to properly test your UI and scripts affecting your dynamic data.

You Cannot Test Your Web UI and Client-Side Script Using a Web Test

A web test will allow you to simulate and test the various HTTP requests that operations in your UI will generate but cannot tell you if your UI is working correctly. For example, you might have a page that has a Submit button that executes some Jscript that then sends a Post request. You can create a web test that has the HTTP Post request that occurs when a user clicks the button (executes the Jscript). But this will not test that the Jscript runs correctly when the button is clicked. This level of UI interaction testing is not currently directly supported in VSTEST.

Dynamic Test Data That Is Affected by Scripts

If your pages have script elements that are required to generate the values used in successive HTTP requests, then you will have to simulate that. If your tests can run correctly with static values, then you can simply record your web test and run it. But often you cannot simply stick to static values for your tests, especially if you will be using the web tests in a load test and running many instances of the test simultaneously.

For example if you have an "add new user" page that takes some data the user enters in and encrypts it and then sends it in a POST request, it is probably not a valid test to record the encrypted string (representing a specific set of data) and use that over and over again in your tests. While this could be a good test of your "user is already in the system" error handling, it will not test your system's ability to add users (except that first time you ran it, which doesn't help when load testing).

In some cases the processing that is done via the page's script does not affect the data that you need to be dynamic, and thus you can keep that value static. This can be handled using the data-driven testing support if the data are easy to put into a DB or CSV file. This allows you to pre-create the data for inclusion into the HTTP request, so that you can either manually create it or have some other process create it. But you are limited to only running as many tests as you have pre-generated data for. This may or may not be a problem depending on your needs (if you are running a load test, e.g., it may be hard to pre-generate enough data for a long-running stress test).

The other option is to dynamically create the data that need to be included in your HTTP request. This can be a much more complicated task and requires that you use a coded web test instead of a regular web test. Another big factor is how complicated it is to generate the dynamic data that you need.

Running a Web Test

All test run settings, for all types of tests, are stored in the Test Run Configuration (which is in a .testrunconfig file). Before running a web test, you need to make sure the correct Test Run Configuration is selected as active and that it has the correct run settings for your web test. If you simply wish to replay the web test on your computer, then you can just use the default configuration that VSTEST has created for you. But if you need to, you can control the various aspects of the test from the configuration file.

Important Settings in the .testrunconfig File

If you select Edit Test Run Configurations from the Test menu or you open a .testrunconfig file from the solution explorer, you will see the Test Run Configuration dialog. This lets you specify all of the settings for running tests in that configuration. Only some of these are interesting for web tests (the others are discussed in the chapters they most relate to).

The only interesting settings for a single web test are in the "Web Test" section. The other sections have settings that do affect web tests (e.g., "Test Timeout," which is usually not important but can be an issue if you are running many iterations so that it takes longer than the default timeout of 5 minutes), but they are general settings and not specifically interesting for web tests.

The following are the run configuration settings specific to web tests:

Setting	Description
Number of Run Iterations	This lets you set a specific number of times to execute the test. You can set a specific number of times to execute, or you can set it to execute the test once per row in the Data Source.
Browser Type	Sets what type of browser the test should simulate. This works by setting the HTTP Request header properties to match what that browser uses so that it appears to your server that it is a request from that browser.
Network Type	Lets you simulate the amount of time that a type of bandwidth would result in. Keep in mind that this does not simulate latency. VSTEST does not actually download the response files any more slowly. It inserts wait times to simulate how long it would have taken with that bandwidth. For example, this would mean that there would be waits inserted in between dependent requests instead of downloading the data as fast as possible.
Simulate Think Times	Each Request has a Think Time property, which is a delay between when the response (the page) finishes loading and when the next request is made. This simulates the time the user spends viewing the page and thinking about it. This usually only affects load testing, and when running a single web test, you usually want to disable think times.

These settings are really only used when running the web test on its own outside of a load test. When running in a load test, the load test's settings for browser type, network type, and think times override the settings in the test run configuration file. And the Number of Run Iterations setting does not apply in a load test scenario since the load test is managing the number of users and duration.

Running the Test

Once the run configuration is set up correctly, simply click the Run Test button (the icon with the green arrow pointing to the right) on the Web Test Editor toolbar, and your test will run.

There are several Run Test variations that are available (pull down the button to see them). For a web test there is no difference between Run Test and Debug Test — both options run the whole test. You can either run the test immediately or pause before running it. If you choose "Pause before starting," VSTEST will prepare everything and open the Results window (the "Web Test Viewer") without starting the test. To start the test at this point, click either the Run button or the Step button. The Step button here allows you to step through the web test.

> **To step through a web test one request at a time, start the test with Debug Test (pause before starting). Then, when everything is loaded and ready, use the Step button to step through the web test one request at a time.**

You can also run a web test from the command line just like a unit test by calling `mstest.exe` and specifying your web test and, if needed, the test run config file.

```
mstest /testcontainer:WebTest1.webtest /runconfig:local.testrunconfig
```

Examining the Results

Of course, once you run the test you need to look at the results. Initially this will be to figure out why the test itself is not working and then later to figure out if a product bug is causing it to fail. There can be a lot of data going back and forth in the requests and responses, especially in a complicated test involving extracting data from one response to be used in a later request and other dynamic operations.

VSTEST has a Results viewer that lets you drill into the details of each response and, to some extent, replay the test looking at what occurred. Figuring out where the problem actually started can be tricky; often a request will fail because an expected value extracted from some previous request's response was not correct.

It is also very important to review what the test is doing to make sure that it is doing what it should be doing. (Is it going to the correct pages? Logging in as the correct user?) Otherwise, the test could be reporting Passing but not really testing what you think it is. It's a good idea to review your web tests occasionally even if they are passing.

Reviewing Each Request and Response in the Web Test Viewer

After running a test, you open the result in the Web Test viewer (usually it opens automatically). The top panel shows all of the HTTP requests that were made in the test, including dependent requests that were not in the actual test but occurred as a result of the responses. Redirects and loading items on a page and any other activity will show up in the test results.

The first thing to look for is any failing requests in the run, which can be easily picked out by the red X-icon on the left. But it is also important to walk through all of the requests at least once before considering the test done and ready for use. It is important to make sure that the test is doing what it is supposed to and is properly reporting passing results. For example, if the "Pass if Text Exists" property is set wrong on your "Verify that no Error message is displayed" validation rule, then the request will show as passing if the Error message is showing.

Request Panel

The top panel displays all of the requests that occurred during the test, including any dependent requests (they will be collapsed under the parent request). There are four columns in this display:

Column	Description
Request	The full request URL.
HTTP Status	The HTTP status returned from the server for this request. This is usually "200 OK" if everything worked fine but could be a redirect (typically 302) or other HTTP status values.
Response Time	The time it took for the web server to respond after the request was sent.
Size	This is the size of the response received back from the server in response to the request.

Details Panel

Below the Request panel is the Details panel. The Details panel has five separate tabs that display the details for the request that is currently selected in the upper panel.

Tab	Description
Web Browser tab	Displays the response as a browser rendered page; note that it does not execute any scripts on the page. This gives you a good idea of which page the request was hitting and its state.
Request	The full contents of the selected Request, including all of the header and body data.
Response	The complete contents of the response to the selected request as text, including all of the header and body data.
Context	This shows all of the current (as of the selected request) context parameter values. This tab is very useful for debugging the web test, especially when investigating extraction rule issues.
Details	The Details tab shows the results of each of the extraction and validation rules executed for that request.

Investigating Failures

Once you run the test and have the Web Test viewer open, you will see if your test passed and which requests (if any) have failed. When a failure does occur, figuring out exactly what went wrong can be tricky. The exact error messages seen and the exact failures will vary quite a bit depending on the details of your web site and how the test runs, but this section covers some of the general or common failures.

Why Requests Fail

There are several reasons that a request could fail — one of which is, of course, that something is wrong with the web site that you are testing. But the failure could also be a problem with the test itself.

Where the Failure Is Occurring

Often the request that failed is failing because something went wrong in one of the previous requests and did not raise an error at that time, but is something the failing request depends on. Because of this, it can be a good idea to walk back through the requests and examine the related data. For example, if the failure is due to a context parameter not being set, then you should look back at the request containing the extraction rule that sets that context parameter and see what happened at that point.

Why does a request fail but not raise an error? Without a validation rule, VSTEST determines a request's Pass or Fail status based solely on the HTTP status returned with the response. It's common practice on many web sites to return custom error pages instead of returning an HTTP error, to make sure that your user sees a nice error message instead of the browser's "page not found." It could also be because there was no error (from the product's perspective); it just returned a different page from what the test expected.

> Having a validation rule for every request helps raise errors as they happen instead of later in the test when they cause other requests to fail.

> The failure could also be in one of the dependent requests. For example, if an image file is missing on a page, then the request will be marked as failing. Remember to check the dependent requests.

What to Look for

It is a good first step to step through the requests with the Browser tab open so that you can visually inspect the page that was returned. Often this will make it clear that the wrong page was returned at some point.

You should also check to verify that the URL of the request is correct; often, due to problems with context parameters or changes to the site, the URL will be incorrect.

Context Parameter Not Found in Test Context

If you see the error message "Context parameter '*<parameter name>*' not found in test context," that means that an extraction rule has failed to extract a value and fill this context parameter. The error appears for the request that is trying to use the context parameter, not the one that failed to extract it. You need to find the previous request that contains the extraction rule.

Many web applications that depend on values being passed from one page to another usually only depend on the values in the previous page. The problem is therefore usually in the previous request. But that request could be failing to extract a value because of an error with a previous request, and so forth.

The easiest way to find the request that extracts this context parameter is to open the web test (not the results) and look through the previous requests for the request that has an extraction rule with the matching Context Parameter Name property. This is the step that failed.

If the problem is that an extraction rule has failed, examine the contents of the response in the Response tab and see if the data are there. If the data are there, then the rule is not set up correctly and needs to be fixed. If the data are not there, then there is likely a problem either with the request or with the web site being tested.

Errors Extracting Hidden Fields

Often you will see the "Context parameter ' < *parameter name* > ' not found in test context" error in relation to a hidden field that is being extracted. This is handled in the same way as other extraction errors except that it is a little trickier to track down where the extraction is occurring.

Hidden Field Context Parameters have a more complicated name scheme, which makes it hard to find the request that is supposed to be extracting the value. Context parameters created by extracting hidden fields have the following name scheme: $HIDDENn.fieldname, where n is a number (usually 1) and fieldname is the name of the hidden field.

When you look at an extract hidden fields rule, its Context Parameter Name property is set to the number in the name. For example, to find the extraction rule that should be extracting the $HIDDEN1.Password context parameter, you need to look for an extract hidden fields rule that has its Context Parameter Name property set to 1.

To make it even more complicated, multiple requests can have extract hidden fields rules with the same name (number). In fact, the default behavior for the Recorder creates all of the extract hidden fields rules with a name of 1. If you have multiple requests with the same extract hidden fields name, then you need to figure out which of those requests is supposed to extract this value. Obviously it's a request before that failing one, with an extract hidden fields rule (with the matching name).

Again, many web applications, especially those that depend on hidden field values being passed from one page to another, usually depend on the values in the response from the previous page. Thus the problem is usually in the previous request. It is a good idea at this point to go back to the test results and look at what is happening in the previous requests to see if one of them appears to have a problem that did not raise an error.

Hardcoded Dynamic Values

One of the most common problems you will run into with your web tests is with values that are dynamically generated by the web application, but are still hard-coded in your web test. Sometimes these values are valid for some amount of time (30 minutes, a day, etc.), which means that you can record a web test, fix it up a bit, re-run it several times, and it all works. Then some time later (after that value has expired), the web test fails.

Usually, if you are familiar with how your web application works, you can spot these by carefully examining all of the form post and query string parameters in the requests. Parameters with names like *Session*, *TrackingID*, and so forth are often clearly dynamic session, user, or state parameters. Also, parameters with values that are GUIDs or long encrypted/encoded strings of data are prime candidates.

If you think you know which parameter may be dynamic, you can look in the response from your recent (failing) test run and see if the response has a different value for it.

The other way to find out what parameters should be dynamic is to simply re-record the test and compare the new recording with the original test. Any static parameters that are different need to be dynamic.

If you find that your test is failing because of hard-coding a dynamic value, you can fix that by adding an extraction rule (on the request that generates the response containing the value) to pull out the value and put it into a context parameter. Then go to the failing request (which is the request that uses this value) and change it from using a hard-coded value to using the context parameter.

Exceptions

Test level exceptions are errors that occur outside of a specific request or inside a custom web test plug-in. Request level exceptions are exceptions that are thrown from a WebTestRequest plug-in or a custom extraction or validation rule. The exception message and any other data from the exception can be found in the Details tab.

Maintaining the Tests

As your site changes during development, you will need to update your tests to work with the new site. As we've mentioned before, because VSTEST uses HTTP requests, your tests should be insulated from many of the changes that your site will go through. Changes to the look and contents of a page, for example, will not affect your web tests. The following changes will require updating your tests:

- ❑ Removing a page.
- ❑ Adding a new page.
- ❑ Changing the URL for a page (e.g., from `http://mysite/home.html` to `http://mysite/main/home.html`).
- ❑ Changing page or response text that you depend on for extraction or validation rules.
- ❑ Changing the "path" for your test case or scenario. For example, your sign-up process was PageA ➪ PageB ➪ PageC and is now PageA ➪ PageC.

In most cases, the difficulty is in finding out that these changes have occurred, not in actually making the updates to the web test.

Coded Web Tests

The other type of web test is the *Coded Web Test*, which is, as you have probably guessed from the name, a web test that is written in code (either C# or Visual Basic) instead of being a list of request objects like the basic web test type. The basic web tests give you ease of creation and use at the expense of some flexibility. With coded web tests there is slightly more work to create and maintain the test, but you gain a great deal of flow control.

Coded versus Basic

While basic web tests are quick to create with the Recorder and have enough flexibility for many web testing tasks, they are limited to running a static list of requests in order. Coded web tests, however, allow you to add the flexibility of conditionals and looping. Basic tests do not support re-using sections of a test — you can copy a set of requests from one test to another, but you cannot have one web test call another. However, in a coded test you can factor out sections of requests and other operations into methods that any test can call.

The disadvantage of coded tests is that they take a bit more work to create and can be harder to maintain. If your web site changes so that the steps to perform the test are different, it will often be more work to update a coded test than it would be with a basic web test.

Converting from a Web Test

The easiest way to create a coded web test is to record a normal web test and then convert it to a coded web test. This creates a code version of your basic web test (in C# or Visual Basic) that can then be edited as a normal test class.

> If you are planning on using any of the dynamic data features in your coded test such as data binding, extraction rules, validation rules, or custom parameters; or if you plan on using a custom plug-in, I strongly recommend that you set that up in the basic web test before generating the code. This allows VSTEST to generate that code for you. It can be fairly complicated and hard to get correct initially but is easier to modify after it is created.

> The code generated is in the language of the test project that the web test is in. For example, if your web test is in a Visual Basic test project, then the generated code will be in Visual Basic.

To generate a coded web test based on an existing web test:

1. Open the web test to be converted.

2. Click the Generate Code button on the toolbar, or right-click on the top-level node (the Web Test) and choose Generate Code.

3. The Generate Coded Web Test dialog appears (see Figure 5-10).

Figure 5-10

4. Enter the name you wish to use for the coded test (it defaults to *WebTestName*Coded), and click OK.

5. A new class file is created and added to the test project containing the web test used to generate the code (and the new code file is opened in the Editor).

Aspects of a Coded Web Test

Writing your web test using code allows for a much greater flexibility compared to the basic (or declarative) web tests but at the cost of a much higher complexity. This flexibility allows you to dynamically control the number of requests executed and alter the flow of the test based on a large number of factors (context parameters, environment variables, load test settings, etc.).

Structure of a Simple Coded Web Test

The newly generated web test consists of a class that inherits from `Microsoft.VisualStudio.TestTools` `.WebTesting.WebTest`. The `WebTest` class contains properties that match those seen in the Properties window for the basic web test, and in the constructor you can see that any of those values that you had set in the basic web test are being set in the code:

```
public class myCodedTest : WebTest
{

    public myCodedTest()
    {
        this.PreAuthenticate = true;
    }
}
```

The main method that performs all of the work is an iterator method called `GetRequestEnumerator()` that defines each request. The Web Test execution engine enumerates through each request, executing it and any execution or validation rules.

Following is an example of a simple `GetRequestEnumerator()` method in C#:

```
public override IEnumerator<WebTestRequest> GetRequestEnumerator()
{
    WebTestRequest request1 = new WebTestRequest("http://localhost/mysite.html");
    yield return request1;

    WebTestRequest request2 = new WebTestRequest("http://localhost/myother.aspx");
    request2.ThinkTime = 6;
    request2.QueryStringParameters.Add("GetAd", "", false, false);
    request2.QueryStringParameters.Add("ADname", "cust1", false, false);
    request2.QueryStringParameters.Add("AdID", "1077", false, false);
    yield return request2;

    WebTestRequest request3 = new WebTestRequest("http://localhost/mySite2.html"");
    request3.ThinkTime = 5;
    yield return request3;

    WebTestRequest request4 = new WebTestRequest("http://localhost/mysite2.html ");
    yield return request4;
}
```

By adding in loops or conditionals, you can create a more complicated ordering of requests instead of a simple list. For example, in the above code the last two requests are the same and could also have been written as in the following code, except now we base the number of times we hit that page on a context parameter named *PageHits* (presumably set before running the test):

```
public override IEnumerator<WebTestRequest> GetRequestEnumerator()
{
    WebTestRequest request1 = new WebTestRequest("http://localhost/mysite.html");
    yield return request1;

    WebTestRequest request2 = new WebTestRequest("http://localhost/myother.aspx");
    request2.ThinkTime = 6;
    request2.QueryStringParameters.Add("GetAd", "", false, false);

    request2.QueryStringParameters.Add("ADname", "cust1", false, false);
    request2.QueryStringParameters.Add("AdID", "1077", false, false);

    yield return request2;

    For (loop = 0; loop < this.Context["PageHits"], loop++)
    {
        WebTestRequest request3 = new
WebTestRequest("http://localhost/mySite2.html"");
        yield return request3;
    }

    WebTestRequest request4 = new WebTestRequest("http://localhost/mysite2.html ");
    yield return request4;
}
```

Using the Web Test Context

In a coded test you can access the `WebTestContext` property bag, which is a simple collection that provides a global property store for the web test. In your coded web test it is the `Context` property, and it is used just like a standard collection:

```
this.Context.Add("Environment", "intperf");

...
WebTestRequest managerRequest = new WebTestRequest(("https://mysite."

                              + (this.Context["Environment"].ToString()

                    + ".com/Manager.html")));
```

Normally the context values would be set in the web test constructor and then accessed in the `GetRequestEnumerator()` method while creating the request.

Web Test Properties

All of the web test properties are accessible from the coded web test and thus can be set in the code and changed dynamically during the test. For example, the following code changes the `Proxy` being used by the test, during the test.

```
this.Proxy = "myProxy.mycorp.com";
```

This can be done with any of the web test properties, allowing for a very flexible and dynamic web test.

Using Transactions in Coded Tests

To set Transactions in your coded test to help get better timing data, simply call `BeginTransaction (string transactionName)` and then `EndTransaction(string transactionName)` to close the transaction. The transaction name must match. This tells VSTEST to track timing data for the time between the begin and end points. You can wrap multiple requests in a transaction. The following code shows a set of coded requests that wraps the first two requests into a single transaction:

```
this.BeginTransaction("Initial Page Load");

WebTestRequest reqPageLoad = new
    WebTestRequest(("https://mysite.com/Default.aspx"));
reqPageLoad.QueryStringParameters.Add("name", this.Context["name"]);
yield return reqPageLoad;

WebTestRequest managerRequest = new
    WebTestRequest(("https://mysite.com/Manager.html"));
yield return managerRequest;

this.EndTransaction("Initial Page Load");

WebTestRequest reqContent = new WebTestRequest("https://mysite.com/Content.aspx");
reqManagedContent.FollowRedirects = false;
reqManagedContent.Method = "POST";
reqManagedContent.QueryStringParameters.Add("Operation", "GetContent");
yield return reqContent;
...
```

Plug-ins

VSTEST allows another level of customization through plug-ins. If your test system needs to do some more complex processing before or after the test executes, or before or after each request, this can be accomplished through a plug-in.

There are two types of plug-ins:

❑ **Web Test Plug-in** — This lets you define code that will be executed before or after the entire web test executes.

❑ **Web Request Plug-in** — This lets you define code that executes before or after each request.

Plug-ins can be used with both basic web tests and with coded web tests. With coded web tests you have a bit more control as to how and when the plug-in code is called, but other than that they work essentially the same way.

Web Test Plug-ins

A web test plug-in allows you to run custom code outside of executing the requests when running the web test. The plug-in is called either before or after the test runs. This is usually used during a load test to track some value or set up one or more context parameters based on a value (often the iteration number or some other load test–related value).

The plug-in must inherit from `Microsoft.VisualStudio.TestTools.WebTesting.WebTestPlugin` and should implement either (or both) the `PreWebTest()` or `PostWebTest()`, depending on whether the code should run before or after the test executes.

```
public override void PreWebTest(object sender, PreWebTestEventArgs e)
{
    e.WebTest.Context["MachineName"] = System.Environment.MachineName;
}
```

Web Test Request Plug-ins

A web test request plug-in allows you to run custom code as each request in the web test is made. The plug-in is called either before or after every request in the test. This is very similar to a web test plug-in.

The plug-in must inherit from `Microsoft.VisualStudio.TestTools.WebTesting` `.WebTestRequestPlugin` and should implement either (or both) the `PreRequest()` or `PostRequest()`, depending on whether the code should run before or after the request executes.

Plug-ins from Coded Web Tests

To use a plug-in from a coded test, you need to have a private instance of the plug-in to be used. Then in either the web test's constructor or in the `GetRequestEnumerator()` method, you hook up the web test's event handlers to use the plug-in's methods.

```
private CustomWebTestPlugin testPlugin = new CustomWebTestPlugin ();
private CustomRequestPlugin requestPlugin = new CustomRequestPlugin ();
```

```
public CodedWebTest()
{
    // In the Web Test constructer hook up the Event Handlers

    //WebTest events
    this.PreWebTest += new
EventHandler<PreWebTestEventArgs>(this.testPlugin.PreWebTest);

    this.PostWebTest += new
EventHandler<PostWebTestEventArgs>(this.testPlugin.PostWebTest);

    //WebTestRequest events
    this.PreRequest += new
EventHandler<PreRequestEventArgs>(this.requestPlugin.PreRequest);

    this.PostRequest += new
EventHandler<PostRequestEventArgs>(this.requestPlugin.PostRequest);
}
```

You can also set the event handler for an individual request, which lets you decide dynamically if you should use the request plug-in. The following code shows setting a request event handler for just a single request based on the return value of the SomeMethod() method (a method that in this case determines if we should use the request plug-in):

```
public override IEnumerator<WebTestRequest> GetRequestEnumerator()
{
    WebTestRequest request = new WebTestRequest("http://myurl");

    if (SomeMethod())
    {
        //Hook up a request plugin handler for just this request
        CustomRequestPlugin requestPlugin = new CustomRequestPlugin();

        request.PreRequest += new
EventHandler<PreRequestEventArgs>(requestPlugin.PreRequest);
        request.PostRequest += new
EventHandler<PostRequestEventArgs>(requestPlugin.PostRequest);
    }

    yield return request;
```

Web Tests and AJAX

For the most part, testing web pages that contain AJAX is not that different once you have the web test. Your web test will still simulate the HTTP requests that occur as a result of the interactions of the user with the page. In other words, when you select an item on an AJAX page, there is an HTTP request made (usually to a web service) that gets some data, but instead of returning it as a new page, those data are then processed into the current page.

Because of the way that AJAX pages work, the Recorder will usually not record the web service calls that make up the bulk of the activity. To create a web test that tests an AJAX page requires manually adding the web service requests.

> If you record a page that is built using AJAX, you will usually get only the calls to load the page the first time (i.e., to navigate to the page) and then when you navigate off of the page. The web service calls made while on the page will not be recorded.

To get around this, you will need to manually add the web service calls that need to be executed. These web service calls can either be captured using an HTTP traffic monitoring tool such as Fiddler, or by understanding how the product/site being testing is supposed to work (reading the specifications, talking to the developer who owns that feature, etc.). Usually a combination of the two is best.

Once you have the web service calls, you simply add them to the web test (see the section "Testing a Web Service" above in this chapter). You should then be able to run the web test and have it exercise your whole site including the AJAX pages.

One option is to test the web service as if it were an API (because it is) and use unit tests instead of web tests. Of course, you still need to know what parameters, values, and so forth you need to call the service with, but in many cases the unit test tools in VSTEST are better suited to this. One thing to keep in mind is that because web tests are optimized for running in a load test, you can usually generate a much higher load using web tests.

Microsoft Fiddler is a freeware tool (an unsupported power toy) that can help determine what traffic is going on in your AJAX application. It is a debugging proxy that logs all HTTP traffic occurring on the computer. It also is able to save its logs as VSTEST web tests, which makes it easy to use it to gather your AJAX traffic and bring it into your VSTEST test system. See Appendix F for where to get Fiddler.

Summary

The Web Test system in VSTEST is very complete and provides support for most of the common scenarios needed to test a web site. With this, it is very simple to record a web test, customize it, and add dynamic data to allow a broad and deep level of test coverage with a minimal investment.

It also provides several extensibility mechanisms that permit a great deal of flexibility, allowing you to execute just about any kinds of tests that you might need to test your web site.

But the true power of web tests really comes into play when they are added to a load test. This combination allows you to simulate thousands of users hitting your web site or web service at the same time, performing a wide variety of tasks.

6

Using Manual, Ordered, and Generic Test Types

In Chapters 3 through 5, we looked at authoring and running unit and web tests. Now we move into a different type of test, what we'll call a *container* test type. These types of tests have the purpose of holding other tests. For example, as we briefly discussed in Chapter 2, an ordered test contains a list of tests in which you can specify the order of execution. Generic tests wrap a command line, providing you with a way to include legacy tests as part of your Visual Studio testing framework. Manual tests are a special animal: They don't have code, and they can be a single test or they can have multiple tests as part of the test description — it all depends on how the author writes those tests. Because manual tests are straightforward and are a unique animal, I've included their discussion in this chapter, and we'll begin with a look at manual tests.

> *The load test type also falls into the category of what we are calling a* container *test type. It, however, is complex enough to warrant a chapter of its own (see Chapter 7). We have also provided a sample walk-through of a load test in Appendix D.*

Manual Test Type

The proper authoring of manual tests is extensively discussed in popular books by such experts as Dr. Cem Kaner (*Testing Computer Software*) and Boris Beizer (*Black-Box Testing*), as well as classes by such software testing experts as Elisabeth Hendrickson (http://www.qualitytree.com). Therefore, we will not focus on the art of writing a manual test; instead, we'll look at the mechanics of how manual tests are created and executed in Visual Studio. A manual test is simply this — a test done by a person manually stepping through a script as opposed to one done by a computer executing source code (also known loosely as an *automated test*).

> *A high-level walk-through of the manual test type can also be found in Appendix E.*

Four examples of where manual tests come into play include:

❑ Tasks that are either too difficult or impossible to automate (e.g., physically unplugging a network cable at a critical moment of your program's execution to verify that it handles error conditions appropriately).

❑ Tasks in which the return on investment (ROI) in time spent to automate the test is not justified (e.g., taking 10 seconds to manually confirm that a UI component is functional in a section of the product that is soon to be replaced — Why spend hours or even days coding and maintaining the test for a soon-to-be retired section of the product?).

❑ Areas that need to be automated but time is not yet available to do the automation work.

❑ Cases in which necessary skills for doing the automation work are not currently available to the team.

The most common reasons for manual tests are the last two bullets — (1) not enough time and (2) currently unavailable skill set. This is where manual tests provide value, allowing testing to be defined and tracked until those tests are either mothballed — because of changes in the product, for example — or taken to the next level. On many teams, manual tests serve as a To Do List of items potentially automatable at a later date, except in the cases where the first two examples — automation impossible or poor ROI — come into play.

Defining a Manual Test Scenario

We will continue with the example mentioned earlier of testing what happens when connectivity is lost and how a program responds in that situation. As we explore the mechanics of creating and running a manual test, keep this example in the back of your mind to remember why we're creating this test and how we're arriving at the content that composes that test.

Our scenario is a simple one, and most tests boil down to a simple set of steps. In this case the user is verifying that Microsoft Outlook 2007 is able to move to a *Disconnected* state, communicate this state to the user, and have no ill effects as a result of that loss of connectivity. We'll also label the area of the application that is being tested as the *send/receive functionality* of the application, for no other reason than that this is what the team started calling this area of the product from the initial design stages.

> *One thing that slows many testers when creating a test is trying to define the perfect test scenario. Don't let this distract you or slow you down — that is, put something down to start with, knowing full well that you or someone on your team will continue to improve on the original test. Avoid writer's block by just putting something, anything, down. For example, in this first scenario, we could do other things as part of the test, including timing how long it takes the application to communicate to the user that the network connection has been lost. This first version of the manual test, however, doesn't address benchmarking a feature's responsiveness as a criterion for whether the test passed or failed.*

When writing the test, we also need to address common mistakes in the testing process; that is, while we are in the moment of writing the test description and its steps, remember that we won't be in that zone later when running those tests. We thus need to be as descriptive and complete as possible right now. Remember, too, that it is very likely that you won't remain the sole runner of this test: Others on your team may run it as part of a larger set of tests, or someone may inherit your tests as your role and areas of responsibility continue to change. Your goal is to be as complete as you can and write not just for yourself but for others. An example of this is to point out that the person running this test, if running from a laptop, needs to remember that unplugging the physical network cable without remembering to turn off their wireless connection may make them think they are seeing an error when, indeed, there is no error; the test was simply run incorrectly. Add these types of notes to your tests.

After describing what your test is doing, the environment and its limitations, or common mistakes that can be made in executing the test, you can finally get into the guts of the test scenario. Specifically, the steps of the test need to be listed. This scenario will be a simple one consisting of only three steps:

1. Run the application.

2. Start the send/receive functionality of the application.

3. Physically unplug the network connection.

With the steps determined, the next piece of the puzzle is describing what the expected outcome is. In this case there is a portion of the UI that updates itself based on whether or not the application has connectivity with the server from where it is sending and receiving e-mails. This UI should change to literally show the word *Disconnected*. This expected behavior needs to be included as part of the test template that you eventually create.

Although we are keeping this example simple, we can go beyond this simple first test scenario by taking into consideration other aspects of testing that can be included in our manual test, including accessibility (in this case ensuring that tools used by users with visual impairments are able to "view" the portion of the UI that changes), usability (running trials with users in a controlled setting to verify they can discover the fact that they are in a disconnected state when they suddenly cannot send or receive e-mail), and security (are there ways for other applications to exploit this feature?), as well as geopolitical issues (when Disconnected *is translated into other languages, will its translation be confusing or even offensive?).*

It is always good to be able to see how a test evolves over time, too. This can be accomplished by providing a section where people updating the test's content can record that they are the ones who made the changes. This makes it easy for other authors to determine to whom to ask follow-up questions when they are executing the test and run into questions.

Now that we have a general idea of what the test scenario looks like, we next need to create the test using the manual test type.

Creating a Manual Test

When creating a new manual test, you have two formats to choose from, as shown in Figure 6-1 — one for straight text and one supporting rich-text, embedded images, and tables, edited using Microsoft Word:

❑   **Manual Test (text format)** (*.mtx) — Text format allows for editing the text for a manual test within the IDE itself. If you do not have Microsoft Word installed, Visual Studio serves as your editor for your manual test.

❑   **Manual Test (Microsoft Word format)** (*.mht) — Microsoft Word serves as your editor for this manual test format, and the richness of that editing experience and the content comes with it. For example, this format supports embedding images and formatting text with different fonts, colors, sizes, and styles.

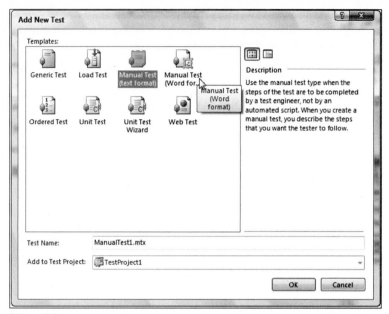

Figure 6-1

Text Format

As you've seen throughout this book, there are various ways to accomplish the same goal. For example, you can create a new test by right-clicking on an existing project in Solution Explorer, or you can select the New Test menu item from the Test menu. Whichever path you select, selecting the Manual Test (text format) test type from the Add New Test dialog box (Figure 6-1) displays the test template shown in Figure 6-2.

Any time a new test type is created, it is immediately opened for editing. As you can see in Figure 6-2, this is no different for the manual test type: The text version of the test is ready for editing in the Visual Studio editor.

Figure 6-3 shows a completed test template using the example of testing the synchronization behavior of Microsoft Outlook 2007 — specifically, how Outlook behaves when network connectivity is lost while a sync is taking place.

Microsoft Word Format

Selecting the Manual Test (Word format) test type from the Add New Test dialog box (Figure 6-1) displays a test template similar to Figure 6-2, except in this case it launches the editing experience specific to this test type — the currently installed version of Microsoft Word (Microsoft Word 2003 or later). Figure 6-4 shows how the experience with a rich-text document can be much more complete than using the simple text version, allowing for embedded screenshots, tables, and formatted text.

> *If you prefer to modify either of the default templates, they can be found in the* `C:\Program Files\`
> `Microsoft Visual Studio 8\Common7\IDE\ItemTemplatesCache\<language>\1033\`

`ManualTestWordFormat.zip\` *directory (where* `<language>` *is* `CSharp, VisualBasic, VisualC,` *or* `Test`*). If you re-run setup, this will overwrite the* `ItemTemplatesCache` *directory; thus a more permanent option is to modify the* `ManualTestWordFormat.zip` *file itself found in the* `ItemTemplates` *directory (you will need to do this for each language).*

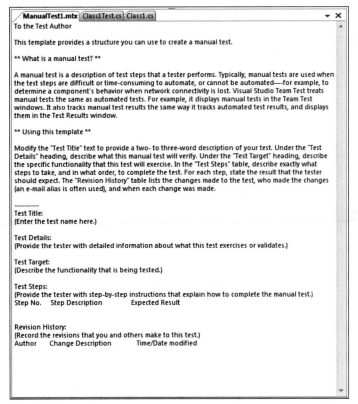

Figure 6-2

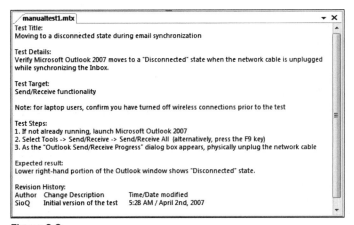

Figure 6-3

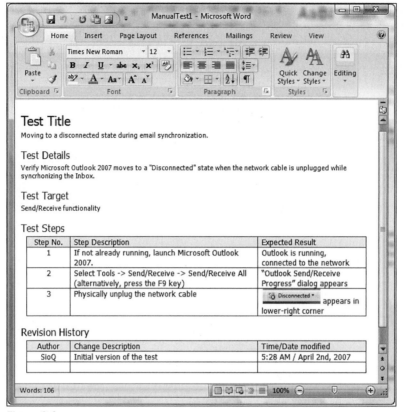

Figure 6-4

Properties of a Manual Test

If not already visible, you can display the Visual Studio Properties window by selecting the Properties Window menu item from the View menu. Single-clicking on a manual test in either the Test View or the Test Manager windows shows the properties of the test in the Properties window, as shown in Figure 6-5.

If you do not currently have the Test View or Test Manager window displayed, this can be accomplished by going to the Test menu and selecting the Windows menu item.

A column can be added to the Test Manager or Test View windows for any properties of a test, allowing you to group or filter based on those property values.

Figure 6-5

The properties for a manual test are as follows:

Property	Editable	Description
Associated Work Items	Editable if part of VSTFS	When working on a team and connected to the Visual Studio Team Foundation Server (VSTFS), a work item can be associated with a test. Work items come in many flavors, including not only an assigned task to be completed, but also reported product defects ("bugs"). Associating a work item with a test provides a way to show that a test maps directly to this particular area of the product. (See Chapter 9 for more details on working with tests when connected to a VSTFS project.)

Continued

Property	Editable	Description
Deployment Items	Editable	Allows you to specify files or folders to deploy with your test run. Specify the full path to the file or folder on one line. Specify each additional file or folder on a separate line. These files are in addition to any files specified in the test run configuration. (See Chapter 2 for a description of the Test Run Configuration dialog box.)
Description	Editable	Use this property to describe what the test is for.
ID	Read-only	The unique identifier for the test. For a manual test type, this is the actual path where the test resides.
Iteration	Editable if part of VSTFS	When working on a team and connected to the Visual Studio Team Foundation Server, an "iteration" can be defined. Consider this like milestones or stages within the software development life cycle (SDLC). This property allows you to specify to which part of the SDLC this test belongs.
Non-runnable Error	Read-only	When a test is part of a test project but for some reason it cannot be included as part of a test run, this property contains a description of the problem. For example, if the file on the local drive does not exist but it is listed in the project, this will contain an error value.
Owner	Editable	Used to list the name or user ID of the person who authored or maintains the test.
Priority	Editable	If your team uses this property, this helps determine which tests need to be run first.
Project	Read-only	This property contains the name of the parent project containing this test.
Project Area	Editable if part of VSTFS	If part of a team project (connected to the Visual Studio Team Foundation Server), the test can be mapped directly to a "project area" specified for the team project.
Project Relative Path	Read-only	The filename of the project containing the test. The path is relative to the location of the solution on the local disk.
Solution	Read-only	This is the name of the solution that contains the test project that holds this test.
Test Enabled	Editable	This allows a test to be excluded from test runs without having to modify a test list that contains this particular test. An example is turning off a test that results in crashing the current build of the program being tested. Once a new build becomes available that fixes the crashing bug, the test can be re-enabled.
Test Name	Read-only	The name of the test, based on its filename.

Property	Editable	Description
Test Storage	Read-only	In the case of a manual test, this is the same as the test ID: the path to the file that contains the test.
Test Type	Read-only	The type of the test — in this case, manual test. Remember that each property can be displayed as a column, allowing tests to be grouped or filtered according to the value of the property. This is a good way to view all manual tests easily when using the Test Manager or Test View windows.
Timeout	Read-only	A manual test does not have a timeout value — that is, its value is infinite. For other test types, this value allows you to specify how long the test can take to run before it is aborted and marked as a failed test if it does not complete on its own in the allotted time.

Again, for more details on working with tests when connected to a Visual Studio Team Foundation Server project, see Chapter 9.

Executing a Manual Test

Recall from Chapter 2 that the two common windows used for executing tests are the Test Manager window (available only with VSTEST) and the Test View window (available in both VSTEST and VSTESD). If the Test View window is not already displayed, select the Windows menu item under the Test menu, then select the Test View menu item. Continuing with the two sample tests from the first part of this chapter, you should see two manual tests — both named *ManualTest1* — in the Test View window, as shown in Figure 6-6.

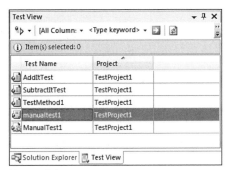

Figure 6-6

Right-clicking on the Test Name column (or any column in the Test View window) allows you to select the Add/Remove Columns menu item from the dropdown ("context") menu. This displays the Add/Remove Columns dialog box shown in Figure 6-7. This dialog box allows you to display any of the properties as a column that can then be used for sorting (accomplished by clicking on the column heading), filtering (by typing in a keyword and optionally selecting a column to apply it to), or grouping (because the window is small, click the "overflow" button on the far right of the Test View's toolbar, then select which property by which to group your tests).

Figure 6-7

To illustrate how adding columns and grouping by a particular property can be helpful, I've added a few more tests to the Test Project, displayed the Owner property as a column, and selected the test type to Group By (see Figure 6-8).

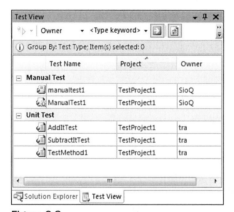

Figure 6-8

These same techniques mentioned for the Test View window also work in the Test Manager, but in that window, as we discussed in Chapter 2, you have the added benefit of grouping your tests into lists.

Execution of a manual test is much the same as any test. Click on a test to select it in the Test View or Test Manager window. To select two or more tests, use the *Shift* key to select a range of tests or the *Ctrl* key to select individual tests.

With the tests selected, click on the Run Selection icon in the Test View or Test Manager toolbar. (Reminder: Use your mouse to hover over the different toolbar buttons to see a description of what each button does.)

Remember that there are many ways to accomplish some of the same tasks in Visual Studio. Look at the toolbars in the window you're working with, as well as right-clicking on columns and objects. Also, many times the main window will have a toolbar that can apply to the current window you're working with. This is true, too, in the case of working with tests: The Test Tools toolbar appears below the main window's menu bar. If it is not currently visible, you can go to the View menu, select the Toolbars submenu, and then select the Test Tools menu item.

Having started the execution of your manual tests, you will immediately see a message box appear alerting you to the fact that the test run you are starting contains manual tests (see Figure 6-9). The reason for this message box is that when a large grouping of tests is executed, the person running those tests may not realize that test execution will pause until the manual test is completed. It can be frustrating to kick off a large test run before heading to lunch only to return and find it paused about 1 minute after you left the office.

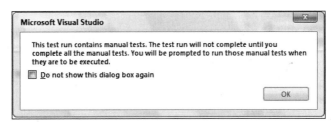

Figure 6-9

As execution begins, Visual Studio refers to the current test run configuration (discussed in Chapter 2) to determine what files need to be copied as part of the test run, whether or not to instrument the application-under-test for gathering Code Coverage Results, and so on. Then Visual Studio works its way down the list of tests to execute. As it reaches a manual test, a message box is displayed that states, "Manual Test 'manualtest1' is ready for execution." Test execution has stopped until a human actually follows the test steps and marks whether they consider the test to have passed or failed. The manual test is presented as a tabbed document in the Visual Studio IDE, looking somewhat close to what's shown in Figure 6-10.

The document has four sections:

- ❑ **Apply toolbar button** — This button becomes active only after the tester has clicked on one of the Pass or Fail option buttons in the Select Result section of the document.

- ❑ **Select Result group** — Two option buttons, Pass and Fail, allow the tester to specify the results of manually stepping through the test script.

- ❑ **Comments textbox** — Saved as part of the test results, the test engineer can provide further details as to why the test was considered a failure.

- ❑ **Test script view** — The bottom portion of the window shows the test script that the tester authored using the Visual Studio text editor or Microsoft Word

Notice how the manual test that was authored using Microsoft Word shows the table and embedded graphic to the tester as the test executes. The text version of the test would have a much more simplified presentation.

Figure 6-10

After the tester specifies the outcome of the test and clicks the Apply button, the Test Results window, shown in Figure 6-11, shows the outcome of that test. The tabbed document window used to present the manual test script to the tester also becomes read-only after the Apply button is pressed. It is now part of the history of the execution of that test run.

Figure 6-11

Lastly, there are a few limitations of the manual test type (other than requiring human interaction). Specifically, these types of tests cannot be included as part of a test run that will execute remotely, they will not execute as part of a test run configured as part of verifying the stability of a team build, and they cannot be executed using the command-line tool (`mstest.exe`) described in Chapter 3. The reason for this is that, because they require human interaction, it is not easy to execute your manual tests remotely; that is, the feature would require the remote computer where the test execution is taking place to stop and prompt a user to take some action before continuing the test. Because of the increased likelihood of causing tests to stop unexpectedly (because it was forgotten that the test contains a manual test) and because the team ran out of time to implement this aspect of the feature effectively, the only recourse is: Take a printout of your manual test to the lab, and run your test on the appropriate machine. Upon completing the test, return to your desk, run the manual test locally, and mark the test as Passed or Failed depending on your findings. Agreed, this is not an optimal approach, but remote execution of a manual test could not be implemented in time for the product to ship.

Ordered Test Type

The ordered test type was created to allow the test author to control in what order tests are executed. While many tests can be written to be self-contained and therefore don't rely on other tests' behaviors, some tests are written to build on a previous test's efforts. For example, one test may change a value in a database table that subsequent tests rely on in their executions.

In this section, we'll look at creating, editing, and executing an ordered test.

Creating an Ordered Test

Add a new ordered test to your test project by right-clicking on the test project in the Solution Explorer and selecting the Ordered Test menu item from the Add submenu.

> *Selecting the New Test menu item from the main window's Test menu or right-clicking on the test project and selecting New Test from the Add submenu will allow you to specify the name of your new test. Using the Ordered Test menu item as described in the above paragraph will name the test for you. You can rename a test by clicking on the file in the Solution Explorer.*

Whenever a new test is added, the editor for that test is opened as a tabbed document in the IDE. In the case of the ordered test type, it presents itself as a form, as shown in Figure 6-12.

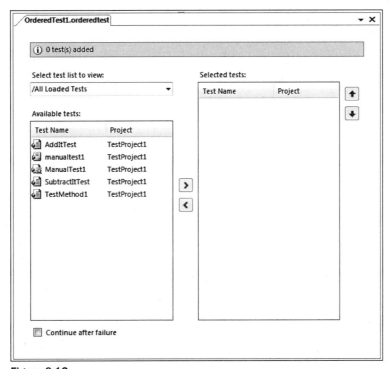

Figure 6-12

The Ordered Test editor has seven components:

- ❑ **Status bar** — Appearing as a light-yellow read-only textbox across the top of the document, this control shows the number of tests that compose the ordered test.

- ❑ **"Select test list to view" dropdown box** — Defaulting to "/All Loaded Tests," this allows you to view the contents of a test list that was created using the Test Manager window.

- ❑ **"Available tests" list box** — Controlled by the Select test list to view combo-box, the available tests are displayed here.

- ❑ **"Selected tests" list box** — Shows the tests that have been selected to be a part of the ordered test. The order in which the tests are listed is the order in which they will execute, from top to bottom.

- ❑ **Left–right arrow buttons** — These buttons allow you to move selected tests from the "Available tests" list box into the "Selected tests" list box or to remove tests from the "Selected tests" list box.

- ❑ **Up–down arrow buttons** — Select a test or tests to move up or down the list of tests. Again, the topmost test in the list executes first, with the test at the bottom of the list executing last.

- ❑ **"Continue after failure" checkbox** — In most cases, an ordered test type is used because it matters in what order tests execute. That is, each test builds on the efforts of the previous test. Therefore, if the previous test fails, usually the rest of the tests should be skipped. However, if the tests are autonomous in their execution, the engineer authoring the ordered test can override the default behavior of aborting the execution of any tests remaining in the ordered test.

To author the ordered test, it's a matter of selecting and moving tests from the "Available tests" list box to the "Selected tests" list box, then arranging those tests into the order in which you prefer those tests to execute. The topmost test will execute first, with execution moving one test at a time down the list.

> *While an ordered test type can contain another ordered test, you are not allowed to have both ordered tests contain each other (resulting in a circular reference). Fortunately, Visual Studio looks for this situation and when encountered, displays a message box with the warning, "Cycle Detected!* <test1> *cannot be added to* <test2> *because this addition would result in an infinite execution loop."*

Properties of an Ordered Test

If not already visible, you can display the Properties window by selecting the Properties Window menu item from the View menu. Single-clicking on an ordered test in either the Test View or the Test Manager windows shows the properties of the test in the Properties window, as shown in Figure 6-13.

> *If you do not currently have the Test View or Test Manager window displayed, this can be accomplished by going to the Test menu and selecting the Windows menu item.*

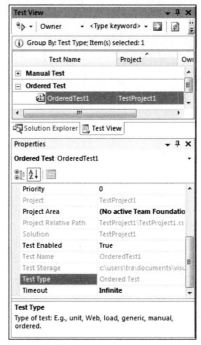

Figure 6-13

A column can be added to the Test Manager or Test View windows for any properties of a test, allowing you to group or filter based on those property values.

The properties for an ordered test are as follows:

Property	Editable	Description
Associated Work Items	Editable if part of VSTFS	When working on a team and connected to the Visual Studio Team Foundation Server (VSTFS), a work item can be associated with a test. Work items come in many flavors, including not only an assigned task to be completed but also reported product defects ("bugs"). Associating a work item with a test provides a way to show that a test maps directly to this particular area of the product.
Continue After Failure	Editable	If False, all tests within the ordered test that follow after a failed test will be skipped. If True, all tests will have their turn at being executed.

Continued

Property	Editable	Description
Deployment Items	Editable	Allows you to specify files or folders to deploy with your test run. Specify the full path to the file or folder on one line. Specify each additional file or folder on a separate line. These files are in addition to any files specified in the test run configuration. (See Chapter 2 for a description of the Test Run Configuration dialog box.)
Description	Editable	Use this property to describe what the test is for.
ID	Read-only	The unique identifier for the test. For an ordered test type, this is the actual path where the test resides.
Iteration	Editable if part of VSTFS	When working on a team and connected to the Visual Studio Team Foundation Server, an "iteration" can be defined. Consider this like milestones or stages within the software development life cycle (SDLC). This property allows you to specify to which part of the SDLC this test belongs.
Non-runnable Error	Read-only	When a test is part of a test project but for some reason it cannot be included as part of a test run, this property contains a description of the problem. For example, if the file on the local drive does not exist but it is listed in the project, this will contain an error value.
Owner	Editable	Used to list the name or user ID of the person who authored or maintains the test.
Priority	Editable	Because a column can be added to the Test Manager or Test View windows for any of the properties, if your team uses this property, it can help determine which tests need to be run first.
Project	Read-only	This property contains the name of the parent project containing this test.
Project Area	Editable if part of VSTFS	If part of a team project (connected to the Visual Studio Team Foundation Server), the test can be mapped directly to a "project area" specified for the team project.
Project Relative Path	Read-only	The filename of the project containing the test. The path is relative to the location of the solution on the local disk.
Solution	Read-only	This is the name of the solution that contains the test project that holds this test.
Test Enabled	Editable	This allows a test to be excluded from test runs without having to modify a test list that contains this particular test. An example is turning off a test that results in crashing the current build of the program being tested. Once a new build becomes available that fixes the crashing bug, the test can be re-enabled.
Test Name	Read-only	The name of the test, based on its filename.

Property	Editable	Description
Test Storage	Read-only	In the case of an ordered test, this is the same as the test ID: the path to the file that contains the test.
Test Type	Read-only	The type of the test — in this case, ordered test. Because each property can be displayed as a column in Test View or Test Manager windows, this property can help you view all ordered tests.
Timeout	Read-only	An ordered test defaults to Infinite for its timeout value. However, this can be overridden by typing in a new value to specify how long test execution waits before aborting the execution of this test. A default value is specified by the test run configuration settings (in this case, 5 minutes), but this property allows the test to override that global setting.

Executing an Ordered Test

The execution of an ordered test is the same as any other test type. Select it in the Test Manager or Test View window, and run it. The biggest difference with an ordered test, however, is that although it contains one or more tests within it, it counts as a single test. If an ordered test contains a mixture of 100 other tests and one of those tests fails, the entire ordered test is considered to have failed. This makes sense when you look at it as it was meant to be used — a single test.

The results of the execution of an ordered test look the same as with any test. However, when you drill down into the results of the test in the Test Results window — either by double-clicking the ordered test in the Test Results window or right-clicking the ordered test result and selecting the View Test Results Details menu item from the context menu — a tabbed document window is displayed similar to the one in Figure 6-14.

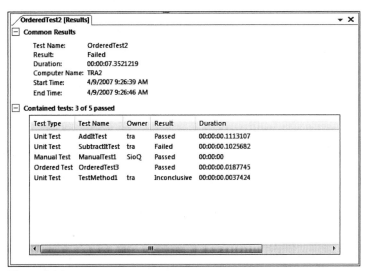

Figure 6-14

In this example, *OrderedTest2* is the name of the test that we executed. The results of all of the tests contained in OrderedTest2 are in the "Contained tests" section of the document. The results of each of these tests can also be viewed through double-clicking an individual test. For example, double-clicking on ManualTest1 opens another tabbed document with that test's results. Closing the ManualTest1 results or clicking back on the OrderedTest2 [Results] tab, you'll note that OrderedTest2 also contains an ordered test named OrderedTest3. The results of OrderedTest3 can also be viewed by double-clicking on it in the "Contained tests" list, effectively drilling down into your test results.

> *Chapter 3 goes into detail about running tests using the command-line tool,* MSTest.exe.

Generic Test Type

The idea of the generic test type is to provide a means for test authors to include their existing tests — created using some other third-party tool that doesn't integrate with Visual Studio — effectively mingling their legacy tests with tests they've authored in Visual Studio Team System. A generic test acts as a wrapper around your other tests by running that third-party test tool using whatever command-line capabilities it provides. Think of generic tests as the poor man's version of extensibility.

> *Generic tests will be different for each third-party tool that you use. That is, the test attempts to work with the third-party tool's command-line utility, assuming such a utility is provided by that tool. Some tools may not provide a means to execute tests via a command line and therefore cannot be integrated into your list of tests using the generic test type.*

While this all sounds well and good, there are some requirements that must be met to allow you to take advantage of this test type:

❑   Your external (third-party tool) tests must be executable from the command line.

❑   A value representing Pass or Fail must be returned by the third-party tool's command-line program.

❑   Preferably (but optionally), the tool saves out an XML file (also known as a summary results file) containing the list of individual tests that were executed.

> *The summary results file allows you to dig into the individual test results of each test executed by your third-party testing tool. If the XML file is not provided by your third-party tests, for example, the generic test will show only that the wrapped list of tests passed or failed as a whole (i.e., if one test fails, the entire generic test is considered to have failed). The summary results XML file allows you to dig down into the individual test results. We'll go into more detail later in this chapter.*

Creating a Generic Test

A generic test is created like any other test type. Use your preferred method of creating a new test type, such as from the Test menu, right-clicking in the list of the Test View window, or right-clicking on the test project in the Solution Explorer window, and selecting the New Test menu item. After naming your test — GenericTest1.GenericTest, for example — a tabbed document window opens, displaying the form used to author this test type, as shown in Figure 6-15.

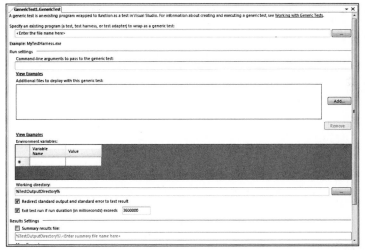

Figure 6-15

Editing the Generic Test Form

While the generic test is defined using a rather large form (see Figure 6-15), remember that its purpose is to work with a command-line utility, and therefore it attempts to gather enough details to allow for that type of interaction. That is, it provides you with the same options you have when working from the command line, such as setting environment variables, passing arguments on the command line, copying files to a directory, before running a test, and setting the current ("working") directory.

The form breaks down into the following controls:

❑ **"Specify an existing program" textbox** — The name of the executable command-line tool to be wrapped by the generic test type. (Note that this is the actual filename of the .exe or .bat file. If the filename is not found in the current working directory or PATH environment variable, you will need to specify the complete path to the file.)

❑ **"Command-line arguments" textbox** — If there are any arguments that need to be passed when running the command-line tool, this is where you specify those arguments. Just as with the actual command line, put quotes around strings, and separate your arguments with spaces.

❑ **"Additional files to deploy" list box** — If there are other files required for the execution of these tests, such as a data file, for example, add those files to this list box.

❑ **"Environment variables" grid** — Just as you could use the SET command to establish environment variables and their values on the command line, you may accomplish the same results using this grid. Some third-party tools use environment variables to locate the program to be tested, directories for storing their own test results, and so on.

❏ **"Working directory" textbox** — This is the same as setting the current directory on the command line prior to running a command-line program. That is, execution is relative to that current directory, also known as the working directory.

❏ **"Redirect standard output" checkbox** — Just as you can re-direct output on the command line using >, this allows you to re-direct any output from the wrapped utility into the test results. This is extremely helpful when diagnosing execution problems or test failures.

❏ **"Exit test run" checkbox** — Represented in milliseconds, this is the maximum amount of time the external command-line tool is allowed to run before Visual Studio moves to the next test (defaults to 1 hour).

❏ **"Summary results file" checkbox and textbox** — If you've updated your tests to write out each individual test's results to an XML file, here is where you specify that summary results file's location and name. Providing this file allows you to dig down into the results of your ordered test instead of seeing a high-level passed or failed result. Although optional, it is very helpful when diagnosing which individual test failed.

If your third-party tool does not provide the required return values to work with the generic test type, consider writing your own simple command-line application as a go-between for Visual Studio and your legacy testing tool. That is, have your command-line application take in command-line arguments from the generic test type, and pass them along to the third-party tool. Also, have your command-line tool interpret the results and pass back the 0 (for Passed) or nonzero number (for Failed). Depending on how you write your go-between application, you might even have it write the XML summary results file (e.g., it may be easier to run each third-party test individually and write out the results of its execution to the XML file).

The Summary Results File

The quandary is how to provide a way to run non-integrated testing tools using VSTEST. The answer the Visual Studio team came up with was the generic test type to wrap a command-line tool for executing those third-party tests. But still, what happens if the single generic test runs a command line that wraps thousands of tests? Having a single result for that generic test — Passed or Failed — isn't all that helpful or representative of just how extensive the wrapped library of tests is. It's especially frustrating when one or more tests fail out of that 1,000 tests and the only result you see from the Visual Studio side of things is, "Failed."

This is where the summary results file comes into play, by providing that helpful level of detail. A schema is provided in the Visual Studio schemas directory, specifically:

```
C:\program files\Microsoft Visual Studio 8\Xml\Schemas\SummaryResult.xsd
```

Using the xsd.exe utility and specifying the above schema file allows you to generate a class in the language of your choice. For example, after setting my current directory to the above path, I typed in the following command line:

```
xsd SummaryResult.xsd /c /l:cs /out:c:\mytemp
```

This example assumes that the directory `c:\mytemp` *already exists.*

This runs the XML Schemas/DataTypes support utility (`xsd.exe`) (see Figure 6-16) against the provided schema (`SummaryResult.xsd`) to generate a class (`/c`) using C# as the language (`/1:cs`) and placing the file generated by `xsd.exe` (`summaryresults.cs`) into my temp directory (`/out:c:\mytemp`). I can then use that class as part of my test code to write out the name of the grouping of tests and the individual test results.

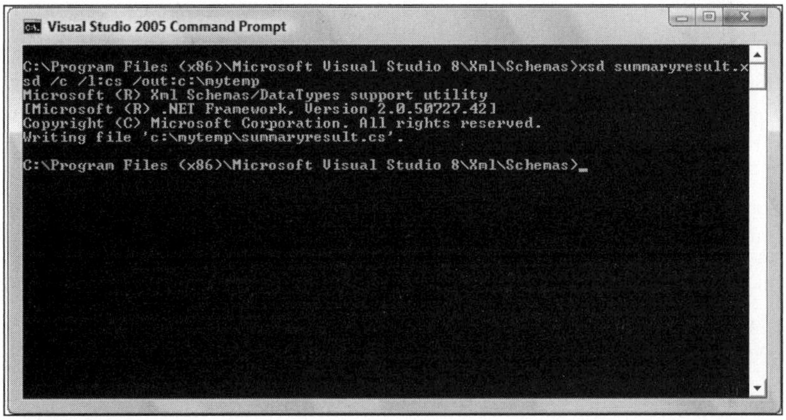

Figure 6-16

Now, if you're truly old school and using a legacy tool that doesn't support any object-oriented languages like C++, C#, or Visual Basic, then you might want to handcraft your own XML file (by "handcraft" I mean to have your legacy tool write out this XML file itself), as shown in the following code:

```xml
<?xml version="1.0" encoding="utf-8" ?>
<SummaryResult>
    <TestName>File Open Dialog Box</TestName>
    <TestResult>Failed</TestResult>
    <InnerTests>
        <InnerTest>
            <TestName>Open a corrupted file</TestName>
            <TestResult>Passed</TestResult>
            <ErrorMessage></ErrorMessage>
            <DetailedResultsFile></DetailedResultsFile>
        </InnerTest>
        <InnerTest>
            <TestName>Open an empty file</TestName>
            <TestResult>Passed</TestResult>
            <ErrorMessage></ErrorMessage>
            <DetailedResultsFile></DetailedResultsFile>
        </InnerTest>
```

```
<InnerTest>
    <TestName>Open a very large file (4gb)</TestName>
    <TestResult>Failed</TestResult>
    <ErrorMessage>Memory fault</ErrorMessage>

    <DetailedResultsFile>c:\mytests\OpenDlgTests.log</DetailedResultsFile>
</InnerTest>
    </InnerTests>
</SummaryResult>
```

Let's dissect the summary results file shown in the preceding code:

❑ `<?xml>` **tag** — Standard XML tag preferred by most programs reading in an XML file.

❑ `<SummaryResult>` **tag** — Represents the entirety of the summary results class.

❑ `<TestName>` **tag** — This is the high-level name of the group of tests that were run.

❑ `<TestResult>` **tag** — The roll-up result of the outcome of the group of tests. That is, if one test failed, the group of tests is considered to have failed.

❑ `<InnerTests>` **tag** — Groups the individual test results together.

❑ `<InnerTest>` **tag** — Represents a specific test's properties:

   ❑ `<TestName>` **tag** — A descriptive name of the actual test.

   ❑ `<TestResult>` **tag** — The result of running that individual test (Passed or Failed).

   ❑ `<ErrorMessage>` **tag** — Any error message relating to the test's execution that you'd like to communicate back to Visual Studio. This is helpful information and is seen by the person digging into the details of why the generic test has failed. Provide good details here.

   ❑ `<DetailedResultsFile>` **tag** — If the test program has additional information about the failure of this test, such as a log file, provide the path to that file to allow the person reviewing the test results to dig even deeper into the cause of the failure.

Be forewarned that changes to the XSD file in future releases will very likely break your XML file formatting.

Properties of a Generic Test

If not already visible, you can display the Properties window by selecting the Properties Window menu item from the View menu, and the Test View or Test Manager windows can be displayed by selecting the Windows menu item in the Test menu.

Single-clicking on a generic test in either the Test View or the Test Manager windows shows the properties of the test in the Properties window, as shown in Figure 6-17.

A column can be added to the Test Manager or Test View windows for any properties of a test, allowing you to group or filter based on those property values.

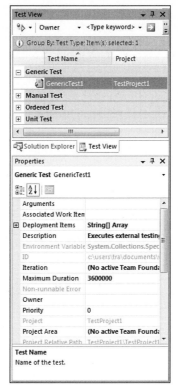

Figure 6-17

Property	Editable	Description
Arguments	Editable	This property is initially set when editing the generic test's form, specifically in the "Command-line arguments to pass to the generic test" textbox. You may also edit the values directly in the Properties window. An example of an argument could be the name of the test file to be executed using the third-party tool being wrapped by the generic test. When you change this argument in either place, it is changed in both places.
Associated Work Items	Editable if part of VSTFS	When working on a team and connected to the Visual Studio Team Foundation Server, a work item can be associated with a test. Work items come in many flavors, including not only an assigned task to be completed, but also reported product defects ("bugs"). Associating a work item with a test provides a way to show that a test maps directly to this particular area of the product.

Continued

Property	Editable	Description
Deployment Items	Editable	Allows you to specify files or folders to deploy with your test run. Specify the full path to the file or folder on one line. Specify each additional file or folder on a separate line. These files are in addition to any files specified in the test run configuration. (See Chapter 2 for a description of the Test Run Configuration dialog box.)
Description	Editable	Use this property to describe what the test is for.
Environment Variables	Read-only	Editable only through the generic test form and not in the Properties window.
ID	Read-only	The unique identifier for the test. For a generic test type, this is the actual path where the test resides.
Iteration	Editable if part of VSTFS	When working on a team and connected to the Visual Studio Team Foundation Server, an "iteration" can be defined. Consider this like milestones or stages within the software development life cycle (SDLC). This property allows you to specify to which part of the SDLC this test belongs.
Maximum Duration	Editable	Defaulting to 60 minutes (3,600,000 milliseconds), this is how long the generic test will be allowed to execute before terminating the test.
Non-runnable Error	Read-only	When a test is part of a test project but for some reason it cannot be included as part of a test run, this property contains a description of the problem. For example, if the file on the local drive does not exist but it is listed in the project, this will contain an error value.
Owner	Editable	Used to list the name or user ID of the person who authored or maintains the test.
Priority	Editable	Because a column can be added to the Test Manager or Test View windows for any of the properties, this allows you to group or filter based on the property values. If your team uses this property, this helps determine which tests need to be run first.
Project	Read-only	This property contains the name of the parent project containing this test.
Project Area	Editable if part of VSTFS	If part of a team project (connected to the Visual Studio Team Foundation Server), the test can be mapped directly to a "project area" specified for the team project.
Project Relative Path	Read-only	The filename of the project containing the test. The path is relative to the location of the solution on the local disk.
Redirect Standard Output And Error	Editable	True or False, this allows you to specify whether or not the output from the third-party command-line tool is included in the test results surfaced in the Visual Studio UI (default: True).

Property	Editable	Description
Solution	Read-only	This is the name of the solution that contains the test project that holds this test.
Summary XML File	Editable	This property is used to specify the path to the summary results file that is optionally provided when executing the third-party tests. Providing this XML file allows the person reviewing the results to dig deeper into which individual test failed and why. (See the section above in this chapter entitled, "The Summary Results File." Also see the "Use Summary XML File" property at the end of this table.)
Target Executable	Editable	The path to the third-party command-line utility that will be used to execute the tests.
Test Enabled	Editable	This allows a test to be excluded from test runs without having to modify a test list that contains this particular test. An example is turning off a test that results in crashing the current build of the program being tested. Once a new build becomes available that fixes the crashing bug, the test can be re-enabled.
Test Name	Read-only	The name of the test, based on its filename.
Test Storage	Read-only	In the case of a generic test, this is the same as the test ID: the path to the file that contains the test.
Test Type	Read-only	The type of the test — in this case, generic test. Because each property can be displayed as a column in the Test Manager and Test View windows, tests can be grouped or filtered according to the value of the property. This is a good way to view all generic tests easily when using those windows.
Timeout	Read-only	A generic test defaults to Infinite for its timeout value. However, this can be overridden by typing in a new value to specify how long test execution waits before aborting the execution of this test. A default value (in this case, 5 minutes) is specified by the test run configuration settings, but this property allows the test to override that global setting.
Use Summary XML File	Editable	If this property is set to True, the path specified in the Summary XML File property (shown earlier in this table) will be used to include additional detail in the test run results for this generic test.
Working Directory	Editable	The third-party program treats this directory as its current directory. Any relative paths it makes reference to will be relative to this directory.

Executing a Generic Test

Execution of the test type is similar to any other test type and can be accomplished using any of the methods for executing tests (i.e., from the Test Manager or Test View windows, as well as re-running tests via the Test Results window or the main window's Test toolbar, already discussed in Chapters 2 through 5).

Similar to the ordered test and, as you'll see in Chapter 7, the load test, these containers of tests allow you to expand their results to see how the tests they contained fared in the test run. For the generic test type, however, this level of detail is not guaranteed. A summary results file must either have been provided by the third-party toolmaker, fashioned by the author of the tests (as described above in this chapter), or created by a go-between application that is executed by the generic test and in turn loops through the third-party tests while writing out the results to the summary results XML file. Whatever the situation, the ability to drill or dig into results cannot be realized without this file.

Summary

In this chapter we looked at three test types: manual, ordered, and generic. The manual test type relies on human interaction, going through steps that must be carried out by a test engineer to verify whether or not the test completed successfully. The ordered test type allows the test author to specify the order in which the tests should execute. When selecting a group of tests that are not part of an ordered test, there is no guarantee in what order those tests will be executed.

A little more involved is the generic test type, which allows you to provide a wrapper around a group of tests that are not integrated into Visual Studio. These include third-party test tools' companies that have not yet integrated with Visual Studio and homegrown tests created and maintained by your testing team. Depending on your implementation of the generic test type, you can have very simple test results that don't communicate much information, or you can have a very detailed and rich set of test results.

In the next chapter we shall look at another test type that we've classified as a container test. This is the load test, which allows you to simulate multiples of virtual testers using your application's functionality at the same time, thereby simulating high user loads on your system.

7

Load Testing

If you have created a set of functional tests — unit tests, web tests, and so forth — running them will tell you if your application works. At least you know it works pretty well for a single user. And for many applications this is all you need, if you are planning on having only one user at a time. But if it's a client/server or a Web-based application or service, then you need to verify that it works under load. Verifying that your application works well when 100 or 1,000 or 1 million users are hitting it at the same time can be very tricky. Even deciding what your definition of "works well" is for these scenarios can be difficult.

VSTEST provides a good set of tools to help you examine your application's functionality and performance under such stress/load conditions. Allowing you to gather and examine these data under various load scenarios will help you make decisions as to whether or not your application is ready for the huge number of customers you will have and will help identify where you need to make fixes and improvements, or buy more hardware.

> **Much of this chapter assumes that you have the Visual Studio 2005 Team Test Load Agent (VSTTLA) product in addition to VSTEST. The Visual Studio Team Test Load Agent product provides the features for setting up and managing multi-computer test rigs with a Controller and several Agent computers. A limited level of load testing can be performed without setting up a test rig (essentially your VSTEST computer acts as the manager, controller, and agent), and many of this chapter's topics still apply in that case.**

Basic Terminology

Load testing is a relatively new type of testing for many software engineers; thus it is probably best if we go over some basic terminology and processes. Next we will move on to some basics of working with the load test test type in VSTEST. Then we can dig into the details of running load tests and analyzing the Result data.

Because load testing is a new enough area for most software engineers and I have frequently seen these terms used differently, it seemed best to go over some of the main load testing terms and how they are being used in this book (and in VSTEST). Many of these terms have a large degree of overlap (many people would include Fault Tolerance testing under Stress Testing, and so forth).

The most commonly used terms are:

❑ **Load Testing** — A general term for testing that involves testing the application "under load," that is, with more than one user. Load testing includes stress testing, performance testing, fault tolerance, and so on. In fact, most often you run a "load test" where you perform a single test run but measure various aspects that fall under each of these categories. For example, during a test run of 10,000 users, you are checking to see that functionally everything works ("stress testing") and that the response times are within design guidelines ("performance testing").

❑ **Stress Testing** — Stress testing is load testing that focuses on the *functionality* of the product when it is running under stress conditions. "Stress conditions" usually means a large number of simultaneous users but can also mean pushing various resources: large data sets (if you have 1 million user records in the database, or DB), file sizes (uploading a 1-GB file), and so forth. It also refers to testing that your application can run for a certain length of time without errors.

❑ **Performance Testing** — Testing that focuses on the speed of the product in terms of throughput and response time. This could be during a load test or not. In this chapter we focus on performance testing in relation to load testing — that is, measuring the product's response times when under load or stress.

❑ **Fault Tolerance Testing** — Testing how well the product performs in terms of both functionality and performance during various error conditions, and also how well the product recovers from error conditions. For example, if you have a web service that uses a clustered SQL server system, what happens when one of the SQL servers in the cluster goes down? Does everything still work? How does this affect the response time (performance) of the product?

❑ **Test Rig** — In VSTEST a *test rig* is the collection of computers used to run the tests. A test rig is made up of a controller and one or more agents. When a load test is run, the controller manages the agents to distribute test execution out to the agents. It is possible to use one computer as both the controller and agent, but this will severely reduce the amount of load (users) that you can generate.

❑ **Agent** — An *agent* is a computer that has been set up to execute individual tests during a load test. Each agent simulates multiple users during the load test, so that you do not need 1,000 agents to simulate a user load of 1,000. The number of users that a single agent can simulate is highly dependent on the capabilities of that agent hardware (mostly memory and processor) and how many resources a test requires to run.

❑ **Controller** — The *controller* manages the agents during a load test and distributes out the tests to ensure that the required user load is achieved. The controller also collects the performance data from the agents and the systems that are being tested.

❑ **Results Store** — The large amount of data that is collected during a load test is stored in a SQL database. The first time you start a "local" run (using your VSTEST system as the controller and manager), VSTEST will create this database for you automatically using the SQL Server Express installation that comes with VSTEST. You can also set the controller to store results in another SQL database that you have set up; this allows you to have multiple controllers all storing their results in the same store.

❑ **Application** — In this chapter, the term *application* refers to the product being tested, usually the server part of a product. Often this is a product that is running on several different systems (e.g., a web server computer and a SQL DB).

While these are the most commonly used terms I've encountered in the teams performing load testing, each company and even teams within companies have their own nomenclature. Now that you know how I'm using the terms, it's time to move ahead and look at how to work with the actual load tests.

Working with Load Tests in VSTEST

A load test in VSTEST is a test type. Just like unit tests or web tests (but much like an ordered test), it is made up of other tests, with additional metadata. A load test can include any test type except for manual tests and other load tests; but it is best to stick to web tests and unit tests. The other test types (ordered and generic) do not work smoothly in a load test.

Web tests are useful for load testing applications with a Web interface (i.e., HTTP requests). Unit tests are good for testing client-side APIs in a client server application, or if you want call the server APIs directly.

Either can be used for load testing a web service. Because web tests are optimized for load testing, using a web test usually allows for generating a larger load than using a unit test. Because unit tests are good at testing APIs, it can be much easier to set up a unit test to test a web service than it is to create the web test for testing the web service.

> *Ordered tests and generic tests can be used in a load test, but have specific problems that make them a bit harder to work with. Because generic tests call some external code via the command line (to allow using legacy testing applications), it can be difficult to execute these tests successfully in a multi-user load test. See Chapter 6 for details on ordered and generic tests.*

Ordered tests are tricky because they can be made up of other test types including types that are not supported in a load test. In addition, it can be harder to examine the results. If an ordered test is made up of only web and unit tests, then it will work pretty well in a load test; otherwise, it's usually more trouble than it's worth. And even if it's only web and unit tests now, someone could add some other test later, say a generic test, that would then break when run in the load test.

A load test takes the tests it is made up of and runs them over and over again for the duration of the test. If you have a single web test in a load test that is set for a user load of 20 users, then when the load test is run, it will execute that one web test in 20 simultaneous instances, simulating 20 users performing the actions of the web test. Note that this does not mean that each user is performing the same step in the web test at the same time — one user may be just starting the test, while another is on a middle step, and so forth. If you add other tests to the load test, then the 20 users will be performing a mix of those tests at any one time.

Creating a Load Test

Creating a new load test is very simple with the New Load Test Wizard, which will walk you through setting some initial properties and picking a base set of tests.

For a more detailed walk-through of the Load Test wizard, turn to Appendix D at the end of this book.

To create a new load test, do the following steps:

1. Select your test project. (To create a new test project, see Chapter 2.)

2. From the Test menu, select New Test (or right-click on the project and select Add ➪ Load Test).

3. The New load Test Wizard appears (see Figure 7-1).

4. Set the Scenario, Counter Sets, and Run Settings properties as appropriate, or take the default values and change the settings later using the Properties window. The next section of this chapter, "Components of a Load Test," goes into all of these properties in detail.

5. After the load test is created, the Load Test Editor will open, displaying the Load Test property tree (see Figure 7-2).

6. Rename your test in the Solution explorer to something more useful than the default name, *loadtest1.loadtest* (but do not change the .loadtest extension).

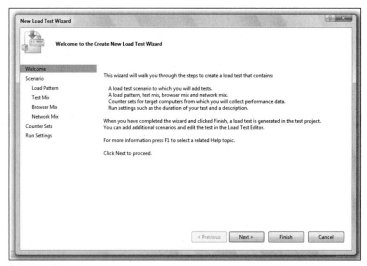

Figure 7-1

Figure 7-2

By going through these six simple steps, you've created a fairly powerful load test. The wizard is extremely helpful in walking you through the creation of your load test. While you cannot edit the load test using the same wizard, you can still tweak the behavior of your load test through the properties that were set when the load test was created.

Components of a Load Test

A load test has several main components that group the large amount of settings that determine the behavior of the test run. This also allows you to vary those settings to re-use the same load test to test various scenarios without having to create new load tests.

Scenarios

A load test has one or more *scenarios*. A scenario groups a set of tests with settings that are used during a load test run. During a load test run, all of the load test's scenarios are run in parallel. In many cases, a load test only has one scenario, but if you need finer control over how tests are run, you can break them into separate scenarios. For example, if you have two tests — TestA, which you want to run with a steady load of 100 users, and TestB, which you want to run starting with 10 users and increasing over time to 1,000 — you obviously would want to run them as separate scenarios. To do this, you would create two scenarios, one for each test with the appropriate user load settings in each scenario. During the load test run, each scenario will be run at the same time, so that at the start of the run you will have a total user count of 110 users (100 from TestA and 10 from TestB), while near the end of the run, you will have a total user count of 1,100 users (100 from TestA and 1,000 from TestB).

Because it is unlikely that all of your users will have the same browser and network connection and perform the exact same operations, each scenario has three components (called *mixes*) that determine what tests will be run during the load test and how they will be run. The mixes all allow you to configure the ratio of different types of users being simulated.

The Edit Mix Dialog Box

There are three mixes: test mixes, browser mixes, and network mixes. Each of the mixes uses the same basic UI (see Figure 7-3) that lists the item on the left, the percentage for that item, Distribution (which is a slider that graphically represents the percentage), and a Lock checkbox. Other than the type of things being mixed (tests, browsers, networks), the dialogs look and operate the same.

To open the Edit Test Mix dialog, simply right-click on the appropriate node (Test Mix, Network Mix, or Browser Mix), and select Edit Mix. The Edit Test Mix dialog will open (see Figure 7-3).

You can set the percentage by typing it into the "%" column, or by dragging the slider in the "Distribution" column. When you do this, the other columns will adjust to keep the percentage total at 100 percent. If the Lock column has been checked for an item, it will not adjust. The unlocked columns will increase/decrease at the same rate.

Hitting the Distribute button will evenly distribute the percentages across all of the items, regardless of the locked state (it changes the locked items as well).

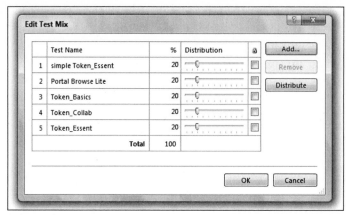

Figure 7-3

Mix Percentage

For all three mixes, the percentage setting determines the probability that a user will pick that setting or test when it starts a new test. In other words, whenever a user starts executing a new test, it randomly selects which test it will run (from the Test Mix), what type of browser (from the Browser Mix), and what type of network connection it should simulate (from the Network Mix). This random selection is based on the percentage set in the mix.

This means that at any particular moment during the load test, there is no guarantee that the actual load produced will exactly match the percentages set. This is a good thing as it better simulates what will happen in the real world. The more users in the load test, the more likely the current load will match the mix percentages.

Also, this allows you to have more tests than users if you want. For example, you could have a single user load test scenario that would pick one of four tests each time it started a new test. This could be useful if you have some operations (say administrative tasks) that do not happen very frequently, but you want to make sure that performing them does not affect normal user functionality or performance.

Test Mix

The Test Mix is the list of tests that are included in this scenario and the ratio of how frequently to run each one. The mix of the tests is set by the percentage. This lets you set one of the tests to be run more frequently than the others in this scenario.

For example, if you have four tests — *Browse, NewOrder, ChangeOrder*, and *CancelOrder* — you probably expect more browsing than canceling orders, thus you would want to set the mix to mimic your expected use. Setting Browse [50%], NewOrder [25%], ChangeOrder [15%], Cancel [10%] will give you that ratio of operations performed by the users.

When you click the Add button on the Edit Test Mix dialog, it opens the Add Tests dialog box, which lists all of the tests in the current test metadata file (.vsmdi) that can be included in a load test (see Figure 7-4). You can use any test lists that exist in the solution's test metadata file to help find the tests you want to include (see Chapter 2 for more on test metadata files).

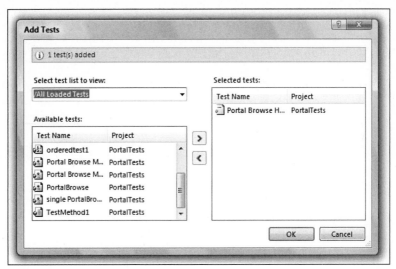

Figure 7-4

Browser Mix

The Browser Mix sets the different browser types to be simulated. This simulation is accomplished by changing the HTTP headers so that the server receives the request as if it were made by a browser of that type. It does not simulate anything on the client side, as there is no actual client-side execution or display.

There are several built-in browser types, but if you need to create a new type, you can do so if you know the header information that you need. The browser templates are stored in: `Program Files\ Microsoft Visual Studio 8\Common7\IDE\Templates\LoadTest\Browsers`. *There is a* `.browser` *file for each browser template. This file is a simple XML file. By copying one of these files and changing the values as appropriate, you can create your own browser templates.*

Network Mix

The Network Mix sets the different network bandwidth types to be simulated during the test. This setting does not actually change the network speed or latency. VSTEST merely adjusts the measured (real) response times based on the settings for a particular speed. In other words, it will tell you how long it would have taken to download that data on a connection of that speed. It does not affect how fast the data were actually downloaded from your server.

This is important to remember, because this can change the load characteristics of how you are affecting the server. Because the actual download is always at the speed of your actual network (and you will usually want this as fast as possible to allow simulating as many users as possible), the server is only spending that long processing the file download.

This could mean, for example, that during the load test the server only has to keep the file handle for a file download open for a second, but in real use if a large percentage of your users have slow connections, the server may have to keep that file handle open much longer, potentially causing deadlocks or running out of resources during higher user loads.

User Load Pattern

There is also a User Load Pattern item of a Scenario that controls how the user load is generated. This allows you to set the various aspects of the user load that this scenario will contribute to the load test.

There are three different patterns to which the User Load Pattern can be set, and each one has a different set of properties.

> *When you expand a scenario in the Load Test Editor, you will see an item named for the current pattern, for example,* Step Load Pattern. *You will not see a "User Load Pattern" item.*

Constant

Constant sets the user load to a constant value throughout the test. The number of users is set and does not change. There is only one property — Constant User Count, which is the number of users this scenario will simulate. This is useful for measuring if your application's performance varies over time with a constant load.

> *If you are considering using a Constant User Count pattern, you should read the boxed text in the following section.*

Step

The Step pattern starts the user load at an initial value and then increases it at intervals up to a maximum amount. This lets you see how your application's performance correlates to increasing user loads. Setting the maximum user count to a very high value (effectively, "keep increasing until the test ends"), you can increase the user load until something breaks (often called a *tip over test* because you are pushing the servers until something fails, or tips over).

The five settings that affect how a load test steps up over time are:

Setting	Description
Initial User Count	The number of users at the start of the test.
Maximum User Count	The point at which to stop increasing the number of users.
Step Duration	The number of seconds to keep the user load the same before increasing it again.
Step Ramp Time	The amount of time, in seconds, to spend increasing the user load. This allows tuning the increase to be more gradual or more abrupt.
Step User Count	The number of users to add during each step.

By setting the Step Duration, Step Ramp Time, and Step User Count appropriately, you can simulate various types of increases. For example, with a step duration of 5 minutes, a ramp time of 30 seconds, and a step user count of 10, you cause the load test to run with a set number of users for 5 minutes, then increase the number of users by 10 over the next 30 seconds.

> When starting a load test run with a very large number of users (or a large number of users per agent), even when you want a constant user load for your test, it is usually better to ramp up to that number rather than asking VSTEST to start all the users at once. For example, to start a run with a constant load of 10,000 users with 10 agents, it is better to set it up as an initial user count of 1,000 users, adding 1,000 users every 10 seconds (with the Maximum User Count set to the desired 10,000).
>
> You can also specify a "warm-up" period in the Run Setting (see below), and VSTEST will automatically increase the load gradually during the warm-up period to the user count.

Goal Based

Setting a Goal-Based user load pattern ties the user load to a performance counter value. The load test will increase or decrease the user load in order to keep that performance counter measurement within a certain range. This lets you run a test like "Run for 2 hours at 80 percent CPU utilization" by linking the user load to the "% Processor Time" performance counter on the server. This is great for finding out how many users your application can handle before hitting some limit on a resource.

Since the Add Scenario Wizard does not support the goal-based user load pattern, to create a scenario with this user load pattern, you need to pick either the Constant or Step pattern in the wizard, change its pattern in the properties, and then set the goal-based pattern settings in the properties window.

The goal-based user load pattern can be very useful but can also be very tricky to set properly to get what you want. If there are factors limiting your application performance other than the one on which you have based the goal, then the user count may keep increasing until the maximum value is reached, or things may start failing well before then.

The goal-based user load pattern has several properties that identify the performance counter to measure for the goal: Category, Computer, Counter, and Instance properties identify the performance counter measure for the goal and the computer on which to measure it.

The other properties for the goal-based user load are:

Property	Description
High End	The high end of the goal range; the user load will be adjusted to keep the specified performance counter below this.
Low End	The low end of the goal range; the user load will be adjusted to keep the specified performance counter above this.
Initial User Count	The starting value for the user load.

Continued

Property	Description
Lower Values Imply Higher Resource Utilization	Tells the load test whether increasing the user load will increase the measured value from the performance counter or decrease it. For most performance counters, a higher measured value means that the resource is being used more, but some counters (e.g., Available MBytes) decrease in value as the load increases. If this property is set to True, then the load test will increase the user load when it needs to decrease the measured performance value to meet the goal.
Maximum User Count	The maximum amount of user load. Even if the goal is not reached, the user load will not exceed this number.
Minimum User Count	The minimum amount of user load. Even if the goal is exceeded, the user load will not be reduced below this number.
Maximum User Count Increment	Sets the greatest amount by which the user load will be increased during a single adjustment.
Maximum User Count Decrement	Sets the greatest amount by which the user load will be reduced during a single adjustment.
Stop Adjusting User Count When Goal Achieved	If this is set to True, then once the goal is reached the user load will be fixed to that constant value for the remainder of the test duration.
	If this is False, then the load test will continue to adjust the user load to continue to keep the performance counter within the goal range.
	The default is False. If you want to see if your application "recovers" from a high load, you can set this to True to see if the resource utilization goes down after some period of time at the load that caused the initial peak value.

Having established the user load pattern, it's time now to explore the properties of a scenario.

Properties of a Scenario

In addition to the mixes and load pattern, each scenario also has a set of properties that control some general aspects of the scenario. These can be set from the Properties window.

The properties are:

❑ **IP Switching** — Determines if IP switching should be used for the tests in this scenario. IP switching allows the tests to use different IP addresses, simulating calls from different client computers. This must be configured and activated on the agents for this setting to have any effect. IP switching is discussed in greater detail later in the chapter; see the "The Agent Properties Dialog Box" section.

❑ **Name** — The name of the scenario.

❑ **Percentage of New Users** — Determines the ratio of cached requests to non-cached requests. The load test engine simulates the standard browser behavior of caching page data to reduce downloads on later visits. For web tests there can be a large difference in behavior between a first-time visit to the page and a second visit (where the browser would normally have cached content and would not download everything). This setting defaults to 100 percent, which means that all web tests will ignore caching and download all content. This should be set based on the ratio of first-time visitors to return visitors that you wish to simulate.

❑ **Think Profile** — This determines if the tests in this scenario should use the think times set in the web test (this is used only by web tests). This is a handy way to switch the think times on or off for a whole set of tests. There are three settings: On, Off, and Normal Distribution. Choosing Normal Distribution will use the think times set in the test as an average, varying the actual think time in each iteration from that average. This can create a more realistic simulation of users hitting a site.

❑ **Think Time between Test Iterations** — This sets the amount of delay between each test iteration, causing that "user" to pause after finishing one test before starting the next, which is especially useful for unit tests that have no other support for think times.

Now that you've established many of the details around how the load test should run, it's time to look at the type of data you want to gather during the execution of the test by looking at counter sets.

Counter Sets

Counter Sets allow you to group a set of performance counters so that you can manage them together. The main use for counter sets is to define a set of counters to collect from a computer operating in a certain "role." For example, you might have a counter set for Back End Database and one for Web Server because you want to monitor different counters on those different types of computers. But a set can also just be a collection of related counters that you want to manage as a unit.

Then in the Run Settings section, you define the mapping between the physical computer and the counter set (or role). If you have several computers operating in the same role, you can manage the counters that are monitored in one place. Computers can have multiple counter sets in case one computer is operating in multiple roles.

By default, all load tests include counter sets for the agent and controller. There are three default sets: LoadTest, Controller, and Agent. Both the Controller and LoadTest counter sets are assigned to the controller computer. The Controller and Agent counter sets are very useful in monitoring the health of the test rig during the run, while the LoadTest counter set includes all of the important test data like User Load, Transaction Time, and test error-related counters. All of these are pretty important, thus you should generally avoid modifying these. If you need to collect additional counters on the agents or controller you will need to add those counters to the built-in counter set (e.g., "Agent"), but you should only delete counters from one of these sets that you have added yourself.

> *VSTEST does not allow you to modify what counter sets the agents or controller collect. The controller always has just the Controller and Load Test counter sets, and the agents always have just the Agents counter set. And you cannot add these counter sets to other computers.*

There are also built-in counter sets that cover common categories of counters, for example, SQL, IIS, and Application. When you add a new computer to the Counter Set Mappings section of a Run Setting, you will see all of the built-in counter sets and any custom counter sets you have created.

Creating a Custom Counter Set

The pre-defined counter sets have been created for common tools and applications (SQL, IIS), and if you are using any of those tools, you will probably want to use these sets. But you will often want to include additional counters that are important for the application you are testing. Also, many applications, especially client server applications, will expose their own custom performance counters.

It is a good idea to create a custom counter set for each "role" in your application, even if those roles can be on the same computer. For example, for a simple customer ordering system with a Web front end, you might have the following counter sets: a Web Server set (or just use the built in IIS set) for the web server, a Customer DB set for the customer database server, and an Order DB set for the order database server. This lets you assign the counter sets to collect based on the roles the computer is performing. If all of these roles are on the same computer, then you add all of the counter sets to that computer. Later when you move to production, or scale up to a separate web server and SQL server, you would assign the Web Server set to one computer and the other two sets to the SQL Server.

Having role-based counter sets allows you to turn counter collection on and off based on what roles you wish to focus on for the current test run. Instead of having to figure out which specific counters are needed, just add or remove the role-based counter sets depending on what roles you want to focus the testing on.

To create your own custom counter set:

1. Right-click Counter Sets.
2. Choose Add Custom Counter Set.
3. A new counter set will appear in the list under Counter Sets.
4. Change the Name property to something appropriate.
5. Add the counters that should be included in this set.

To remove a counter set, simply right-click on it and choose Delete.

Adding a Counter to a Counter Set

In some cases you may wish to modify a counter set you or a teammate has previously created. It's pretty easy to add another counter into the existing set (and a fairly common practice until you get it dialed in just the way you like).

To add a counter to your custom counter set:

1. Right-click on the counter set to which you wish to add the performance counters.
2. Choose Add Counters.
3. The Pick Performance Counters dialog appears (see Figure 7-5).
4. Select the computer to scan for performance counters.

   This does not have to be the actual computer that will be used during testing, but it does need to have the same set of performance counters installed on it that you wish to add to the counter set.

5. Select the "Performance category" of counters (e.g., Active Server Pages).
6. The left pane will be populated with all of the available counters in that category, while the right pane will have all of the instances.

7. Either select all of the counters and instances you wish to include (it supports multi-select), or choose the "All counters" and/or "All instances" radio buttons above the lists.

Figure 7-5

After you close the Pick Performance Counters dialog, the counters and instances that you added should appear under the counter set to which you added them. If you expand the Counters node under the Counter Set, you will see all of the counters in that set (see Figure 7-6).

To remove a counter or an instance, simply right-click on it and choose Delete.

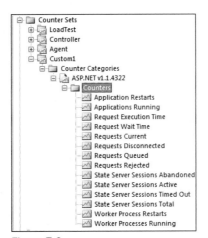

Figure 7-6

Whether you've created your own counter set or plan to use one provided for you, next you'll likely want to modify what levels a counter can reach before it starts to report an issue. This topic is covered next.

Setting a Threshold Rule for a Counter

During a load test run, especially a long duration test run, it can be very useful to raise a warning when a performance counter exceeds some value. For example, raising a warning if the SQL server's CPU utilization ever goes above 80 percent allows you to easily see where you have potential stress issues on your SQL server. You set threshold rules for each counter individually, and each threshold rule has a "warning" and a "critical" level of alert.

> **Any defined threshold rules are applied to all instances of the counter that are in the counter set.**

There are two types of thresholds:

❑ **Compare Constant** — which compares the performance counter measurement with a set value.

❑ **Compare Counters** — which compares the performance counter measurement to another performance counter, on the same computer or a different one. This lets you raise a warning when the counter value is over/under some other counter. For example, if your SQL server's CPU is ever higher than the web server's CPU, raise an alert.

To add a threshold rule, follow these steps:

1. Right-click on the counter to which you wish to add the threshold rule.

2. Choose Add Threshold Rule.

3. The Add Threshold Rule dialog appears (see Figure 7-7).

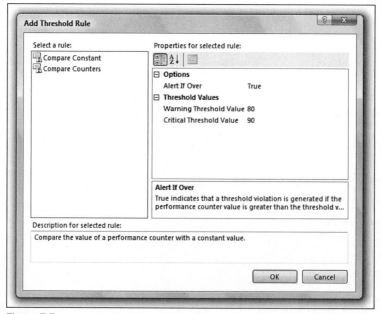

Figure 7-7

4. Set the "Properties for selected rule" for the warning you want:

❑ **Alert If Over** — True causes an alert to be raised if the value of the counter ever goes above the threshold value. False causes the alert to be raised if the value ever falls below the threshold value.

> The default value for Alert If Over is False, which is not what you want for most of the common performance counters like CPU utilization.

❑ **Warning/Critical Threshold Values** — These are the values that determine the levels for raising a warning alert or a critical alert during a load test. They work slightly differently for the two different types of rules.

For Compare Constant–type rules, this is a simple threshold — if it is over (or under, depending on the Alert If Over property) this value, then an alert is raised.

For Compare Counters, the threshold values are used as a ratio for comparison between the dependent counter and the counter to which the rule is applied. For example, if the Warning Threshold Value is set to 0.8, then a warning alert will be raised if the counter ever goes above (DependentCounter * 0.8), that is, if (Counter >= (DependentCounter * 0.8)) is ever true. If the value is set to one, then it is a straight (or equal) comparison; in other words, the alert is raised if the value is greater than the Dependent Counter.

Your counters are now in place, and you've modified the thresholds to alert you to issues as they arise. Next you'll look at what you can control for the overall execution of the load test by looking at a Run Setting.

Run Settings

Run settings allow you to group a variety of settings that determine a test run. A run setting controls overall test run properties like the duration of the run, how often to sample the performance counters, and so forth.

> A load test can have multiple run settings, but only one is active at any time.

Run settings provide an easy way to re-target the load test to different test environments and also allow the same load test to be re-used for different variations of the same test. Each run setting defines the mapping of counter sets to actual computers, thus if you have multiple test environments, you can create a run setting for each environment and set the correct counter set mappings for each environment separately. Also, you can have one run setting that defines a short test run that collects a large amount of data including SQL traces and so forth and another run setting that runs the same tests but over a much longer duration and scales back the amount of data collected.

Counter Set Mappings

If you click the Manage Counter Sets button on the Load Test Editor tool bar, the Manage Counter Sets dialog appears, where you can manage the mappings of physical computers to the counter sets that should be collected from them (see Figure 7-8).

1. From the dropdown at the top, choose the run setting that has the computers you wish to edit.

2. Use the Add Computer button to add a new computer to the list, if needed.

3. For each computer, check the counter sets that should be collected from it during a run.

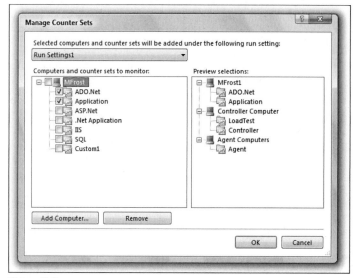

Figure 7-8

The computers do not need to exist or be accessible when managing counter set mappings; they only need to be accessible during the test run.

Context Parameters

In addition to the counter set mappings, a run setting can also define context parameters. These context parameters set (and override if they are set in the web test) the context parameters of the individual tests. This is very useful if you have parameterized the web servers in your web tests, as you can set the web server context parameters in the run setting, allowing you to re-target all of the tests in the load test by simply changing the active run setting.

To add a context parameter to a run setting, just right-click on the run setting, and choose "Add context parameter." A *context parameter* is a simple Name/Value pair — to set the Name and Value, simply select the context parameter, and set the properties appropriately.

Run Setting Properties

Last, but as you'll see, certainly not least, are the Run Setting properties. This fairly extensive list of values offers even more flexibility in how the test is executed. These properties control a wide range of settings from the amount of data collected and how often, to how the user pool is managed.

The Run Setting properties are

❑ **Description** — A description of this run setting, useful as documentation for what this run setting is intended for.

❑ **Maximum Error Details** — The maximum number of error details (for failed requests or tests) that is stored during the run. Error details can take up a large amount of space in the Results Store.

❑ **Name** — The name of the run setting. This is what appears in the Load Test Editor tree.

❑ **Validation Level** — Sets the highest level of validation rule that will be executed for web tests during the load test. (See Chapter 5, "Web Tests," for more detail on validation rules.) Only validation rules with a level equal to this or lower will be executed. For example, if the Run Setting Validation level is set to Low, then only the validation rules with a level of "low" will be executed.

❑ **Storage Type** — Sets how to store the Results data. The choices are None (don't store data) and Database, which stores the data in a Results Store.

❑ **Timing Details Storage** — Setting that determines the level of detailed Result data that is stored. The timing detail data include timing details for each individual test/transaction/page in the load test: the time to execute each individual test, transaction times, and so forth. This can create a large amount of data (and increases the time required at the end of the run to store the data into the repository). But if you need to dig into deep details or wish to perform detailed analysis on the data in the SQL database, this is useful.

    ❑ **None** — The default. Does not collect or store any of the detailed timing data.

    ❑ **StatisticsOnly** — This collects the timing data during the run and then processes it to generate the overall statistics. But the detailed data are not stored, only the generated statistics.

    ❑ **AllIndividualDetails** — Collects the timing data during the run and then processes it to generate the overall statistics. All of the detailed data are then kept in the Results Store.

    The next few properties are related to collecting SQL trace data, which is covered in more detail below in this chapter.

❑ **Minimum Duration of Traced SQL Operations** — This sets the minimum length of time (in milliseconds) a SQL operation must take before it is recorded; any SQL operations that take less than this time will be ignored and not appear in the SQL trace log. This lets you tune what appears in the SQL trace log to longer-running (i.e., slow) operations.

❑ **SQL Tracing Connect String** — This is the connection string used to connect to the database being traced.

❑ **SQL Tracing Directory** — This is the location, usually a fileshare on the SQL Server being traced, where the SQL trace logs are placed. The account that the SQL Server being traced is running as must have write permissions at this location, and the account that the controller is running as must have read permissions.

❑ **SQL Tracing Enabled** — Turn SQL tracing on (True) or off (False).

❑ **Run Duration** — The duration of the load test run (in hh:mm:ss format). When this time is reached, tests are shut down, and then all of the test run data are collected and stored in the Results Store.

❑ **Sample Rate** — This is the interval for capturing performance counters. A shorter interval gathers more detailed and accurate data, but creates substantially more Result data. A longer interval creates less data but risks missing events (if the CPU spikes for 10 seconds, you could miss it with a 30-second interval). The default of 5 seconds is generally good for shorter runs (a few hours), but for longer runs, this value should be increased. Also, if there is a large number of computers being monitored, it may be necessary to increase the sample rate because of the amount of data collected and the time required to collect a sample.

❑ **Warm-up Duration** — This sets a length of time at the beginning of the load test run where data are not collected. Also, the user count is gradually increased during the warm-up period to avoid flooding the application as it is starting up. For many applications the initial start-up period has very different performance characteristics from a normal running state (the application may be loading files into a cache, pre-compiling files, loading settings, etc). In most real world operations, this occurs rarely enough that it is unimportant for testing and can create noise in the test results, especially on shorter runs. By doing a simple load test run with a steady user state, you can get a good idea of how long it takes your application to reach a steady state.

> Data collected during the warm-up duration will be displayed in the Load Test Analyzer while the test is running so that you can see the activity, but those data are not saved.

❑ **WebTest Connection Model** — This setting controls how the web tests use the connections on the agent. This can be very important when performing a load test run with a large number of users per agent. There are two connection models:

❑ **ConnectionPerUser** — Most accurately simulates a user with a real browser. Each user in the load test creates one (or sometimes more) connection dedicated to that user at the start of each web test (adding more during the web test if needed). The connections are only re-used during that web test and are closed at the end of the web test. This can result in a large number of connections open on the agent computer (usually up to twice the number of users being simulated on the agent computer). This adds processing time to the web test to open and close the connections and increases the amount of resources required per user.

❑ **ConnectionPool** — This is a less realistic simulation of the "real world" but conserves resources on the agent computer, allowing more users/agent and therefore a higher load. With this setting, there is a set number of connections on the agent (the WebTest Connection Pool Size), and all of the virtual users share these connections. This reduces the amount of resources required per user and avoids having to open/close the connections before and after every test iteration. But there is a danger of this setting causing your tests to run slower if the connection pool is not large enough. Because all of the users on the agent are sharing the connections in the pool, if the pool is too small, then some users will have to wait for a connection to be freed up; this can reduce the load being generated.

❑ **WebTest Connection Pool Size** — This is the maximum number of connections to keep open on an agent when using the ConnectionPool model. Increasing this value reduces the contention for connections between the users on the agent but increases the resources consumed by the connections.

> When using the ConnectionPool model, it is important to monitor the "Avg. Connection Wait Time" load test performance counter on each of the agent computers. This value is the average amount of time that a user is waiting for a connection to be freed up and represents the delay to your tests that the ConnectionPool model is creating. It should be as low as possible. Increasing the WebTest Connection Pool Size will reduce the wait time.

It is usually best to start with the ConnectionPerUser model and only switch to the ConnectionPool model if you are hitting resource limitations on your agents that are preventing you from increasing the user load to where you need it.

SQL Tracing

The SQL tracing features built into a load test allow you to easily gather tracing details from a SQL server that is part of your application. This can be very useful for identifying the SQL bottlenecks in your application. The integrated SQL tracing in a load test is not as detailed as using SQL Profiler, but having the data integrated into the test allows easy correlation of the data. Even if you need to fall back to using SQL Profiler to examine the SQL operations in more detail, the integrated SQL tracing can identify the main performance bottlenecks and long duration operations occurring during a load test, helping to pinpoint the best places to examine in detail with SQL Profiler. And often the SQL trace data from the load test are enough to uncover and fix the SQL bottleneck.

Requirements for SQL tracing include the following:

❑ The account that the controller is running as must have permissions in the SQL database to perform SQL tracing.

❑ Both the account that the SQL server being traced is running under and the Controller's account need access to a location to store the trace log files. The SQL server account must have write access, but the controller account only needs read access.

❑ Set the SQL Tracing Run Settings properties appropriately. (See "Run Setting Properties" above in this chapter.)

SQL Tracing Specific Run Settings

As was mentioned above in the "Run Setting Properties" section, a run setting has some properties that directly affect how SQL tracing occurs during the test run. Using these properties, you control how, when, and where SQL tracing collection occurs during the test run.

Using the "Minimum Duration of Traced SQL Operations" Run Setting property, you can specify how long a SQL operation has to take before it is recorded in the trace log. This lets you filter out the quicker operations and focus on the longer-running SQL operations. It is usually best to start this off with a larger value (e.g., 1 to 5 minutes) during your early testing to surface the really slow operations and then reduce this as they are taken care of.

The SQL Tracing Connect String is the connection string used to specify what server and database the tracing will be done on. Currently VSTEST only allows tracing one SQL database during a test run. If you have more than one database in your system, then you can create multiple run settings for each database you will wish to trace. This does not allow tracing multiple databases during the same run but does make it easier to trace one and then start another run to collect traces from the other.

The SQL trace logs are stored in a directory, set using the SQL Tracing Directory run setting. It is necessary that the SQL server account can write to this location and that the controller can read from it.

The other run setting that affects SQL tracing is the SQL Tracing Enabled setting. This simply turns SQL tracing on and off. With this property set to False, no SQL tracing is done during the test run.

Viewing SQL Trace Data

Once the test run is complete, as part of viewing the results of the test run, you can see the trace logs. This lets you view the SQL activity that was occurring during a specific slice of time or to look for SQL operations that are taking a long time.

When you view the SQL trace data in the load test results, you can see:

❑ **TextData** — This is the text of the SQL operation being executed, for example, `EXECUTE myStoreDB.sp_SubmitOrder`.

❑ **Duration** — How long this operation took (in milliseconds when tracing a SQL Server 2000 instance and in microseconds when tracing a SQL Server 2005 instance).

❑ **StartTime** — The time the operation started executed, useful for comparing to the other performance counters to see what else was happening around this time.

❑ **EndTime** — The time the operation completed.

❑ **Reads** — The number of reads that were performed on the server for this operation.

❑ **Writes** — The number of writes that were performed on the server for this operation.

❑ **CPU** — The CPU time (in milliseconds) used to execute the operation.

❑ **EventClass** — An integer that identifies the SQL type ID of the event class for the operation. This corresponds to a class (or type) of SQL event such as `SQL:BatchStarting`. For more details, see the SQL server documentation and the SQL Server Profiler documentation.

These data can be used to identify activity that was occurring during a specific time (using the StartTime and EndTime columns) and also to find operations that are taking a long time to perform. For example, if your load test shows a performance problem occurring at a certain time (e.g., response time becomes unacceptably slow), you can look at the SQL trace data of operations occurring at that time to see exactly what operations the database is executing. It is also a good idea to simply sort the list of operations and examine those that are taking the most time and/or CPU to complete.

It is also a good idea to examine any SQL operation where one of these data points is unusually high compared to other SQL operations. Anything with a high number of Writes may be a problem. A large difference between the duration and the CPU time shows that the operation spent a great deal of time waiting (blocked by SQL locks, CPU contention, etc.) and can signal a bottleneck.

It is important to remember that you are not seeing all of the SQL activity. Depending on what you have set "Minimum Duration of Traced SQL Operations" to, there may be some operations that are occurring too quickly to show up in the trace. Usually this is OK and you want to filter them out, but it is possible for a million quick operations to overload the server, causing a single operation to take longer. In that case, that single operation will appear in the trace, but it's just the symptom, not the cause.

As you can see by this list, the SQL Tracing features gather extremely helpful details that help identify the SQL bottlenecks in your application.

Using a Test Rig

> In order to set up a test rig with multiple computers, you need the Visual Studio 2005 Team Test Load Agent product in addition to VSTEST.

A *test rig* is the set of computers used to run the tests. It consists of a controller and one or more agents. You can run all of these on a single computer, but there are serious limitations to using a single computer for your test rig. Having the controller and agents all on the same computer will limit the amount of user load you can simulate because of the resources being taken up by the different components.

However, the single computer "test rig" can be very useful for testing your tests, making sure that the load test you have set up works, and identifying and fixing any problems your test might have. Once you know that the load test is set up and working the way you want in the single-computer scenario, you can move it to the test rig.

But in most cases, you will want to have a set of computers for use as a test rig. Usually this is a single controller with several agent computers. I have not seen any real problems with having the Results Store database and the controller on the same computer that you are using to manage the runs.

Determining Hardware Requirements

One of the first difficulties you will face when starting to do load testing is deciding what kind of test hardware you will need to use for your load testing rig. This is an issue both for the application hardware (where the application being tested will run) and for the test rig hardware. For the application hardware, you should try to be as close to your production hardware as possible (see the section "Best Practices" below in this chapter). But it can be tricky deciding what your hardware needs are for the test rig.

Estimating the hardware needed for your test rig can be difficult. MSDN lists some recommendations for a test rig based on the number of users you need per agent. However, there is such a huge variation depending on what your tests are like (unit tests vs. web tests, how long average test execution time is, etc.) that these recommendations are really only useful in the most broad and general sense. For example, we have some load test runs that max out the agent CPU at just a few hundred users (processor-intensive unit tests with no think time between tests), but on the same agent computer, we can run 1,500 web tests (with think times during and between the tests).

The think time setting in your tests has a huge impact on what your agent hardware supports. This makes sense because "think time" is essentially just a pause during test execution or between tests. More pauses result in less resource usage so that you can have a higher overall user load. But keep in mind that greater think times reduce the "load pressure" you are putting on the application. Therefore, be careful to set the think times so that they reflect your best estimate of how customers will use the application.

The Best Way to Determine Hardware Needs

Remember that you are stress-testing the entire system, and that this includes the test rig that you have set up. It is easy to max out what your test system can handle, and if you are not paying attention, you may think that you are testing at a higher level than you actually are.

> **You should always monitor the controller and the agent computers during a test run to make sure that you are not hitting any limitations in your test rig.**

By default, the counter sets created in VSTEST include sets for the controller and the agents. It's a good idea to get in the habit of monitoring these performance counters during and after a load test run, to make sure that you are not maxing out any of the major counters on any of your test computers. You can monitor this in the Load Test Analyzer window during and after the test run by adding the appropriate performance counters (CPU%, available memory, etc.) for the agents to the graph. You should also make sure to set thresholds for the various counters on the test rig computers so that you will be warned if the limits are ever exceeded. Again, VSTEST has the defaults correct on this for the most part, but you may need to fine-tune them a bit for your exact scenario. Any threshold violations will be flagged in the Load Test Analyzer window so that you can find them even if you have not added them to the graph. If any of these test rig thresholds are exceeded, then you should probably question the validity of the test run, if not of the whole run then at least of the data in the time around the threshold being exceeded.

Limiting Factors

In general, the obvious applies to determining what hardware you need. The higher the performance of each part of the system is, the better things will run. The better the agent hardware is, the more users you can simulate on a single agent. The better the controller hardware is, the less missed performance counter collections you will have. Also CPU and memory are the main limiting factors for both the agent and the controller. Be aware that the network bandwidth on the agent can be a limiting factor in some cases. For example, if the requests or responses are large and there is a large enough user load, you can max out the agent's network connection.

Agents

The exact needs for your agent computers can vary quite a bit, depending on exactly what kinds of tests you are performing. For example, if you have web tests that are requesting large pages (or other chunks of data), then the network throughput may be a bigger factor than the CPU.

In many cases, what happens when an agent computer is overloaded in some aspect is that it doesn't appear to provide the load that you want or expect. The number of users may say 200, but if the network throughput is overloaded and it is taking longer to get the response data from the system under test, then you will see the requests stacking up. This can look just as if your application is performing slowly.

By default, a load test includes counters that monitor the agent's "health" during the test run. It is always a good idea to check these values to make sure that the test is running correctly. If any of the agents has more than 80 percent CPU utilization, then it is overloaded and you need more agents to provide the load you want. You should also make sure that the agent's memory stays above 10 percent available.

> **If any of the agents were overloaded during the test run, then the Result data are suspect and should be used with caution, especially data collected during the times when the agents were overloaded.**

> In general, an agent with 2–3 GHz of CPU speed (single processor) and 1–2 GB of memory should be able to handle several hundred users.

Multi-Processor Agent Computers

Another thing that can limit the agent's ability to generate load is the speed at which it runs a test and cleans up afterward. This means that the garbage collection process on the computer can be a crucial factor in how much load the agent can generate. The standard .NET garbage collector is optimized for "normal" operation, where the computer has some idle time, thus it tends to avoid interrupting current work, opting to wait until the system is idling to do its cleanup. But when you are doing a load test, you are usually running the agent computer at near its maximum capacity for long periods of time. This can cause the garbage collector not to run for long periods, which results in memory filling up on the agent and other issues (sudden slowdowns when the garbage collection finally does run). The Server Garbage Collector is designed for multi-processor servers that might not have any idle time.

If your agent computers (or the single computer used to run load tests if you do not have a test rig) are multi-processor, you should configure them to use Server Garbage Collection. This is a much more efficient garbage collector designed for use with multi-processor systems and can have a huge effect on how many users the agent will support.

> If you are using multi-processor computers for your load testing agents and are not able to generate the user load you expect, you should enable Server Garbage Collection.

Setting your system to use the Server Garbage Collector is slightly different for agents in a test rig (i.e., the computer is just an agent or is just an agent and controller) and when there is no test rig (the single computer with just VSTEST installed). The only difference is which .config file needs to be edited — the setting change is the same. Note that for agents in a test rig, you should make this change on every agent that has multiple-processors.

To configure a single computer test rig for Server Garbage Collection, follow these steps:

1. Edit the `<Program Files>\Microsoft Visual Studio 8\Common7\IDE\VSTestHost.exe.config` file. (This is in the location where VSTEST is installed on the computer.)

2. In the `<runtime>` section of the config file, add the following line:

```
<gcServer enabled="true" />
```

To configure an agent in a test rig for Server Garbage Collection, follow these steps:

1. Edit the `<Program Files>\Microsoft Visual Studio 2005 Team Test Load Agent\LoadTest\QTAgent.exe.config` file. (This is in the location where the Visual Studio Team Test Load Agent is installed on the computer.)

2. In the `<runtime>` section of the config file, add the following line:

```
<gcServer enabled="true" />
```

Controller

The controller is usually not the limiting factor, but does need more resources, especially hard drive space, as the user load increases. Also as you increase the number of performance counters being collected, the controller will need more hard drive space and, to a much lesser degree, processor and memory.

Results Store

Since the Results Store is just a standard SQL server database, for the most part the hardware requirements are just the standard SQL server requirements. In fact, while it is always better to have the Results Store on a separate computer, I have seen the Results Store run on the controller computer just fine. But if you have a large number of agent computers, or if you are going to have multiple controllers (for simultaneous test runs), then you should have a separate Results Store. See the "Results Store" section below in this chapter for how to create a new Results Store.

> If you are using SQL Express (the default from a Visual Studio install), then you will be limited to 4 GB of storage, which can severely limit your ability to perform longer stress runs (this depends on how much data you collect in a run and how long you keep results around).

Setting Up the Test Rig

Before you can run a load test across multiple agent computers, the test rig needs to be set up and configured. The computer designated to act as the controller needs to have the VSTEST Controller software installed on it; then the Agent service needs to be installed on each of the agent computers.

> During the setup of an agent computer, you need to specify the controller that will be managing the agent computer. The Agent setup program then sets up the link between the computers. Therefore, the controller needs to be set up first and running and accessible from the agent during the Agent install.

Security

Before starting to install the controller and agents of your test rig, you need to create the following accounts (the setup program will ask you for them during install):

- ❑ **Controller Service Account** — This is the account that the controller service runs as. It must have access to read performance counters (member of the Performance Monitor Users group) from all of the computers being tested (the application computers) and from all of the agent computers. If the test rig is set up in a workgroup, then every computer needs to have the same local account (same username/password) created on it.

- ❑ **Agent Service Account** — This is the account that the Agent service runs as on the agent. This account does not need to be the same for every agent computer (but it is easier to manage that way). By default, this is the account that the tests run as on the agent computer. If you are using IP switching, the Agent service account must have administrator privileges.

> All computers that you wish to collect performance counter data from need to have the Remote Registry service running. On non-Windows Vista OS's, this service is set to start automatically. On Windows Vista, this service is not set to start automatically and will need to be set to start automatically (or start it manually before a load test run).

Controller

One question about your setup is, will you want to run Visual Studio on the controller for managing a test and viewing results? You can install just the Controller software on the computer and use another computer (with the full VSTEST installed) to manage the run and view results.

The Controller installation creates three local user groups on the controller computer. The Agent service group is handled automatically by the Agent setup program. The other two groups allow you to control who can administer and operate the test rig.

- ❑ **Team Test Controller Admins** — This group governs who has permission to administer the test rig.

- ❑ **Team Test Controller Users** — This group governs who has permission to run tests using the test rig.

- ❑ **Team Test Agent Service** — This group includes all of the Agent Service Accounts and is automatically added to during the Agent setup.

Agents

Each agent is set up for a specific controller, and if you need to re-target an agent to a different controller, you will need to either re-install the Team Test Load Agent software or run the `agentconfigutil.exe` (a command-line utility for re-targeting the agent, installed with the agent on the agent computer).

To use the command-line tool to connect an agent to a different controller, use the following command line:

```
AgentConfigUtil /controller:NewController:6901 /agentserviceusername:AgentUser
```

where *NewController* is the name of the controller that you want to own this agent, 6901 is the port (6901 is the default port used by the VSTEST Load Controller), and AgentUser is the account that the Agent service on this computer runs as (which needs to be added to the Team Test Agent Service user group on the controller).

Managing the Test Rig

Once the test rig is set up, there are a variety of administrative tasks that will need to be taken care of before you start a load test run. The administration controls in VSTEST let you take care of most of these without have to log into the agent computers, allowing you to perform tasks like restarting the Agent service on all of the computers in the test rig with one click.

The Administer Test Controller Dialog Box

All of the Test Rig administration work is handled through the Administer Test Controller dialog box (see Figure 7-9). The Administer Test Controller dialog box is opened by selecting Test menu ⇨ Administer Test Controllers. Because each test rig has a single controller, the test rig is specified by the controller.

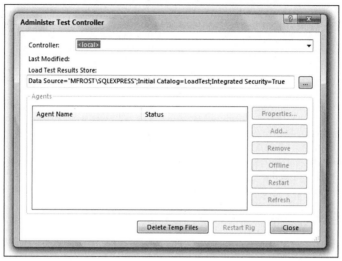

Figure 7-9

Following are some of the more important buttons and fields of the Administer Test Controller dialog box:

❏ **Controller** — This dropdown lists the available controllers; if the controller you want to manage is not listed you can just type in the computer name of the controller

❏ **Load Test Results Store** — This is the connection string for the Results Store and determines where all of the results generated through this controller are stored. By default, this points to the SQL Express instance on the controller that was created during the controller install. If you have created a new Results Store, this should be changed to point to your new Results Store.

❏ **Delete Temp Files** — This cleans all of the deployment files off all of the agents and the controller (cannot be used if a test run is in progress).

❏ **Restart Rig** — This restarts the load test services on all of the agents and on the controller. If a test run is in progress, this will halt the run (you are asked to confirm the re-start in this case).

The Agents section of the Administer Test Controller dialog lists all of the agents owned by the selected controller. The Agent list also displays the current status of each agent:

Agent Status	Description
Ready	Agent service is running and the agent is connected to the controller, but no tests are running.
Running Test	The agent is currently involved in a test run.
Offline	The agent has been taken offline so that it will not participate in any test runs. You can take an agent offline to remove it from test runs or if there are issues with the computer.
Disconnected	The agent is not connected to the controller.

The buttons in the Agents section let you manage the various aspects of the agents:

- ❑ **Properties** — Brings up the Agent Properties dialog (see below) for the selected specific properties for the agent.

- ❑ **Add** — Adds a new agent computer. This brings up a blank Agent Properties dialog. In most cases, you do not need to use this since usually the agent registers itself with the controller during setup.

- ❑ **Remove** — Deletes the Agent entry from this controller.

- ❑ **Offline/Online** — Sets the status of the selected agent to Offline (or back to Online if it is currently offline).

- ❑ **Restart** — Stops and then starts the Agent service for the selected agent. Will abort any tests currently running on the agent.

- ❑ **Refresh** — Re-scans each Agent to update its status.

In normal use you will not need to use this dialog very frequently for anything more than checking the status of the rig before starting a load test.

The Agent Properties Dialog Box

The Agent Properties dialog lets you set the various properties for an agent. There are three main properties of an agent, and they each manage features that enable a great deal of control and flexibility in your test rig. There are three main properties that are configurable on an agent: *weighting*, which controls how the user load is distributed across agents; *IP switching*, which allows the agent to simulate multiple IP addresses during the test run; and *attributes*, which allows tagging an agent with a custom value.

Weighting

Unless all of your agent computers are exactly the same hardware (which you should try for, but which is often difficult to achieve), it is unlikely that each agent in the rig can support the same user load. An agent's "weighting" determines how to distribute tests across the agents. This number (which defaults to 100) is relative to the other agents in the test rig. If all of the agents have a weighting of 100, then the user load will be distributed evenly.

For example, if you have three different types of agents, you might set the weighting of the low-end agents to 50, the medium agents to 100, and the high-end agents to 200. With these weightings, during a test run the tests will be distributed in a 1:2:4 ratio.

While the Weighting feature supports picking any integer, you could have your agents set to 59, 73, 97, 113, and so forth. This is really not that useful as it's hard to understand the weighting and it does not really affect the actual load distribution. I would recommend picking a few categories for the different types of agent hardware in your test rig (e.g., Low, Medium, High) and picking easy numbers to match the distribution you want (Low = 66, Medium = 100, High = 150). Also, because 100 is the default, it should be used for whatever is the most common agent configuration.

IP Switching

IP switching allows the tests to use different IP addresses, simulating calls from different client computers. This is often important if your application bases its behavior on the IP address of the incoming request. For example, since many systems perform load balancing based on the incoming IP address, if all of the requests from an agent come from the same IP address, you will not properly test the load balancing.

> The load test's scenario turns this feature on or off for the tests in the scenario, and if enabled, then the test will use an IP address based on the IP switching settings for the agent the test is running on.

This sets the parameters for IP switching for this agent:

❑ **NIC** — Selects the agent computer's network card (if there is more than one) to which the IP addresses should be added during the load test. After the test run these addresses are removed from the network card.

❑ **Base Address** — This sets the base (unchanging) part of the IP address.

❑ **Start/End Range** — These set the range of IP addresses the IP switching should cycle through.

For example, if you want this agent to use IP addresses in the 192.68.1.0–192.68.1.155 range, then you would set the Base Address = 192.68.1, the Start Range = 0, and the End Range = 155.

> Make sure that each agent in the test rig has a unique range of addresses that does not overlap with any of the other agents.

> For IP switching to work, the Agent service account (the user account that the Agent service runs as on the agent computer) must have administrator privileges so that it can configure the network card.

> It is a good idea to verify that the IP switching is working properly by looking at the IIS (or similar) logs on your application to make sure it is seeing a variety of IP addresses.

Attributes

An agent can be tagged with one or more attributes. Each attribute is a simple Name/Value property. This simple feature allows a couple of very useful operations. The main use for this is that in the Test Run Config file, when you select the test rig that the load test will run on, you can also specify properties that an agent is required to have to be used in the test run. This allows a fine-grained control over which agents are used in the test run.

One use for this feature is to filter out agents with or without a necessary configuration. For example, if you want to perform a load test run using only the agents with Windows Vista installed, and if each agent in the test rig has an OS attribute, then by setting OS = Vista in the Test Run Config file, the load test would only use those agents.

Another use is to allow executing more than one test run at the same time on a single test rig. By starting one test run using agents with Group == A and another test run using agents with Group == B, you can run both test runs at the same time. The controller is doing the same amount of work as if it were managing a single run using all of the agents and collecting performance counter data from all of the computers under test in both runs.

Results Store

Load test runs can collect huge amounts of data, even during short runs. To store all of these data, each controller is configured to use a Results Store. All of the data collected during a load test is stored in the Results Store database. More than one load test run's data can be stored in the same Results Store. Also, more than one controller can use the same Results Store to store its load test data, which is very useful if you have more than one test rig and want to have all of your load testing data in one place.

The Results Store is a SQL Server–based database. By default, a Results Store using a SQL Express instance is created on the Controller during the Controller install. So by default, every controller stores the data for load tests that it executes in a local Results Store.

> **SQL Express has a 4-GB size limit that can be pretty easy to hit after only a few test runs if you are doing load testing of any reasonable size or duration.**

If you run out of space in the Results store during a load test run, your test will abort and much of the data may be lost. This can be very frustrating if this happens near the end of a long test run.

Running the Results Store locally (on the controller) also uses up resources (CPU, memory, drive space) on the controller, which can interfere with your ability to generate load. Also, if you are setting up multiple test rigs (and therefore multiple controllers), it is much easier to have all of your results stored in a central Results Store instead of spread out on each controller.

Because of these reasons, if you are planning on doing any large-scale testing (long duration, many agents, or more than one controller), it is a good idea to move your Results Store to a separate system with a full install of SQL Server. This will free up resources on the controller, avoid results storage limits, and allow you to store all of the data from multiple controllers in one place.

Creating a Results Store in an Existing SQL Server

To create a new Results Store on an existing SQL Server, you just need to run the SQL script provided by VSTEST. Note that this creates a database on the server named *LoadTest* and does not support multiple Results Stores on the same SQL server instance. If you are setting up your Results Store on a full SQL Server, it is unlikely that you will need to create a second Results Store. You can store Results from multiple controllers and load test runs in the same Results Store.

> **Unless you are only going to be performing small-scale runs with a single controller, it is a good idea to set up a new, larger Results Store.**

To create a new Results Store database, do the following:

1. The script (`loadtestresultsrepository.sql`) is located at: `\Program Files\ Microsoft Visual Studio 8\Common7\IDE`. (This is your VSTEST install location.)

2. From the Visual Studio command prompt, execute the following command line:

```
SQLCMD /S ServerName -U <UserName> -P <Password> -i loadtestresultsrepository.sql
```

where UserName/Password is the info for an account that has permissions to run scripts (and create databases) on the ServerName SQL server. If the account you are currently running as has these permissions, you can leave out those parameters. Since the option flags (the /S, -U, -P, -i) are case-sensitive, make sure you type them as they are shown here.

After this is done, you can set the Load Test Results Store property of your test rigs to connect to the new Results Store, and they will store load test results in the new Results Store.

Results Store Database Schema

The Results Store has a somewhat complicated schema but not so much that it's hard to access directly for more detailed reporting using SQL (or other tools). Here we are only going to provide a brief overview of the schema and not get into details about each column. For more detailed information, see Bill Barnett's excellent MSDN blog article at http://blogs.msdn.com/billbar/articles/529874.aspx, where he describes each column.

Table	Description
LoadTestRun	Summary information for each load test run. One record for each load test.
LoadTestCase	Stores the data describing each individual test included in the load test, also links the test case to the scenario it is in.
LoadTestScenario	The load test scenario data.
LoadTestRunAgent	Name of the agent computer used in the load test.
LoadTestTestDetail	Stores the timing details for each individual test iteration. There is a row for each completed test in the test run.
LoadTestTestSummaryData	Summarizes the data in **LoadTestTestDetail** for each test defined in the load test. Includes the total number of tests executed, average execution time, and so forth.
LoadTestPageDetail	Stores the timing details for each individual web test page request. There is a row for each web test request completed in the test run.
LoadTestPageSummaryData	Summarizes the data in **LoadTestPageDetail** for each unique page requested during the load test. Includes the total number of times the page was requested, average load time, and so forth.
LoadTestMessage	The data for each Error that occurred during the test run.
LoadTestThresholdMessage	The data for each threshold violation that occurred during the test run.
WebLoadTestErrorDetail	The detailed error information for each web test error.
WebLoadTestRequestMap	Describes the unique URIs used by the web tests in the load test.
WebLoadTestTransaction	The names for all of the transactions defined in the tests that are in the load test. Despite the name, this includes transactions in unit tests.

Continued

Table	Description
LoadTestPerformanceCounter	Describes a performance counter that was colle during the run, one record for each performance counter/computer.
LoadTestPerformanceCounterSample	Where the collected counter data are stored.
LoadTestRunInterval	A performance counter collection interval. All of the **LoadTestPerformanceCounterSample** records with the same **LoadTestRunIntervalID** were collected at the same time.

This only covers some of the tables in the load test Results Store, but as you can see, there is a large amount of detail being collected during a load test. This amount of data can easily be overwhelming, especially if you are new to load testing, if you do not follow some simple "best practices."

Best Practices

Stress and performance–related testing is a new type of testing for many people, and it is very different from standard functional testing. In many ways, it is more of an art than "normal" functional testing is. There is often no clear "Failure" during a load test. If the response time for a particular web request drops from 1 second to 2 seconds when the load increases from 1,000 users to 10,000 users, is that bad? Maybe, maybe not. At its basic level, load testing will provide you with data (often too much data) to help you make the decision.

Frequently I see a product team starting to do load testing and falling into several traps and not ending up with actionable data and/or not knowing what to do with their testing results. There are several practices that can dramatically improve the value of your load testing.

Working from Clear Goals

It's a very good idea to have some stress/performance goals before you start doing any testing. These goals can be somewhat vague at the start and fine-tuned as you get some actual data, but should be based on your product needs and come from the product design team (including marketing). If the expectations are that an average user load is 1,000 simultaneous users, you should use that for your goals. You should also have several goals that detail as much as possible what you need to verify.

Examples of some goals include:

- No performance degradation up to 2,000 users.
- No performance degradation after 48 hours with a constant user load of 1,000 users.
- Handle (i.e., no errors/crashing, etc.) a peak load of 10,000 users for 10 minutes.

Usually each of these goals will become at least one load test that you run to verify the goal. *Performance degradation* would then need to be defined in terms of average response time and requests/second (and/or other appropriate measures), so that before you really start load testing in earnest, you have goals like:

- ❏ Maintain an average response time less than 0.5 second up to a load of 2,000 users generating 30 requests/second.

- ❏ Maintain an average response time less than 0.5 second for 48 hours with a constant user load of 1,000 users generating 20 requests/second.

- ❏ Handle (i.e., no errors/crashing, etc.) a peak load of 10,000 users for 10 minutes.

Goals like these are much easier to measure and verify than trying to measure your application's performance under a load and trying to decide if that "looks OK."

Often a product team will start its stress and/or performance testing with a "Let's see how things look first and then set goals" approach. One problem with this is that it can lead to setting the goals based on how the product currently performs and not based on how it needs to perform in order to meet the customer's needs.

While not having detailed goals does not prevent doing initial load testing work, it is much easier to do the testing based on specific goals. And testing without goals is a slippery slope that leads to continuing to just report the stress/performance results without being able to make any quality judgments. If you start without specific stress/performance goals, you should have as your top priority determining what the goals should be. In other words, if you cannot determine stress/performance goals before you start the testing, your initial testing should be focused on gathering the data that you need in order to set those goals. Without goals at the start, you can only report your stress or performance data. Not having specific goals to meet will make it harder to identify where you have problems. You can only report the data you have gathered but won't know if it's good enough for release. It will help you identify areas of potential problems, usually in comparison with other areas ("this page takes 10 times longer to load than the other page"), but it makes it much harder to know if you are ready to ship.

It's fine to alter the goals as you go along (deciding that meeting the original goal is not possible in this release, or that it's not good enough), but it is much better always to have stress/performance goals that you are verifying, even if they are changing, and these changes should be based on how the application compares to the current goals.

Also, having at least ballpark goals at the start will help you determine what kind of test rig you will need to set up. If you discover midway through that you really need to simulate 2,000 simultaneous users and you need to buy five more agent computers, you will be delayed while those are being ordered and set up. If you have an initial goal, then you can even stress-test your test rig before the application is ready, to make sure that your rig should be able to handle the number of users and tests that you think you will need.

These goals should be based on an estimated user load, number of customers, usage patterns, and so on. The more data you have as to customer usage and load, the better your goals will be.

Understanding Your Test Environment

One of the common ways stress/performance-related bugs are missed and let into a release is through differences between the test environment and the production environment. Obviously, if you can set up a test environment that is an exact duplicate of your production environment, then this is not an issue. But in most cases this is not possible because of resource constraints around money, space, or other issues.

It is then very important to understand all of the differences between your test environment and planned production environment as much as possible and track any assumptions being made. These assumptions are around how the results from the test environment translate into the production environment, such as, "We will have twice as many computers in production so we expect the production system to handle twice the user load as the test environment." Whenever possible you should test those assumptions even if you cannot test the final setup. For example, if your final production server is an 8-processor server but your test server is only 4-processor, you might assume that you will be able to handle twice the load in production that your tests show. But you could test that assumption by comparing the test system running as a 2-processor with the test system running as a 4-processor.

It is easy and dangerous to make assumptions about how the product will change based on changes to the hardware configuration, and one of your load testing goals should be to verify those assumptions. It may seem obvious that putting the business layer of the application onto a separate computer from the SQL database will improve your performance, but it is possible that this will cause a network connection bottleneck or some other issue.

Knowing When to Load Test

Another decision is when to start load testing your product. There is a "Catch-22" situation here because, for the most part, you cannot do stress or performance testing until the product (or at least a feature) is mostly functional. Obviously until a feature works in the basic single-user case, you cannot test how well it scales to a thousand users. But stress and performance–related problems, particularly those related to scaling to large numbers of users, often require deep architectural changes to fix. If you therefore wait until you are mostly ready to ship and discover that you need to make a fundamental design change, you could be in trouble.

To make matters worse, many stress/performance issues involve interactions between the product's different features. Perhaps it can handle 1,000 users browsing their order status or 1,000 users submitting a new order, but not 500 users browsing orders and 500 users ordering at the same time. If the order-browsing feature does not come online until late in the product cycle, you may not find this until later.

Unfortunately there is no good way to avoid this, but if you keep it in mind you can reduce the surprises. If you make sure to have your testcase creation keep pace with the feature development, then you can add tests for newly finished features into your load tests as soon as they are ready. And you should include stress/performance testing concerns into the product work schedule. Any feature that has stress or performance concerns should be finished sooner rather than later.

Walk Before You Run

"Walk before you run" is a good strategy both for getting your load testing system set up and working and for your actual testing strategy. For setting up your test system (the test rig, the tests, and the load test definitions), it's good to work your way up to what you want. This also applies to your testing strategy — instead of trying to test the whole system on a large scale, focus on the small scale first.

Scaling Up Your Test Infrastructure

Always try things out on a smaller scale first; this can save you quite a bit of wasted time. Jumping directly to a 10,000 user load test made up of 30 different tests and using 10 agents collecting counters from 10 application computers for a week is almost guaranteed to fail, or worse run for the week but not collect the right data. It's best to scale up your testing, increasing as few variables at one time as possible. For example, starting with one test with 100 users on a single agent for 10 minutes will let you work out any basic agent setup issues and any counter collection issues. Then adding more tests (but not increasing the user load or duration) will let you check for any issues with running the tests. If you do these "test" test runs with a short duration, you can quickly ramp up your test system to where it needs to be to start your testing while making it easy to identify and fix any issues you run into.

Make sure that all of the individual tests in the load test work by themselves, outside of a load test. Then make sure that they run inside a load test. And keep in mind that just because the test worked with last week's build of the product, it might not work with the more recent build. It's always a good idea to check that the tests still work before kicking off that long-duration run.

In fact, a very good habit to get into is, before starting a long-duration run, do a run with the exact same settings except for a short duration, around 10 minutes. When it's done, examine the data completely, just as if it were the "real" run. In fact, you can often notice performance problems in just that short run and save yourself waiting the week for the run to finish. This gives you a quick end-to-end verification that all of the aspects of your load test are working. It doesn't take more than one ruined week-long test run with a problem that wasn't immediately noticed when the run started (e.g., SQL traces not being collected) to convince you that a short-duration pre-test is a good idea.

Scaling Up Your Testing

The "walk before you run" strategy applies as much to your actual testing strategy as it does to getting your test infrastructure set up and working. Your testing strategy is about what you test and when — what sorts of things you are looking for at any particular point in your product cycle. The temptation is to begin trying to load test all of your features at the same time (actually the biggest temptation is to hold off on load testing until late in the product cycle, but that's a different problem), and while you do need to load test all of the features working together at some point, your first test run may not be the best time for it.

One major problem with load testing is the huge number of factors that can affect the test run. Starting with small-scale testing can help reduce all of these variables and allow you to focus on the problem. "Small scale" here does not really mean testing with a small number of users; the idea is to start off with your load testing more focused on the small scale of your product. Starting with focused component level testing and then moving to cross-feature tests lets you identify the more obvious problems without clouding the issue with a lot of other factors. For example, running a load test specifically around your application's Add User functionality lets you see how many Add User operations it can support (while nothing else is happening). Any problems will be much easier to identify and fix. Then do the same with Edit User, and then Delete User, and so forth. Then once all of the component-level issues have been resolved, do a test run that combines all of them.

Another advantage of this strategy is that it allows you to componentize the testing work. In the above example the User Management team could own the "User" component testing, while the Order Management team owns the "Owner" component testing. The core stress/performance team then just needs to gather all of the individual team's tests and combine them for the big, application-wide runs. Note that the "team" here could be the single developer who is writing that feature.

Scaling up your testing also includes starting with shorter test runs. Not only do longer runs require you to wait a longer time before you can really look at the data, there's also a lot more data to look at. It's easier (and often quicker) to do a short run (15 minutes or an hour) and investigate that first.

Once you've worked through all of the "obvious" issues that appear in a short run, you can do a longer run and can then focus on the issues that are caused by a long-term load.

Running a Load Test

Once you have the test rig set up and the load test defined, actually running the load test is pretty simple. Simply set the Active Run Configuration you want and then click Run Test.

Important Settings in the .testrunconfig File

If you select Edit Test Run Configurations from the Test menu or you open a .testrunconfig file from the Solution Explorer, you will see the Test Run Configuration dialog. This lets you specify all of the settings for running tests in that configuration. Only some of these pages are interesting for load tests (the other setting's pages are discussed in the chapters they most relate to).

The main page of interest is the Controller and Agent page in the designer (see Figure 7-10). This lets you select the test rig (or "local" if you want to run using just the local computer) on which you want to run the load test.

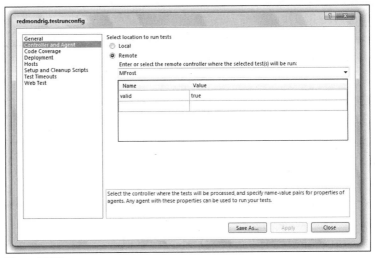

Figure 7-10

This selects the controller (and therefore the test rig) to use for this test run. You can also set attribute requirements to filter the agents used in the run. (See "The Agent Properties Dialog Box" section above in this chapter.)

You can also start a load test from the command line just like any other test type. For load tests the Test Container is the .loadtest file (instead of a test assembly).

```
mstest /testcontainer:LoadTest1.loadtest/runconfig:RigSettings.testrunconfig
```

If you do not specify a /runconfig, then MSTest.exe will execute the load test run locally (not using a rig). To run a load test on a test rig, you must always specify a .runconfig file.

Starting the Load Test

To start the load test from the Load Test Editor, simply click the Run Test button in the Load Test Editor toolbar.

As the load test starts, the Load Test Analyzer window will appear, showing the detailed graph of the current status of the run (see Figure 7-11). You can use the Load Test Analyzer to monitor the current status of the run and the various computers involved in the run.

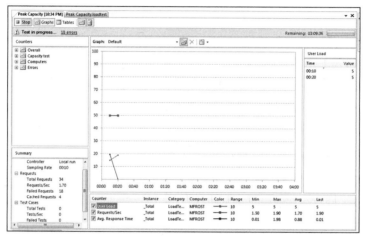

Figure 7-11

> If you are using a test rig, then you can close Visual Studio or the Load Test Analyzer window while the test is running without affecting the test run. You can then reconnect at any time.
>
> If you are running a load test without a rig (locally), then you cannot close the Load Test Analyzer window (or Visual Studio) without halting the test run.

Examining in Progress Test Data

For long-running test runs, you probably do not want to leave your Visual Studio system connected and monitoring the run. It does not affect the run, but you probably have better things to do.

To connect to either remote (test rig) run that is currently in progress, follow these steps:

1.   Open the Test Runs window from the Test ➪ Windows main menu (see Figure 7-12).
2.   In the Select dropdown at the upper left, pick the controller or <local>.
3.   If the controller you want to connect to is not in the list, choose Local or Connect to Remote at the bottom of the dropdown list. This will open up the Connect to Controller or Local Results dialog (see Figure 7-13).

   From this dialog you can enter another controller name, select an already known controller, or pick a local Test Results directory (containing the .trx files from the runs).

4. The grouped table in the Test Runs window should now show all of the runs that are stored in the Results Store associated with the controller that was selected.

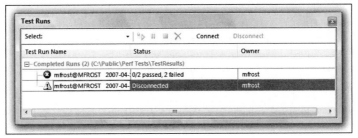

Figure 7-12

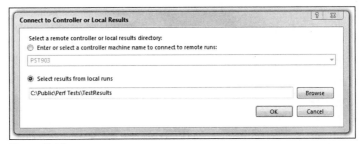

Figure 7-13

5. An in progress run will be listed under Active Runs, while runs that have finished will be listed under Completed Runs. Find the test run that you wish to examine.

6. Select the test run you want, and click the Connect button on the toolbar. The status field for the run will change from Disconnected to the actual status of the run.

The Test Results window will show all of the test runs that have been connected to.

7. Open the Test Results window. (Right-click the test run, and choose View Results, or select from Test ➪ Windows ➪ View Results.)

8. If the test run you want to view is not displayed, use the dropdown box at the left of the Test Results window toolbar to select it (or All to list all of the currently connected test results).

9. Double-click the test run or right-click it, and select View Results Details.

The Load Test Analyzer window will open with the detailed data and graph view. From here you can monitor the status of the run, watching for any errors or threshold rule violations.

> While the run is in progress, you will not be able to view all of the Result data. A small set of data is available to view in the Load Test Analyzer until the run completes.

Using the Load Test Analyzer

The *Load Test Analyzer* has several panels and generally requires a full screen to use it effectively. The main pieces are the counters, the graph, and the tables. This lets you monitor any of the aspects of the currently executing run to see how things are going. This is also the same screen that is used to analyze the results of a completed test run.

You can control which of these panels are displayed using the toolbar at the top of the Load Test Monitor (see Figure 7-14). Each of them can be turned on or off independently, except for graphs and tables.

Figure 7-14

The Counters Panel

This pane on the upper left of the Load Test Analyzer has a hierarchical list of all of the performance counters being collected from this run. These counters are grouped into three main categories, plus a group for each scenario:

❑ **Overall** — These are the load test–specific counters and include things like User Load, "Transaction response times," and so forth.

❑ **Scenario** — There will be a top-level counter group for each scenario in the load test. The name of the scenario is the name of the group. These are the counters specific to the scenario including counters for each test in the scenario.

❑ **Computers** — These are performance counters from the various computers involved in the load test (the test rig and the application computers under test). These counters are the "standard" performance counters like processor utilization.

❑ **Errors** — These are load test–specific counters that measure various error conditions such as validation rule failures, requests timing out, or HTTP errors.

Double-clicking on a specific counter (a leaf node in the tree) adds the counter to the graph and the legend.

If there were any threshold rule violations during the test run, the Counters tree view will show a warning icon on any nodes that have threshold violations (see Figure 7-15). This helps you quickly identify areas where problems occurred.

Figure 7-15

The Graph Panel

The main part of the Load Test Analyzer is the *Graph panel*, which displays sets of counter data graphically. You can add performance counters to a graph from the Counters panel.

The Graph panel has its own toolbar at the top that lets you switch between graphs, and control various graph options (see Figure 7-16).

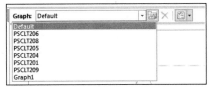

Figure 7-16

You can create more than one graph and switch between them using the dropdown at the top of the Graph panel and the button just to the right of the dropdown. By default, there are several graphs pre-created, a "default" graph and one for each computer in the test rig.

The rightmost pull-down button on the Graph toolbar lets you set various options for the Graph display.

The Graph panel has two subpanes, the Legend and the "Plot Points table." These can be turned on or off using the rightmost pull-down button on the Graph toolbar.

❑ **Plot Points Table** — If the Show Plot Points setting is on, then you will see a table to the right of the graph. This lists the data points for the currently selected graph line. There are two columns, "Time" and "Value."

❑ **Legend** — If the Show Legend setting is on, then you will see a legend at the bottom of the graph. Selecting an item will cause its line on the graph to be bolded, and its plot points will be displayed in the Plot Points table (if it is visible). Each item on the graph is listed here. Each item has a checkbox that determines if it is drawn on the graph. This lets you overlay several counters and quickly un/hide them as you are examining the data.

The data values displayed in the graph are all normalized to fit together on the same graph. Looking at the graph, you will see that the vertical axis goes from 0 to 100. This is used for all of the counters displayed. Each line on the graph has its own scale. In the Legend there is a Range listed for each item — this is the value that the 100 (the top of the graph) represents.

By default, the range (and therefore the scale) changes dynamically based on the values for that counter that need to be displayed in the current view (the ranges are all powers of 10). Thus if you are watching a running test, you will often see a line shift (appearing to become smaller) because incoming values have changed the range that needs to be displayed. Likewise when you are zooming in the graph, you will see the scale for the items changing, sometimes dramatically. This can be a little confusing since it might appear that one value is lower than another because they have different scales. But this can be turned off (fixing the range to a set value).

Plot Options

By right-clicking on an item in the Legend and choosing Plot Options, you will open the Plot Options dialog, which lets you specify the line color and style for that counter in the current graph.

You can also turn the automatic range adjustment on or off. If the automatic adjustment is disabled, then you will need to specify the range manually. This is useful when you wish to compare two data sets but one of them has some data points putting it into the next range, or if the counter has a spike putting it just into the next range. For example, if the Requests Current counter is usually under 10 but at one point it goes to 11, the auto-scaling will set the Range to 100 to fit the "11" on the graph, but it is easier to examine the data at the 10 scale with the one data point off the scale.

Zooming in the Graph

Once a load test has finished and all of the Results data have been compiled, you can zoom in to a specific range of time using the slider bars at the bottom of the graph. The Zoom bar (see Figure 7-17) is like a scroll bar in that you can move it left and right to scroll through the test, but you can also re-size the bar (by grabbing the handles on either side) to define how large a time slice you want to view.

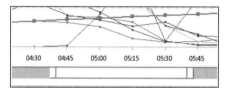

Figure 7-17

You can also zoom in to a specific slice of time by highlighting that region with your mouse. This is very useful when you want to zoom into a specific time slice based on the data displayed in the graph.

The Tables Panel

The Tables panel lets you see data that is better displayed as a list of records instead of changing values over time (which the Graph view is better for). For example, the Agents table (see Figure 7-18) lists a row for each agent that contains summary data for each agent (total requests processed by the agent, number of failed requests, etc.).

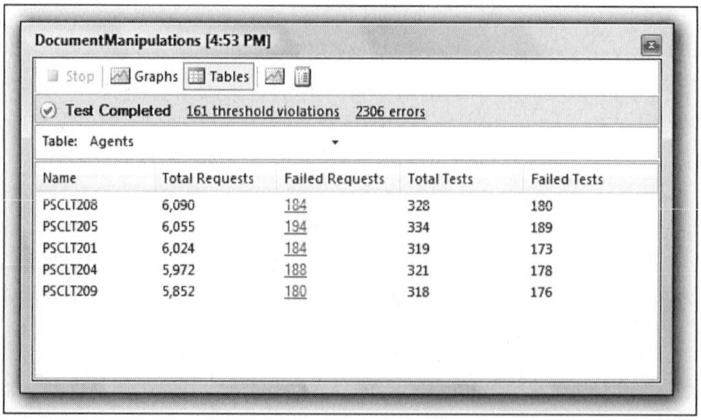

DocumentManipulations [4:53 PM]

Stop | Graphs | Tables

✓ Test Completed   161 threshold violations   2306 errors

Table: Agents

Name	Total Requests	Failed Requests	Total Tests	Failed Tests
PSCLT208	6,090	184	328	180
PSCLT205	6,055	194	334	189
PSCLT201	6,024	184	319	173
PSCLT204	5,972	188	321	178
PSCLT209	5,852	180	318	176

Figure 7-18

This gives you the ability to view the data in different slices (by agent, by test, by errors, etc.). The drop-down at the top of the Tables panel lets you select which table to view.

The Errors table (listing all of the errors that occurred) and the Thresholds table (listing the threshold violations) are two very important tables for investigating issues with the test run.

The SQL Trace table is only available if SQL tracing was enabled for the test run and only after the test has completed.

Several of these tables have an "Error" or "Failed" column that lists the total number of failures related to the current table (e.g., the Agents table has a "Failed Requests" column that shows the number of failed requests on each agent). These fields are links that open up a Load Test Errors window with the details of the individual errors (see Figure 7-19).

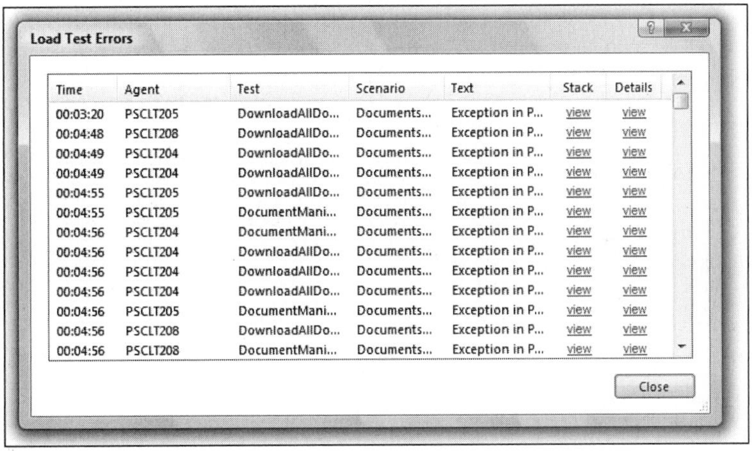

Figure 7-19

This lets you examine the details of each of the errors, including the time the error occurred, the test that failed, and the details of the error. For some errors, a stack trace is available (which is a link that opens a Stack Trace window). The Details field (when available for web request failures) opens the Error Detail window (see Figure 7-20).

This window shows all of the details of the HTTP Request and Responses that occurred as part of the web request that failed. This window works just like the Web Test Details pane in the Web Test Viewer used when running an individual web test (see Chapter 5, "Web Testing").

The other tables (Tests, Transactions, Pages, and Requests) can be very useful for comparing timing data. Often it is useful to find the specific page (or Test/Transaction/Request) that is slowest. Much of the timing data collected by VSTEST and displayed in the graphs is an average value; that is, the counter shows the average time for that operation so far in the test run, which could mean that everything is generally slow or that one operation is very slow.

For example, if you noticed that the overall "Avg. Page Time" is slower than you expect, you can go to the Pages table and sort by "Avg. page time" to see which page is the slowest, on average. You could then also check to see if there is a large difference between the average time it takes to load this "slowest page" and the overall average page time, and the next slowest page. This works the same with Transactions and Tests — you can use all of these tables to quickly find the unusual items and compare them with other items.

Figure 7-20

When looking at the counter data, some of the different time counters can be a bit confusing. The "Avg. Page Time" is the average time it takes to fetch a page (where "page" is the primary request and all of its dependent requests), in contrast to "Avg. Response Time," which averages together all requests including the dependent requests. This means that if a page has 10 dependent requests that take 0.01 second to fetch and its primary request takes 0.1 second to fetch, then the "Avg. Page Time" would be 0.2 [0.1 + (0.01 * 10)] second, the sum of all the requests required to completely fetch the page. That same page would have an "Avg. Response Time" that was the average of those 11 requests, or about 0.02 second.

The Summary Panel

This panel shows a very high-level summary of the load test run. This lets you see, for example, if there are any failed tests and the current total number of tests and the test rate (tests/second).

Investigating Results

With the huge amount of data that can be collected and the wide variety of ways to view the data, it can seem overwhelming. Once you've gathered all of this data, how do you tell where the problems are? Sometimes it can even be difficult to tell if the load test "passed" or "failed." Load testing is more of an art than functional testing, where you perform an action and verify that the result is what you expect, and if it fails it's usually obvious, and you can track down the problem by debugging and so forth.

Load testing has several issues that make it much harder to identify and track down problems and how to fix them. For one thing, it's very hard (often effectively impossible) to debug the code while it is failing. If the failure only occurs after 40 hours with a load of 1,000 users, attaching a debugger at that moment is usually not an option.

Understanding Your Application

It is very important to understand the application you are testing and how it works. Knowing what resources are crucial for your application (or at least having a good starting set of assumptions) lets you know what performance counters to focus on. This includes understanding the resource needs for the underlying infrastructure in terms of your application. For example, if your application has a SQL server, then you will probably want to pay attention to various SQL performance counters (Cache Hits, Locking, etc.), but exactly which ones may depend a bit on what is important to your application.

The better you know your application, the better you will be able to dig into the data and track down where the failure is actually occurring. Because of the interrelatedness of most server applications, problem symptoms may show up in one performance counter but actually be caused by something else (even on a separate computer). The fact that the Request Execution Time has increased past an acceptable limit may be caused by on overload on the web server or on the SQL server behind it.

Using Rules

Probably the best way to identify issues in a load test (especially a long-duration one) is to look for threshold violations that have occurred. But, of course, to do that you need to have set the threshold rules on the counters before the test starts.

> **Threshold rules define your product requirements and are one way you define Passing or Failing for a test.**

Many of the "standard" counters like CPU Utilization have default threshold rules, and in many cases those are fine (>90% CPU, etc.). But there are usually other counters that are important for your specific application. These should also have threshold values.

The goals that were defined for the product usually translate into threshold rules, if your goals are:

- ❑ Maintain an Average Page Response time of less than 0.5 second up to a load of 2,000 users generating 30 requests/second.

- ❑ Maintain an Average Response time less than 0.5 second for 48 hours with a constant user load of 1,000 users generating 20 requests/second.

- ❑ Handle (i.e., no errors/crashing, etc.) a peak load of 10,000 users for 10 minutes.

This would mean that you should have threshold rules for Average Page Time (which is approximately how long a user would see it take for the page to load) and Requests/Second (at a minimum). Note that the Requests/Second are actually measured on the agents and are there to verify that you are generating the load that you expect.

If there were any threshold rule violations during the test run, the Counters tree view will show a warning icon on any nodes that have threshold violations (see Figure 7-21). This helps you quickly identify areas where problems occurred and drill into them.

Also make sure that you have validation rules for all of the requests that need them in your web tests. Without these it can be difficult to tell if the web test passed and exactly where the failure was.

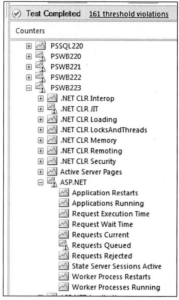

Figure 7-21

Checking the Test Computers

If there is an issue with the test computers, such as being overloaded, then your Result data are suspect. If your requests/second suddenly drops, is that because the server you are testing has become overloaded and slow to respond or because the agent has become overloaded and slow to send the request? Often the problem is in the test rig, but it causes subtle changes in the aspects of the test.

For each agent (and the controller) you should always check:

❑ Is the user load what is expected?

❑ Are its memory and CPU usage within acceptable limits?

❑ Are the requests/second what you expect (for the user load at the time)?

❑ Does the "Avg. Connection Wait Time" stay near 0 (if you are using connection pooling)?

> It is important to check the agents to make sure they are performing even when there are no errors in the test run. Problems on the agents may be reducing the load and making your application's performance seem better than it is.

"Checking" these counters is best done using threshold rules on the agent performance counters. Thus in most cases you do not really need to manually check every one of these on each agent. But it is a good idea to at least verify that the user load is what is expected.

But remember that even if the user load is what you expect, it may not be driving your application as hard as you want. In the same way that a load of 1,000 users with a 10-second think time between tests can be less stress on your application than 100 users with no think time, if there is something on the agent that is slowing things down (e.g., overloaded network connection), your 1,000 users may really only be stressing the application as if they were 100.

Analyzing a Test Run

Once your run is finished and you have all of the results, assuming you have set up all the necessary threshold rules and validation rules, you need to analyze the results data. Going over the data and then drilling in where necessary is where most of the interesting (and challenging) work is.

The first thing to check is if there were any errors or threshold violations. Checking for threshold violations is easy in that the Counters panel will show an icon on any Counter Group that contains a counter with a threshold violation.

You can also see the errors and threshold violations displayed at the top of the Result window. If there were errors or threshold violations, then the count of each is displayed as a link to the table for that data. This lets you quickly jump to examine the raw data for the errors and view the specific threshold violations. In the Table view it can be easier to see any commonalities or clustering, for example, if the errors all occurred on the same agent, or if they all occurred around the same time.

As for which is more important to investigate, errors or threshold violations, and which should be looked into first: There is not really a huge difference between the two, and I generally consider threshold violations as user-defined errors. True — with an actual error you know that something has definitely gone wrong, whereas the CPU hitting 100 percent does not mean that something has gone wrong for sure. Thus errors are the first place to start your investigation, but you need to consider the threshold violations in that investigation, since either one can be the cause or a symptom of the other. Sometimes it's better to start the investigation with the first problem that appeared, whether it's an error or a threshold violation.

If there were errors (and this includes test failures), the first thing to do is find out exactly what happened by going to the Errors table and examining the error details. From this you can (usually) determine what the exact error was, and sometimes you will find other important data. For example, if there were a large number of errors all at the same time across all of the agents, then it's more likely a problem in the application being tested; whereas if all the errors are on the same agent and none of the other agents show any errors, I would be inclined to suspect the test or a problem on the agent. Even if it's not obvious what the problem is from the error information, the Error message and details, especially the timing, should give you a good set of clues as to where to look further.

If there were threshold violations, graph that counter and see when the problems occurred. In this example, the ASP.NET:Requests Queued counter has a threshold violation (see Figure 7-22). (We should never have any queued requests, thus the threshold rule is set to 0.)

You should also check the Test Failures counters and the Errors counters. Including them on the graph with the threshold violation is a good idea as well (see Figure 7-23).

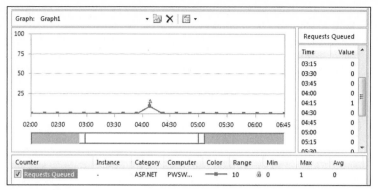

Figure 7-22

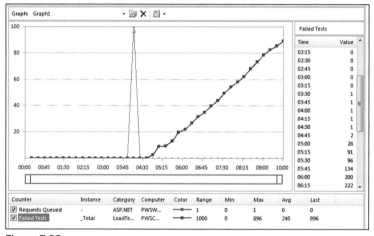

Figure 7-23

Here, since the test failures seem to start up right about when the threshold violation occurred, they are probably connected.

If you are looking at the test failures, don't forget to look at the passing tests as well. Comparing the two can be very informative. An important question if there are failures is whether or not there are any passing tests. In this case if we look at the Total Passed Tests (see Figure 7-24) to see if there were any passing results after we started seeing the failures, we see that there were some passing tests but not very many.

One thing to remember when looking at the test-related counters (Passed/Failed Tests) is that this value is incremented when the test finishes, thus if your tests take a while to execute, there could be a delay or shift in the counter data.

From just looking at the graph, it looks like there were no passing tests after the error occurred (assuming that the short period where it increases is tests that were in progress finishing). But if you look at the Plot Points table to the right of the graph (see Figure 7-25), you can see the actual data, which show that while there were not many passing tests after the error, there were a few.

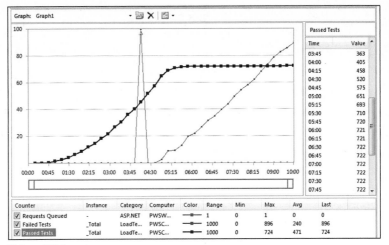

Graph: Graph1											Passed Tests	
											Time	Value
											03:45	363
											04:00	405
											04:15	458
											04:30	520
											04:45	575
											05:00	651
											05:15	693
											05:30	710
											05:45	720
											06:00	721
											06:15	721
											06:30	722
											06:45	722
											07:00	722
											07:15	722
											07:30	722
											07:45	722

Counter	Instance	Category	Computer	Color	Range	Min	Max	Avg	Last
☑ Requests Queued	-	ASP.NET	PWSW...		1	0	1	0	0
☑ Failed Tests	_Total	LoadTe...	PWSC...		1000	0	896	240	896
☑ Passed Tests	_Total	LoadTe...	PWSC...		1000	0	724	471	724

Figure 7-24

Passed Tests	
Time	Value
04:15	458
04:30	520
04:45	575
05:00	651
05:15	693
05:30	710
05:45	720
06:00	721
06:15	721
06:30	722
06:45	722
07:00	722
07:15	722
07:30	722
07:45	722
08:00	722
08:15	723
08:30	723
08:45	723
09:00	723
09:15	723
09:30	723

Figure 7-25

Possibly these are stragglers, tests that took a very long time to run (possibly because of the error) and that started before the error but didn't finish until much later. To check that, you can look at the "Avg. Test Time" counter, which is the average amount of time that the tests are taking to execute (this is the cumulative average for the entire test run) (see Figure 7-26).

Since the Avg. Test Time is decreasing, that means that the tests are executing quicker. But it's an average, and it's possible that the failures are happening faster than a passing test. Looking closely at the Plot Points table for the two counters, you can see that when the Passed Tests value increases, the Avg. Test Time jumps up quite a bit (considering that it is an average value). In this case, the few passing tests that finished after the error were just tests that took a very long time.

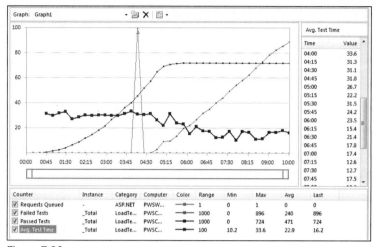

Figure 7-26

This is an interesting piece of data. Looking at the Avg. Test Time early on in the test (before the error), you see that the average time was around :30, which means that if a test took from around the time of the error (4:15) to near the end of the test (8:15) that it is taking substantially longer to execute. Or possibly there were a few passing results even after the error (but very very few).

The next step is to start investigating what else is going on at that time that is related to this error. A good first step is then to graph some of the standard counters for the computer where the issue is occurring — for example, adding the CPU, memory, and so forth for the computer.

Looking at those (see Figure 7-27), we see that there does not seem to be any obvious problem on this computer (the web server for the application).

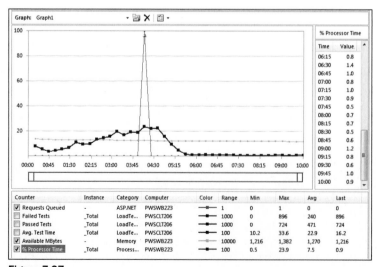

Figure 7-27

Let's start with a few other ASP.NET counters. You can right-click on a group of counters (e.g., ASP.NET) and add them all to the graph at once, and then remove the ones that are not interesting. If this adds too many to see what's going on, you can uncheck them in the legend to see a few at a time and turn some on or off. In this case, most of the ASP.NET counters were constant throughout the test run, thus we remove those (see Figure 7-28).

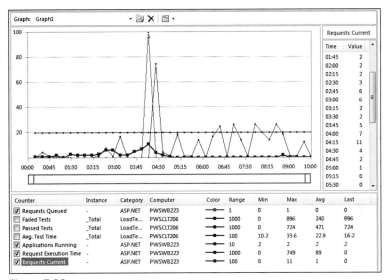

Figure 7-28

Here we see that the ASP.NET Request Execution Time increases dramatically after the error. But the number of Current Requests drops. Interestingly the error occurred right when the number of ASP.NET:Requests Current hit 11 (its maximum value). Here we see the Graph and the Plot Points table zoomed in on the error time.

Thus our current theory is that there is a correlation between the Requests Current exceeding 10 causing the requests to be queued, which then causes continuing failures in our application.

To be sure, we should examine the performance counter data from the SQL Server computer. The problem could easily be on that computer with the symptoms only visible on the web server front-end. In this case, looking at the counter data for the SQL Server does not show anything obviously interesting; therefore we stick with this theory.

The next steps should be to:

❑ Add a threshold rule to the ASP.NET:Requests Current counter to raise an alert if it ever goes above 10. This will help us see if this value really does correlate to the error. The alert makes these occurrences more visible so that we can see if we get this error and the test failures every time this happens, only sometimes, or never (again).

❑ Set up some tests specifically to reproduce this problem under more scrutiny. Varying the user load, trying slightly different mixes of tests, turning think times on/off, and so forth. This gathers more data about the problem so that you can fine-tune your search.

Discuss this with the expert on this feature area (if this is narrowed down enough to a feature), and examine the code to see if there is an issue. In this case, that probably also means investigating the ASP.NET Request Queue handling.

If There Are No Errors

Assuming that you have set up your rules correctly, this is a very good sign. Even so, you should still spend some time analyzing the results. You should verify the health of the agents throughout the test run. (Usually you would see threshold violations, but it's good to be paranoid if everything seems too good to be true.)

Then you should check that all of the metrics that are important for your goals are what they should be:

❑ Was the user load what you needed?

❑ Are the requests/second what you need or expected? If you are seeing a much lower number of requests/second than you expect, that could be the sign of a problem. Even if it is not, it may mean that you are not stressing your application the way you intended.

❑ Were there any failing tests?

❑ Do you trust the results? Often it is good to do a general "gut-feeling" check of some of the data. Does the CPU utilization on the SQL Server look correct? Do the web server requests data track with the user load? Spot-checking some of these things can make sure that you don't miss something that maybe is not being caught by a rule.

Once you get to this point — a test run with no errors, threshold violations, or test failures and that you are (mostly) sure is a good run — you still need to tell everyone. Summarizing all of these data into a reasonable report will help make the decision as to whether or not the product performs well enough to release.

Reporting Results

There is no real reporting built into the Load Test system in VSTEST. But there are a few options:

❑ You can make the .TRX file available. For this to work, everyone must have VSTEST installed and have access to the database where the actual load test result data are stored. This gives them full access to all of the data and the ability to drill in and examine the data using the VSTEST Load Test Analyzer. But this is probably too much data for a managerial-level report.

❑ You can download the *Load Test Reports* package written by Sean Lumley (a member of the VSTEST Web/Load Testing team). At the time of this writing, the location of this tool is changing, but there should be current information on it at Sean's blog: `http://blogs.msdn.com/slumley`.

❑ You can create your own reports against the database. See the "Results Store" section above in this chapter for an overview of the database tables.

If you have set all of your rules (validation and threshold) and made sure that the test run is a good measure of your stress and performance goals, it should be easy to tell when you have met those goals. But, of course, even when you do meet those goals, there is going be a need for reporting the data, and even collecting more data — marketing wants some specific data, someone wants to know how many more users can be handled if a SQL cluster is used, and so forth.

Summary

Load testing is as much an art as a science and can require quite a bit of detective work. The good news is that the VSTEST Load Test system takes care of a large amount of the legwork for you. Even so, there can still be an overwhelming amount of data to sift through.

The keys to successful load testing are knowing what you need to verify and measure ahead of time, focusing on those metrics by setting rules, and having a solid understanding of your application. Load testing can take a long time; thus be sure to account for that in your testing schedule, and start your load testing as soon as possible during development. Even if you only have a few tests working, you can do some component-level stress testing.

8

Using Code Analysis and Dynamic Analysis

In this chapter, we're going to look at the code analysis tools in VSTESD. These are tools that allow you to verify the correctness of an application without executing it. After we've looked at these tools and the benefits/drawbacks associated with them, we will take a look at the dynamic analysis tools that allow for performance profiling and analysis of your application. As with code analysis tools, these are only available in VSTESD. We will examine Code Coverage, a component of Dynamic Analysis that is available in VSTEST, as well as in the full Dynamic Analysis toolset that is in VSTESD.

Code Analysis

One of the components of VSTESD, but not VSTEST, is the collection of static analysis tools — more commonly referred to as *code analysis*. These tools perform static analysis (versus runtime analysis via profiling) of the code that you have written. They analyze your code for common patterns that are dangerous for stability, security, and maintainability. The code analysis tools in VSTESD take this to the next level by including "rules" that validate your code for performance, design, globalization, naming, and other sets of rules that help maintain a high level of code quality without having to perform code reviews.

Static Analysis Tools

The tools that are part of VSTESD are not a new class of tools. They've been around for many years in many forms, mostly as source-based tools that will lexically analyze the source code, much like a compiler. These tools perform various tasks on the "tree" that is built from the source — analyzing the relationships between statements, functions, classes, variables, and other code constructs.

It is important to note at this point that the managed code analysis tools in VSTESD are not language-specific. They work on the compiled code (assemblies) at the level of the MSIL (Microsoft

Instruction Language). There is no need to build a parser that is capable of parsing individual languages, because the static code analysis tools can read the "machine readable" MSIL. This also means that there is a richer set of information from the metadata.

PREfast

One of the tools that ships with VSTESD is PREfast, a tool that is combined with the C++ compiler. It was created around the time that Microsoft was having its large post-Window XP security push. It is a very complex application, with a large knowledge base built around common coding conventions in the Win32/native programming world.

The most recent version (shipped in Visual Studio 2005) included a set of annotations that can be applied to the code to ensure that the intentions and expectations in functions are validated at compile time rather than being found as security issues after your application is in production.

As the focus of this book is on managed programming, we won't cover PREfast.

FxCop

Before the creation of VSTESD, the CLR team at Microsoft wanted to create a tool to ensure that the BCL (Base Class Library) met the basic design guidelines. The result of their efforts was a free tool called FxCop. This tool became the basis of the managed code analysis tools that are in VSTESD. It's important to realize that one of the driving forces behind the creation of FxCop was to enforce design guidelines around software components. These design guidelines are embodied in "Design Guidelines for Developing Class Libraries" on Microsoft's MSDN site (http://msdn.microsoft.com).

Coding Standards

Part of the goal of code analysis tools is to enforce coding standards, but it's important to note that these are not coding standards of source style (e.g., Kernigan and Richie), but of overall style around the way you implement your application.

Some sample rules include

❑ **CA1062: Validate the arguments of public methods** — This means that you need to ensure that the supplied parameters to a method are validated, for example, "Not Null," "Counts greater than 0."

❑ **CA1707: Identifiers should not contain underscores** — When you are declaring classes, fields, properties, and methods, you should not include "_" characters in the name. This makes them difficult to read when surrounded by other code.

The rules are all categorized according to the type of coding standard that they are attempting to enforce. There are hundreds of rules included in the product, and with each new release, Microsoft adds new rules and new categories.

Enabling Code Analysis

With VSTESD, enabling rules is significantly easier than before the IDE integration. Previously when FxCop was an external tool, there was a separate UI that allowed you to load rule sets and assemblies to perform analysis (see Figure 8-1).

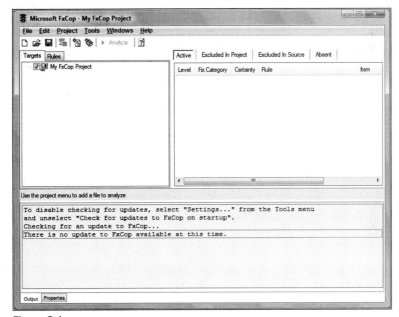

Figure 8-1

With VSTESD, this process has become significantly simpler thanks to code analysis being integrated directly into the project system. It's now as easy as checking a checkbox on your project properties (Figure 8-2) and (optionally) selecting Rule sets that you wish to validate against.

The actual validation happens at build time, as part of the IDE build process, as well as from the command line when using MSBuild. After your code has been successfully built, the code analysis phase begins to validate your code. Any errors will be reported in the Error List window in Visual Studio.

To enable code analysis:

1. Right-click on the project for which you wish to enable code analysis.
2. Select Properties.
3. Select the Code Analysis tab (Figure 8-2).
4. Check the Enable Code Analysis checkbox.
5. Close the Property page.

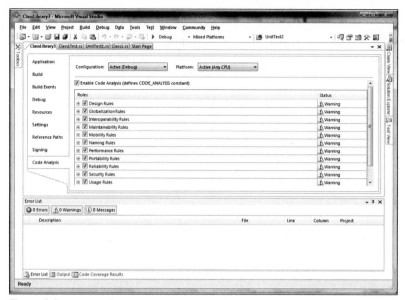

Figure 8-2

One extra step you can take when configuring how the validation failures are reported is that they may be reported as either a warning or an Error. When you select a warning, your build will not fail; however, when Error is selected, your build will fail. This means that when you hit *F5* to debug your current active project, the application won't start, and you'll be unable to debug. You need to weigh your options of being blocked by a simple typo against potentially ignoring many warnings until they have snowballed into a level that has become very difficult to bring back under control without significant effort. All the available errors are displayed on the Code Analysis property page, accessed via the preceding steps. Additionally, it is possible to force a violation to be reported as an error rather than just as a warning. This can be performed by single-clicking the "!" icon or double-clicking the text next to the specific rule.

Understanding Errors

Two of the most difficult problems that you face when you encounter a number of code analysis errors are trying to understand them and trying to rectify their cause. Some of them (as in the examples mentioned previously) are simple to fix — simply change the name or add some additional code. However, some are much more complex and are not immediately clear from their one-line description. This creates a problem: Without being able to understand what the error means, you are unable to rectify this issue.

However, the very first step to understanding what the errors mean is seeing what the errors are. This is done through the Error List window (Figure 8-3), as with other build errors. Just like normal syntactical issues that show up as both warnings and errors, code analysis errors show up in the Error List window as warnings or errors, depending on how you configure the individual errors.

Within the Error List window, there are several categories — Informational, Warning, and Error. Errors are issues that have caused the build to fail. Traditionally, errors are syntactical issues (depending on the warning level of your compiler) such as assigning one type that is incompatible with the target type. These are the errors we know and love (or maybe not). Warnings are issues that, while they won't stop a program from running completely, may cause problems in the future (such as potential for overflows in integer values). You can choose to ignore these, but at your peril. Informational messages tend not to show up at build time, but as part of editing documents in the IDE — maybe an XSD violation, for example.

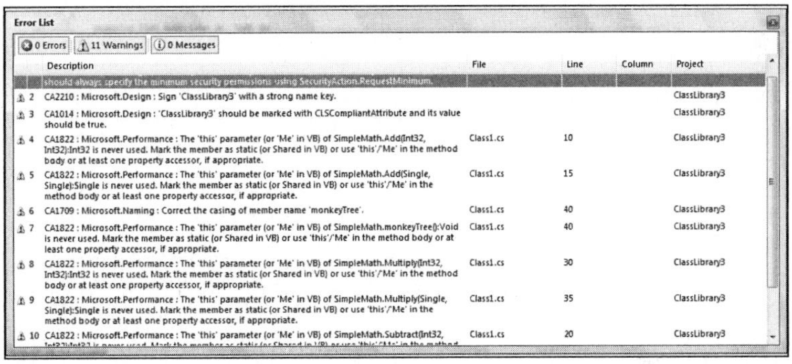

Figure 8-3

For all the messages that show up in the Error List window, be they compiler or code analysis messages, "help" is available. While the generally held belief is that Help is not helpful, the error information for these issues is very reasonable and goes the extra mile to help you understand the cause of the issue. The easiest way to get to this information is to press *F1*, or if you aren't willing to do that, perform an Internet search for the error code. No matter which route you choose, you should see a page containing information similar to Figure 8-4.

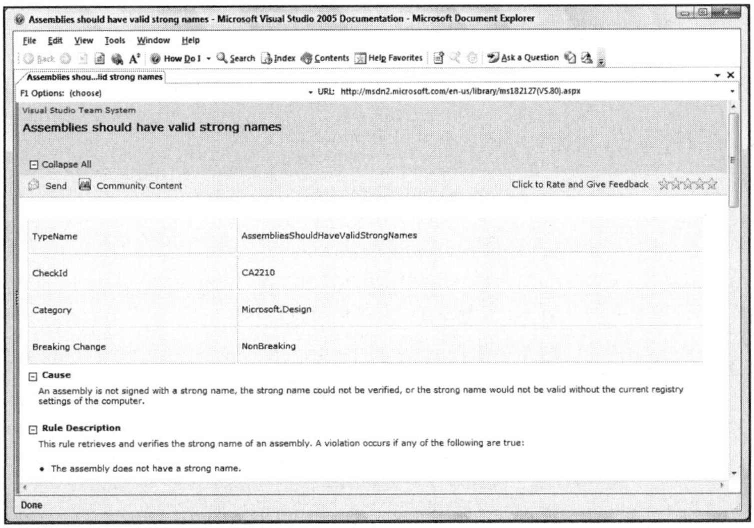

Figure 8-4

What the Errors Actually Mean

Let's take a look at an example code analysis error; in this case, it's CA2209. This is one of the errors that you will always encounter when you first enable code analysis.

This error (CA2209: "Assemblies should declare minimum security") is related to security demands that an assembly can make before it is executed. This enables the .NET Framework (and any code that consumes that specific assembly) to validate the demands of an assembly before it tries to execute any code within that assembly. Also, an assembly can refuse a set of security permissions to ensure that no second-level dependencies gain higher permissions than would be safe.

Several different permissions can be requested by an assembly. These include, at the basic level, executing, as shown here:

```
[assembly: SecurityPermission(SecurityAction.RequestMinimum, Execution = true)]
```

However, there are more complex and intricate security demands that an assembly can make, such as File permissions (including quotas in isolated storage), Link Demands, IP Connectivity, and many others. For example, see the following code:

```
[assembly:IsolatedStorageFilePermission(SecurityAction.RequestMinimum,
    UserQuota=1048576)]
[assembly:SecurityPermission(SecurityAction.RequestRefuse, UnmanagedCode=true)]
[assembly:FileIOPermission(SecurityAction.RequestOptional, Unrestricted=true)]
```

Security demands can also be defined by your code to ensure and validate any security demands. This is not a simple process and is well outside the scope of this book.

Another common error is CA1709: "Identifiers should be cased correctly," which is a design guideline that is specifically about ensuring a consistent naming convention for your public methods, properties, and classes. Examples of "bad" names include

- ❏ Accountfinder
- ❏ illShowyouAbadMethod
- ❏ iAmtheMethod

With each of these methods, notice that each word is not always capitalized. To rectify this issue, you would have to change the above names to

- ❏ AccountFinder
- ❏ IWillShowYouABadMethod
- ❏ IAmTheMethod

With the changes made, the errors will go away. It is important to again note that these are very easy to suppress. This is one of those cases where suppression is wholly dependent on your personal preference.

Suppressing Errors

When running code analysis on an empty project, you will see three errors for a normal C# class library. This is before you've written one line of code. It should be clear from this that not all errors in code analysis are valid, actionable errors that require resolution. Sometimes you will just want to suppress — hide — the rule in a number of different scopes: project, assembly, class, or specific method/property where the rule is broken. It's important that you understand the specific error and why it has occurred before you choose to suppress it.

The simplest, easiest, and most sweeping way to suppress an error is merely to stop the rule from being used within that project. This can be done by editing the rule set for the project (refer back to Figure 8-2 to understand what the UI looks like), which can be performed on the Code Analysis tab of project properties. You can check single rules or whole categories, depending on your aim.

However, when you do this, you are removing all possibility that other errors of this class will be caught. You are asserting that you do not care, in any way, about the error that has been found in your code base. This is a dangerous assertion to make, and you should only make it with full understanding of the error and the code that is causing it.

An alternative way is to add an assembly-level attribute to suppress the error by placing code similar to the following into the source code. Additionally, you can right-click an item in the Error List window and select Suppress Error. This will automatically insert the code into the project in the appropriate place.

```
[assembly: System.Diagnostics.CodeAnalysis.SuppressMessage("Microsoft.Design",
    "CA2210:AssembliesShouldHaveValidStrongNames")]
```

This has the same effect as suppressing for the project — you will never see an error for that rule again. In certain cases, this is obviously the only choice. This is the case with the following example:

```
[SuppressMessage("Microsoft.Naming", "CA1709:IdentifiersShouldBeCasedCorrectly")]
public class aspecialClass
{ }
```

My personal opinion is that you should suppress assembly-level errors with attributes rather than removing the rules from the project. Having the suppressions declaratively marked up is a much clearer way to remove the rule than some opaque project file with a difficult-to-locate UI. This is only possible with non-member-specific errors; if you wish to suppress an entire class of errors and those errors are not assembly level, you do need to remove the error as part of the project, rather than as an inline declaration.

For other scopes, the attachment is based on the location of the attribute (e.g., on the method or class). When you attach the suppression attributes, the scope will be that of the construct to which it is attached. For example, here the attribute is attached to a class:

```
[SuppressMessage("Microsoft.Naming", "CA1709:IdentifiersShouldBeCasedCorrectly")]
public class aspecialClass
{ }
```

Here the attribute is attached to a method:

```
public class aspecialClass
{
    [SuppressMessage("Microsoft.Naming",
    "CA1709:IdentifiersShouldBeCasedCorrectly")]
    public void terribleTerrance()
    { }
}
```

With these additional scopes, it's possible to pick and choose the rules that you ignore with much more conviction and certainty that you are excluding only the specific violations that you understand and not hiding other potentially more dangerous (and valid) occurrences.

When to Suppress?

With so many errors on any reasonably sized existing project, ensuring that all errors are dealt with is an impossible task. You potentially have to evaluate hundreds of errors for validity. In one project I evaluated, there were more than 80,000 specific violations in that code base. It is impossible to fix each and every one of those errors, and you have to do two things: prioritize and suppress. These two tasks are very tightly bound because part of the suppression process is going to be prioritizing those that you care about. A primary example of this is CA2209; your application may always run in Full Trust and be designed to run like that. In that situation, there is little to be gained by including those attributes ensuring the correct permission sets. Thus in that case, it makes sense to suppress the errors rather than trying to rectify them. When starting with a clean slate, it is possible to pay the code analysis tax as you go, rather than as one large code later on. One still has to evaluate rules, but you end up suppressing significantly less because the cost is much more incremental.

However, the suppression of these low-hanging fruit will only remove a certain number of errors and potentially leave you with a large number requiring attention. In these cases, there are probably a large number of "common" errors that are being seen widely across your project (CA1709 is a good example). This is where you need to be able to understand and accept the implications of suppressing those errors. In the case of CA1709, this is something that on the surface is easy to dismiss, but it does require you and your management team to make a decision about how you expect your classes and methods to be exposed to other people. I personally believe that the specific error is mostly ignorable, but the *spirit* of the message is very valid. You need to ensure that your identifiers are consistent in their naming. If they aren't, your publicly exposed API will be confusing and have an unprofessional feel to it.

It is in this part of this discussion that we can see the crux of the issue: Just because a specific error is bad, that does not mean that the root intention of that message is invalid, and you need to be careful when you suppress that error in terms of the implications further down the line. A good way to help you draw the proper conclusion is to follow some simple guidelines:

1. Evaluate the actual scope of the error. Is it an assembly-wide error (CS2209)? Or locally scoped to a method?

2. Are the errors about how you have named your identifiers? Do you have a different company policy?

3. Are the security errors irrelevant to your application's usage?

The key point to take away is that you need to understand the meaning of the error for your particular application, which also means that you need to be comfortable with the architecture and implementation of your application. Without this understanding, you are going to make wrong decisions.

Dynamic Analysis

In contrast to static analysis, *Dynamic Analysis* tools examine your application while it is actually executing. This means that it has much greater impact on the execution of your application than static analysis, which is only performed on the binary of your application rather than actually executing it. This is often not a simple case of it taking a few more seconds to execute, and in certain situations it can be very expensive, slowing the performance of your application to a snail's pace. However, despite this, the information that can be garnered from using dynamic analysis tools can be immensely useful in solving any performance problems your application might have.

Dynamic analysis has two main purposes: profiling and code coverage. Profiling is about gaining an understanding of what your application did when it was executed — how long a method took, how much memory it used, how often it was called. This means you can see which methods are being called the most and, more importantly, taking the most time, to enable you to focus on those areas to resolve any problems. Code coverage is finding out which lines of your application code were actually executed while the application was running, enabling you to find dead code and code that you do need but that is not being tested.

It is important to realize that profiling is not the first step in diagnosing a performance problem. There is no point in trying to resolve a performance issue if you don't actually have one or do not understand *why* you have a performance problem. Just blindly changing code to make the issue go away will not be productive in the long run. But how do you know whether you have a performance problem and get a hint of where it might be? Well, the first question is often easily answered: You have to define goals for performance, and if you do not meet those goals, you have a performance problem by definition. It is very important to set goals for your performance, since without knowing what you are aiming for, you cannot know where you need to get your performance to.

Other Tools to Use

Within the basic Windows operating system, there are two primary tools that can be used to analyze the performance of your application before bringing out the big guns of dynamic analysis. While the range of features and some of the user interface elements change between Windows 2000, XP, 2003, and Vista, the fundamentals that are covered here are shared across all versions of Windows. Note that these tools are not available on Windows 9x and Millennium (nor do the dynamic analysis tools run there).

Task Manager

While Task Manager is primarily for monitoring specific processes on your system and killing those processes when they behave badly, it can also be useful for monitoring applications to understand what they are doing. This applies to the usual (and default) set of processor usage and memory properties, as well as more complex concepts such as page faults and read/write performance. Also, you can view other performance properties of the computer. This includes networking (introduced in XP), overall system memory usage, individual CPU usage, pagefile usage, and several other metrics about your system.

You can access Task Manager in various ways (some of which depend on how you have your system configured):

❑ *Ctrl + Shift + Esc* (when domain-joined; if not joined to a domain, this will show the start menu).

❑ *Ctrl + Alt + Del*, then click the Task Manager button.

❑ Right-click on the taskbar, and select Task Manager.

After pressing these, Windows Task Manager will appear, looking like Figure 8-5.

Figure 8-5

It will show whichever tab you last had selected. If it is your first time using Task Manager, it will show the Applications tab listing all the applications/windows that are also showing in your taskbar. However, this tab provides little value when examining the performance of your application. The tabs that we are interested in are Processes (see Figure 8-6) and Performance (see Figure 8-7).

The Processes tab lists all the processes currently executing on your system, along with the details about their CPU usage, memory usage, and other metrics.

> *It is important to note that if you are not an administrator, you will only be able to see your own processes and not those of others. Often this is not a problem. However, if you are trying to examine a service, it will likely be running under another identity.*

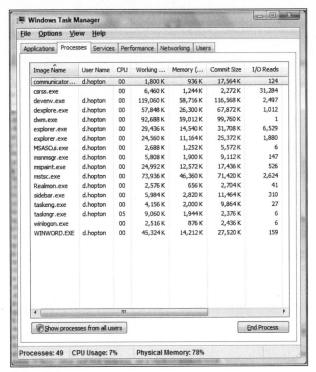

Figure 8-6

Additionally, if you are running on Windows Vista, you need to run Task Manager as "elevated" to see all the other processes. Within Task Manager, on the Processes tab, there is a button named "Show processes from all users." When used, this button will start Task Manager as an elevated process with the usual Vista prompts.

When the Processes tab is shown, take a look at the information about some of the processes that you know and love, such as DevEnv.exe (Visual Studio) or Notepad. Note the "Memory" usage and "CPU" usage columns and the values in them. Move the Task Manager window to the side of your screen, enough to see the Task Manager window while you use your other application. Once you've done this, start using the application, paying careful attention to the CPU and memory numbers for that application. As you use the application, the CPU usage should change, as should the memory (try opening, and then closing files within that application). It's important to note that across the various versions of Windows, the "Memory" column has slightly different meanings, but it is a good indication of how much physical memory your application is using at that point in time. However, an application may also allocate significantly more memory, but that memory is paged out to disk ("Working Set" versus "Allocated"). For a greater discussion of these values and their meanings, see a Windows internals' book.

You can show and hide other columns using the View/Columns menu item. There are a large number of choices here, and I suggest using the Windows Help and also Internet searches to understand what each of the different columns means in the context of your application. The ones I find interesting in general are Threads, Memory, Virtual Memory, Page Faults, Handles, IO Reads, and IO Writes. With these values being shown for my process, I can see the application changing over time as it runs and understand what (if any) issues it may be having. (For example, Handles going up and not coming down could indicate leaking handles.) An interesting thing to note is that there is no history here. You merely see the values at that instant in time. There also is no logging support in Task Manager.

The other tab that is of interest is the Performance tab (see Figure 8-7):

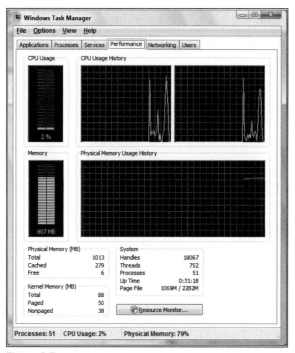

Figure 8-7

The Performance tab provides a general overview about the system, with no specific process information. However, it's very useful for understanding what effect your application may be having on the overall performance of a system, with minimal historic data for memory and CPU usage (per CPU). The values that are most interesting here are mostly the CPU and Page File Usage History. Other values can be interesting but are often only useful in very unique scenarios.

Performance Monitor

While Task Manager provides a snapshot in time of the metrics of the applications running on your system, there are no historical data, and also, Task Manager is about the local system, not a remote system. This is where the Reliability and Performance Monitor steps in (Performance monitor on non vista platforms). It provides the ability to view even more performance metrics about a system and its applications, while allowing logging and also viewing remote systems. All of this is in an easy-to-use graphing interface (see Figure 8-8).

The Performance Monitor and Task Manager are built on top of the performance counter infrastructure in Windows. This infrastructure is a common, consistent interface (both from an API and UI perspective) that allows you to read many metrics about your system — memory usage, network packets, .NET garbage collection generations, message per second, and many others. These counters can be added to by your application if it has a need to be monitored (maybe in a data center scenario, e.g.).

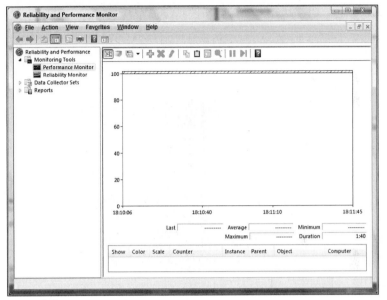

Figure 8-8

You can access the Performance Monitor in several ways:

❑ Start ⇨ Run ⇨ Perfmon.

❑ Right-click My Computer ⇨ Manage ⇨ System Tools ⇨ Performance Monitor.

❑ Start ⇨ All Programs ⇨ Administrative Tools ⇨ Performance Monitor.

❑ Start ⇨ Control Panel ⇨ Administrative Tools ⇨ Performance Monitor.

Once you've started the Performance Monitor, you'll be presented with something similar to Figure 8-8.

The screen shots here have been taken with Windows Vista. While it looks different, the basics are exactly the same on Windows 2000, XP, and Server 2003.

If you just leave the Performance Monitor as is and use your system (reply to e-mail, surf the Web) for a few minutes, you should see the graph peak and trough in time with the use of the system (see Figure 8-9).

On Vista, there are no default counters. To be able to see graphs, you need to add counters.

However, these are unlikely to be the performance counters that you need to measure to understand the performance of your application. You will need to add other counters by using the Add Counter button on the toolbar. You will be presented with a list of all the categories of counters, along with the counters in the currently selected category and the instances of each counter (such as per process, per network card, per disk). You can then add them to the list of tracked counters (see Figure 8-10).

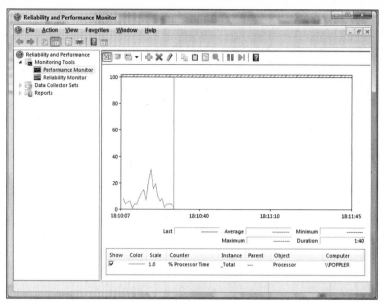

Figure 8-9

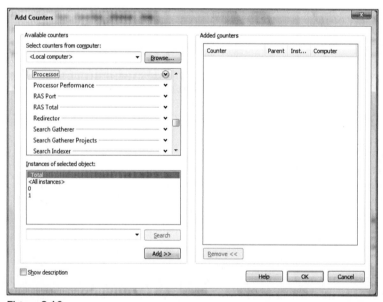

Figure 8-10

There is no specific way to know from the value of a specific counter that you have an issue. As stated previously, you need to have set goals before deciding if you have a problem. However, the Performance Monitor can help you see where and when you have problems with your application. For example, if you are seeing high memory usage, you can see if you are leaking managed memory by adding ".NET

CLR Memory" and "Gen 2 Heap Size" counters, and seeing if your high memory usage is due to objects making it into Generation 2 (e.g., a reference to an instance has been left in a dictionary and thus can't be garbage collected). Or, if you think you are CPU-bound, see the peak CPU usage of your application over time.

There are so many ways to slice and dice the data and what you need to look at that there is no definitive answer as to which counters to look at. This is where the Task Manager and Performance Monitor come into play as a pair: The Task Manager can clue you in to there being an issue, and the Performance Monitor can be used to narrow it down without having to bring out the profiler.

Profiling

When trying to analyze the specific performance of your code, it is very difficult to understand specifically what is taking its time. Is it a for loop? Network access? Disk IO? You can spend hours just taking stabs in the dark looking at code that doesn't look "optimal" or that might not be the best performing method, and while those may not be the most efficiently written lines of code, if they are not the ones causing your problem, then you are merely re-writing code for the fun of it, and you won't be seeing any real performance benefit. This is where Profiling comes in. It shows what functions were called, when they were called, and how long they took. "How long" includes both that specific function (exclusive time) and any other functions that were called from it (inclusive time). The mechanisms for obtaining these data are complex and can take one of two paths — Sampling and Instrumentation.

Additionally, the Profiling engine will collect trace events (ETW, Event Trace for Windows) from the operating system in any of the discovered categories. These can then be correlated with your method calls later during analysis. This provides a great way to see the repercussions of your code executing.

> *Profiling requires a specific set of privileges; however, these are not administrative rights. On XP/2000/ Server 2003, standard users have these privileges assigned to them. On Windows Vista, user account control removes this privilege. This issue resolved with the Visual Studio on Vista patch released in March 2007.*

> *When trying to profile a library or application, you cannot get accurate, or arguably useful, information without the PDBs or symbols for your application. If you are building the application yourself, ensure that the symbols are created at build time. This can be done for both debug and release flavors. If you are not building the application but still need to profile, contact your component vendor for the symbols. Microsoft provides symbols for almost all its applications online for free. Find more information at* http://support.microsoft.com/kb/311503.

Sampling

Most modern CPUs have hooks and counters that can be used to measure the time it takes certain things to happen. The application that wants to measure this information must sample these counters on the CPU over the period of time that measurement is required. This has less impact on the application, but it can also be less accurate. It also can give a more real-time estimate of how long things are taking, rather than an affected time in the case of instrumentation.

Sampling analyzes the performance of the whole application, and can be started/stopped on an already running application, if you have a specific scenario that you need to analyze.

Instrumentation

While sampling can have an impact on the real-time performance of your application, it does not actually modify it. It merely uses the CPU-based counters to read the information it needs. However, this is only as accurate as the periods over which you are sampling. The alternative form is instrumentation, which changes your built binaries before running.

Because of the way that instrumentation works, you get a much more accurate sense of what was called and how long it took. This is because when a binary is instrumented, all the method entry and exit points are changed to include calling a hook that sends data and information to the profiling runtime infrastructure. As the hook is called, the Profiler builds its database of what was called and how long it took.

Using the UI

Within the Profiler there are two main areas of UI — the Performance Session window and the Results window. The Performance Session window allows you to see what targets you have set up (DLLs, EXEs, web sites) to measure the performance of, as well as any previous runs.

Performance Wizard

To create a new performance session using the Performance Wizard, you can do one of two things — either use the Tools ⇨ Performance Tools ⇨ Performance Wizard, or if you have the Performance Explorer open, click the Performance Wizard button. You will see the Performance Wizard as in Figure 8-11.

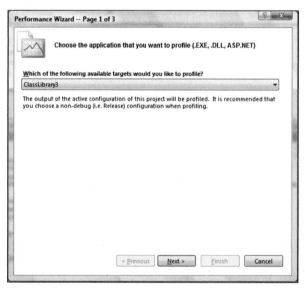

Figure 8-11

Here, you can select which of your projects to profile, or an EXE, DLL, or even a web site. Depending on which of these you select, you may be presented with a page asking you to locate the DLL, EXE, or web site. After you do that, you will be presented with a page asking to choose between Sampling and Instrumentation (see Figure 8-12).

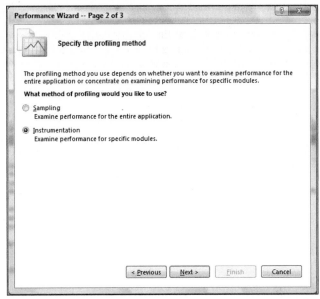

Figure 8-12

The next page is a confirmation page, where you can click Finish to create the performance session.

If you don't wish to use the Wizard to create a performance session, then you can just create a new performance session from Performance Explorer and add targets yourself.

Performance Explorer

This tool window allows you to manipulate all the properties and settings for your performance session. It also allows you to see all the performance reports that you have collected with this session over time. This is very useful for tracking your performance improvements (e.g., naming the reports after each change you make). A default window should look something like Figure 8-13.

There are two main sections to this window: targets and reports. Targets are the binaries you are trying to profile, whether they are a single DLL, multiple DLLs, applications, or web sites. While the Performance Wizard only adds one target, with Performance Explorer you are able to add many more. You do this by right-clicking on the Targets node and selecting the appropriate option from the context menu:

❑ Add Target Binary.

❑ Add Target Project.

❑ Add Existing Web Site.

If you have only one project in your solution and that project is, in fact, in the performance session as a target already, the Add Target Project option will be grayed out and not selectable. When you select any of the other options, you will be asked to locate a file or directory to be added as the target.

The Reports node is much simpler, only allowing you to add .vsp (report) files to be listed, as well as to manipulate currently existing reports (rename, delete, and exporting of results).

Figure 8-13

The toolbar (see Figure 8-14) provides several useful shortcuts for working with your performance sessions:

❑ **Performance Wizard** — Creates a new performance session using the Wizard (as previously discussed).

❑ **New performance session** — Creates a new, blank, performance session where you will need to add targets as you see fit before you can profile anything.

❑ **Launch** — Starts the target in the profiling environment (with the collection monitors, drivers, and auto instrumentation) and waits for the application to complete execution.

❑ **Instrumentation/Sampling combo box** — Allows you to change the session from instrumentation to sampling quickly and easily.

❑ **Stop** — Stops the currently running target (if there is one) and starts analyzing any collected data.

❑ **Attach/Detach** — Allows you to attach to or detach from any application on your system (providing you have the right privileges) and perform sampling profiling on that application until you stop the session, the application terminates, or you detach the Profiler.

Figure 8-14

It is also possible to have more than one performance session open in the Performance Explorer at a given time. You can do this by opening other .psess files or by adding additional new performance sessions.

Integration with Unit Testing

One useful integration point with profiling is the ability to use a test result to profile your application. This means that if you have created a test to follow a specific scenario, you can measure its performance quickly and easily. To do this you need to have successfully run the test and have the result in the Test Results window. Then, simply right-click the result, and select Create Performance Session. This will start the Performance Wizard for that test and allow you to proceed through the Wizard as you normally would. After this, running that performance session will ensure that your test is executed and profiling information is collected. There is no way to create a performance session for a test without having first executed it. You must use these steps to create that performance session.

Advanced Options

As well as the simple options (what to profile and how to profile), there are several more complex options (see Figure 8-15). These allow for significant customization of the profiling process in three main ways.

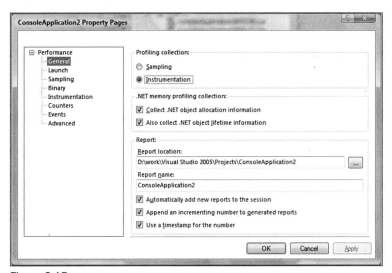

Figure 8-15

❑ **Pre- and Post-instrumentation events** — These are just like build events that you set for pre- and post-build. Typically for build events, you copy files over that are needed to build, or run some sort of post-build processing tool (adding a Windows manifest for UAC, e.g.). In the case of profiling, this might be placing the file in a different location.

❑ **What to collect (CPU counters, trace events)** — There are several different counters available on the CPU and also many different trace events. While in some situations it may be easy to collect all the information for all of the counters and events, this might not always be the case. Because of this, you can use these property pages to select the individual counters and events to collect.

❑ **Advanced options** — Some options are not ON by default and require you to change them here — specifically, the collection of allocation data for .NET managed objects. Also, not all the options that are available with profiling are surfaced in the UI. This setting allows you to specify additional command-line options that you would pass to the command-line tools if you were doing these steps by hand. These options are covered in the "Off-Roading on the Command Line" section below in this chapter.

Most, if not all, of these advanced options are only needed when you are pushing the envelope of the profiling functionality.

The Results UI

The Results UI, titled "Performance Report Summary," as seen in Figure 8-16, is primarily table-based, showing you data organized by method that can be sorted by various customizable columns. There are also several different tabs in the Results UI, allowing you to see different subsections of the collected data.

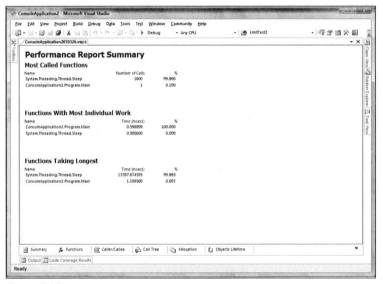

Figure 8-16

It's important to note that if you are collecting allocation information, that is all that will be shown. You won't be able to see function call time information at the same time.

Of the six tabs, the last two (Allocation and Object Lifetime) do not have information collected for them by default, and you are required to enable them using the property pages for the performance session.

❑ **Summary Page** — There is a large amount of information that is collected, and sometimes a lot of it is noise. The Summary page attempts to cherry-pick the important pieces of information or the information that is likely to be most significant to you and bring it to the Summary page. If you have Allocation Collection turned off, it will show Most Called Functions, Functions With Most Individual Work, and Functions Taking Longest (see Figure 8-16). If you have Allocation Collection turned on, then you will see Functions Allocating Most Memory, Types With Most Memory Allocated, and Types With Most Instances.

By default, these items only show the top three items; however, by using the Tools ➪ Options ➪ Performance Tools options page, you can change this number to show as many as you see fit. Personally, I think that three items is more than enough to get you focused in on the problem, rather than potentially showing you a lot of noise. You cannot customize the columns that are shown in the summary sections.

❑ **Functions Page** — When collecting allocation information, this shows you information about allocations, including the number of allocations (inclusive and exclusive) and bytes (inclusive and exclusive). When collecting performance information (see Figure 8-17), this will show six columns by default.

Figure 8-17

❑ **Function Name** — The name of the function is sorted by module, and then you can expand to see the function. This is very useful when you have many components that make up your application, as you can expand it to see which function in a specific module is most expensive.

❑ **Number of Calls** — The number of times that function was called.

❑ **Elapsed Exclusive Time** — The amount of time that this function (but not its children) spends executing. This includes any time that may have been spent executing in kernel mode (e.g., performing an operation that required a transition to kernel mode).

❑ **Application Exclusive Time** — Amount of execution time spent in this function (but not its children), excluding any time that may have been spent in kernel mode. This, in combination with exclusive time including kernel time, allows you to see if your problem is being slowed by a user/kernel mode transition.

❑ **Elapsed Inclusive Time** — It is rare that a function only executes within itself and never calls any other functions. This represents the time it took for the entire function to complete, including the time it took to call all other functions (all the way down the call stack) in that function.

❑ **Application Inclusive Time** — Time that was spent actually in the application and called functions, and not in kernel mode waiting on objects or other kernel mode calls.

❑ **Caller/Callee Page** — Within any application there is a call stack. As methods call other methods, the stack slowly gets bigger. Each time there is a discrete set of methods that are called from one function. This view allows you to walk down the call stack (see Figure 8-18), seeing which functions are called at each step of the way, how long they took, which other functions called that function, and which functions it called. As with the Functions page, this page includes the same set of timings.

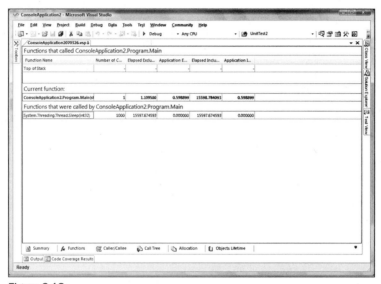

Figure 8-18

You can return back through the call stack using the "Functions that called this function" section at the top of the page.

❑ **Call Tree Page** — This is the most straightforward and simple view in the selection of views of the profile data. It provides a tree view of the application or profiled module as a tree. Each entry point into the module is listed, and all its child's calls, and those childrens child's calls, and so on. The same columns are shown here as in the Functions and Caller/Callee pages.

❑ **Allocation Page** — This shows each type that was allocated and where it was allocated (the function that allocated it), along with how many times the type was allocated (broken down by function and by type), how many types (also by function and type), and finally what percentage of the overall allocations for the application were in those types (by function and type).

❑ **Objects Lifetime Page** — Within the managed world, we have been blessed with a garbage collector for memory allocations. This means that when you make use of a new instance or cause memory to be allocated in the managed domain in some way, you do not need to remember to "free" or "release" that memory. The CLR will do it for you when it detects that there are no more references to that instance. However, it is very easy to "lose" a reference to an instance. The simplest example of this is putting something into a hash table and not storing the key into the hash table. If you do this, your instance is left hanging there for the lifetime of the application. You don't access it, because you no longer have the key to index into the hash table, and the run time won't release it because it sees that there is something that still has a reference to it. Thus, you have the potential of a memory leak.

When looking at the memory usage of your application, you may determine that it is using too much memory over the lifetime of its execution. But it can often be very unclear as to why this is. Is it simply because you are allocating more memory than is needed, but correctly disposing of it, or are you "leaking" memory somewhere? This is where the Objects Lifetime page comes into play. This will list all the instances of types within your application and how long they stayed alive. Because of the nature of the garbage collector in the CLR, it is generational. That is to say that as time goes on, the garbage collector will mark the "age" of a type by which generation it is in — how many times it has been passed over for release. When you see that types are making it to Generation 2 in large numbers, it suggests a memory leak. If you are seeing nothing make it even to Generation 1, then you are probably just allocating too much memory for no reason.

Understanding Results

With so much data telling you so many things, it can be difficult to interpret results. The key to being able to make productive use of the information the Profiler collects is to take it step by step and analyze the information being given to you. Start with the Summary page. It's telling you what's taking the longest to execute across your entire application. If you are looking at these numbers and they are not significant chunks of the execution time, then it suggests a deeper, more complex issue than assuming that someone did something foolish when they wrote the function, and you may need to examine the overall architecture of your application for a performance issue at that level.

Additionally, when looking at the timing of a function, it is important to compare and contrast the inclusive and exclusive times. This can help you narrow down the area at fault better than assuming that it is somewhere in the call stack with no real focus.

Remember, profiling doesn't tell you what is broken, only where things are spending their time. You only have a performance problem if your application is not meeting the goals that have been set for it. If you have no goals, you have no problem.

It is up to you to gain an understanding of your application to a level that the information gathered by the profiler can help you see how your application behaves and see how it is going awry.

> *Only make one change at a time. Never make multiple changes at a time, since this will inhibit your ability to know which change improved performance (or hurt performance). Profile after every change, and use this to compare your results manually over time to see whether your performance is trending up or down.*

Code Coverage

Part of instrumentation in profiling is about finding how often functions (or lines within a function) are executed. The side effect of this functionality is that you can see which lines within your application have and have not been executed, enabling you to detect dead and untested sections of your application. This means better testing, and if you find real dead code, you can remove it, which will result in less code to maintain.

Code Coverage with Tests

One of the integration points between VSTEST and VSTESD is the ability to collect code coverage information automatically every time you run a test. This is immensely useful as you build up a set of unit tests, for example, enabling you to maintain a high level of code coverage over the development of a class library. Other than checking a box to say "these assemblies should be used for coverage," everything is seamlessly integrated into the normal test run infrastructure.

1. To enable code coverage, you need to open up your run configuration from the Solution Explorer, and select the Code Coverage dialog box (see Figure 8-19)

2. In this dialog, all your currently loaded projects (some can have coverage measured; not all can) are listed, and can be checked. A check in the box indicates that the binary for that project will be instrumented when the test is executed. You can add additional assemblies here if they are not outputs of projects.

3. There are two other options in this dialog: "Instrument assemblies in place," and "Re-signing key file." *Instrument in place* means that the assembly will be instrumented where it currently is located (e.g., bin\debug). If you uncheck this option, the binaries will only be instrumented for coverage in the test run directory.

4. *Re-signing* is more significant and is tied to the original signing state of the assembly for which you are seeking coverage information. If your assembly was not signed, this value need not be set. However, if you signed your assembly, you will need to provide a key here; otherwise your assembly will be unable to load during the test run. The changes made by instrumentation will cause your assembly to fail the strong name check, and thus the private key used to sign the assembly in the first place is needed here. Providing the path to the key file (.snk) is all that is needed, and the re-signing will happen transparently.

5. After you have saved the run configuration, you can run the tests to collect the coverage information. When the test run has completed, you can click the Show Code Coverage Results button on the Test Results toolbar (see Figure 8-20) to see the code coverage window (Figure 8-21).

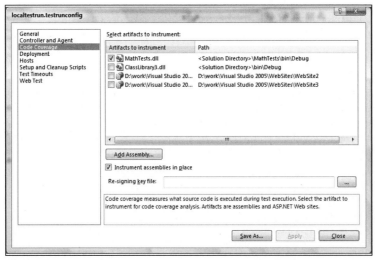

Figure 8-19

Figure 8-20

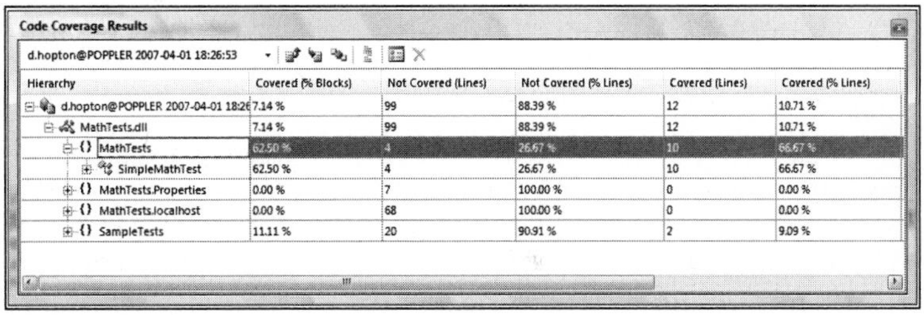

Figure 8-21

Blocks, Lines, and Partial Coverage

Code coverage is measured using two main measures — lines and blocks. Lines are exactly what one expects them to be: the lines in your source code. However, blocks are not quite what one may interpret them to be — blocks of source. Blocks are sections of control within the compiled binary. These blocks may not be manifested in the source code anyway, which is an example of why you may find it difficult to attain 100 percent coverage. The uncovered blocks have no source construct to interpret to write additional tests. These blocks are inserted by the compiler and are for housekeeping purposes. Example results from a test run with coverage can be seen in Figure 8-21.

When one is looking at lines, there are three states that a line is in — covered, not covered, and partially covered. The first two states are clear: Either your line of code was executed, or it was not. However, with a "partially" covered line, it is not completely covered. This is the case with a multicondition if-statement, whereby you have many clauses that are not evaluated at every execution; tertiary statements are also an example of these statements. Finally, if you place many lines on one line, these also will show up as partially covered if something causes the statements to not be executed (e.g., an exception being thrown).

```
Random rand = new Random();
Int rand1 = rand.Next(1, 10);
Int rand2 = rand.Next(1, 10);
If((rand1 < 5) && (rand2 > 5))
{
    Console.WriteLine("Random number in range")
}
```

When you execute this code, for example, by placing it in a unit test and executing that unit test (with coverage enabled for the test project), viewing the results in the Code Editor will show that the if-statement is only partially covered using colored highlighting with the source code itself. An example of results in the code editor for a partially covered statement is shown in Figure 8-22 (albeit using different code than the preceding example).

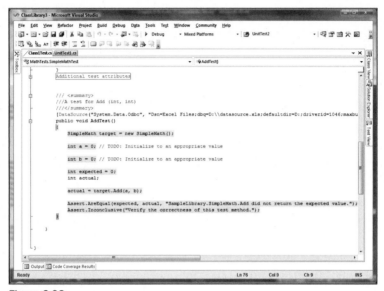

Figure 8-22

This means that after evaluation of the first clause proved that the entire condition could not be evaluated to True, the second statement is not executed — therefore only "partially covered." While in this contrived example this seems unimportant, in the case of the two clauses requiring two method calls to be evaluated, it can have a significant impact on what you are actually testing. You can see the opposite effect with "or" clauses, where it will not evaluate the second clause because the first has evaluated to True.

When to Care, When Not to Care

Code coverage is measured in percentages — the percentage of all lines in the chosen binary that are executed over a specific execution of that binary. While at first it seems that you should aim for 100 percent, this turns out to be a bad idea, because as your application grows both in size and complexity, it becomes increasingly difficult to maintain that 100 percent coverage. One specific example of this is trying to ensure coverage of error handling code. It can be very difficult to cause error conditions to occur, and in many cases it can be impossible without the addition of fault injection tools, which can be very costly.

If you set a goal of 100 percent at the beginning of the project, when the inevitable missed goal occurs, it will be a precipitous fall from that goal, rather than a momentary lapse. It's under these circumstances that you usually have the epiphany that while code coverage is very significant in ensuring that the important parts of your application are being tested, it cannot prove that your application has been tested.

For a moment, let's suppose that your application or library has 100 percent coverage — every line of your application has been executed, and all your tests have passed. What does this tell you? That your application is bug free? That you are successfully testing all the possible paths through your application? It doesn't tell you either of these things. The coverage number is a good "canary in the mine" metric; it can tell when things are mostly okay and when things are definitely going bad (no coverage is a bad sign). What it doesn't tell you is whether your QA team is testing the right part of the application, in the right way. They could just be calling all the functions (private and public), or they could just be making sure that the error conditions are occurring and being tested.

Take as an example the following code snippet:

```
MyType myInstance = null;
If(OtherCondition())
{ myInstance = new MyType(); }
myInstance.DoWork();
```

When you get 100 percent coverage on this snippet, it is missing a very important code path that would create a NULL-reference exception after the if-statement. But because of the false security of 100 percent coverage, it won't be found until much later in the product cycle, where it is more expensive to fix, test, and release.

The key takeaway from this is that 100 percent coverage does not mean your application is being fully tested. It means that all lines of code have been executed and that some different paths through the code require more investigation to ensure that they are correctly tested. It is a canary in a mine, not a conclusive answer.

Off-Roading on the Command Line

While the IDE integration of the profiling and code coverage tools is good, sometimes it doesn't satisfy your needs. As such, there are several tools provided to allow you to profile your applications manually, as well as providing more advanced options and fine-grained control of the collection engine. Additionally, if you have a complex set of performance tests or technology, the command-line tools can be integrated into your automated processes for monitoring of performance across builds.

There are four tools that can be used on the command line. They perform the same functions as the UI (Instrumentation, Collection, and Report Viewing) but from the command line. The tools are VsInstr (for instrumenting binaries), VsPerfCmd (for managing a performance session that is in progress), VsPerfMon (for collecting data), and VsPerfReport (for exporting report data on the command line).

VSInstr

This tool is used for instrumenting a binary before either profiling (nonsampling) or code coverage collection. The simplest use of this tool is by supplying the assembly that you wish to be instrumented.

By default, this will instrument your application for profiling rather than coverage (the markers that are inserted differ for profiling and coverage collection). An example of output is seen here:

```
D:\SampleLibrary\bin\Debug>vsinstr SampleLibrary.dll
Microsoft (R) VSInstr Post-Link Instrumentation 8.0.50727 x86
Copyright (C) Microsoft Corp. All rights reserved.

File to Process:
    D:\SampleLibrary\bin\Debug\SampleLibrary.dll --> D:\SampleLibrary\bin\Debug\
    SampleLibrary.dll
Original file backed up to D:\SampleLibrary\bin\Debug\SampleLibrary.dll.orig

Successfully instrumented file D:\SampleLibrary\bin\Debug\SampleLibrary.dll.
Warning VSP2013 : Instrumenting this image requires it to run as a 32-bit
    process.  The CLR header flags have been updated to reflect this.
```

The warning at the end is because currently profiling is only supported on 32-bit assemblies. You can remove this warning with either the /NOWARN switch., or by ensuring that your assembly is marked as 32-bit only (if appropriate) rather than as "Any CPU" in your build configuration To instrument an assembly for coverage, supply the /coverage switch on the command line.

There are several advanced options available on the command line related to the placement of instrumentation markers and callbacks within your assembly, allowing you to include/exclude specific functions. This is a very advanced topic and won't be covered here. If you use vsintr /?, you can see the switches related to this functionality.

VsPerfMon

Collection happens as an asynchronous task to the execution of your application and is logged in the background by vsperfmon. This is actually the same tool that is run by the UI when you start a performance session from the IDE. In the general course of using the command-line tool, you don't need to start this tool yourself; however, you can. When executing vsperfmon by hand, there are some powerful options for running against other user identities, inside other window "sessions" (in the case of remote desktops or terminal servers), and across sessions. Use vsperfmon /? to see the specific syntax for these options.

When you are using vsperfmon manually, you still need to use vsperfcmd to shut down the monitor and ensure noncorrupt report data. You can do this by using vsperfcmd /shutdown.

VSPerfCmd

This is the all-encompassing tool for management of your collection from the command line. It enables you to start and stop collection, select which counters to collect for sampling, attach/detach, and manage the security of the driver (such as who can and cannot perform profiling). I will not be covering the management of security here because the command-line help from vsperfcmd /? is self-explanatory.

To start collection, merely use vsperfcmd /start:trace /output:<filename>, where trace is one of trace, coverage, or sampling (the profiling type), and <filename> is the filename for the output of the collection. After you start the monitor, you will see the banner outputted and no other information.

At this point, you would execute your application throughout the scenario you are trying to investigate (or run tests in the case of coverage). When you have completed running through the steps you need to perform, you need to shut down the monitor and allow it to write out any collected information. You do this with `vsperfcmd /shutdown`. You should see output like the following if it is successful:

```
Microsoft (R) VSPerf Command Version 8.0.50727 x86
Copyright (C) Microsoft Corp. All rights reserved.


Shutting down the Profile Monitor
-------------------------------------------------------------
```

You can now examine the .vsp file either in the IDE or using the vsperfreport tool (which is discussed in the next section).

If you wish to collect allocation information in managed applications, you need to use the /GC switch. By default, this will only track allocations and not the lifetime of objects. If you specify `/gc:lifetime`, then both allocations and lifetime of objects will be collected as part of profiling.

You can also verify the current status of the monitor by using the `/status` command. If the monitor is not currently running, you will see it say that it is not running. However, if it is running, more information about the state of the monitor will be displayed. This includes the current output file, collection mode, size of buffers, and the current access rights:

```
Microsoft (R) VSPerf Command Version 8.0.50727 x86
Copyright (C) Microsoft Corp. All rights reserved.


Process and Thread Status
=============================================================
Output File Name            : D:\foo.vsp
Collection mode             : COVERAGE
Maximum Processes           : 64
Maximum Threads             : 256
Number of Buffers           : 258
Size of Buffers             : 65536

=============================================================
Maximum Number of Processes : 64
Number of Active Processes  : 0
Global Start/Stop Count     : 1
Global Suspend/Resume Count : 0
=============================================================
Users with access rights to monitor:
UserName (SID)
NT AUTHORITY\SYSTEM (S-1-5-18)
BUILTIN\Administrators (S-1-5-32-544)
```

VsPerfReport

When you collect data with vsperfcmd, you will end up with a vsp file. VsPerfReport can be used to export these data into a manipulatable form such as CSV or XML. You cannot export coverage data using this tool. You need to use the IDE for this.

When you execute vsperfreport without any command-line switches and supply a .vsp file, the tool will generate a summary header file of that report. This CSV will have some very simple information about the performance session and nothing of any value. For really useful information, you need to use the /summary switch, which allows you to generate a specific report (or all reports). These reports contain the basic information you see in the UI, along with all the other optional columns that are hidden (but can be shown) by default. The report types are the same as those in the UI. Use VsPerfReport /? to see the full syntax for these options. Once you have a CSV (or XML, using the /XML switch), you can process the output in another tool such as a database or a spreadsheet.

Summary

In this chapter, we've seen the static analysis tools, which allow you to catch stylistic, design, security, and other categories of errors at build time before they get into the product, or even soon after, depending on your check-in model. We've seen that they can be very powerful, but also very distracting.

Also, we've learned about performance profiling and code coverage metric for your application. We've seen how to use the coverage tools with VSTEST, as well as seeing how the different types of profiling can be used.

VSTEST and VSTESD within the Software Development Life Cycle

With the software testing and developer analysis tools added to Visual Studio Team Edition introduced in the earlier chapters, we turn to look at when and where these tools can be applied in a software development life cycle (SDLC) and how they intersect with the Team Foundation System.

> *While we will look at integration points for VSTEST and VSTESD tools, this chapter does not go into great detail about the Visual Studio Team Foundation Server (VSTFS). For greater detail on installing, configuring, deploying, and managing VSTFS, please refer to the book* Professional Team Foundation Server, *published by Wrox and authored by Jean-Luc David, Mickey Gousset, and Erik Gunvaldson.*

We'll begin by looking at what VSTFS has to offer and why your team would consider adding it as a tool. Next, we'll look at the software development methodologies, move on to collaborating with your team using VSTFS, and finish with how the different development tools plug in to VSTFS.

VSTFS at a High Level

Before we talk about how the developer and tester tools integrate into the Visual Studio Team Foundation Server, we want to discuss what exactly VSTFS is at a high level. Typically at the start of a project, the team comes up with (or is handed) an idea of some software that needs to be created. For younger teams in smaller companies, this typically means that everyone works to cobble together a number of tools to help the entire project flow a little bit better, especially when there is more than just one person involved.

Instead of trying to bring several tools together from different tool vendors and then write thin layers to get those applications to connect in some fashion, VSTFS provides a solution in which all of the tools are provided and are already aware of each other.

Specifically, VSTFS provides the following:

❑ **Process Templates** — Every project I've been on in a new team requires templates to be created for functional specifications (for the Project Manager), design documents (for the developer), and test plans (for the test engineers). In addition, everyone must agree upon how things flow from conception to design and testing to final release. These templates are provided to you by VSTFS so that you have a starting point.

❑ **Version Control** — This is an easy concept to sell for anyone who has ever been on a project with a large number of people. Allowing you to merge changes together, to verify you're not overwriting each other's changes, and to put work on hold ("shelving," in VSTFS terms) while you work on a previous or newer version of the same file are all capabilities of this type of tool. Your project administrator can even set up "check-in policies" requiring you and your teammates to run specific tests prior to checking in your new or modified source code. If you are new to version control, the simplest way to think of it is as being able to save your game as many times as you like; you can always go back to the previously saved version in case your character dies. Now, imagine how nice this is in a team setting when someone else kills your character.

❑ **Issue/Work Item Tracking** — Commonly known as a bug tracker, this feature allows you to keep track of all of your work items, software defects, requirements, and so on. You can even add your own types of work items, should you choose. Remember that we did say at the very beginning that this is an integrated approach: You can associate any work item (e.g., bugs) with any source code change you make as it is being checked into the version control system (more on this later). In addition, as new tests are written, they can be associated with the bug that identified the previously unknown issues. This comes in handy especially when looking at metrics and determining how many of your bugs have an associated test to verify that the bug does not recur.

❑ **Metrics/Reporting** — The program managers and people footing the bills for the project have not been forgotten. Included with VSTFS is a reporting engine allowing you to see the health of your project by looking at defect trends, effectiveness of testing (also known as code coverage tracking), tests that verify that requirements continue to be met, and so on. Pretty charts, graphs, and tables abound.

❑ **Build Management** — Also a key ingredient of VSTFS is the ability to manage a team build. Imagine a team of 100 developers all checking in their code by a particular weekly (or nightly) deadline, having run their tests to confirm that their changes haven't broken the build. Now compile it into one large build that takes hours to complete, run a key set of tests against that project, and then confirm the next morning whether or not it's worthwhile for the test engineers to take it for testing. This is the promise of the team build capabilities of VSTFS.

❑ **SharePoint/Team Collaboration** — Included with VSTFS is Microsoft SharePoint, the collaboration software that allows your team to create its own intranet site for storing the aforementioned documentation, team calendars, links to popular reports, and so on. If you are new to collaboration software, it's a simple concept but very powerful in allowing you to create a single portal for your team to go to for key project information.

❑ **Integration with Other Tools** — VSTFS also provides you the ability to import your work items (bugs, tasks, requirements, etc.) into Microsoft Excel and Microsoft Project. The key thing here is that it keeps the items *linked*. We're not talking a simple import/export; these items are tied together so that as work items change in either the VSTFS database (also known as the *warehouse*) or the client application, the changes are kept in synch.

As you can see, VSTFS is all about providing a way for the team to work and play together while staying in sync and communicating with one another and avoiding losing any key pieces through the cracks. A big part of putting these tools to use, of course, is in following some kind of process. In our world, this is the Software Development Lifecycle, or SDLC, which we will look at next.

The Software Development Life Cycle

There are many different approaches to running a project and following a preferred process. There is no one perfect approach; they all have their pros and cons. What is important, however, is to pick a process, understand it as a team, and follow it, bending it to meet your team's needs and leveraging your teammates' strengths.

Some of the more popular SDLCs include such models as Waterfall, Spiral, MDD (Model-Driven Development), Top-down and Bottom-up design, Chaos, and Agile (e.g., eXtreme Programming). Many companies selling software development tools have cobbled together their own approaches that borrow from one or more models, most notably IBM/Rational and the Rational Unified Process (RUP, an iterative development process) and Microsoft and their Microsoft Solution Framework (MSF, also an iterative approach, but including sets of processes, principles, and proven practices).

Because it always seems that everyone has strong opinions and feelings around one SDLC methodology over another (also known as religious battles), we will forgo the battle of picking an approach and instead look at the common ground shared among many of the more mainstream practices.

If you hunger for more information on the topic of SDLCs, Wikipedia has a great entry worth reading: http://en.wikipedia.org/wiki/Software_development_process.

Common activities in any SDLC include

- ❑ **Gathering Requirements** — Determining the goals and outcome that the customer wants.
- ❑ **Creating Functional Specifications** — Pulling together a description of how the product will work based on the assembled requirements.
- ❑ **Designing the Architecture** — Also a form of specification, this is created by the software development engineer to lay out what needs to be created "under the hood" to meet the requirements and goals of the functional specification.
- ❑ **Coding** — Writing the code to actually create the defined architecture.
- ❑ **Testing** — Verifying that the written code is working as designed or specified and that the requirements are still being met. Test engineers are also, in my opinion, one of the last lines of defense when it comes to championing customers' needs.
- ❑ **Documenting** — End-user documentation, whether it's for how APIs are called or the UI components are used. You could even consider comments within the source code a form of documentation. Also, never forget the translation needs if you are shipping to multiple markets.
- ❑ **Supporting** — When customers don't want to read the documentation (or if the documentation is lacking), Customer Support through training, e-mail, and even phone calls needs to be provided (in many software companies, especially smaller ones, the "supporting" step is an

afterthought and not considered a part of the SDLC). Do not forget to schedule time to train your support engineers for new features and to bring your support sites online in time to meet your product ship dates.

❑ **Maintaining** — If the software is successful, users will want updates prior to the next version. These are typically provided through patches or service releases and need to be taken into account as part of the work being done as part of the next major release.

Now, before someone points out that this is a typical Waterfall approach, I argue that these steps are taken no matter what the methodology being followed is. Whether the requirements, specifications, and architecture work is done in individual 20-page formal documents, on a bar napkin (been there, done that, and even have the napkin), on a whiteboard, in wikis, through ad hoc hallway discussions, or your private mental ruminations, the fact is that a certain amount of planning goes in before a substantial amount of code is written.

An Iterative approach means that the project is broken down into multiple coding and testing milestones. This allows everyone to come up for air midway through the project to make sure that the project is tracking to the requirements/goals and so that (hopefully) minimal course corrections can be made — this instead of the early days of software projects, where it was one long slog to design, then code, code, code, then test, test, test, and finally fix, fix, fix, to hit a single, final end date.

Microsoft's approach with Visual Studio Team Suite is to allow you to apply whichever process you prefer, as strict or loose as your team decides, while supporting the common needs of a development project: source code management (aka: version control), requirements and work item tracking (aka: bug database), integration with development and testing tools, and finally, metrics reporting.

Collaborating with Your Team

Thus far in this book, we've looked at how the tools are used in a stand-alone setting. To explore how these developer and testing tools work in a team-level collaborative environment, we must connect to your team's existing project. To do this, you must first install the Team Explorer utility that integrates with Visual Studio.

Installing Team Explorer

Included with the Visual Studio Team Foundation Server installation that is purchased separately from the Visual Studio Team Suite is Team Explorer, a plug-in that allows you to join a team project and utilize the benefits of the Visual Studio Team Foundation Server (including source code control, work item/bug tracking, publishing test results for rolled-up metrics reports, and more). Running the Visual Studio Team Foundation Server installation shows an initial page similar to Figure 9-1, where you have the option of installing Team Explorer.

For a detailed walk-through of what it looks like to install Team Explorer, see Appendix A. Also, documentation for Team Explorer is included with the MSDN Library for Visual Studio 2005.

After successfully installing Team Explorer, the Connect to Team Foundation Server menu item will appear under the Tools menu, as shown in Figure 9-2.

Figure 9-1

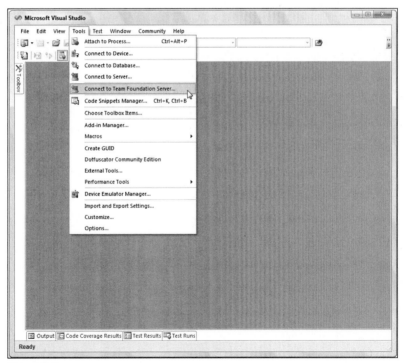

Figure 9-2

Connecting to a Project

Using this new menu item, you may now connect to your team's project. Sharing source code, work items, team documents, team builds, metrics reports, and a shared approach to the software development life cycle are the key benefits, as we discussed above in this chapter (see Figure 9-3). In Figure 9-3 you can see the Microsoft Solution Framework approach to Agile Software Development as displayed in the team's project portal, which was created as part of the new VSTFS team project. Note, too, the new Team Explorer window on the right side of the main window showing the team project named msvstest_tra.

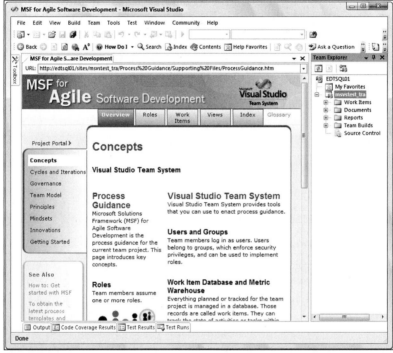

Figure 9-3

The high-level concepts and key definitions can be found in the document selected in Figure 9-3. Much of the work has been done for your team in advance, and you can tweak the provided templates to best suit the group's needs.

It's through the Team Explorer view and its folders that you can access the components that define the entire project. In this example, the server is named *EDTSQL01*, and the project on that server is called *msvstest_tra*. The server can hold multiple projects; this is but one project we've chosen to view.

For detailed steps on installing Team Explorer, as well as creating and connecting to a team project, see Appendix A.

High-Level View of the Project

Continuing with the example of the project called *msvstest_tra* on the EDTSQL01 server, we have five areas to look at, as shown in Figure 9-4:

- ❑ Work Items
- ❑ Documents
- ❑ Reports
- ❑ Team Builds
- ❑ Source Control

Figure 9-4

Work Items

Going far beyond a simple bug tracking database, using the Microsoft Solutions Framework's "Agile" template, we have five types of work items:

- ❑ Bug
- ❑ Quality of Service Requirement
- ❑ Risk
- ❑ Scenario
- ❑ Task

The project also comes stocked with common queries and allows you to specify your own queries, as shown in Figure 9-5. These queries work with the previously mentioned work item types. For example, the Active Bugs query will display all defects that have not yet been fixed, verified, and closed. The All Tasks query will display all tasks within the project database, no matter what their status (i.e., active or closed will both be displayed). In the My Queries folder, each team member has the ability to create his or her own private queries, as I have done in Figure 9-5. Here I can see what my teammates have assigned to their folders.

Figure 9-5

Documents

One of the biggest tasks that I find when starting a new project is figuring out what documentation we need and what each of those documents should contain. I've seen people keep their documents from past jobs to use as templates simply because they didn't want to create the template again and again. When the project is created in Visual Studio Team Foundation System, the process template selected when creating a new team project creates a default set of documents, as shown in Figure 9-6.

These templates provide you a starting point in such areas as the process your team will follow, files useful to project managers, requirements based on particular customer types (also known as *personas*), security considerations prior to releasing your software, and, of course, a test plan or approach to how quality will be measured and verified on the project.

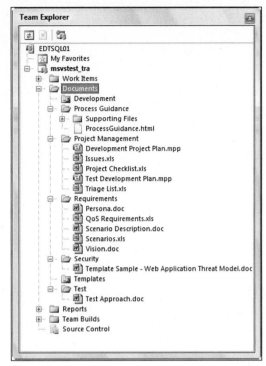

Figure 9-6

Reports

One of the cool things about the Microsoft Visual Studio team is that they actually used their tools as they were creating them. A bit of a chicken-and-egg scenario, as the tools matured through their iterative development process, they started to bring new features online. What better way to find real-world bugs than to use the product on one's own team? Another benefit was that when reports were needed to get an understanding of where things were with the project, those reports were later polished and added as the default reports created when a new team project is added to a Visual Studio Team Foundation Server. While you can author your own reports, Figure 9-7 shows the standard reports included with a new team project.

These reports can be very simple in nature, such as listing all bugs by their degree of criticality (priority). Or they can get a little more involved by showing trends such as bug rates to help your team understand if you're on an upward slope (more bugs being opened than fixed) or downward slope, as you shoot for your release date.

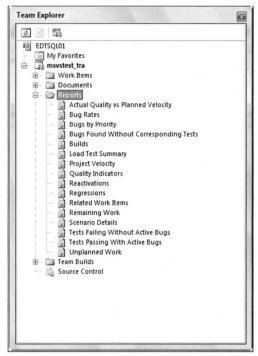

Figure 9-7

Team Builds

Part of being on a team project is collaborating with your teammates and sharing documents and files. This includes coordinating changes to your source code so that a build can be created for testing purposes. Woe unto the person who "breaks the build" and requires a new build to be kicked off. (With large builds taking many hours to complete, a broken build has a direct impact on the test engineers' schedule for their test pass.) The goal of a team build is to help coordinate a large build that comprises all teammates' changes. In addition, a team build can be configured to run a set of tests after the build completes, allowing the test team to determine immediately if the build is worth taking or rejecting. Figure 9-8 shows where the team builds appear in the Team Explorer window.

Figure 9-8

Below in this chapter we look at how creating a team build that incorporates tests as part of verifying a build is worthwhile.

Source Control

Source control is the feature that allows you to have a single library utilized by your entire team for storing the project's source code. This is helpful to avoid people changing the same file at the same time and overwriting each other's changes. It also helps in merging changes together. Lastly, one of the nicer features is the ability to "shelve" one's work. That is, imagine you've checked out a file to work on, but someone wants you to verify a change they've made in the same file. You can temporarily shelve your work, check out the file that has your co-worker's changes, verify their fix, and then unshelve your work to continue where you left off. Later, when you check it in (if you didn't allow for mutually exclusive checkouts), you can merge your changes into the file. Figure 9-9 shows where the Source Control files will appear in your Team Explorer window.

Figure 9-9

Double-clicking on one of the source controlled files will then check out the file and open it for editing.

How the VSTEST and VSTESD Tools Fit

Companies that create tools are constantly finding customers using those tools in scenarios that never occurred to them. While you look at how these tools can fit into a SDLC, remember that there may be other ways to leverage a tool beyond its originally intended purpose.

In this section I've roughly listed the different tools covered in Chapters 3–8 in the order that you would likely use them on your project. For example, static analysis is listed first because as you set up a new project, the benefits of using this tool are shown from the very beginning. Testing, depending on how you go about creating your tests (i.e., Do you follow an Agile method of creating tests first?), likely comes next. Complementing your testing efforts is the code coverage functionality.

As your project matures and you look to streamline its performance, dynamic analysis comes into play to help you identify and address performance bottlenecks. With the project maturing and more developers coming into the fold, you will likely create a build process where everyone checks in by a particular time so that a single build can take place. Last in the list, but arguably an on-going necessity, is reporting to help those footing the bill and those managing everyone's efforts to get the big picture of where everything is at.

While writing this chapter, I was going to create a table to show when each of these tools comes into play. It didn't make sense to create that table, however, because as it turns out all of the tools can be used throughout the entire life cycle (that is, soon after coding begins). Regardless, I've still attempted to discuss how they work with VSTFS in the order that you will likely encounter them when initially creating a project and getting some code written. The point to take away, though, is that these tools should be used early and often to keep your expenses low. You've heard the adage again and again, I'm sure, that the earlier you find a problem, the cheaper it is to correct it. These tools will help you find those problems, so use them early and often.

Team Project Source Control Policies

One of the key integration points for the developer tools and testing tools is the ability to create a source control policy. These policies are accessed through the top-level Team menu that was added to Visual Studio when a team project was joined on VSTFS, as shown in Figure 9-10.

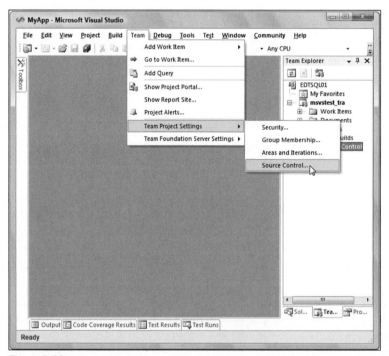

Figure 9-10

After selecting the Source Control menu item from the Team Project Settings submenu in Figure 9-10, the Source Control Settings dialog box for your selected team project is displayed, as shown in Figure 9-11.

If you are currently working with more than one team project, be sure that you have clicked on that team project's name in the Team Explorer window before going to this dialog box. Its context is based on the currently selected team project.

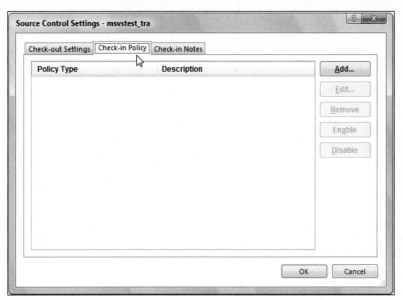

Figure 9-11

The Source Control Settings dialog box for your selected team project has three tabs:

❑ **Check-out Settings** — Currently there is only one option on this tab: whether or not you want to allow your team to be able to exclusively check out a file or allow multiple people to check out a file at the same time. (They've left the door open for expansion as this feature matures.)

❑ **Check-in Policy** — This tab, shown in Figure 9-11, allows you to create various policies that come into play when someone attempts to check a file into the source control for your project:

   ❑ **Code Analysis** — A policy that requires the static analysis tool to be used prior to checkin.

   ❑ **Testing Policy** — Requires that a specific list of tests are executed successfully prior to checkin.

   ❑ **Work Items** — Ensures that at least one work item (i.e., a task, bug, or other work item type) is associated with the engineer's checkin.

❑ **Check-in Notes** — This allows the Team Project administrator to specify what type of notes are required with each checkin. Visual Studio Team System provides for notes from three reviewer roles: code reviewer, security reviewer, and performance reviewer.

Now we will look at how to create check-in policies for the code analysis and testing tools. (We won't go into the work item policy, as a discussion of it is outside the scope of this book.)

Adding a Code Analysis Check-in Policy

As you'll recall from Chapter 8's in-depth introduction to the static analysis tool — a tool used for early detection of security and performance issues — right-clicking on the project in the Solution Explorer window displays a menu similar to the one shown in Figure 9-12.

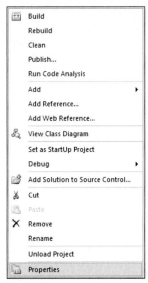

Figure 9-12

Clicking the context menu's Properties menu item and then the Code Analysis tab in the resulting window (see Figure 9-13) allows you to modify the static analysis rules available for your project.

If you are familiar with FxCop, you already understand the concept of static analysis, except now it is integrated into Visual Studio. See Chapter 8 for a look at this functionality.

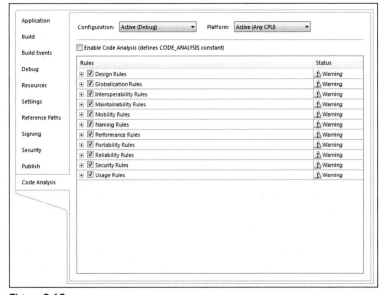

Figure 9-13

On a team of developers it's not uncommon to have someone check in code that results in a compilation error, thereby breaking the build — frustrating, to be sure, especially when your project gets to the size that it requires hours for a build to complete. Worse is code that compiles but hits runtime errors that are caught as part of the testing tools that can be added as part of the build process, increasing the time it takes to get an intact build out for test engineers to start using.

This is where the static analysis tool can help in a team setting. Setting up a check-in rule to discourage developers from checking in code that fails the static analysis validation rules is a big step toward minimizing team build breaks. Build breaks can still occur, of course, especially as there is a way to override the policy.

> *The check-in policy is merely a way to remind team members to take certain actions prior to checking in their changes. There are ways around it including explicitly choosing to override the policy via its message box as well as the* `[ConditionalAttribute("CODE_ANALYSIS")]` *attribute to suppress a rule violation. (See Chapter 8 for more details about this attribute.)*

As we saw above in this chapter, the Source Control Settings dialog box (see Figure 9-11) is displayed by selecting the Source Control menu item found under the Team menu's Team Project Settings submenu. Clicking on the Check-in Policy tab and then on the Add button displays the Add Check-in Policy dialog box, shown in Figure 9-14.

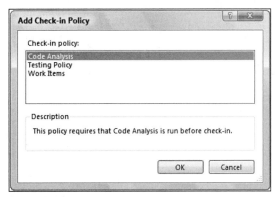

Figure 9-14

Of the available policies, for this section we are interested only in the Code Analysis item. Clicking the OK button with the Code Analysis item selected displays the Code Analysis Policy Editor, shown in Figure 9-15.

The Code Analysis Policy Editor dialog box allows the administrator of the team project to determine exactly how stringent the policy is for checking in source code. (For more details on the different types of rules, see Chapter 8 as well as the MSDN online Help.) There are three checkboxes found on this dialog box that are of interest:

❑ **Enforce check-in to only contain files that are part of the current solution** — This checkbox helps the developer be explicit in what he or she is checking in. The theory goes: if it's important enough to check in, then it's important enough to be part of the solution. Otherwise, keep it out of the Source Control database. Most teams would rather not block extra files being checked in, and as a result this option defaults as "unchecked." (Also, keep in mind that automated tests can be part of the check-in process, meaning that check-in policies would also apply when this checkbox is set.)

❑ **Enforce C/C++ Code Analysis** — This invokes the PreFast functionality of the Code Analysis feature that is specific to C and C++ source code.

❑ **Enforce Code Analysis For Managed Code** — This utilizes the FxCop functionality associated with managed source code.

Figure 9-15

It is possible to add multiple code analysis check-in policies and then enable or disable them depending on the current project needs.

With the Code Analysis Policy in place, a developer going through the usual steps of adding his or her solution or individual file to source control will be required to first have his or her source analyzed against that policy. For example, adding a new project or file into the team project's source control can be done by right-clicking on the project or file in the Solution Explorer window, as shown in Figure 9-16. (In this example, we're adding a Project named *MyApp*.)

After the files are added, the Pending Changes window is displayed, as shown in Figure 9-17.

The Pending Changes window has the following icons running vertically on the left side of the pane:

❑ **Source Files** — Provides a view of the list of source files available to be checked into the source tree. (The previous steps did add the files to the team project's source control library, but they've not actually been checked in.)

❑ **Work Items** — Part of the check-in process allows work items to be associated with the checkin. For example, you can associate the added or changed files with a task or bug type of work item (or any type of work item, for that matter).

❑ **Check-in Notes** — Notes can be entered for later clarification of what work was done that resulted in this checkin of files. Note, too, that unless a policy has been created requiring these notes, they are optional.

❑ **Policy Warnings** — This tab is what we're most interested in at the moment. It shows what policies have not been addressed as part of the check-in steps.

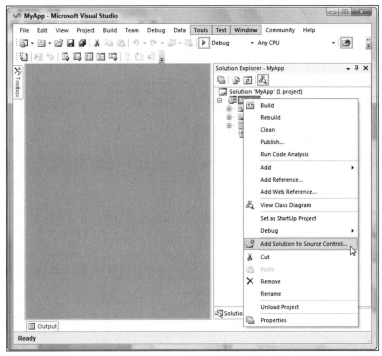

Figure 9-16

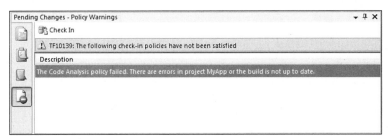

Figure 9-17

Because we've added a project ("MyApp") with a bunch of new source files to the team project's source control library and not run the code analysis beforehand, Figure 9-17 shows the warning we receive that a check-in policy is being violated.

Even though we are seeing a policy violation prior to checking in our source files, we can continue our checkin. In our example we have not addressed the violation and a Policy Failure dialog box is shown, similar to the dialog displayed in Figure 9-18.

Figure 9-18

With a policy failure we have two options:

❑ We can cancel out of this dialog box and run code analysis prior to checking in the files.

❑ We can move ahead with the checkin and override the policy. In this example, the team member has chosen to move ahead with his checkin, aware that he could break the build but willing to take the risk.

On our team you had to have a very good reason for not following policy because you risked breaking the build and holding up the rest of the team. The end goal is to have zero policy warnings so that the Policy Warnings list in your Pending Changes window resembles Figure 9-19: "All check-in policies are satisfied."

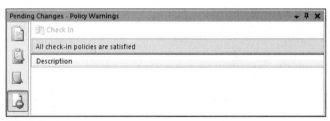

Figure 9-19

Adding a Testing Check-in Policy

Referring back to Figure 9-11 shown above in this chapter, we will look at how to add a check-in policy that requires a list of tests to run and pass prior to allowing the source code to be checked in. This policy ensures that a set of tests have helped to verify that key aspects of the project have not been compromised as a result of the developer's efforts. While you or your teammates are likely to do your own testing prior to attempting to check in changes, all too often even the simplest changes can affect other aspects of the code base. Some teams refer to these types of automated tests as *build verification tests* (BVTs) — in this case, run on your local computer instead of on a larger team build — *smoke tests*, or even *sanity-check tests*.

The common scenario here is that you or someone on your team has added a test project to your team's overall project. If someone else has added a new test project to be shared with everyone, the result is that when you synchronize the latest files by right-clicking on the solution in the Solution Explorer window and selecting the Get Latest Version (Recursive) menu item (see Figure 9-20), you will have a test project appearing along with your MyApp project. In this case, the test project is called *OurTeamTests*, as shown in Figure 9-21.

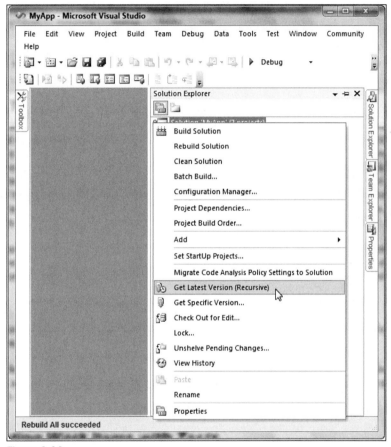

Figure 9-20

With the test project comes your team's tests and, more importantly, the .vsmdi file (also known as the test metadata file) used by your team that holds the groupings of tests also known as test lists (refer to Chapter 2 for creating a test list). This .vsmdi file can be seen in the Solution Items folder for your team project, also shown in Figure 9-21.

With a test project part of the team's project, you may now move forward with creating a testing policy used as part of the check-in process. Recall that to reach the dialog box shown in Figure 9-11, we select the Source Control menu item found under the Team Project Settings submenu in the top-level Team menu (see Figure 9-10 to see the actual menu structure). Clicking the Add button within the Source Control Settings dialog box, we will select the Testing Policy list item shown in Figure 9-22.

Figure 9-21

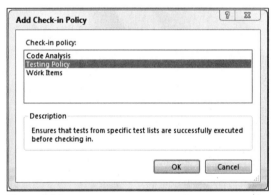

Figure 9-22

After selecting Testing Policy and clicking the OK button, you can browse to the checked-in .vsmdi file, shown in Figure 9-23.

In the dialog shown in Figure 9-23, we have browsed into the team project msvstest_tra, and drilled down through the MyApp project to reach the .vsmdi file that is part of the MyApp solution. Selecting the file and clicking the OK button displays the Testing Policy dialog box (see Figure 9-24) populated with the test lists found in the MyApp.vsmdi file. Here we've selected just one of the seven test lists, specifically one used by the team called *Team Check-in Tests*.

Putting a checkmark next to the test list to be used as part of this policy and clicking the OK button takes us back to the Source Control Settings dialog box, shown in Figure 9-25. To keep things simple and deal with only one check-in policy at a time, I've also chosen to temporarily disable the Code Analysis policy while I verify that the Testing Policy is working as expected.

> *The ability of adding, deleting, enabling, and disabling check-in policies is an administrative-level action. If you are not the VSTFS administrator for your team, you will not be able to do this. See your VSTFS administrator for any changes you need to make to the team's check-in policies.*

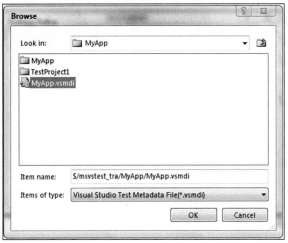

Figure 9-23

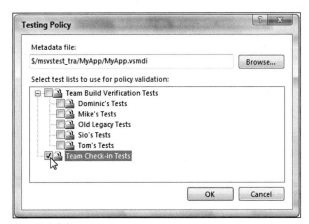

Figure 9-24

With the testing policy in place, we've edited one of the source files in the team's MyApp project. After we save changes, the file is ready to be checked in. Right-clicking on the source file in the Solution Explorer window and selecting the Check In context menu item displays the Check In dialog box, shown in Figure 9-26.

In this dialog box we've already clicked on the Policy Warnings view prior to clicking on the Check In button. Here we can see that two tests found in the Team Check-in Tests test list have yet to be run or have run and failed. As with our Code Analysis rule, we have two options: Exit the dialog and complete the required tasks (in this case, successfully executing your tests and getting a Passed result) or override the policy and check in the source file, as is shown in Figure 9-18. Before overriding the policy, however, remember that it was established for a reason: to avoid teammates breaking the build (that includes you!). On most teams, if you override the policy, you'd better have gotten lots and lots of buy-off so that you're not standing alone if issues arise.

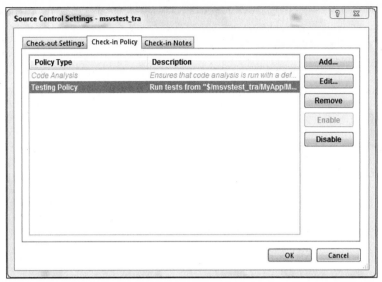

Figure 9-25

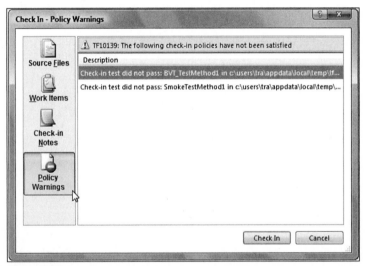

Figure 9-26

The Check In dialog box is very similar to the Pending Changes view. The difference is that the dialog box requires steps be taken to complete the action (in this case, selecting the Check In menu item), whereas the Pending Changes view is simply a current view onto the state of your source controlled files. Useful in different work modes, they provide similar functionality.

Associating Tests with Work Items

One of the properties of each of the test types is the Associated Work Item property. The value stored in this property is the identifier for the work item to which this test applies. OK, so what does that mean?

For example, I was on a project for Microsoft Consulting Services where the client was very meticulous about verifying that each requirement was met. To do this, there was a test that was run to demonstrate that each of the requirements was met. In addition, the client wanted 70 percent of the bugs found to be placed into tests to verify that they did not recur. Therefore, each test written should be associated with one or more work items, whether it's referencing a bug, task, requirement, or some other work item type.

Associating a test with a work item is very straightforward. First, of course, you must be connected to a team project so that you have access to the database containing the work items. Next, open the project that will contain the tests you want to associate with the different work items. In our example, the association is done at the time the test is authored (because you'd not be writing a test unless you first had a requirement, task, or work item directing you to write that test), but you can always change properties throughout the lifetime of the test.

> *There is a one-way association from tests to work items. That is, although a test may be referencing a work item, the work item does not know of the reference. You cannot go to a work item to determine which tests are referencing it. This also means that the state of the work item is unaffected by results you obtain when you run the test, unless you change the work item's state manually after running the test (i.e., if your test fails, it won't re-open a currently closed work item).*

In either the Test View or Test Manager window, click to select the test you wish to associate with a work item. Next, in the Properties window, scroll to the top of the list of properties until you find the Associated Work Items entry, as shown in Figure 9-27.

Figure 9-27

Notice that as you select the property name and move to the right column in the Properties window, a button with ellipses (...) appears. Click on this button to display the Associated Work Items dialog box. Clicking the Add button in this dialog box presents the user with the Work Items Picker dialog box shown in Figure 9-28.

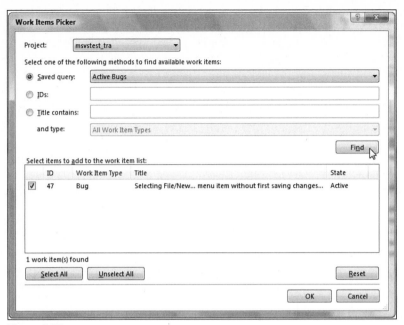

Figure 9-28

In the Work Items Picker dialog box, you can search for one or more work items that you'd like to associate with your test using one of three methods:

❑ **Saved query** — Use one of the queries that comes by default with your Team Project or one of the queries you or someone else on your team has created and saved.

❑ **IDs** — Type in a comma-separated list of work item IDs that you already know and would like to have displayed in the search.

❑ **Title contains** — Type in a substring you'd like to use in searching the titles of the work items in the team database. With this option, you can also further define your search by specifying the type of work item you are looking for (e.g., Bug).

Once you have specified the search criteria, clicked the Find button, and located the work item you wish to associate with your test, check the checkbox next to the work item and click the OK button (in Figure 9-28, we've already found and checked the box for bug ID 47, e.g.).

Because you are editing the property of a test, if those tests are checked into a source control database, they will need to be checked out. Assuming default team project settings, this checkout will occur automatically, so be certain to check those files back in.

Where this comes in very handy is when you inherit tests later from others or when you are trying to remember what exactly it was that you were trying to accomplish with a particular test. In the case of bug ID 47, for example, if you later click on the Associated Work Items property (Figure 9-27) to display the Associated Work Items dialog box, you can then click its Details button to display more information about that particular work item, as shown in Figure 9-29.

Properties are set in different ways depending on the test type. For a manual test in Word format, a property is added to the file alongside its other properties (e.g., author, version, etc.), which you can view in the Properties window of Visual Studio. For the unit test type, the WorkItem property is added to the TestMethod attribute. For example, [TestMethod] *becomes* [WorkItem(47), TestMethod].

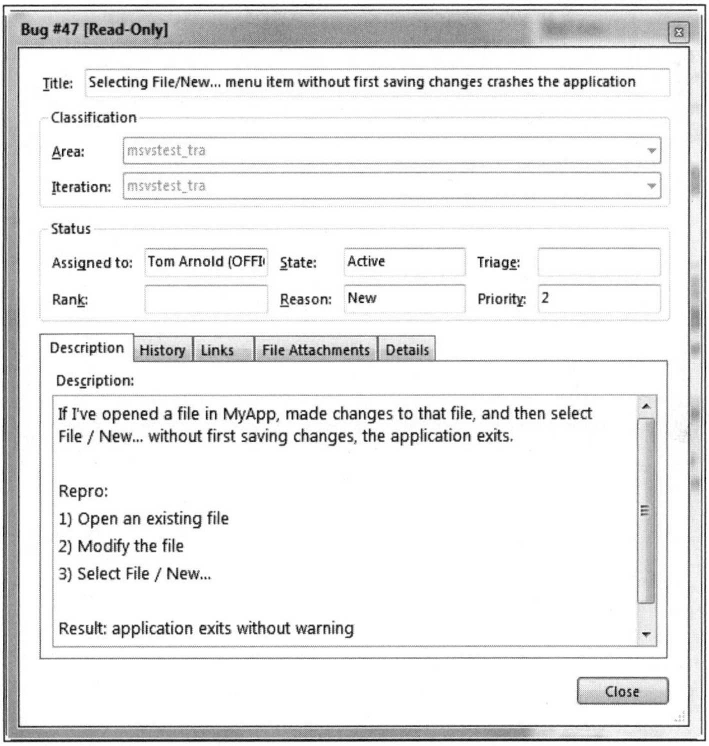

Figure 9-29

Team Build Process

One necessity that comes from being on a large development and testing team is having a single build where everyone's code can be compiled at a predetermined time. To do this, VSTS has the concept of a team build.

There are at least two development and testing tools' integration points when it comes to a team build:

❑   Test lists can be associated with the build (just as a check-in policy uses a test list) to allow for verification that the build is worth taking and testing.

❑   A build number is created that can be referenced by test results, work items, and reporting.

Creating a team build is accomplished by using the Team Explorer window, which is shown in Figure 9-30.

Figure 9-30

Right-click the Team Builds folder in the Team Explorer window, and select the New Team Build Type menu item from the context menu. This displays the New Team Build Type Creation Wizard, which is shown in Figure 9-31.

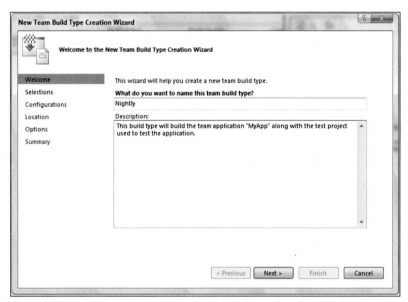

Figure 9-31

Because we're looking only at the integration points for the VSTEST and VSTESD tools, I'll quickly summarize the different views of the New Team Build Type Creation Wizard.

The New Team Build Type Creation Wizard steps are:

1. **Welcome** — This is where you specify a name and description of what this build will be used for. For example, if it is for a specific platform (e.g., 64-bit machine running Windows Vista), that kind of information should be provided here.

2. **Selections** — In this step you are able to select which of your projects you'd like to have built.

3. **Configurations** — Specify which type of configurations you'd like built in this step. That is, is this a debug build or a release build? What CPU are you building for?

4. **Location** — Specify the name of the machine that will be doing the build, what directory will be used, and the final "drop" location of the build so that team members have access.

5. **Options** — Shown in Figure 9-32, this step allows you to specify which Test List(s) to run when the build completes. It also allows you to specify whether or not code analysis will be used during the compilation of the build.

6. **Summary** — This final view in the Wizard allows you to see in one place a summary of all of your selections. Take care that you have configured your build correctly because editing it after you exit the Wizard is only achievable by editing the XML file created by the Wizard.

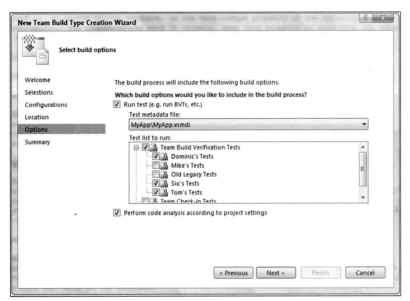

Figure 9-32

After creating a successful build type called *Nightly* and running that build type, the build computer will synchronize the latest files. Once it has the latest files, it will use the project's settings for the code analysis step as part of the compilation process. What this means is that if particular rules were switched off as part of the project, those rules will be skipped.

Finally, when the build completes, it is copied into a common share directory (in this example, \edtsql101\drops) where others can access the build. It is also a good idea to check the health of the build, first — that is, how well it did in running tests against the resulting binaries. Because we expanded the number of tests to run, we had 157 tests in the selected Test Lists, 92 of which passed and 42 of which failed, as can be seen in Figure 9-33. [The other 23 were either marked as Completed (for a load test) or Inconclusive (for a unit test that has the assert.inconclusive() method still in the code).]

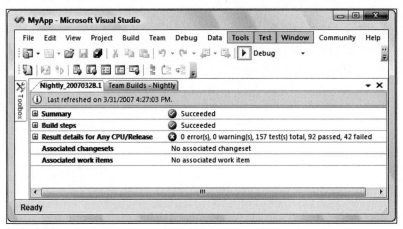

Figure 9-33

Further drill-down into the test results to determine why a test has failed is possible by expanding the "Results details for Any CPU/Release" item and clicking on the individual test result link. This will open the test results in the Test Results window, allowing you to look at the details as if you'd executed those tests on your local machine.

> *For more details on using the Test Results window to drill into the details of test execution, see Chapter 2.*

Associating Work Items with Test Results

Another integration point with VSTFS and the testing tools is the ability to associate a work item with the results of a test run. Let's say you have a test that uncovered a crashing issue as part of a test run. When filing a bug, instead of including the steps of how to go about downloading, setting up, and re-running the tests, you can instead attach the actual test results to the bug work item. The first step is shown in Figure 9-34: opening the bug and clicking on the Links tab.

Clicking the Add button displays the Add Link dialog box, which has, among other options, a Test Result type of link, as shown in Figure 9-35.

After adding the link to the bug and saving these changes, anyone viewing the bug can go to the Links tab and view the linked test results. These results will open in the Test Results window, allowing the person looking at the bug to drill deeper into the whys and wherefores of the issue.

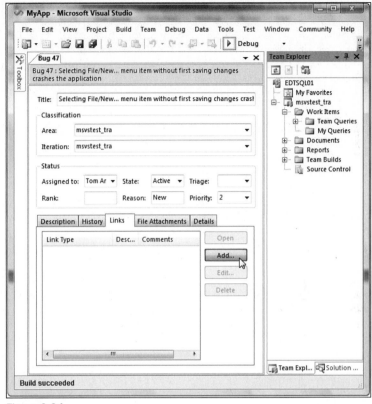

Figure 9-34

Figure 9-35

Publishing Test Results

In addition to the work item database and source code control database, there is a database available for reporting. These reports look at anything from bug metrics to code churn (i.e., how much new code is added) to test results. For this book, however, we are concerned only with publishing our results from testing on our project.

The publishing of test results is simple. After you have completed a test run that you wish to have incorporated into the overall team reports, you can use the Publish button found on the Test Results window's toolbar, shown in Figure 9-36.

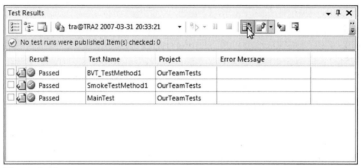

Figure 9-36

The Publish Test Results window is then displayed, allowing you to select which test run you want to publish, which build the test results apply to, the type of build it was (such as debug or retail, e.g.), and whether or not to include the code coverage data if they were gathered during the test run (see Figure 9-37).

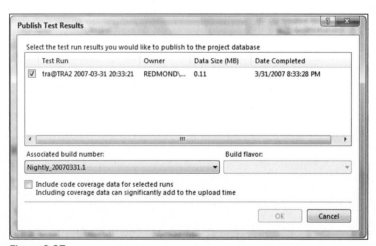

Figure 9-37

Each team member's results are added to VSTFS. In some cases, merging takes place, such as when code coverage data are gathered. For example, if one engineer runs tests against feature A on the project, and another engineer runs against feature B, the merged code coverage data allow the reports to show the combined code coverage for a particular build based on data from multiple teammates.

For a detailed look at reporting and VSTFS, please refer to the book, Professional Team Foundation Server, published by Wrox and authored by Jean-Luc David, Mickey Gousset, and Erik Gunvaldson.

For details on using code coverage as part of your test execution, see Chapters 2 and 8 in this book.

Summary

In this chapter we looked at where the new testing and development tools fit into the software development life cycle. Instead of picking a single SDLC approach, we looked at the commonalities shared by most practices and how VSTS works with these tasks, specifically around the new tools.

We looked at the many touch-points where the different tools integrate into VSTFS. However, there was a fine line around how deep to dive into the use of VSTFS. That is, we've shown you how the tools complement VSTFS and left additional features of VSTFS (i.e., work item tracking, source control, reporting, document templates, and team site) alone as they are covered in great detail in another Wrox book. Instead, we looked at how, when a team project exists, the different tools can plug into VSTFS and leverage work that's already been done.

Plugging testing and code analysis tools into check-in policies, publishing team-wide test results into a common database for richer reporting, associating tests with work items, and linking work items to test results, all add significantly to the bigger picture of working on a team and using VSTFS.

Installing Team Explorer

Coding an application and writing manual and automated tests to verify its functionality is a small part of a much larger picture when working in a team environment. The Visual Studio Team Foundation Server (VSTFS) is another piece of the complete Microsoft Visual Studio Team System toolset. If you are on a team that uses VSTFS, there are several opportunities that open up to you in sharing your tests and reporting on their results. Some of these scenarios as they apply to the tester and developer tools addressed in this book are discussed in Chapter 9.

With your team running a Visual Studio Team Foundation Server, you can join the party by installing Team Explorer. This appendix goes through the steps of getting that particular utility added to your installation of Visual Studio.

Installing Team Explorer

The following steps assume that you have VSTEST or VSTESD already installed on your computer. Running the setup program then adds Team Explorer to your installation.

1. Run the Visual Studio Team Foundation Server setup program found on your team's copy of VSTFS, and click on the Install Team Explorer link as shown in Figure A-1.

2. Click the Next button on the Welcome to Setup wizard page.

3. On the Ready to Install wizard page, you will see a summary of the components that are about to be installed. The main one you want to see is the Microsoft Visual Studio 2005 Team Explorer component. You may also see the Microsoft Visual Studio 2005 Premiere Partner Edition as well as Microsoft Office System 2003 Primary Interop Assemblies components, as shown in Figure A-2.

You will typically install the files into the same directory as your other Visual Studio application files.

Figure A-1

Figure A-2

4.   Click the Install > button, shown in Figure A-2, to begin your installation. The installation progress is displayed as shown in Figure A-3.

5.   On the Setup Completed Successfully wizard page, click the Finish button to complete your setup.

6.   Run your already installed copy of Visual Studio.

Figure A-3

7. Under the Tools menu, you will now see a new menu item entitled "Connect to Team Foundation Server." Select that menu item, as shown in Figure A-4, to begin the process of connecting to your team's VSTFS server.

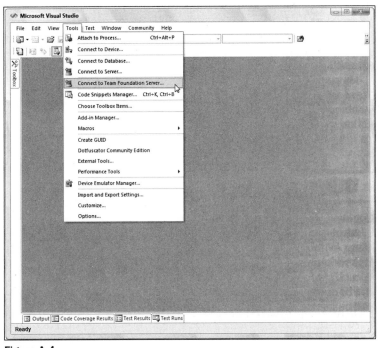

Figure A-4

8. The Add/Remove Team Foundation Server dialog box is displayed showing the different servers to which you are currently connected. If you've just installed Team Explorer, this is a blank list. Click the Add button.

9. After clicking the Add button in Step 8, the Add Team Foundation Server dialog box is displayed, as shown in Figure A-5. Type in the name of the server that your VSTFS administrator used when setting up the box. In this example, our team's VSTFS box is named EDTSQL01 and the default connection details, determined by the VSTFS Administrator, are typically used.

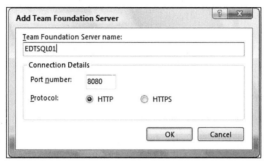

Figure A-5

10. Click the OK button in the Add Team Foundation Server dialog box to return to the same dialog box mentioned in Step 8. Under Team Foundation Server list, you see your newly added server, as demonstrated in Figure A-6.

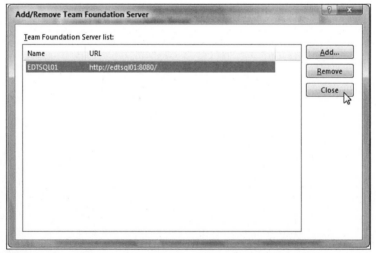

Figure A-6

11. Click the Close button on the Add/Remove Team Foundation Server dialog box to return to the Visual Studio main window.

At this point, you may either open an existing project or create a project of your own. To show you more of the UI, this example continues by showing you how to create a project to be added to the VSTFS server you just joined.

12. Now that you are joined to a Visual Studio Team Foundation Server, you can open existing team projects or create new team projects to be shared with your teammates. To create a new team project, go to the File menu, and select the New menu item. There you will see a new submenu item named Team Project. Select that menu item, as shown in Figure A-7.

The addition of a new window — Team Explorer — accompanies the installation of the Team Explorer utility. This window shows all projects you've opened on the Visual Studio Team Foundation Server to which you are connected. If you are running into issues with seeing a particular team project or creating a new project, contact your team's VSTFS Administrator.

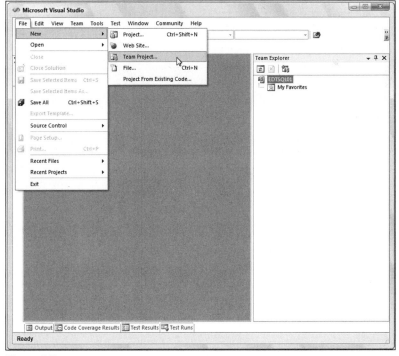

Figure A-7

13. Selecting the Team Project menu item under the New submenu on the File menu displays the New Team Project wizard, as shown in Figure A-8. Here you decide on the name of the project that will be used by the team when interacting with your files and reports. Enter a file name, and click the Next > button to proceed.

Figure A-8

Figure A-9

14. The next screen of the New Team Project wizard, shown in Figure A-9, allows you to select which development methodology your team will follow for this project. The template provides default workflows, project files, and process guidance to help you get started quickly with your team. Here we've selected the Microsoft Solution Framework (MSF) Agile Software Development template, which comes in-box with VSTFS.

15. Click the Finish button to start Visual Studio on its way to creating a new Team Project for you, as shown in Figure A-10. This will take some time as it creates and assigns new groups and permissions, provisions a new version control library, creates a new Microsoft SharePoint site for your team, adds a project reporting site, and performs a host of other details to create a well-integrated experience.

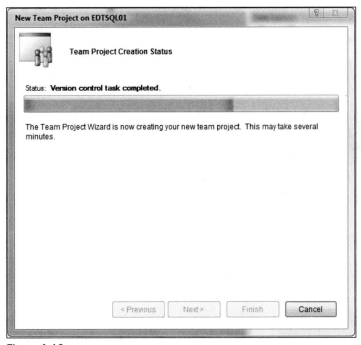

Figure A-10

16. After all services are provisioned, click the Close button on the Team Project Created screen of the New Team Project wizard, ensuring that the checkbox is selected that gives the option, "Launch the process guidance for more information about running the team project." As the wizard closes and your project opens, you are rewarded with a new Team Project, as shown in Figure A-11. The web site with your process guidance appears in the editor window, and your new project and its associated folders and files are in the Team Explorer window on the right.

Figure A-11

With the Team Explorer installed, turn to Chapter 9 to see how the developer and tester tools integrate into the Visual Studio Team Foundation Server provided to your team.

B

Creating and Running a Web Test: A High-Level Walk-Through

We have selected some tests to give you a quick introduction to some of the tools in VSTEST and VSTESD. This is meant to help you quickly see some of the UI around this feature to help you decide if you want to explore the topic further. To go into greater depth on the web test type, read Chapter 5.

To begin with, we need a test project. This can be accomplished by either creating a completely new test project, or adding it to an existing solution. Adding it to a solution works particularly well if the solution already contains the source code for the web project you are about to test. In this example, a completely new test project has been created and is the only project in the solution.

1. Select the File ➪ New ➪ Project menu item (see Figure B-1).

2. In the New Project dialog box, click on the Test project type under C# on the left side of the dialog box, verify that the Test Project template is selected on the right side of the dialog box, type in the name "WebTestExample" in the Name text box (see Figure B-2), and click OK.

3. The Solution Explorer window opens, displaying the new test project (see Figure B-3).

4. From the top-level Test menu, select the New Test menu item (see Figure B-4).

5. In the Add New Test dialog box, select the Web Test template (see Figure B-5), and, for this example, leave the *Test Name* the default value, `WebTest1.webtest`. Also verify that the Add to Test Project dropdown shows the new project we've just created, "WebTestExample." Then, click the OK button.

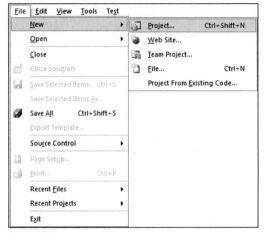

Figure B-1

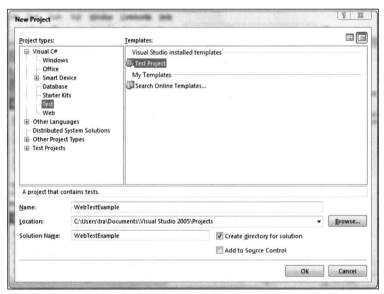

Figure B-2

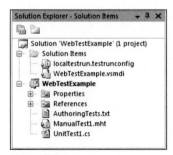

Figure B-3

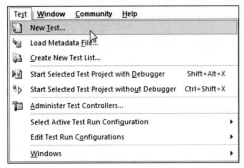

Figure B-4

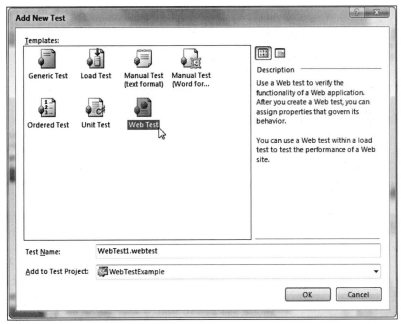

Figure B-5

6. After clicking the OK button, an instance of Microsoft Internet Explorer opens in a new window (see Figure B-6) with the Web Test Recorder pane showing on the left of the window. Typing in a URL in the address bar (e.g., http://www.msvstest.com) and pressing Enter records your navigation to the site. Clicking around within the site records each URL you've clicked on. In this example, the links About Us, Contact Us, and Site Map were clicked on and their URLs added to the Web Test Recorder pane.

7. Click the Stop button in the Web Test Recorder pane in Microsoft Internet Explorer (see Figure B-6). This stops the recording session and places the results in Microsoft Visual Studio's editor window, as shown in Figure B-7.

Figure B-6

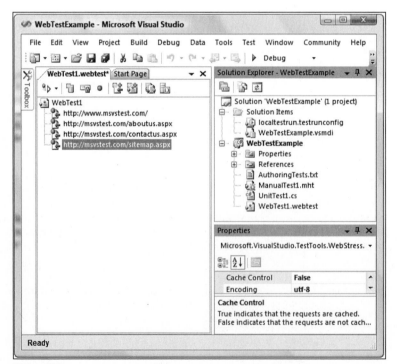

Figure B-7

If the Web Test Recorder pane does not appear in Internet Explorer, go to the View menu, and select the Web Test Recorder menu item found under the Explorer Bar submenu.

8. Press *Ctrl+S* to save the test, then click on the Run Test button in the upper-left corner of the document that shows the test you've recorded. (I've minimized the Solution Explorer and Properties windows to provide more room to view the WebTest1.webtest document window.) See Figure B-8.

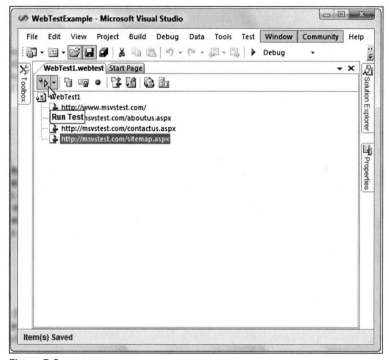

Figure B-8

9. Figure B-9 shows the results of running the test. The top portion of the editor shows the URLs that were executed based on the original recording. The middle section has five tabs that allow you to explore more details about the execution of the test (in this example, the Response tab is showing the Headers and Body sent back as a result of navigating to the `http://mstest.com/sitemap.aspx` URL). The bottom portion of the IDE shows the Test Results window and that no issues were encountered in executing the test.

What to do when issues are encountered as part of executing a Web test can be found in Chapter 5. Details about the Response tab and the other four tabs mentioned above are also discussed in Chapter 5.

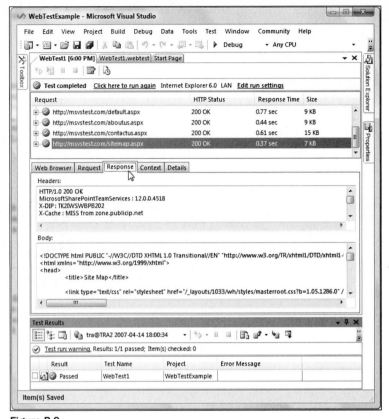

Figure B-9

As you can see, the creation and execution of a Web test is a pretty simple process. This test may now be included in your overall collection of tests as described in Chapters 2 and 5. Chapter 7 and Appendix D also go into detail about how a web test can be included in a load test type to simulate high user activity on a website.

C

Creating and Running a Unit Test: A High-Level Walk-Through

We have selected some tests to give you a quick introduction to the tools in VSTEST and VSTESD. This is meant to help you quickly see some of the UI around this feature to help you decide if you want to explore the topic further. To go into greater depth on the unit test type, read Chapters 3 and 4.

This example begins by opening an existing project called SimpleMath — a library containing methods for adding, subtracting, multiplying, and dividing numbers. Through the course of this example, we will add a test project to the solution, autogenerate tests against the methods in the SimpleMath class, modify the tests, and finally execute the tests to see the results.

While we've not provided the source code anywhere for this example, it's a simple matter of creating a new Windows library and typing in the lines of code found in Figure C-3 should you wish to follow along in a hands-on way.

1. Select the Project/Solution menu item from the File menu and Open submenu (see Figure C-1).

2. In the Open Project dialog box, we search for the project for which we want to create unit tests. In this example, we're using a project we quickly concocted called SimpleMath (see Figure C-2).

3. Opening our project displays the code on the left side of the IDE and the Solution Explorer on the right, as shown in Figure C-3.

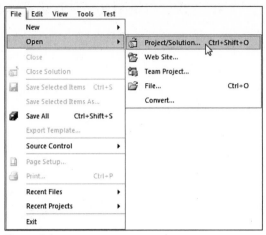

Figure C-1

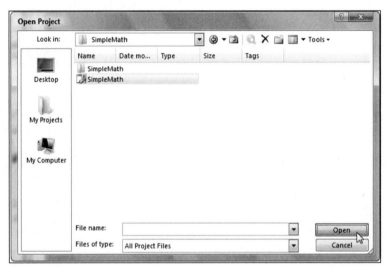

Figure C-2

4. The easiest way to create unit tests is to let Visual Studio do the code generation for you. Even though we've not yet created a test project, we'll be prompted to do so as part of the process. We begin by right-clicking on a method, class, or namespace in the code on the left side of the IDE. I want tests for everything in the MathClass1 class, thus I've right-clicked on the class name and will select the Create Unit Tests menu item from the context menu, as shown in Figure C-4.

5. Because a test project is not part of the SimpleMath solution we've opened, the Create Unit Tests dialog box affords us the option of specifying what type of test project to create so that the generated unit tests can be saved. We've selected C# as the language in which we'd like the unit tests rendered, as seen in Figure C-5, but we could also have selected Visual Basic or Visual C++. Click the OK button.

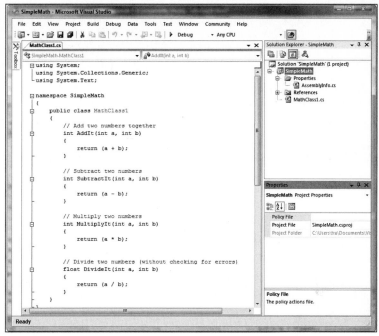

Figure C-3

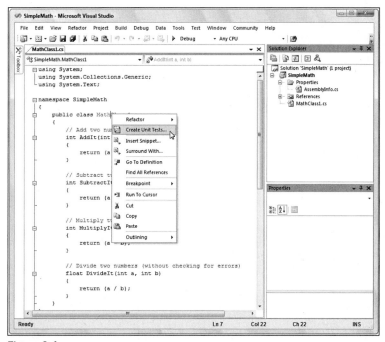

Figure C-4

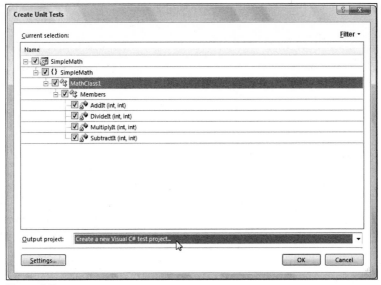

Figure C-5

Tests can reside only in test projects. If the SimpleMath solution already had a test project, that project would be available in the Output project dropdown list. Because a test project does not yet exist, however, we've instead selected a language to use in creating a new test project.

The language you select for writing unit tests does not need to be the same language as the code you are testing. For example, the code we are testing was written in C#, but we could write our tests in Visual Basic if that is the language that's more familiar to the test author.

6. Clicking the OK button on the Create Unit Tests dialog box after specifying C# as the language to use when creating our test project results in the New Test Project dialog box being displayed, as shown in Figure C-6. The project holding the code to be tested is called *SimpleMath*, and therefore I've named the test project *SimpleMathTest*. Click the Create button to add the new test project and source code for your tests to the current solution.

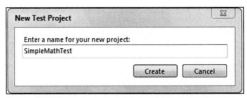

Figure C-6

7. A lot of things just happened, including generating tests against the SimpleMath class and adding the test files to the new SimpleMathTest project that is now part of the SimpleMath solution, as shown in Figure C-7. Also notice the Test View window in the lower right-hand corner of Figure C-7. This shows the tests that were autogenerated by the Create Unit Tests dialog box.

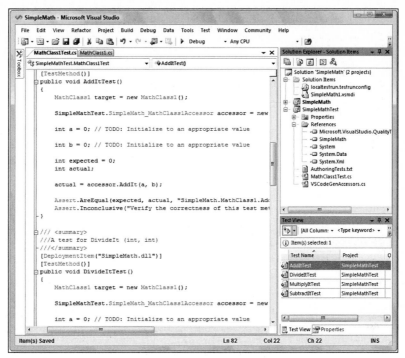

Figure C-7

If the Test View window is not currently displayed in your window, you can show it by going to the top-level Test menu and selecting the Test View menu item under the Windows submenu.

8. In the code editor window, scroll to the generated method `AddItTest()` and modify the `int a = 0;`, `int b = 0;`, and `int expected = 0;` lines to replace the zeros with the values 2, 3, and 5, respectively. Also, remove the entire line of code that begins `Assert.Inconclusive`.

The feature for creating new unit tests can only do so much; that is, it can do the busy work of creating the test project and writing the initial code for your tests, but it does not have the smarts to figure out what test values you'd like to use and the expected return value based on the values passed to the method being tested. Thus, you need to provide those pass values and expected results.

9. Scroll next to the `DivideItTest()` method; set a = 8 and leave b = 0. Leave the `expected` variable equal to 0, and remove the `Assert.Inconclusive` line of code.

When the test runs, this will result in a divide-by-zero error, something we want to test for to see if the code being tested handles this scenario.

10. Move next to the `MultiplyItTest()` method, and set a = 2, b = 3, and expected = 6. Remove the entire line of code that begins `Assert.Inconclusive`.

You'll be happy to know that there is a way to create data-driven tests wherein you can tie a data file full of values for the a, b, and expected variables so that you can tweak your data file to include new values for new test scenarios instead of modifying the code all of the time. This is discussed in Chapter 3.

11. Leave the final test, SubtractItTest(), as it is. Don't modify the values, and do not remove the Assert.Inconclusive line of code.

The Assert.Inconclusive method is used to communicate that the test method has not yet been modified from its originally autogenerated version. Instead of the default values of 0 minus 0 equaling 0 reporting a passed result, this will instead report an inconclusive result to show that a human has not yet reviewed the test.

12. In the Test View window in the lower-right corner of the IDE, use *Shift + Click* to select all of the tests in the list, and then click the Run Selection button in the upper-left corner of the Test View window, as shown in Figure C-8.

Figure C-8

13. As the tests execute, the outcome of each test is shown in the Test Results window, as shown in Figure C-9. Two of the tests — AddItTest and MultiplyItTest — passed. DivideItTest failed because of the divide-by-zero error. (You found a bug! The developer needs to add an error check for that condition.) SubtractItTest is Inconclusive because the Assert.Inconclusive line of code wasn't removed, and therefore it concludes that the person writing the test didn't modify this method yet. Double-click the failed DivideItTest in the Test Results window. (Alternatively, right-click the test, and select the View Test Results Details menu item on the context menu.)

14. Having double-clicked the failed DivideItTest test in Step 13, the details of the results of that test's execution can be seen in Figure C-10, helping the test author to track down what exactly went wrong. That is, was it a problem with the test itself or an actual bug in the code?

After going through these 14 steps, the value of the unit test type should be pretty clear. Not only can you add tests by typing them in directly, but you can also generate tests against existing source code and let Visual Studio do the heavy lifting. You need only go in and tweak it further.

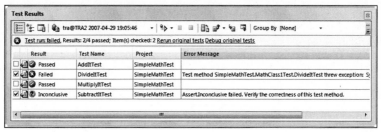

Figure C-9

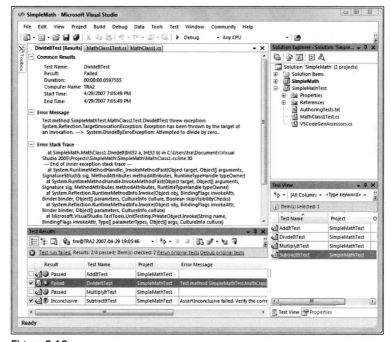

Figure C-10

For many more details on this particular test type, refer to Chapters 3 and 4. Be sure also to review Chapter 9 to see how tests like these can be included as you and your team work together to build and release a quality software product by sharing tests and requiring them as part of the check-in process.

Creating and Running a Load Test: A High-Level Walk-Through

We have selected some tests to give you a quick introduction to some of the tools in VSTEST and VSTESD. This is meant to help you quickly see some of the UI and workflows around using this feature to help you decide if you want to explore the topic further. To go into greater depth on the load test type, read Chapter 7.

This example takes you through the creation of a test project, refers to adding automated test types as shown in Appendixes B and C, and then puts those test types to use by creating a load test using the Load Test wizard. Lastly, it shows you how to run the load test and examine the results. This will help you understand the flow of this test type, but more detail about this test type is found in Chapter 7.

1. Select the Project menu item under the New submenu within the top-level File menu, as shown in Figure D-1.

An alternative is to create a new Team Project. See Chapter 9 and Appendix A if you prefer this option.

2. In the New Project dialog box (see Figure D-2), expand the Visual C# node, select the Test project type in the left list box, and the Test Project item in the Templates list box. Next, name the project `LoadTestExample`, and click the OK button.

Depending on the environment settings you selected the very first time you ran Visual Studio, these nodes may appear different from Figure D-2. If this is the case, just look through the nodes until you find the C# project, or select Visual Basic or C++ if you prefer those languages over C#. You can also open an existing test project and add your load test to that.

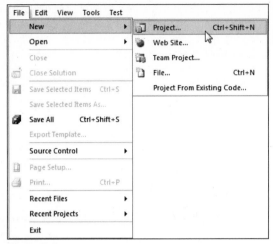

Figure D-1

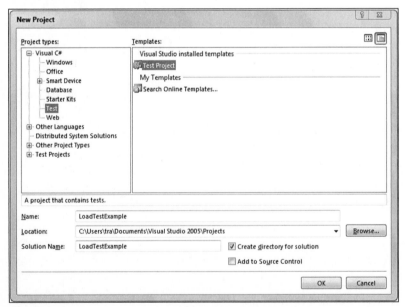

Figure D-2

Your integrated development environment (IDE) should now look similar to the one shown in Figure D-3. Depending on your configuration, there will be some slight differences, but the general idea is that you now have the LoadTestExample project showing in the Solution Explorer window, likely on the right-hand side of the Visual Studio main window.

3.   Add one or more automated tests to your new test project, such as a web test (see Appendix B) and optionally a unit test (see Appendix C). Also, delete the template files that were added to your new test project by default: AuthoringTests.txt, ManualTest1.mht,

and `UnitTest1.cs` (*Shift + Click* the items in the Solution Explorer window, right-click on the selection, and select the Delete menu item from the context menu). Your Solution Explorer window will resemble Figure D-4. (I've elected only to add a single web test that is discussed in great detail in Chapter 5.)

> *The load test type is what we've referred to in this book as a* container *test type; that is, its main purpose is to act as a wrapper around other automated test types. Other test types that wrap tests are the generic and ordered test types, both described in Chapter 6.*

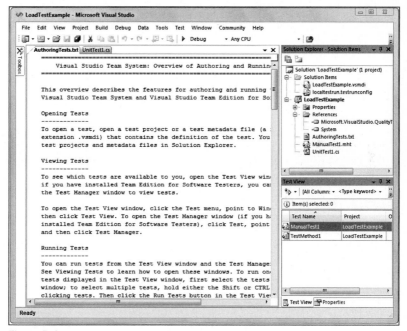

Figure D-3

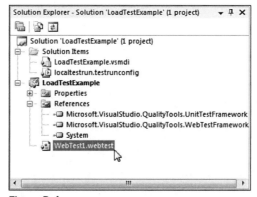

Figure D-4

4. Select the New Test menu item from the top-level Test menu, as shown in Figure D-5.

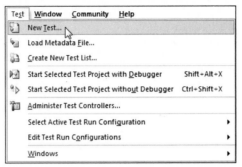

Figure D-5

5. In the Add New Test dialog box, click the Load Test icon in the list of Templates, as shown in Figure D-6. Keep the default name for this example, and click the OK button to start the New Load Test Wizard.

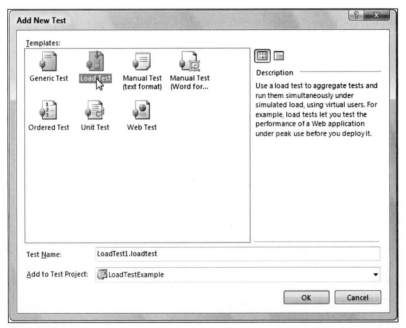

Figure D-6

6. Click the "Next" button on the Welcome to the Create New Load Test Wizard screen (see Figure D-7).

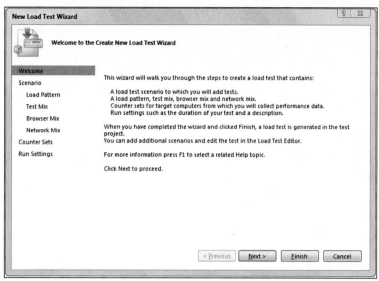

Figure D-7

7. Keep the default settings on the Edit settings for a load test scenario screen, which should resemble Figure D-8. Click the "Next" button to continue to the next screen.

> *"Think times" allow you to choose to keep the actual pauses recorded during the creation of the web test, go with an average delay between each step, or skip think times altogether. More details on this option are in Chapter 7.*

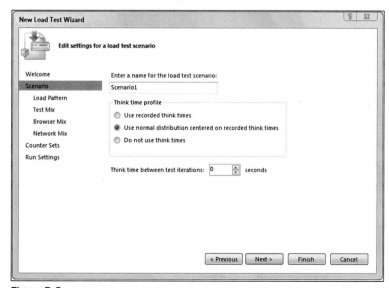

Figure D-8

8. On the next wizard screen ("Edit load pattern settings for a load test scenario"), click "Step load," and set the four fields to 10, 10, 10, and 200 (see Figure D-9). Now click the "Next" button.

> *Stepping up the load allows you to set the test to start at a small number of virtual users and increase that over time. The Step Load settings let you define the starting number of users and the frequency and size of the increase, up to the maximum user count.*

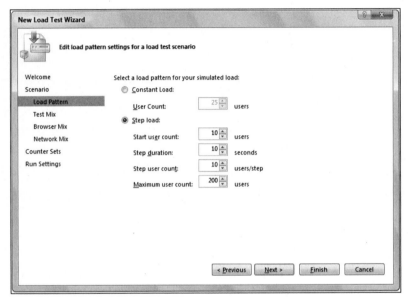

Figure D-9

9. The next screen of the wizard is "Add tests to a load test scenario and edit the test mix." Click the Add button to display the Add Tests dialog box shown in Figure D-10.

10. Click the WebTest1 item in the Available tests list box (see Figure D-10), then click the "Next" button to add it to the Selected tests list box. If you have other automated tests that you added as part of completing Step 3, you may select those tests now to add them to this load test. When you're done, you should have one or more tests on the right side of the dialog box, as shown in Figure D-11. Click the OK button.

> *If you have a manual test in your test project, you will not be able to add that to your load test because it doesn't make much sense to have 100 virtual users attempt to run a manual test (or even only one user).*

11. If you have two or more tests, you can move the Distribution slider control (see Figure D-12) to specify what percentage of your virtual users will be running which test. You can also click the Distribute button to spread it out evenly across all tests added to this load test. When you're done specifying the distribution, click the "Next" button.

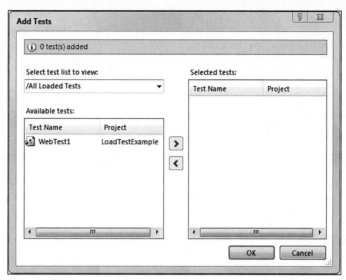

Figure D-10

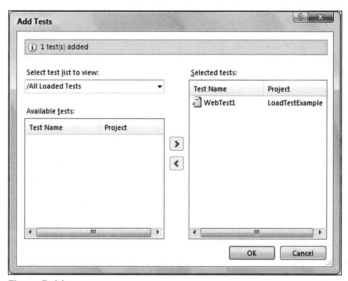

Figure D-11

12. The "Add browser types to a load test scenario and edit the browser mix" screen allows you to add browser types to your load test and then specify the browser mix. Click the Add button four times for a total of five browser types added to this screen (see Figure D-13). You can now control the distribution of what percentage of which browser will be used when sending a HTTP request for your web test type. Once you have things set the way you like, click the "Next" button.

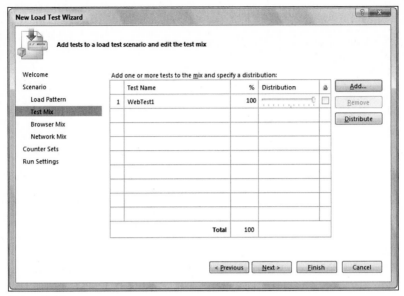

Figure D-12

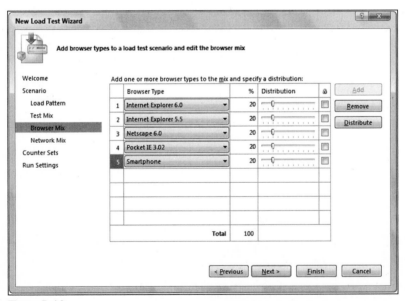

Figure D-13

13. The "Add network types to a load test scenario and edit the network mix" screen allows you to specify which network type to use and by what percentage of the virtual users during the test run. Click the dropdown for the first item in the Network Type column, as shown in Figure D-14, and select T1. Click the "Next" button to continue.

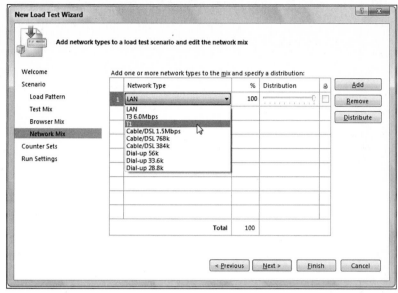

Figure D-14

14. Figure D-15 shows the next screen in the wizard that allows you to specify which computers to monitor during the execution of the load test. Click the Add Computer button, and type in the name of the computer to be monitored. For example, I'll be running this simple test on my local computer named *TRA2*. Click the "Next" button.

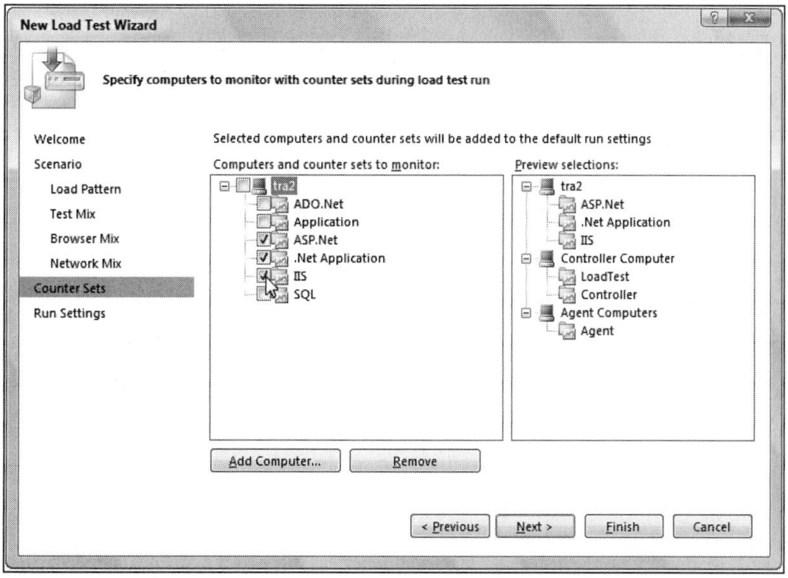

Figure D-15

15. The final screen of the New Load Test Wizard, shown in Figure D-16, allows you to specify the run time of your test among other settings. Change the Run duration setting from 10 minutes to 1 minute for this example, and click the Finish button.

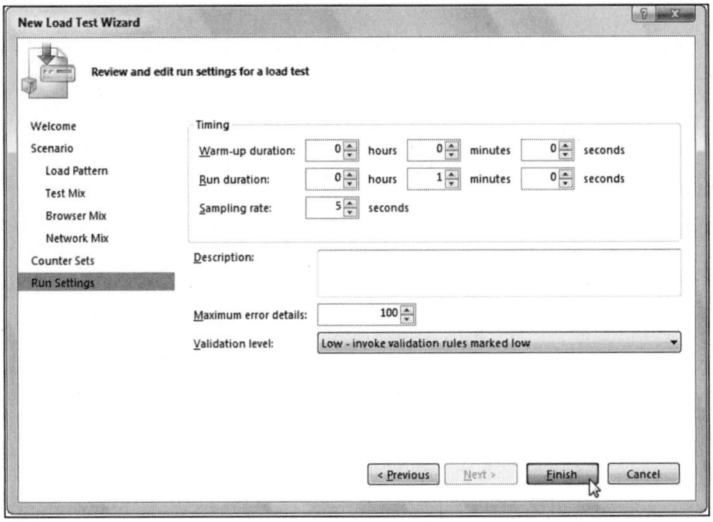

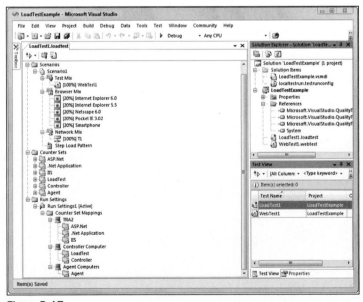

Figure D-16

Having clicked the Finish button on the final screen, Visual Studio now takes all of your settings and places them into a new test file called LoadTest1.loadtest. Should you wish to make changes to any of the settings, you can now do this by opening the file and changing the individual properties for any of the nodes, as shown in Figure D-17.

Figure D-17

16. To run the test, click on the LoadTest1 test item in the Test View window to select it, then click the Run Selection button in the upper-left portion of the same window, as shown in Figure D-18.

If you do not have the Test View window showing in your main window, you can display it by selecting the Test View menu item in the Windows submenu of the top-level Test menu.

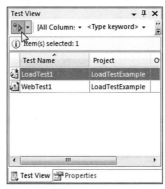

Figure D-18

17. As the test starts to run, the Test Results window is displayed. Double-click the LoadTest1 item in the Test Results window to get a detailed view of the test. If the test is still executing, you will see live updates based on measurements it's taking. If the test has completed, as is the case in Figure D-19, you will see the final results of that test's execution.

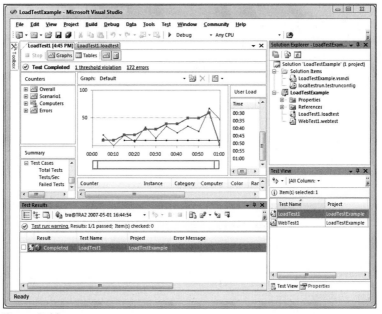

Figure D-19

Creating tests to simulate multiple users working with an application was previously a daunting task. Writing the code, distributing the tests to multiple computers, determining what data to collect, and viewing the results took a lot of thought up front as well as time at the end to sift through the results. Microsoft has taken the approach of providing a simple wizard with default values of what you want to watch and how you can run your tests, which allows you to tweak those settings as you better understand how to use these tools.

For greater depth and detail on how to put the load test type to use, read Chapter 7.

Creating and Running a Manual Test: A High-Level Walk-Through

We have selected some tests to give you a quick introduction to some of the tools in VSTEST and VSTESD. This is meant to help you quickly see some of the UI and workflows around using this feature to help you decide if you want to explore the topic further. To go into greater depth on the manual test type, read Chapter 6.

This example takes you through the creation of a test project, refers to adding a manual test, and then executes that test. This will help you understand the flow of this test type, but more detail about this test type is found in Chapter 6.

The manual test type is available only in the VSTEST installation of Visual Studio. If you've installed the full Visual Studio Team Suite, then you have VSTEST.

1. Select the Project menu item under the New submenu within the top-level File menu, as shown in Figure E-1.

2. In the New Project dialog box (see Figure E-2), expand the Test Projects node, and select the Test Documents project type in the left list box and the Test Project item in the Templates list box. Next, name the project `TestProject1`, and click the OK button.

In the walk-through examples in Appendixes B, C, and D, we created test projects based on a particular programming language. If you are writing manual tests and uncertain which language to select, you can use the Test Documents project type as shown in Figure E-2.

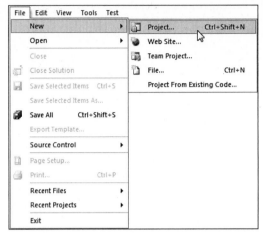

Figure E-1

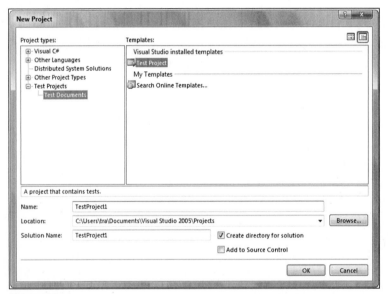

Figure E-2

3. As shown in Figure E-3, the new project is created, and `AuthoringTests.txt` is displayed to help you understand some of the options available to you. Read through this text file if you want a quick introduction. Next, double-click on the `ManualTest1.mht` (a manual test file) in the Solution Explorer window found in the upper-right corner of Visual Studio.

> *If no manual test file is displayed, create one. To do this, right-click your test project, point to Add, and click New Test. In the Add New Test dialog box, select "Manual Test (Word format)", and click the OK button. [If you do not have Microsoft Word installed, select "Manual Test (text format)" instead.]*

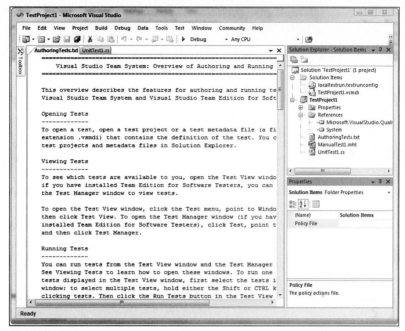

Figure E-3

4. If you have Microsoft Word installed, the manual test `ManualTest1.mht` is opened in the installed version of Microsoft Word (in this case, Microsoft Word 2007), as shown in Figure E-4. If Word is not installed, the manual test opens in Notepad; a manual test in text format has the extension `.mtx`.

5. Delete the paragraphs before the Test Title heading, and replace the highlighted text with information that you want displayed to the person who will run the manual test, as shown in Figure E-5.

6. Save the `ManualTest1.mht` file, and close Microsoft Word.

7. Back in Visual Studio, delete from TestProject1 the files `AuthoringTests.txt` and `UnitTest1.cs` by right-clicking each file individually and selecting the Delete menu item from the context menu, as shown in Figure E-6.

8. Display the Test Manager window by selecting the Test Manager menu item from the top-level Test menu under the Windows submenu, as shown in Figure E-7.

9. In the Test Manager window, click the checkbox next to the `ManualTest1` test to select it for execution, then click the Run Checked Tests button found on the toolbar on the upper-left corner of the Test Manager window, as shown in Figure E-8. This will start the execution of the selected tests. In this case, only one test was selected: `ManualTest1`.

   A quicker way to execute this test would be to use the Test View window as was illus-trated in Appendixes B, C, and D. However, I wanted to make sure we had an example of using the Test Manager window. For more details on using the Test Manager window, see Chapter 2.

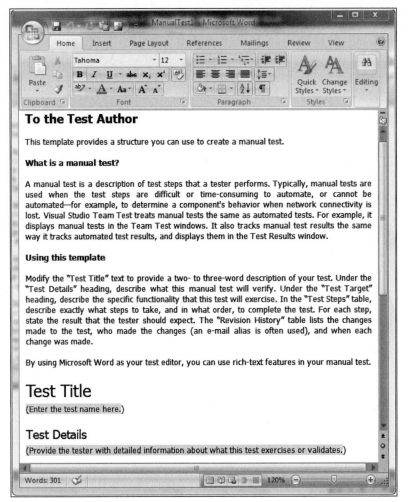

Figure E-4

10. As the test is executed, the contents of ManualTest1.mht are displayed as part of a form allowing you to type comments explaining the outcome of the test. In this example, the file transfer did not complete as expected and is therefore marked as a Failed test. Type in any comments you find helpful, select the Fail option button, and then click the Apply button at the top of the form, as shown in Figure E-9.

> *I've minimized the Solution Explorer and Properties windows on the right side of the main window to give a better view of the manual test being executed, as shown in Figure E-9.*

> *In Figure E-9 the Test Results window at the bottom of the Visual Studio main window shows the test as Pending. This is because the Apply button had not yet been clicked. In Step 11, however, the Test Results window now shows the outcome of clicking the Apply button, as shown in Figure E-10.*

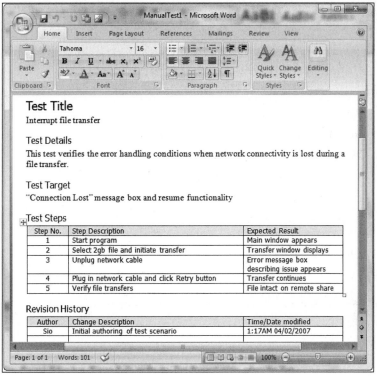

Figure E-5

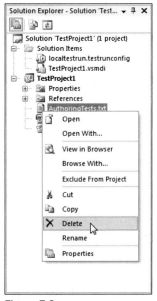

Figure E-6

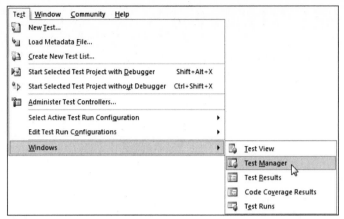

Figure E-7

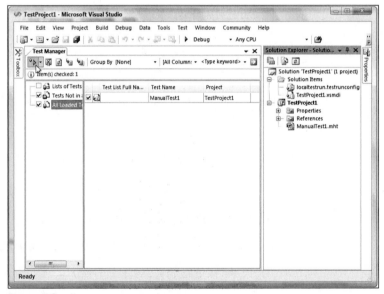

Figure E-8

11. Double-clicking the Failed test in the Test Results window, shown in Figure E-10, or right-clicking the Failed test and selecting the View Test Results Details menu item in the resulting context menu, will once again display the test form used in the execution of the manual test. However, it will be read-only.

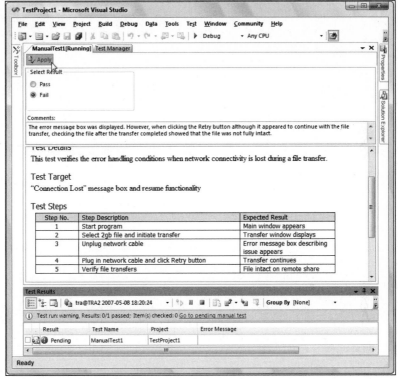

Figure E-9

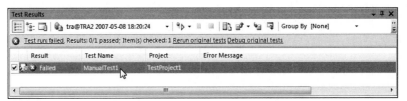

Figure E-10

As you can see, manual tests are simple to create and have as part of your test project. They can be included alongside your other tests as part of running an overall test pass. They can also be included as part of an ordered test type, also discussed in Chapter 6. However, they cannot be part of a load test, which works only with automated test types. See Chapter 6 for more details on authoring, executing, and working with manual tests on your project.

Other Sources of Information

Because of how quickly information changes, it's important to have links to other sources so that not only can you find more details on the topics addressed in this book, but also look beyond to software development and testing communities that you might not yet know about.

Author Sites

The following are sites provided by some of the authors of this book.

- ❏ www.msvstest.com **(Tom Arnold)** — Training and links to other things relating to Microsoft Visual Studio Team Edition for Software Testers.

- ❏ www.vsTeamSystemCentral.com **(Andy Leonard)** — A community dedicated to Visual Studio Team System and Visual Studio Team Foundation Server users.

- ❏ p2p.wrox.com — For author and peer discussion, visit this site and its Web-based forums.

Blogs

Hear it straight from people using the tools, in some cases people on the teams that have created those tools.

- ❏ blogs.msdn.com/vstsloadtestblog/default.aspx — VSTS Load Testing Team blog.

- ❏ blogs.msdn.com/slumley — Sean Lumley's blog on web and load testing. (Sean is a software developer at Microsoft on the VSTS team.)

- ❏ blogs.msdn.com/billbar — Bill Barnett's blog on web and load testing. (Bill is a software developer at Microsoft on the VSTS team and also one of the technical editors for this book.)

- ❏ blogs.msdn.com/edglas — Ed Glas is a group manager for the web and load testing team at Microsoft.

Forums

Community plays a key role in not only helping you find information to grow in your skills, but also in helping others who are struggling with issues you've also grappled with in the past. Help your fellow developers and testers out at some of these forums.

❑ p2p.wrox.com — For author and peer discussion, visit this site and its Web-based forums.

❑ www.testdriven.com — Test-driven development (TDD) community.

❑ www.qaforums.com — Proclaims itself to be "the most popular Software Testing and Quality Assurance discussion site" (and they very well might be).

❑ www.theserverside.net — "Your Enterprise .NET Community."

❑ www.sqlservercentral.com — "A Microsoft SQL Server community of 447,609 DBAs, developers, and SQL Server users and growing."

❑ msdn2.microsoft.com/en-us/teamsystem/ — The home page for Visual Studio Team System on the Microsoft MSDN (Microsoft Development Network) web site.

Conferences

Here is a list of some of the more popular and worthwhile conferences worth exploring. Be sure to visit www.msvstest.com for updates.

❑ msdn.microsoft.com/events/pdc/ — Microsoft Professional Developers Conference.

❑ www.associationforsoftwaretesting.com — "A nonprofit professional organization dedicated to advancing the understanding and practice of software testing."

❑ www.icse-conferences.org — International Conference on Software Engineering.

❑ www.microsoft.com/events/ — Tech Ed Conference and other events hosted by Microsoft.

❑ www.sdexpo.com — Dr. Dobb's software conferences.

❑ www.sqe.com — Software Quality Engineering hosts both the "Better Software Conference & Expo" as well as the Software Test Analysis and Review (STAR) conferences.

Other

These are other interesting sites that didn't necessarily fall into the above sections. There are several gems here, including free open source hosting, free debugging software, and more.

❑ www.AutomationJunkies.com — An index to web sites, books, professionals, conferences, and more, all centered around software test automation.

❑ www.codeplex.com — "CodePlex is Microsoft's open source project hosting web site. You can use CodePlex to create new projects to share with the world, join others who have already started their own projects, or use the applications on this site and provide feedback."

❑ www.fiddler2.com/fiddler2/ — HTTP debugging proxy that is freeware.

❑ www.gotDotNet.com — "The Microsoft .NET Framework Community."

❑ www.stickyminds.com — "StickyMinds.com is the online companion to Better Software magazine and together they are the most comprehensive resource for helping you produce better software."

Index